A DOCTOR
ACROSS BORDERS

RAPHAEL CILENTO AND PUBLIC HEALTH FROM
EMPIRE TO THE UNITED NATIONS

A DOCTOR
ACROSS BORDERS

RAPHAEL CILENTO AND PUBLIC HEALTH FROM
EMPIRE TO THE UNITED NATIONS

ALEXANDER CAMERON-SMITH

Australian
National
University

PRESS

PACIFIC SERIES

ANU PRESS

Published by ANU Press
The Australian National University
Acton ACT 2601, Australia
Email: anupress@anu.edu.au

Available to download for free at press.anu.edu.au

ISBN (print): 9781760462642
ISBN (online): 9781760462659

WorldCat (print): 1088511587
WorldCat (online): 1088511717

DOI: 10.22459/DAB.2019

Cover design and layout by ANU Press.

Cover images: Cilento in 1923, John Oxley Library, State Library of Queensland, Neg: 186000. Map of the 'Austral-Pacific Regional Zone', Epidemiological Record of the Austral-Pacific Zone for the Year 1928 (Canberra: Government Printer, 1929), State Library of New South Wales, Q614.4906/A.

Contents

Abbreviations

AITM	Australian Institute of Tropical Medicine
BSCHB	Brisbane and South Coast Hospitals Board
CDH	Commonwealth Department of Health
CSR	Colonial Sugar Refining Company
DDT	dichlorodiphenyltrichloroethane
EAM	National Liberation Front (Greece) [Ethniko Apeleftherotiko Metopo]
ECOSOC	United Nations Economic and Social Council
ELAS	Greek People's Liberation Army [Ethnikós Laïkós Apeleftherotikós Stratós]
FEATM	Far Eastern Association of Tropical Medicine
IHB	International Health Board
ILO	International Labour Organization
LNHO	League of Nations Health Organization
MP	Member of Parliament
NHMRC	National Health and Medical Research Council
NLA	National Library of Australia
OIHP	Office International d'Hygiène Publique
PCIRO	Preparatory Commission of the International Refugee Organization
UN	United Nations
UNESCO	United Nations Educational, Scientific and Cultural Organization
UNRRA	United Nations Relief and Rehabilitation Administration
WHO	World Health Organization

Map and plates

Acknowledgements

First and foremost, I dedicate this book to my mother, father and sister, whose support and belief have been unfailing.

The encouragement and guidance of Alison Bashford and Warwick Anderson have been crucial to this project over the years, while a chance encounter with Christine Winter provided an essential new impetus to publication a few years ago. I thank also the great many staff and postgraduate students of the University of Sydney, past and present, whose constructive readings and conversations enriched this book.

A great many archivists and librarians provided the foundations for this book, especially the staff of the National Archives of Australia, the Queensland State Archives, the Fryer Library at the University of Queensland, and the United Nations Archives and Records Service. I thank John and Heather Seymour, who generously established the Seymour Scholarship, which I was awarded at the National Library of Australia (NLA) in 2008. Special thanks are thus also due to Margy Burn, Marie-Louise Ayres and the rest of the staff of the NLA, who were so welcoming and supportive during my time there.

Introduction

When Raphael Cilento drafted his unpublished autobiography, he called it 'The World, My Oyster'. Some of the other titles he considered—such as 'Confessions of an International Character', '20th Century Spotlight', 'Mankind in the Raw' and 'Tapestry of Humanity'—similarly evoked his international career. Other alternatives—such as 'Topical Confessions of a Tropical Doctor', 'Where the Fever Lurks, There Lurk I' and 'The Southern Cross is Hard to Bear'—instead suggest how Cilento, an Australian doctor, colonial official and administrator, remained preoccupied with health and sickness across the tropical spaces of northern Australia, the Pacific Islands and South-East Asia.[1] Like many public health experts in the twentieth century, Cilento enjoyed significant mobility across the imperial and international professional networks of the time. Between 1918 and 1950, he studied and worked in northern Australia, British Malaya, New Guinea and other Pacific Island colonies, as well as Europe, the United States, Latin America, Palestine and other states in Asia and the Middle East. He stayed for several years in some places, as in the Mandated Territory of New Guinea in the mid-1920s, while elsewhere he simply passed through as a student, a conference participant or a member of an international health survey.

Cilento's memoir titles and the breadth of his colonial and international experience are, at first glance, striking for a man who dedicated his career to national health and racial fitness. In the 1920s, even as knowledge of the causes and preventability of disease spread among the medical profession and the public, the belief that European residence in tropical climates led to sickness in the short term and to racial deterioration over a few generations still cast doubt on the realisation of the White Australia

---

1   Raphael Cilento, 'The World, My Oyster,' n.d., Papers of Sir Raphael Cilento [hereinafter Cilento Papers], UQFL44, Box 1, Item 4, Fryer Library, University of Queensland.

Policy.[2] As a senior Commonwealth Medical Officer between 1922 and 1934, and then as Director-General of Health and Medical Services in Queensland until 1946, Cilento was part of a cohort of reformers who challenged this lingering orthodoxy and pursued a white Australia through state-provided medicine and hygiene.[3] He wrote extensively for public audiences about race and health in the tropics, intervened in the medical policing and segregation of Aboriginal people, and vocally urged the state to enlarge its role in organising health and medical services. Gendered anxieties about racial decline and impurity were central to his thought and action, as time and again he returned to the importance of cultivating both the whiteness and the virility of Australia. Cilento thus emerged as the foremost champion of the view that individual hygiene knowledge and discipline, racial segregation and the organisation of health and medical services by the state would ensure Australia remained a 'white man's country'.

Cilento's memoir titles are nevertheless a reminder that his experience and vision stretched across the Pacific Islands, Asia and, ultimately, the world. In fact, his nationalist public health agenda in Australia was rooted in larger fields of colonial and international discourse and practice. In his 1926 book, *The White Man in the Tropics*, Cilento sourced much of his advice on personal and domestic hygiene from British, French and American texts on colonial life in Asia and Africa. Cilento spent his early working life in New Guinea and Malaya and, for much of the 1920s, it was Australia's imperial role in the Pacific that held his attention.

2   Russell McGregor, 'Drawing the Local Colour Line: White Australia and the Tropical North,' *The Journal of Pacific History*, 47(3), 2012, pp. 329–46.
3   There has been much study of this aspect of Cilento's work. See Suzanne Saunders, 'Isolation: The Development of Leprosy Prophylaxis in Australia,' *Aboriginal History*, 14(2), 1990, pp. 168–81; Suzanne Parry, 'Tropical Medicine and Colonial Identity in Northern Australia,' in Mary P. Sutphen and Bridie Andrews (eds), *Medicine and Colonial Identity* (London: Routledge, 2003), pp. 103–24; James Gillespie, *The Price of Health: Australian Governments and Medical Politics 1910–1960* (Cambridge: Cambridge University Press, 1991); David Walker, 'Climate, Civilization and Character in Australia, 1880–1940,' *Australian Cultural History*, 16, 1997, pp. 77–95; Andrew Parker, 'A "Complete Protective Machinery": Classification and Intervention through the Australian Institute of Tropical Medicine, 1911–1928,' *Health and History*, 1, 1999, pp. 182–201; Alison Bashford, '"Is White Australia Possible?" Race, Colonialism and Tropical Medicine,' *Ethnic and Racial Studies*, 23(2), 2000, pp. 248–71; Alison Bashford, *Imperial Hygiene: A Critical History of Colonialism, Nationalism and Public Health* (Basingstoke, UK: Palgrave Macmillan, 2004); Warwick Anderson, *The Cultivation of Whiteness: Science, Health and Racial Destiny in Australia* (Melbourne: Melbourne University Press, 2002); Diana Wyndham, *Eugenics in Australia: Striving for National Fitness* (London: The Galton Institute, 2003); Rosalind Kidd, *The Way We Civilise* (Brisbane: University of Queensland Press, 2005); Meg Parsons, 'Fantome Island Lock Hospital and Aboriginal Venereal Disease Sufferers 1928–45,' *Health and History*, 10(1), 2008, pp. 41–62.

He explicitly linked public health in Australia to wider networks of colonial knowledge and practice, often claiming that his training in London and experience in the Pacific and South-East Asia uniquely positioned him to tackle tropical hygiene in Australia. 'Probably no man,' acknowledged *The Mail* in Brisbane, 'medical or otherwise, knows more about the habits and customs of the aborigines of Queensland and the nearer islands of the Pacific than does Dr. R. W. Cilento.'[4] He recommended on several occasions that specific strategies for surveillance and management of indigenous people in New Guinea be adopted across Aboriginal reserves and missions in Queensland. National security and the preservation of indigenous populations against Asian migration and microbial invasions were, moreover, the central premises of Australian engagement with international health in the Pacific.

In Cilento's thought and practice, the threads of race, gender, food, land and population both bound together and distinguished national and colonial spaces of government. In working among colonised peoples in foreign and testing environments, experts in tropical medicine such as Cilento could believe they exemplified white masculinity, leading the kind of productive, physical, vigorous and commanding life that Theodore Roosevelt and others had promoted.[5] Such beliefs had grown in part from anxiety about racial deterioration in Europe and settler-colonial societies. For some politicians, scientists and reformers, evidence of declining physical and mental quality among the urbanised masses in the late nineteenth century made the deepest impression.[6] Others dwelt on stagnant fertility rates and depopulation, especially in settler-colonial societies and the Pacific Islands, where the fear of invasion or other foreign demands on unoccupied land loomed large.[7] Cilento wrote in 1944 that 'we cannot preserve our frontiers unless we can effectively occupy the lands we claim'—a geopolitical situation that demanded an increased birth rate.[8] He always insisted, however, on steering a middle

---

4   *The Mail*, 22 October 1933, National Archives of Australia [hereinafter NAA]: A1928, 4/5 SECTION 1.
5   Michael Roe, 'The Establishment of the Australian Department of Health: Its Background and Significance,' *Historical Studies*, 17(67), 1976, pp. 186–7; Marilyn Lake and Henry Reynolds, *Drawing the Global Colour Line: White Men's Countries and the Question of Racial Equality* (Melbourne: Melbourne University Press, 2008), p. 104.
6   Deborah Dwork, *War is Good for Babies and Other Young Children: A History of the Infant and Child Welfare Movement in England, 1898–1918* (London: Tavistock Publications, 1987), pp. 3–9.
7   David Walker, *Anxious Nation: Australia and the Rise of Asia 1850–1939* (Brisbane: University of Queensland Press, 1999), p. 113; Anderson, *The Cultivation of Whiteness*, pp. 159–60.
8   Raphael Cilento, *Blueprint for the Health of a Nation* (Sydney: Scotow Press, 1944), p. 94.

road between unbridled pronatalism and eugenic control.[9] Where some doctors and scientists emphasised eugenic intervention in reproduction, Cilento's proposals for public health reform in the 1930s were in keeping with mainstream international thought on the social and environmental roots of sickness.[10] He argued that beyond the preservation of racial purity, the state must safeguard and maximise the health of white Australians, and therefore national efficiency, against the effects of modern food production, industrial working conditions, urban housing and cultural decadence. In this sense, Cilento echoed longstanding apprehensions about the effects of industrial urban modernity on national and racial health.[11]

If Cilento moved comfortably through imperial and international networks, much of his work was also grounded in place. A new biographical study can thus deepen understandings of how public health took shape across connected imperial spaces in Australia and the Pacific. In embracing biography, historians have insisted on taking it beyond a traditional focus on the agency and achievements of high-profile individuals. The job of the historian as biographer, it is said, is not to simply narrate the life of an individual, but to also describe and analyse in detail their relationships to local communities, larger societies, culture and material exchanges.[12] The individual subject, in other words, serves as a hook to gather historical threads that might otherwise remain separate or overlooked. The scale of biographical studies of such relationships can thus range from the family or neighbourhood to the movement of people and ideas across regions, empires or even the globe.

---

9   ibid., p. 98.
10   Paul Weindling, 'Social Medicine at the League of Nations Health Organisation and the International Labour Office Compared,' in Paul Weindling (ed.), *International Health Organisations and Movements, 1918–1939* (Cambridge: Cambridge University Press, 1995), pp. 109–33; Dorothy Porter (ed.), *Social Medicine and Medical Sociology in the Twentieth Century* (Atlanta: Rodopi, 1997).
11   See, for example, Paul Weindling, *Health, Race and German Politics between National Unification and Nazism, 1870–1945* (Cambridge: Cambridge University Press, 1989), p. 11.
12   Nick Salvatore, 'Biography and Social History: An Intimate Relationship,' *Labour History*, 87, 2004, pp. 188–9; David Nasaw, 'AHR Roundtable: Historians and Biography—Introduction,' *American Historical Review*, 114(3), 2009, pp. 576–7; Alice Kessler-Harris, 'Why Biography?,' *American Historical Review*, 114(3), 2009, pp. 626–7; Barbara Caine, *Biography and History* (Basingstoke, UK: Palgrave Macmillan, 2010), pp. 1–6.

Tracing Cilento's career relates tropical medicine and public health in Australia to a larger web of connections in the Pacific. Fedora Gould Fisher based her conventional biography of Cilento on thorough research of published works and a range of personal, government and institutional archives. She endeavoured to situate Cilento's work within wider historical contexts of medicine and public health. Yet her work remains a traditionally heroic narrative of his achievements as an individual, centring Cilento as an autonomous subject intervening in the world. She left aside, for the most part, a detailed and critical examination of his work. In New Guinea, for example, Fisher focused on Cilento's role in building a public health system in difficult political and environmental circumstances. In doing so, she largely reproduced Cilento's own image of himself as a pioneer: 'Cilento's work in New Guinea was of a magnitude much greater than can be described here.'[13] The emphasis here is on the scale and extent of Cilento's individual mission. Even though Fisher acknowledged conflict within the New Guinea administration, she represents this as an obstacle that Cilento had to overcome rather than the main subject of analysis.[14] Fisher lists policies and practices that Cilento introduced in New Guinea without scrutinising their governmental objectives and discursive frames.[15] This book instead examines those discourses and practices of tropical medicine, as well as the connections between colonial government in the Pacific and Australia. There is thus great value in writing about Cilento in an extensive fashion again by adopting critical approaches in biographical history that focus on relationships between subjects and their contexts.

Cilento framed and enacted public health in ways that make postcolonial accounts of the entanglement of nations and empires obvious.[16] Historians have been trying to escape the confines of the nation-state for some time, hoping to understand a wide array of past connections, subjectivities

---

13   Fedora Gould Fisher, *Raphael Cilento: A Biography* (Brisbane: University of Queensland Press, 1994), p. 55.
14   ibid., p. 52.
15   ibid., pp. 52–6.
16   Ann Laura Stoler, 'Tense and Tender Ties: The Politics of Comparison in North American History and (Post) Colonial Studies,' *The Journal of American History*, 88(3), 2001, p. 848; Catherine Hall, *Civilising Subjects: Metropole and Colony in the English Imagination 1830–1867* (Cambridge: Polity Press, 2002), p. 12; Angela Woollacott, 'Postcolonial Histories and Catherine Hall's *Civilising Subjects*,' in Ann Curthoys and Marilyn Lake (eds), *Connected Worlds: History in Transnational Perspective* (Canberra: ANU E Press, 2006), pp. 63–4.

and spatial imaginaries.[17] 'Transnational' has emerged as a particularly popular catch-all term for such studies of international or global history.[18] Yet the meanings of all these terms have veered from reframing specific national histories to attending to mobilities and diasporic communities that transcended or defied the nation-state.[19] Critics have also suggested that transnational and global histories tend to reproduce neoliberal claims about the smooth flow of ideas, people, capital and goods, while ignoring the channels, frictions, adaptations and blockages arising from the material power of nation-states and modern empires.[20] These critical readings of 'transnational', as well as reminders of the insights of postcolonial thought, resonate with Cilento's career, which itself illustrates the expanding scientific and intergovernmental networks that allowed health officials to move between imperial territories and places.[21] The surveillance, management and cultivation of individual subjects and populations were shared aspects of public health everywhere in the

---

17   See Akira Iriye, *Global Community: The Role of International Organizations in the Making of the Contemporary World* (Berkeley: University of California Press, 2002); Erez Manela, *The Wilsonian Moment: Self-determination and the International Origins of Anticolonial Nationalism* (New York: Oxford University Press, 2007); Adam McKeown, *Melancholy Order: Asian Migration and the Globalization of Borders* (New York: Columbia University Press, 2008); Mathew Connelly, *Fatal Misconception: The Struggle to Control World Population* (Cambridge, MA: Harvard University Press, 2008); Mark Mazower, *Governing the World: The History of an Idea* (New York: The Penguin Press, 2012); Glenda Sluga, *Internationalism in the Age of Nationalism* (Philadelphia: University of Pennsylvania Press, 2013); Alison Bashford, *Global Population: History, Geopolitics, and Life on Earth* (New York: Columbia University Press, 2014); Mark Harrison, 'A Global Perspective: Reframing the History of Health, Medicine and Disease,' *Bulletin of the History of Medicine*, 89, 2015, pp. 639–89.
18   Anne Curthoys and Marilyn Lake, 'Introduction,' in Anne Curthoys and Marilyn Lake (eds), *Connected Worlds: History in Transnational Perspective* (Canberra: ANU E Press, 2006), pp. 5–9.
19   On national reframing, see Ian Tyrrell, 'American Exceptionalism in an Age of International History,' *American Historical Review*, 96(4), 1991, pp. 1031–55; Lake and Reynolds, *Drawing the Global Colour Line*, pp. 184–222. On larger communities and connections, see A. G. Hopkins (ed.), *Globalization in World History* (New York: W. W. Norton & Co., 2002); Kevin Grant, Philippa Levine and Frank Trentmann (eds), *Beyond Sovereignty: Britain, Empire and Transnationalism, c. 1880–1950* (Basingstoke, UK: Palgrave Macmillan, 2007); Desley Deacon, Penny Russell and Angela Woollacott, 'Introduction,' in Desley Deacon, Penny Russell and Angela Woollacott (eds), *Transnational Ties: Australia Lives in the World* (Canberra: ANU E Press, 2008).
20   Sarah Hodges, 'The Global Menace,' *Social History of Medicine*, 25(3), 2011, pp. 719–28; Warwick Anderson, 'Making Global Health History: The Postcolonial Worldliness of Biomedicine,' *Social History of Medicine*, 27(2), 2014, pp. 374–8; Alecia Simmonds, Anne Rees and Anna Clark, 'Testing the Boundaries: Reflections on Transnationalism in Australian History,' in Alecia Simmonds, Anne Rees and Anna Clark (eds), *Transnationalism, Nationalism, and Australian History* (Singapore: Palgrave Macmillan, 2017), pp. 1–14.
21   On imperial networks, see David Lambert and Alan Lester, 'Imperial Spaces, Imperial Subjects,' in David Lambert and Alan Lester (eds), *Colonial Lives Across the British Empire: Imperial Careering in the Long Nineteenth Century* (Cambridge: Cambridge University Press, 2006), pp. 21–4; Tony Ballantyne and Antoinette Burton, 'Empires and the Reach of the Global,' in Emily Rosenberg (ed.), *A World Connecting: 1870–1945* (Cambridge, MA: Belknap Press, 2012), pp. 285–431.

twentieth century, not just colonial territories.[22] Cilento's experience of public health administration in New Guinea and his engagement with larger networks of colonial research and legislation shaped his general understanding of health and disease. The ways in which he represented diet, health and race in Australia rested on an understanding of how a modern, imperial world order had transformed relationships between populations and their environments on a global scale. In turn, Cilento's nationalist ideal of racial homogeneity informed his understanding of colonial government and international health. In many ways, therefore, he embodied the postcolonial claim that empire was a 'spatialized terrain of power'.[23]

Rather than tell a comprehensive story of a life, the chapters of this book focus on examples of how Cilento's work connected tropical hygiene, international health and social medicine across the colonial spaces of Australia and the Pacific. The first explores how Cilento joined a growing number of students passing through imperial institutions in London, Liverpool and elsewhere in the twentieth century, absorbing knowledge and ideas while bearing a particular political and cultural subjectivity.[24] Cilento was born in Jamestown, South Australia, in 1893, but his grandfather Salvatore had arrived in Adelaide from Italy in 1855. Instead of sweeping his heritage under the rug, Cilento would reconcile his Italian background with a white Australian subjectivity throughout his life. His path to the

---

22   David Arnold, *Colonizing the Body: State Medicine and Epidemic Disease in Nineteenth-century India* (Berkeley: University of California Press, 1993), p. 9; Shula Marks, 'What is Colonial about Colonial Medicine? And What Has Happened to Imperialism and Health?,' *Social History of Medicine*, 10(2), 1997, pp. 205–19; Warwick Anderson, 'Postcolonial Histories of Medicine,' in Frank Huisman and John Harley Warner (eds), *Locating Medical History: The Stories and their Meanings* (Baltimore: Johns Hopkins University Press, 2004), pp. 299–300; Waltraud Ernst, 'Beyond East and West: From the History of Colonial Medicine to a Social History of Medicine(s) in South Asia,' *Social History of Medicine*, 20(3), 2007, pp. 505–24.
23   Antoinette Burton, 'Introduction: On the Inadequacy and Indispensability of the Nation,' in Antoinette Burton (ed.), *After the Imperial Turn: Thinking with and through the Nation* (Durham, NC: Duke University Press, 2003), p. 5.
24   Michael Worboys, 'The Emergence of Tropical Medicine: A Study in the Establishment of a Scientific Speciality,' in Gerard Lemaine, Roy MacLeod, Michael Mulkay and Peter Weingart (eds), *Perspectives on the Emergence of Scientific Disciplines* (The Hague: Mouton & Co., 1976), pp. 75–98; Michael Warboys, 'Manson, Ross, and Colonial Medical Policy: Tropical Medicine in London and Liverpool, 1899–1914,' in Roy Macleod and Milton J. Lewis (eds), *Disease, Medicine, and Empire: Perspectives on Western Medicine and the Experience of European Expansion* (London: Routledge, 1988), pp. 21–37; John Farley, *Bilharzia: A History of Imperial Tropical Medicine* (Cambridge: Cambridge University Press, 1991), p. 17; Mark Harrison, *Public Health in British India: Anglo-Indian Preventive Medicine, 1859–1914* (Cambridge: Cambridge University Press, 1994), pp. 150–58; Ryan Johnson, 'The West African Medical Staff and the Administration of Imperial Tropical Medicine, 1902–14,' *The Journal of Imperial and Commonwealth History*, 38(3), 2010, pp. 419–39.

London School of Tropical Medicine emerged out of chance and initiative. After serving briefly as an army medical officer in occupied German New Guinea, Cilento grew bored of private practice in Adelaide and applied for an advertised position in the Federated Malay States. While he was there, the nascent Commonwealth Department of Health (CDH) offered him the job of Director of the Australian Institute of Tropical Medicine (AITM) in Townsville, Queensland, on the condition that he study for a diploma in London. These years shaped Cilento's professional identity as a mobile expert in tropical hygiene who could adapt a body of portable colonial knowledge to particular places. Yet these years also sharpened his sense of Australia's particular situation in the world as he began to engage in a more conscious way with contemporary discourses about health, race, population and conflict.[25]

Cilento returned to New Guinea in the mid-1920s as Director of Public Health in the Mandated Territory, while he was also nominally head of the AITM. His appointment was part of a plan to expand the Commonwealth's activities from quarantine to responsibility for a unified medical service for the Australian tropics and territories. As Chapters 2 and 3 show, public health in New Guinea under Australian administration was enmeshed in exchanges between empires of knowledge, ideas and practices. As elsewhere, in New Guinea, public health aimed to govern populations through forms of surveillance—by justifying and enforcing racial segregation and devising systems for managing labour.[26] Yet, while in New Guinea, Cilento also began to conceive of health and difference in terms of social and environmental histories beyond strictly hereditary conceptions of race, especially in his growing interest in nutrition.[27]

---

25 Cilento, like other Australians, was very interested in the work of Charles Pearson, Lothrop Stoddard, J. W. Gregory and others. See Raymond Evans, '"Pigmentia": Racial Fears and White Australia,' in Dirk A. Moses (ed.), *Genocide and Settler Society: Frontier Violence and Stolen Indigenous Children in Australian History* (New York: Berghahn Books, 2007), p. 119; Lake and Reynolds, *Drawing the Global Colour Line*, pp. 314–19; Bashford, *Global Population*, pp. 109–12.

26 See, for example, Donald Denoon, *Public Health in Papua New Guinea: Medical Possibility and Social Constraint, 1884–1984* (Cambridge: Cambridge University Press, 1989); Megan Vaughan, *Curing their Ills: Colonial Power and African Illness* (Stanford, CA: Stanford University Press, 1991); Arnold, *Colonizing the Body*, p. 9; Lenore Manderson, *Sickness and the State: Health and Illness in Colonial Malaya, 1870–1940* (Cambridge: Cambridge University Press, 1996), pp. 1–5; Warwick Anderson, *Colonial Pathologies: American Tropical Medicine, Race, and Hygiene in the Philippines* (Durham, NC: Duke University Press, 2006).

27 See Veronika Lipphardt and Alexandra Widmer, 'Introduction: Health and Difference— Rendering Human Variation in Colonial Engagements,' in Veronika Lipphardt and Alexandra Widmer (eds), *Health and Difference: Rendering Human Variation in Colonial Engagements* (New York: Berghahn Books, 2016), pp. 1–19.

In formulating policies and practices for workers' rations and racial segregation, Cilento looked to Asian, African and Pacific colonies for guidance. At the same time, Australia administered New Guinea under a League of Nations mandate that gave Cilento a language with which to critique existing colonial policies and promote his expert knowledge. While the practical efficacy of the mandate system was itself minimal, the discourse surrounding the status of the mandated territories shaped public health politics in New Guinea through the initiative of officials such as Cilento.

Cilento's emphasis on surveillance, hygienic discipline and racial segregation in New Guinea extended to Queensland, where a variety of colonial intersections shaped the discourses and practices of Australian tropical hygiene, examined in Chapter 4. *The White Man in the Tropics*, Cilento's major work in the mid-1920s, drew from Asian and African colonial texts to advise on clothing, diet, bathing, exercise, housing and patterns of work and leisure that would keep white settlers healthy both in northern Australia and in Australian territories in the Pacific. The Australian Hookworm Campaign of the 1920s, which sought to instruct working-class communities in better personal and domestic habits, was funded by the International Health Board (IHB) of the Rockefeller Foundation and relied on methods it used in campaigns across the southern United States, Latin America and Asia.[28] In the ongoing colonisation of northern Australia, white working-class communities in Queensland thus became subjects of hygienic scrutiny and discipline in ways that drew on ideas and practices from colonial Asia and the Pacific Islands.

As Cilento sought to cultivate white settler health in the tropics, he simultaneously sought to reform and reinforce racial segregation on the basis of hygiene. In promoting changes to the institutionalisation of Aboriginal people, Cilento appealed to his own experience of tropical hygiene in the Pacific and South-East Asia. As in New Guinea, he reimagined and reorganised the segregation of Aboriginal people in Queensland as the hygienic management of labour, yet on a much more extensive and profound scale. In keeping with conventions of tropical medicine, Cilento described Aboriginal communities as 'reservoirs' of disease, either because they harboured pathogens or because they created environments

---

28 Robert Dixon, *Prosthetic Gods: Travel, Representation and Colonial Governance* (Brisbane: University of Queensland Press, 2001), pp. 24–46; Anderson, *The Cultivation of Whiteness*, pp. 139–46.

in which they might flourish.[29] His construction in the late 1930s of a new leprosarium on Fantome Island to separate Aboriginal inmates from Europeans patients at the Peel Island institution is indicative of his segregating impulses.[30] Yet this regime of racial hygiene developed relative to wider imperial concerns and practices. Health officials had long blamed Chinese immigrants and indentured Melanesian labourers for introducing leprosy and hookworm to Aboriginal communities in Queensland.[31] Cilento argued further that the growth of mixed communities of Aboriginal, Melanesian and Asian peoples—'indistinguishable' from 'native communities in the Pacific Islands'—meant that public health problems in the urban spaces of Queensland were little different from those of Rabaul or Suva.[32] Indeed, the health problems of such colonial spaces seemed to arise from historical relationships between them. The focus of Queensland's existing *Aboriginals Protection and Restriction of the Sale of Opium Act* (1897) on a narrow definition of 'Aboriginal' meant that the state was unable to effectively control these heterogeneous communities. Cilento thus defined problems of race and health in Queensland as typically colonial, collapsing racial categories into an idea of the 'native' as a broad social and administrative category familiar in the Pacific.[33] Amendments to the Act in 1934, which gave the state more control over a broader range of 'half-caste' groups, followed soon after Cilento's reports, although the Queensland Government had many more reasons to change the law.[34]

To Australian health officials, the Pacific Islands seemed like stepping-stones for diseases brought from Asia on steam ships. Cholera or smallpox could invade Australia directly from the islands, but they might

---

29   Anderson, *The Cultivation of Whiteness*, p. 145.
30   Gordon Briscoe, *Counting, Health and Identity: A History of Aboriginal Health and Demography in Western Australia and Queensland, 1900–1940* (Canberra: Aboriginal Studies Press, 2003), pp. 319–20; Bashford, *Imperial Hygiene*, p. 94; Meg Parsons, 'Spaces of Disease: The Creation and Management of Aboriginal Health and Disease in Queensland 1900–1970,' (PhD Thesis, University of Sydney, 2008), pp. 325–43.
31   A. T. Yarwood, 'Sir Raphael Cilento and *The White Man in the Tropics*,' in Roy MacLeod and Donald Denoon (eds), *Health and Healing in Tropical Australia and Papua New Guinea* (Townsville, QLD: James Cook University, 1991), p. 55.
32   Raphael Cilento, 'Report of a Partial Survey of Aboriginal Natives of North Queensland,' p. 3, NAA: A1928, 4/5 SECTION 1.
33   See Stewart Firth, 'Colonial Administration and the Invention of the Native,' in Donald Denoon with Stewart Firth, Jocelyn Linnekin, Malama Meleisea and Karen Nero (eds), *The Cambridge History of the Pacific Islanders* (Cambridge: Cambridge University Press, 2004), pp. 253–88.
34   Regina Ganter, *Mixed Relations: Asian–Aboriginal Contact in North Australia* (Perth: University of Western Australia Press, 2006), p. 81.

also catastrophically depopulate the islands of Melanesia. As prospects of further Australian territorial expansion dimmed, the Department of Health organised the first International Pacific Health Conference, in Melbourne in 1926, where delegates from New Zealand, several Pacific Island colonies and various Asian states met with Australian officials to discuss the potential of a regional epidemiological intelligence service, standardisation of quarantine regulations, training programs for medical officers and coordinated research in the Pacific Islands. By the mid-1920s, such practices had become the standard repertoire of international health under the Office International d'Hygiène Publique (OIHP) in Paris and the League of Nations Health Organization (LNHO) in Geneva.[35] For Cilento, the explicit aim of such practices was to define a space in the Pacific in which an Australian institution, not an international organisation, would determine the development and administration of public health. In shaping medical knowledge and health practice in the region, Australia would enhance its epistemic authority, prestige and security. Chapter 3 thus explores how Australia—much like the United States in Latin America—sought to turn northern Australia and the Pacific Islands into a distinct space of hygiene governance and a sphere of influence for Australian imperial dreams.[36]

While the direct connections between hygiene in the Pacific Islands and in northern Australia reflected an ongoing colonial project, an imperial mentality remained central to Cilento's contributions to national public health in the 1930s. As Director-General of Health and Medical Services in Queensland from 1934, he often framed his proposals for national reform in terms of 'social medicine'. Although it had a long genealogy, it was not until the 1920s that health officials and medical schools across

---

35   Martin David Dubin, 'The League of Nations Health Organisation,' in Paul Weindling (ed.), *International Health Organisations and Movements, 1918–1939* (Cambridge: Cambridge University Press, 1995), pp. 56–80; Lenore Manderson, 'Wireless Wars in Eastern Arena: Epidemiological Surveillance, Disease Prevention and the Work of the Eastern Bureau of the League of Nations Health Organisation, 1925–1942,' in Paul Weindling (ed.), *International Health Organisations and Movements, 1918–1939* (Cambridge: Cambridge University Press, 1995), pp. 109–33; Mark Harrison, 'Disease, Diplomacy and International Commerce: The Origins of International Sanitary Regulation in the Nineteenth Century,' *Journal of Global History*, 1, 2006, pp. 197–217; Anne Sealy, 'Globalizing the 1926 International Sanitary Convention,' *Journal of Global History*, 6, 2011, pp. 431–55.
36   See Alexandra Minna Stern, 'Yellow Fever Crusade: US Colonialism, Tropical Medicine, and the International Politics of Mosquito Control, 1900–1920,' in Alison Bashford (ed.), *Medicine at the Border: Disease, Globalization and Security, 1850 to the Present* (Basingstoke, UK: Palgrave Macmillan, 2006), p. 41–2; Ana Maria Carillo and Anne-Emmanuelle Birn, 'Neighbours on Notice: National and Imperial Interests in the American Public Health Association, 1872–1921,' *Canadian Bulletin of Medical History*, 25(1), 2008, pp. 225–54.

Europe, the United States and much of Asia widely embraced the idea that sickness had social and environmental roots.[37] Cilento drew extensively on cross-Atlantic exchanges of articles, surveys and official reports, and shared widespread anxieties about declining fitness and fertility in imperial and settler-colonial societies.[38] British inquiries and texts, for example, conflated national and imperial decline against a backdrop of population growth and anticolonial agitation in Asia.[39] As Chapter 5 shows, however, Cilento's articulation of social medicine also spoke to specific nationalist and Pacific colonial contexts. His commitment to state supervision of collective and individual health in New Guinea, through surveillance and preventive practices, differed little in principle from social medicine elsewhere. Nutrition was a central element of social medicine in the 1930s and became a major topic of international discussion, especially through the LNHO.[40] Cilento's own belief in the importance of nutrition, however, came directly from his practical experience in New Guinea, while colonial research in South and South-East Asia had produced much of the basic nutritional knowledge on which he and others relied.

Race was fundamental for Cilento throughout all these spaces, where it worked as a global organising concept and a prism through which to view anxieties about transformation and decline.[41] As he moved through Queensland and the Pacific Islands, Cilento constructed white, Aboriginal, Asian and Pacific Islander peoples in relation to each other. If the superiority of white men and the importance of racial homogeneity were articles of faith for him, whiteness also seemed to be always changing or under threat. Cilento had made it his mission to show that tropical climates did not themselves cause disease or degeneration. Yet in *The White Man in the Tropics*, he also had to admit that:

---

37 Dorothy Porter, 'Introduction,' in Dorothy Porter (ed.), *Social Medicine and Medical Sociology in the Twentieth Century* (Atlanta: Rodopi, 1997), pp. 4–5; Warwick Anderson and Hans Pols, 'Scientific Patriotism: Medical Science and National Self-fashioning in Southeast Asia,' *Comparative Studies in Society and History*, 54(1), 2012, pp. 98–9.

38 Gillespie, *The Price of Health*, p. 51; Dorothy Porter, *Health, Civilization and the State: A History of Public Health from Ancient to Modern Times* (London: Routledge, 1999), pp. 165–93.

39 Dwork, *War is Good for Babies*, pp. 6–10; Connelly, *Fatal Misconception*, pp. 34–5.

40 See E. Burnet and W. R. Aykroyd, 'Nutrition and Public Health,' *Quarterly Bulletin of the Health Organisation of the League of Nations*, 4(2), 1935, pp. 323–474; Commonwealth of Australia, *First Report of the Advisory Council on Nutrition* (Canberra: Government Printer, 1936); Joseph L. Barona, 'Nutrition and Health: The International Context during the Inter-war Crisis,' *Social History of Medicine*, 21(1), 2008, pp. 87–105; Bashford, *Global Population*, pp. 206–10.

41 Christian Geulen, 'The Common Grounds of Conflict: Racial Visions of World Order 1880–1940,' in Sebastian Conrad and Dominic Sachsenmaier (eds), *Competing Visions of World Order: Global Moments and Movements, 1880 – 1930s* (New York: Palgrave Macmillan, 2007), pp. 69–72.

The race is in a transition stage, and it is very apparent that there is being evolved precisely what one would hope for, namely a distinctive tropical type, adapted to life in the tropical environment in which it is set.[42]

This new type was 'tall and rangy', with 'long arms and legs', but also 'moves slowly', which in women 'becomes a gracefulness of movement that reminds one of those nations of the East that live in similar environments'.[43] Although not explicitly Lamarckian, Cilento clearly represented race, fitness and health as historically and environmentally contingent. Remarking on indigenous population decline in New Guinea, Cilento suggested that nutrition shaped both the health of individuals and 'the place to which a tribe or race has won in manliness, energy, and soldierly instincts'.[44] In later arguing against climatic determinism, Cilento reminded readers that 'belief in national superiority has been a universal delusion'. Civilisation was instead 'ephemeral', the product of 'maintained accord between man and his environment'.[45] This of course meant that races and societies could also deteriorate if such a balance was lost.

In public lectures and journal articles in the 1930s, Cilento dwelled on cycles of progress and decline that linked sickness in New Guinea and urban Australia within a causal network of empire. The importance of a stable relationship between populations, local agriculture and diet remained a central theme in Cilento's writing about national health. In fact, he argued, Australians and Pacific Islanders shared a dietary deficiency that underpinned their poor physical development, 'instability of the nervous system', fatigue and lack of resistance to infectious disease. This, he suggested, 'may explain the decay of primitive and sophisticated alike, for there is no less evidence that the same conditions occur in people resident in cities'.[46] In addition to situating Australian health reform in international networks of knowledge and practice, Chapter 5 thus also examines how empire lay at the heart of Cilento's construction of the white Australian subjects of public health.

---

42 Raphael Cilento, *The White Man in the Tropics: With Especial Reference to Australia and its Dependencies* (Melbourne: Government Printer, 1926), p. 74.
43 ibid., p. 74.
44 Raphael Cilento, 'Report on Diet Deficiencies in the Territory of New Guinea,' n.d., p. 1, NAA: A1, 1925/24149.
45 Raphael Cilento, 'The Conquest of Climate,' *The Medical Journal of Australia*, 1(14), 8 April 1933, p. 424.
46 Raphael Cilento, 'Some Problems of Racial Pressure in the Pacific,' *British Medical Journal (Supplement)*, 1 February 1936, pp. 42–46.

These themes of equilibrium, mobility and disruption are keys to how Cilento thought about race, national health and world order. After volunteering for the United Nations Relief and Rehabilitation Administration (UNRRA) in 1945, he joined the United Nations itself, where population growth and migration animated much international discussion and research on demography, public health, agriculture, education, family planning and other fields.[47] The final chapter explores Cilento's time as director of the social welfare program of the UN Department of Social Affairs, which worked with various government departments and universities to provide fellowships and expert consultants in welfare legislation, social work training and other related fields when governments requested them. These practices—which also underpinned the UN Technical Assistance program of the 1950s—recognised and promoted the nation-state as the fundamental unit of world order.[48] For his part, Cilento continued to express settler-colonial anxieties about the threat of Asian population growth to Australian nationhood and peace in the Pacific. The larger aim of the UN social welfare program was, in his view, to ameliorate regional and global effects of population growth across a decolonising Asia, which would in the future make these people 'a threat to every specialized frontier of culture and civilization'.[49] Since is was impossible to arrest such growth, it was vital for international organisations, through social and economic programs:

> To direct the activities, the intentions and the ideas of the peoples of these huge undeveloped areas in such a way that ... their actions will be along lines that experience has proved to be the most progressive socially.[50]

Cilento's understanding of the aims of UN social welfare and development programs thus stemmed from his old preoccupations with race, population and empire. His ideal world order was static—one of arrested cycles of decline and progress and of settled peoples, 'rooted in the soil'.[51]

---

47   Connelly, *Fatal Misconception*, pp. 115–55; Bashford, *Global Population*, pp. 267–354.
48   See also Sunil Amrith, *Decolonizing International Health: India and Southeast Asia 1930–65* (Basingstoke, UK: Palgrave Macmillan, 2006) p. 76–83.
49   Raphael Cilento, 'Underdeveloped Areas in Social Evolutionary Perspective,' *The Milbank Memorial Fund Quarterly*, 26(3), 1948, p. 299.
50   ibid., p. 298.
51   Raphael Cilento, 'A Correlation of Some Features of Tropical Preventive Medicine, and their Application to the Tropical Areas under Australian Control' (Doctor of Medicine Thesis, University of Adelaide, 1922), p. xiii.

While many scholars have recently shown how imperialism and racial thought influenced the United Nations and its specialised agencies, Cilento eventually concluded that the United Nations represented a rupture with the imperial world order he had worked within.[52] Rapid economic development and modernisation, human rights and Cold War politics seemed to him a decisive break with gradual colonial development of the kind represented by the League of Nations mandates.[53] He felt increasingly out of step with these trends in liberal internationalism and decolonisation, and said so in a letter to Robert Menzies shortly before resigning from the United Nations.[54] Decolonisation was, in reality, a protracted process, while policies of racial segregation and immigration restriction remained in place in Australia and South Africa well after World War II.[55] By the 1970s, however, the Australian Labor Party had dropped the White Australia Policy from its platform, while the admission of students and refugees from Asia ushered in the policy's final collapse. In one of his last public statements, Cilento prepared a recorded lecture for the far-right League of Rights in 1972 on the subject of 'Australia's Racial Heritage', warning about the 'incompatible racial clots that might end in disaster' if biological and social racial mixing continued.[56] Cilento clearly felt the world was changing beyond recognition. He had worked with Labor governments in Queensland in ways that contributed to comparatively expansive public health services in Australia, which made medical services more widely available, and yet he was enmeshed in empire. If many of the institutions and practices of contemporary public health took shape in Cilento's time, few now would frame their purpose in his terms.

---

52   Mark Mazower, *No Enchanted Palace: The End of Empire and the Ideological Origins of the United Nations* (Princeton, NJ: Princeton University Press, 2009), p. 40–1; Glenda Sluga, 'UNESCO and the (One) World of Julian Huxley,' *Journal of World History*, 21(3), 2010, pp. 405–7; Bashford, *Global Population*, pp. 301–4.

53   Susan Pedersen, *The Guardians: The League of Nations and the Crisis of Empire* (Oxford: Oxford University Press, 2015), p. 299.

54   Raphael Cilento to Robert Menzies, 11 September 1950, p. 1, Cilento Papers, UQFL44, Box 4, Item 11.

55   Lake and Reynolds, *Drawing the Global Colour Line*, pp. 352–6.

56   Raphael Cilento, *Australia's Racial Heritage* (Adelaide: The Australian Heritage Society [Australian League of Rights], 1972), p. 4.

1

An education in empire: Tropical medicine, Australia and the making of a worldly doctor

When Raphael Cilento was a student at the London School of Tropical Medicine in 1922, his classmates included British colonial officers, indigenous members of the Indian Medical Service, missionaries and doctors from Europe and the United States. In August of the previous year, he had represented Australia at the Far Eastern Association of Tropical Medicine (FEATM) in Batavia, where delegates from across Asia gathered to share and discuss medical research and public health practice in the region. His presence there came after the nascent Commonwealth Department of Health (CDH) had offered him a position in Australia while he was working as a medical officer in the British colonial service in the Federated Malay States. His work there was the fruit of his own initiative, having responded to vacancies for medical officers advertised in medical journals such as *The Lancet*. Cilento's introduction to tropical medicine and the cultivation of his professional identity thus depended on a network of British colonies and imperial institutions. It also illustrates how individuals could travel across these connections in many different ways.

A wide variety of people participated in these imperial exchanges, but Cilento's mobility reflected and sharpened his sense of emerging Australian nationhood. After gaining a medical degree in 1918, his first experience of tropical health practice came in the former German colony of New Guinea, which Australian forces had occupied since 1914. These new colonial responsibilities in the Pacific and Australia's relationship to Asia became central to Cilento's nationalism. World War I seemed to have shattered impressions of European superiority, amplifying old fears about population growth and anticolonial agitation in Asia.[1] This was highly relevant to Australia, where the settlement and development of the tropical north had been slow and, to some, remained impossible with white labour. Local and international observers argued that if white Australians could not make progress in the tropics, it was immoral for racial immigration restrictions to prevent the redistribution of people from areas of high density to the less populous spaces of the globe. War, in fact, would, in their view, be the inevitable outcome of restrictions such as the White Australia Policy.[2] Cilento was well aware of these discourses as he travelled the world for his studies. In contrast to pacifist calls for a redistribution of population, Cilento embraced the opposing determination to maintain global white supremacy and preserve settler societies as white men's countries.[3] In this way, Cilento presented tropical hygiene as one of the foundations of a white Australia.

An Italian–Australian patriot

One of the earliest entries in Raphael Cilento's medical school diary consisted of verses submitted to a national song competition, which he might have seen reported in Adelaide's *The Advertiser*.[4] Held in 1913 under the auspices of the Musical Association of New South Wales, the competition offered £100 to the winner and ultimately received 722 entries. Professor Thomas G. Tucker from the University of Melbourne and Mungo William McCallum of the University of Sydney acted as

---

1   See, for example, Lothrop Stoddard, *The Rising Tide of Color Against White World-supremacy* (New York: Charles Scribner's Sons, 1921), p. 16. See also Michael Adas, 'Contested Hegemony: The Great War and the Afro–Asian Assault on the Civilizing Mission,' *Journal of World History*, 15(1), 2004, pp. 31–63; Mazower, *No Enchanted Palace*, pp. 34–6.

2   Sean Brawley, *The White Peril: Foreign Relations and Asian Immigration to Australasia and North America 1919–1978* (Sydney: UNSW Press, 1995), p. 12; Alison Bashford, 'Nation, Empire, Globe: The Spaces of Population Debate in the Interwar Years,' *Comparative Studies in Society and History*, 49(1), 2006, pp. 173–5; Alison Bashford, 'World Population and Australian Land: Demography and Sovereignty in the Twentieth Century,' *Australian Historical Studies*, 38(130), 2007, pp. 217–20.

3   See especially J. W. Gregory, *The Menace of Colour* (London: Seeley Service & Co. Ltd, 1925), pp. 150–60.

4   *The Advertiser*, [Adelaide], 1 August 1913, p. 8.

judges.[5] The winning entry was submitted by Sydney resident Arthur H. Adams and described the land as 'God's demesne'—a 'vast … heritage … splashed with sun and wattle gold'. To achieve its potential and secure it for 'our race', Adams wrote, required courage.[6] Adams was actually born in New Zealand, studied in Otago and served as a war correspondent during the Boxer rebellion in China.[7] Racial subjectivities thus tended to spill over national political boundaries in the British Empire.

The promise and beauty of the land were nevertheless prominent themes in Australian cultural nationalism. Sun and wattle were common symbols of the nation's health and wealth. It was important, wrote one *Herald* correspondent, that the winning song 'awaken patriotic fervour, and become the national air'.[8] A spokesman for the Musical Association acknowledged that, insofar as Australia was a part of the British Empire, there was already a national anthem, but he argued that there was still a need for an 'Australian song, vital with hope, exhortation, and patriotism' that would reflect 'the energy of new ideas and new enthusiasms that may lead this youngest of nations to a great and glorious future'.[9] Youth, health, energy and progress were thus all central to a nationalism that many expected and desired in Australia.

Much like Adams's, Cilento's verses evoked the promise of the land, the progressive work of the rural pioneer and the imagined classlessness of Australian society. In lines that echo the present national anthem, he celebrated Australia as 'Neptune's dimpled daughter fair/By azure oceans all embraced' and blessed with a 'thousand novel beauties'. The squatters 'riding through their fields' and the miners in their 'clayey claims', both of whom were striving to colonise and develop this land, were 'brothers, when abreast they stand/to guard their fair Australian land'. These twin themes of national development and defence, and the relationship of the people to the nation-state, would become central to Cilento's work in public health. Referencing Henry Parkes, he proclaimed that the 'crimson thread of kinship' bound 'Australia's welfare unto all', from bushmen to statesmen.[10] One might suppose, given his pennilessness at the time, that

---

5   *Sydney Morning Herald*, 2 August 1913, p. 13.
6   *The Argus*, 20 November 1913, p. 8.
7   *The Advertiser*, [Adelaide], 20 November 1913, p. 15.
8   *Sydney Morning Herald*, 21 November 1913, p. 11.
9   *Sydney Morning Herald*, 13 September 1913, p. 7.
10   Raphael Cilento, Diary: Medical School, September 1913 – October 1914, 30 September 1913, Cilento Papers, UQFL44, Box 11, Item 16.

he may have entered the competition simply in the hope of winning the prize money. Yet Cilento's diary betrays the real fervour of his nationalism. Travelling by rail to work as a fruit picker in Renmark near the Victorian border, he described the sunset:

> From one dark cloud the beams fell on the quiet earth gently as a benison, and those long golden fingers seemed to touch with tender hope the face of this new and virgin land.[11]

Richard Waterhouse has noted that representations of the bush in the twentieth century similarly eschewed an earlier nostalgia and willingness to recognise the history of Indigenous dispossession in favour of a more triumphal emphasis on potential and progress that elided social stratification. Waves of strikes and labour militancy had marked the 1890s and persisted well after federation of the colonies. The creation of a new Commonwealth and the establishment of a legal framework to harmonise relations between labour and capital belied entrenched class-consciousness.[12] The Australia that Cilento imagined in his song was thus emptied of Indigenous voices and of class struggle.

The song competition was one small manifestation of nation-building among all the social legislation, economic development and cultural production in the years after Federation in 1901. As prime minister, Alfred Deakin committed the Commonwealth to constructing an Australian navy and instituting compulsory military training.[13] Federal parliaments produced a raft of progressive social legislation, including old-age and invalid pensions and a maternity allowance. The Commonwealth Arbitration Court, created under the supervision of liberal political figures such as Deakin, Charles Kingston and High Court Justice H. B. Higgins, was designed to determine a living wage and arbitrate in industrial disputes.[14] The state also took a prominent role in developing industries, as in the case of the Newcastle steelworks of Broken Hill Proprietary Company Limited (BHP).[15] All these measures in economic

---

11   Cilento, Diary: Medical School, 24 December 1913, Cilento Papers, UQFL44, Box 11, Item 16.
12   Richard Waterhouse, *The Vision Splendid: A Social and Cultural History of Rural Australia* (Fremantle, WA: Curtin University Press, 2005), pp. 90–2.
13   Richard White, *Inventing Australia: Images and Identity, 1688–1980* (Sydney: Allen & Unwin, 1981), p. 114; Evans, '"Pigmentia",' p. 106.
14   Stuart Macintyre, *The Oxford History of Australia: The Succeeding Age, 1901–1942. Volume 4* (Melbourne: Oxford University Press, 1986), pp. 101–2; Stuart MacIntyre, *A Concise History of Australia* (Cambridge: Cambridge University Press, 1999), pp. 150–1.
15   White, *Inventing Australia*, p. 115.

development, security and social welfare were part of a largely middle-class, liberal project of creating a progressive nation-state that obscured persistent class-consciousness and conflict in Australia.[16] Beyond legislative and industrial measures, a cultural nationalism rooted in the middle class flourished in this time, drawing especially on environmental and Aboriginal imagery. Native flowers and animals, as well as boomerangs and the call of 'Cooee', for example, featured prominently in literature, art and advertising. Depictions of the land emphasised its beauty, fecundity and wholesomeness and thus the promise of Australia—exemplified in articles and images published in *The Bulletin* and *Lone Hand*, and in social movements such as the Wattle Day Leagues that emerged after 1909.[17]

Progressive Australian nationhood was ideologically conditional on racial purity and improvement, but in ways that underscore an emerging sense of transnational racial kinship binding white settler nations in solidarity.[18] The arrival of Chinese migrants in the western United States and Australia in the 1840s and 1850s led to sustained agitation for immigration restrictions from the labour movement, academia, the media and politicians on both sides of the Pacific. The goldfields were the primary attraction for immigrants, but Chinese merchants also established businesses, married local women and aspired to residence. This was a tiny fraction of a much larger story of migration in the nineteenth century, when 50 million Chinese and 30 million Indians travelled for work, business or education. Most of these people went to South-East Asia through imperial systems of indentured labour, but many travelled freely to North America and Australia within the framework of the British Empire or international treaty obligations.[19] The surge in Chinese migration to California and Victoria in the 1850s, however, was met with growing hostility that manifested in discriminatory taxes on miners and mob violence.[20]

---

16   ibid., p. 114.
17   ibid., pp. 117–23.
18   ibid., pp. 112–14; Michael Roe, *Nine Australian Progressives: Vitalism in Bourgeois Social Thought, 1890–1960* (Brisbane: University of Queensland Press, 1984), p. 19; Helen Irving, *To Constitute a Nation: A Cultural History of Australia's Constitution* (Cambridge: Cambridge University Press, 1997), p. 100.
19   Patrick Manning, *Migration in World History* (New York: Routledge, 2005), pp. 146–9; Lake and Reynolds, *Drawing the Global Colour Line*, pp. 20–30; McKeown, *Melancholy Order*, pp. 48–58.
20   Charles A. Price, *The Great White Walls Are Built: Restrictive Immigration to North America and Australasia 1836–1888* (Canberra: Australian Institute of International Affairs/Australian National University Press, 1974), pp. 61–9.

This was an important moment in the emergence of new and explicit racial identities and assertions of national sovereignty. As Marilyn Lake and Henry Reynolds have shown, the commitment to freedom of movement embodied in British and American treaty arrangements with China clashed with a powerful sense of national democratic sovereignty emerging in white settler-colonial societies such as the United States and the Australian colonies.[21] Governments and newspapers in California and the Australian colonies observed each other closely for precedents and inspiration in the ideology and legislative practice of immigration restriction. Migration, moreover, encouraged the emergence of 'white' as an explicit transnational subjectivity, in which assumptions about the racial basis of the capacity for self-determination implied an inalienable national sovereignty. Labour movements in the United States and elsewhere were beginning to reimagine work in terms of rights and individual self-rule. Asians, it was said in both California and Australia, were collectivist, servile and accepted wages and working conditions that undermined white livelihoods.[22] Whiteness, in other words, came to mean independence and the capacity to participate in representative democracy.

Liberal political discourse similarly saw racial unity as the condition for peaceful democracy, and the architects of the legal, social and cultural frameworks of Australia were a part of this tradition. Academic and political proponents of this view in Britain, America and Australia cultivated strong personal connections and shared ideas about the racial foundations of democratic self-determination and its institutions. Oxford fellow James Bryce had strong ties to the United States and was prominent in identifying the roots of social problems and conflict in racial heterogeneity.[23] Deakin and Higgins shared similar personal connections and identified strongly with American democracy and republicanism.[24] These were powerful influences on the men who did much to shape the political, legal and social character of post-Federation Australia. In the 1880s and 1890s, the Australian colonies passed legislation that explicitly restricted Chinese entry, while there had been similar efforts in the United States and Natal. Australian colonial legislation was sometimes explicitly racial, such the Alien Restriction Bill introduced to New South Wales in 1896.

---

21 Lake and Reynolds, *Drawing the Global Colour Line*, pp. 26–7.
22 McKeown, *Melancholy Order*, pp. 69–72.
23 ibid., p. 54.
24 ibid., pp. 41–2.

The Colonial Office in Britain was uneasy with the explicit racism of this legislation, being anxious to protect commercial interests in China and honour the Anglo–Japanese treaty of 1895. They also remained committed to ideals of free movement within the empire. In 1896, a proposed US Immigration Restriction Act failed to pass, while another such Bill became law in Natal. Both of these relied on the mechanism of a literacy test, which required immigrants to write out a passage in a given language to demonstrate their desirability or otherwise. This mechanism appealed to the Colonial Office, since the literacy criteria avoided the explicitly racial discrimination that angered China and Japan while still satisfying settler interests.[25] The New South Wales Alien Restriction Bill, now based on the Natal literacy test at the suggestion of the Colonial Office, was passed in 1897 as the *Coloured Races Restriction and Regulation Act*.[26] By the time of Australian Federation, the principles and strategies of racial exclusion had thus been refined.

Immigration restrictions and the deportation of Pacific Islanders were high priorities in the early sessions of the Commonwealth Parliament. Higgins, while debating the Pacific Island Labourers Act as a Commonwealth Member of Parliament (MP), claimed: 'There are no conditions under which degeneracy of race is so great as those which exist when a superior race and an inferior race are brought into close contact.'[27] In this he echoed Bryce's observations on the United States and, like Deakin, warned of the need to protect Australian democracy against the supposedly degrading influence of multiracial societies.[28] The White Australia Policy, embodied particularly in the *Immigration Restriction Act* (1901) and the *Pacific Island Labourers Act* (1901), became the dominant ideology across the political spectrum, and remained so until the 1960s.[29]

Cilento's subjectivity was more complex than the typical Protestant, imperial and Anglo-Saxon loyalties inscribed in the texts of Australian nationalism.[30] His grandfather Salvatore Cilento arrived in Adelaide in 1855, having taken part in revolts against King Ferdinand II in 1848. This familial connection to Italian language and history was an emotionally

---

25   ibid., pp. 129–31.
26   Walker, *Anxious Nation*, p. 75.
27   H. B. Higgins quoted in Marilyn Lake, 'White Man's Country: The Transnational History of a National Project,' *Australian Historical Studies*, 34(122), 2003, p. 360.
28   See also Lake and Reynolds, *Drawing the Global Colour Line*, pp. 142–52.
29   See Brawley, *The White Peril*, pp. 297–8.
30   White, *Inventing Australia*, p. 112.

powerful one that sometimes served to compensate for his social marginalisation. In his second year in medical school, Cilento confessed to feeling that his once friendly classmates now regarded him, 'in the cheap delirium of 1st year success', as a 'parvenu'.[31] As if to reassure himself, he imagined a patrician Etruscan lineage that he must honour in Australia:

> [H]ere our name is now implanted. Mine let it be to enwreathe it with glory! Mine let it be to hand on to my children (if I am so blessed) brilliant with achievement, resplendent with honours.

On the death of his grandfather, Cilento lamented how his passing cut 'the bond that united us to Italy' and, noting his father's impending overseas journey, prophesied: 'So will I one of these days leave my adopted land to walk on the soil of my Etruscan ancestors.' This identification put Cilento at odds with the more extreme expressions of the White Australia Policy. The British Immigration League, for example, opposed the migration of Southern European labourers, and Cilento himself was well aware in later years of prejudice against Italians in north Queensland.[32] That Cilento would remain one of the most vociferous advocates of the ideal of white Australia shows he was able to accommodate his Italian identity within a predominantly Anglo-Saxon racialist nationalism.

Tropical medicine and the circuits of empire

As dominant as the white Australia ideology was, centuries of experience elsewhere in the tropics seemed to rule out permanent European settlement in the north of the country. British colonisation in the Caribbean, India and West Africa from the mid-eighteenth century generated a corpus of medical knowledge about sickness and health in warm climates. According to naval surgeons, soldiers, explorers and traders, anyone displaced from the climate that had shaped their constitution would likely fall ill. This view rested on ancient Hippocratic and Galenic theories in which health depended on the correct balance of bodily fluids, or humours, as well as the knowledge that the tropics were home to all manner of influences that

---

31   Cilento, Diary: Medical School, 6 March 1914, Cilento Papers, UQFL44, Box 11, Item 16.
32   Walker, *Anxious Nation*, pp. 116–17. See Raphael Cilento to Phyllis Cilento, 7 July 1929 and 12 July 1929, Cilento Papers, UQFL44, Box 11, Item 21. It is also worth noting that Italians and other southern and eastern European people were the chief objects of late nineteenth- and twentieth-century immigration restriction legislation in the United States; see Lake and Reynolds, *Drawing the Global Colour Line*, p. 129.

might upset this balance. Increased sweating in the heat might disorder certain organs, while the abundance of plant life and swamps produced sickly vapours, or miasmas. The injunction to build European outposts on high ground away from swamps and in cooler temperatures became a universal mantra of the texts on hot-climate medicine.[33]

The experience of tropical settlement in Australia seemed to confirm this conventional wisdom. Dysentery and unspecified fevers forced the abandonment of three separate military outposts on the Cobourg Peninsula and Melville Islands between 1827 and 1849. The settlement at Moreton Bay also struggled with disease in the late 1820s. Physicians attributed these outbreaks to climate for the most part, although cultivation of the land at Moreton Bay seemed to promise healthier conditions if settlers could overcome the initial fever shock. Yet even after squatters moved their sheep on to the Darling Downs and Brisbane attracted more free settlers in the 1840s, climate still seemed a barrier to the settlement of a large working population.[34] Visitors to Queensland after its separation from New South Wales in 1859 declared that white occupation and development of the colony would depend on non-white workers. The Queensland sugar industry indeed began importing indentured labourers from the Pacific Islands. These workers, numbering nearly one-third of the Queensland population, had established more than 24,000 hectares of sugar cane by 1900.[35] Even as medical thought drifted away from older climatic theories, doctors, travellers and residents continued to represent the tropics as having a distinctive, racially attuned pathology.[36] Although many in the Australian tropics were alert to the presence of bacteria and parasites after 1890, they were convinced the tropical climate had cultivated a unique community of pathogens to which settlers would be especially vulnerable.[37]

---

33   James Lind, *An Essay on Diseases Incidental to Europeans in Hot Climates: With the Method of Preventing their Fatal Consequence*, 5th edn (London: J. Murray, 1792); James Johnson, *The Influence of Tropical Climates on European Constitutions*, 2nd edn (London: T. & G. Underwood, 1818). See also Philip D. Curtin, '"The White Man's Grave": Image and Reality, 1780–1850,' *The Journal of British Studies*, 1(1), 1961, pp. 94–110; Mark Harrison, *Climates and Constitutions: Health, Race, Environment and British Imperialism in India, 1600–1850* (Delhi: Oxford University Press, 1999); Ryan Johnson, 'European Cloth and "Tropical" Skin: Clothing Material and British Ideas of Health and Hygiene in Tropical Climates,' *Bulletin of the History of Medicine*, 83(3), 2009, pp. 536–8.
34   Anderson, *The Cultivation of Whiteness*, pp. 76–8.
35   ibid., p. 79.
36   ibid., pp. 73–5.
37   ibid., pp. 83–4.

The growing dominance of germ theories of disease nevertheless meant that nationalist public health officials could begin to argue that there were no climatic barriers to white Australia. J. S. C. Elkington, the Public Health Commissioner in Tasmania, declared in a 1905 polemic that all previous warnings about tropical climate, sickness and deterioration were unfounded. Around the words 'tropical' and 'climate', he wrote, had been 'woven a tissue of incorrect inferences, of superstitions, and of prejudices'.[38] Instead of inevitable degeneration, permanent settlement of the tropics was possible with the careful design and application of sanitary regulations, improved infrastructure and hygiene education. Improvements in army sanitation were a clear example, Elkington argued, of how 'the formulation and observation of sanitary laws, and the adoption of a more reasonable manner of living' could ensure health anywhere.[39] James Barrett, a prominent figure in the Melbourne medical community, asserted in 1918:

> The people of Australia are ... realising that the proper use of their northern possessions is vital to national existence, since we are quite unable to keep a valuable part of the earth's surface idle.[40]

Like Elkington, Barrett claimed that the primary cause of sickness among Europeans in the tropics was not climate but infectious diseases, 'which may be almost completely suppressed if certain precautions are taken'.[41] The emphasis here on legislation and individual knowledge and behaviour reflects how a shift in medical discourse from climate to microbe and hygiene made health a matter of 'modern citizenship'.[42] Barrett's and Elkington's comments exemplify this shift, not least in the latter's suggestion that alcoholism was a more important factor in sickness in the tropics than climate.[43]

Elkington was one of many who called for more direct scientific investigation of white health in the tropics. The deportation of indentured labourers under the *Pacific Island Labourers Act* (1901) had necessitated

---

38   J. S. C. Elkington, *Tropical Australia: Is It Suitable for a Working White Race?* (Melbourne: Commonwealth of Australia, 1905), p. 4.

39   ibid., p. 4.

40   James W. Barrett, *The Twin Ideals: An Educated Commonwealth. Volume II* (London: H. K. Lewis & Co., 1918), p. 283.

41   ibid., p. 281.

42   Warwick Anderson, 'Geography, Race and Nation: Remapping "Tropical" Australia, 1890–1930,' *Historical Records of Australian Science*, 11(4), 1997, p. 458.

43   Elkington, *Tropical Australia*, p. 5.

white labourers in sugar production when doubts still lingered over whether they could do such work in the tropics.[44] The establishment of the Australian Institute of Tropical Medicine (AITM) in 1910 was a response to these doubts. Initially administered by the University of Sydney, the institute had financial support from the Commonwealth and Queensland governments and the endorsement of the universities of Melbourne and Adelaide. In his first survey report as the AITM's director, Dr Anton Breinl, formerly of the Liverpool School of Tropical Medicine, reiterated the fundamental question: 'Is the white man able to stand the strain of cutting cane in the tropical parts of North Queensland without having his health permanently injured?' It was, he wrote, a question of 'vital importance for the development of the sugar industry in North Queensland' and for the 'White Australia question generally'.[45]

The imperative of claiming the newly defined and bounded space of the nation through white settlement shaped the work of the institute for the rest of its existence, although its technical work shifted over time.[46] Breinl and his staff focused on two broad research agendas: studies of the common parasites and insects of northern Australia and investigation of the effect of climate on the physiology and physical development of white people in the tropics. The latter included measurement of the body temperature of Queensland dockworkers and the blood composition of white schoolchildren.[47] The 1911 Australasian Medical Congress had resolved to review the results of the institute's research at its next meeting in Brisbane, which did not occur until 1920.[48] With the weight of the institute's positive research results and wartime statistics on the fitness of Queensland recruits behind them, nationalist health officials at the 1920 congress seized the moment to assert that there were no inherent barriers to 'the permanent occupation of tropical Australia by a healthy indigenous white race'.[49]

44   Lorraine Harloe, 'Anton Breinl and the Australian Institute of Tropical Medicine,' in Roy MacLeod and Donald Denoon (eds), *Health and Healing in Tropical Australia and Papua New Guinea* (Townsville, QLD: James Cook University, 1991), p. 35.
45   Anton Breinl, *Tropical Diseases: Report by Dr Breinl, Director of the Australian Institute of Tropical Medicine, Townsville, on the Results of his Journey to the Northern Ports of Queensland* (Melbourne: Commonwealth of Australia, 1910), p. 2.
46   Bashford, '"Is White Australia Possible?",' pp. 253–4.
47   Australian Institute of Tropical Medicine, *Collected Papers* (Townsville, QLD: Australian Institute of Tropical Medicine, 1914–30). See also Anderson, *The Cultivation of Whiteness*, pp. 117–18.
48   *Transactions of the Australasian Medical Congress*, 9, 1911, p. 122.
49   *Transactions of the Australasian Medical Congress*, 11, 1920, p. 45.

This official declaration belied the continuing—and now dissenting—belief among local practitioners that the climate of the Australian tropics was unhealthy for white settlers, particularly women and children.[50] Dr Richard Arthur accused the subcommittee that drafted the congress resolutions of being overly committed to the political ideal of racial purity.[51] When the Yale University geographer Ellsworth Huntington visited north Queensland in 1923, he heard the 'chorus of praise' for the health of the Australian tropics, but saw in the poor condition of some homes an 'undertone' telling of the effect of the tropics on the standards of the community.[52] These criticisms did not dent the confidence of the nationalist cohort. J. H. L. Cumpston, the Director of the Commonwealth Quarantine Service and future Director-General of the CDH, argued that high rates of infestation by filarial worms in Queensland were what impeded economic development in the Australian tropics. 'It is all very well to have a white Australia,' he cautioned, 'but it must be kept white. There must be immaculate cleanliness.'[53] As Anderson has noted, the promoters of tropical settlement demanded not only the exclusion of contaminating aliens, but also the positive cultivation of a fit white race behind the *cordon sanitaire*.[54] In this way, health officials positioned hygiene as a key element in racial and national fitness.

As director of the AITM in the 1920s, after it had come under the control of the CDH, Cilento became the most vocal evangelist for tropical settlement and the fulfilment of a white Australia. His 1926 book, *The White Man in the Tropics*, outlined a complete hygiene program for white settlement, ranging from housing to food, clothing, exercise and leisure.[55] Australian tropical medicine was thus engaged in a national social project. Yet Cilento's introduction to tropical medicine, and his articulation of Australian nationhood, took place within larger imperial contexts. His formal training came through an international network of imperial medical institutions that had developed since the late nineteenth century. His experience of Australian colonial government in New Guinea

---

50   ibid., pp. 54–8.
51   ibid., p. 60.
52   Ellsworth Huntington, *West of the Pacific* (New York: Charles Scribner's Sons, 1925), pp. 340–1.
53   *Transactions of the Australasian Medical Congress*, 11, 1920, p. 49.
54   Anderson, *The Cultivation of Whiteness*, p. 94.
55   Yarwood, 'Sir Raphael Cilento and *The White Man in the Tropics*,' pp. 47–63; Bashford, '"Is White Australia Possible?",' pp. 248–71; Anderson, *The Cultivation of Whiteness*, pp. 135–52.

also played a crucial role in the way he formulated the agenda of tropical medicine. For Cilento, the national significance of tropical hygiene for Australia indeed derived from political and social transformations across empires in Asia and the Pacific.

Plate 1.1 Raphael Cilento and other graduates from the Faculty of Medicine, University of Adelaide, 1918

Cilento is third from the right in the back row. Phyllis McGlew, his future wife, is in the centre of the picture.

Source: Courtesy of the University of Adelaide Archives, Series 1151, No. 196.

There was little indication in Cilento's early education that tropical medicine would define him. He studied for his medical degree at the University of Adelaide, where his lack of prerequisite science subjects made admission a real challenge. His father, who had encouraged him to do law, refused to fund a medical education, forcing Cilento to work as a trainee teacher, fruit picker and newspaper writer while studying for exams. He was fortunate to win a state bursary for his first year, when academic success led to a scholarship that funded the rest of his studies.[56] The curriculum was a basic one, covering anatomy and bacteriology, the

---

56   'Interview with Sir Raphael Cilento, Tropical Medicine Specialist,' Interview by Mel Pratt, Transcript, 7 March 1971, pp. 7–8, National Library of Australia [hereinafter NLA], Canberra. See also Fisher, *Raphael Cilento*, pp. 7–10; Mark Finnane, 'Cilento, Sir Raphael West (Ray) (1893–1985),' *Australian Dictionary of Biography*. Online Edition (Canberra: The Australian National University, 2006), available from: www.adb.online.anu.edu.au/biogs/A170212b.htm.

A DOCTOR ACROSS BORDERS

preparation of slides, the use of microscopes and drawing.[57] It was thus a world away from the colonial administration and social medicine that were to become his career and professional identity.[58]

Historians often trace tropical medicine as a distinct academic and professional discipline to about 1898 with the founding of schools of tropical medicine in London and Liverpool and the start of American territorial expansion in the Philippines, Cuba and Puerto Rico. The rush of bacteriological and parasitological discoveries after the 1870s, including the identification of insect vectors, led imperial governments to invest more in medical knowledge and trained personnel at the turn of the century. There were thus new career opportunities for young doctors. Much of the knowledge of bacteria and parasites had in fact developed in colonial contexts before major institutions of tropical medicine existed. Patrick Manson, the founding head of the London School of Tropical Medicine, conducted his research on the transmission of filarial worms at the Chinese treaty port of Amoy while a member of the Imperial Maritime Customs Service in the 1860s and 1870s.[59] Alphonse Laveran identified the malaria parasite *Plasmodium* in French Algeria in 1880.[60] Ronald Ross discovered the mosquito vector of the malaria parasite in India after consulting with Manson on a return visit to England in the 1890s. Mark Harrison has suggested that tropical medicine in India actually developed separately from the wider British Empire through local responses to plague epidemics in the 1890s.[61]

The eventual establishment of the schools of tropical medicine in Liverpool and London reflected growth of research across the British Empire. The London school trained students from a wide variety of backgrounds, not just those destined for colonial service.[62] The second cohort of students at the London school included three missionary women heading to India and China. In fact, missionaries continued to make up a proportion of the

57   Medical School Notes, Cilento Papers, UQFL44, Box 11, Item 16.
58   'Interview with Sir Raphael Cilento,' p. 11.
59   Douglas M. Haynes, *Imperial Medicine: Patrick Manson and the Conquest of Tropical Disease* (Philadelphia: University of Pennsylvania Press, 2001), pp. 18–20.
60   Warboys, 'Manson, Ross, and Colonial Medical Policy,' p. 24.
61   Harrison, *Public Health in British India*, p. 150.
62   Heather Bell, *Frontiers of Medicine in the Anglo-Egyptian Sudan 1899–1940* (Oxford: Clarendon Press, 1999); Michael Worboys, 'The Colonial World as Mission and Mandate: Leprosy and Empire, 1900–1940,' *Osiris*, 15, 2000, pp. 207–18.

student body.[63] A significant number of Indian students also studied at the school, as the Indian Medical Service increasingly included indigenous personnel in public health work and laboratory research.[64]

American tropical medicine at first developed within the US Army during the Spanish–American war and subsequent conflict with indigenous guerilla forces in the Philippines, Cuba and Puerto Rico.[65] As in previous conflicts, yellow fever and malaria contributed significantly to mortality among American troops. Yellow fever killed 15 soldiers a day during July 1898 in Santiago, Cuba.[66] In the Philippines, 700 soldiers died of disease between 1898 and 1900; 100 more than were killed in battle.[67] In response to these losses, the US Army's surgeon general George Sternberg set up a number of research commissions for tropical diseases.[68] These studies fed back into public health campaigns aimed at cementing regional economic and cultural dominance, most famously in William Gorgas's work in maintaining the health of workers building the Panama Canal. Research on yellow fever in Cuba had demonstrated that mosquitoes were responsible for transmitting the virus, and Gorgas subsequently deployed preventive measures in the canal zone based on those developed in Havana.[69] Interest and expertise in tropical medicine quickly spread beyond the Army Medical Corps. Doctors in Philadelphia founded the American Society of Tropical Medicine in 1903, and a few years later private funding helped to establish the School of Tropical Medicine at Tulane University in Louisiana.[70]

As states began to recognise the value of medicine and hygiene, private contributions to imperial tropical medicine were also increasingly important. Indeed, much of the agenda, finances and institutions of colonial medicine and international health came from the health branch of the Rockefeller Foundation. The foundation's International Health Commission, established in 1913, and successively renamed the International Health Board (IHB) and the International Health Division, had grown out of hookworm programs in the American South. John D.

---

63   Lise Wilkinson and Anne Hardy, *Prevention and Cure: The London School of Hygiene and Tropical Medicine—A 20th Century Quest for Global Public Health* (London: Kegan Paul, 2001), p. 10.
64   Harrison, *Public Health in British India*, p. 163.
65   Farley, *Bilharzia*, p. 31; Stern, 'Yellow Fever Crusade,' pp. 41–3.
66   Farley, *Bilharzia*, p. 36.
67   Anderson, *Colonial Pathologies*, p. 14.
68   Farley, *Bilharzia*, pp. 40–1.
69   Stern, 'Yellow Fever Crusade,' pp. 45–9.
70   Farley, *Bilharzia*, p. 43.

Rockefeller, Snr, had wanted to do philanthropic work since the 1890s and, in 1909, having already founded a research institute in New York, he established the Rockefeller Foundation. Its ambitious aims were to:

> Promote the well-being and to advance the civilization of the peoples of the United States and its territories and possessions and of foreign lands in the acquisition and dissemination of knowledge, in the prevention and relief of suffering, and in the promotion of any and all of the elements of human progress.[71]

National, imperial and global spaces were thus all brought into the potential ambit of the foundation's aims.

Under the influence of Rockefeller's advisor Frederick Gates, medical research and public health became a special focus. The Sanitary Commission, created in 1909 under the direction of Wickliffe Rose to tackle hookworm in the southern United States, established a model public health campaign. It aimed to not only eradicate the disease in local areas, but also educate local authorities, general practitioners and the public in preventive hygiene through special lectures and exhibitions.[72] In this way, they hoped to leave behind a health consciousness that would translate into more active public health activities and institutions. When Rose became the first director of the International Health Commission, he sought to export this model, especially throughout the British Empire. After dining with Colonial Office officials in London in 1913, Rose received permission to initiate projects in British Guiana, and was later invited to consider campaigns in Egypt, Ceylon and the Malay States.[73] British colonies were expected to be self-sufficient on tight budgets and so were reluctant to conduct significant public health campaigns on their own. Colonial medical officers thus tended to welcome Rockefeller funding as an opportunity to do something more ambitious.

As its policies developed, the commission's emphasis on education shifted towards establishing schools of medicine and hygiene around the world. After visiting potential locations at Harvard and Columbia, the commission selected Johns Hopkins Medical School as the site for its new School of Hygiene and Public Health. Although the prospective

---

71   John Farley, *To Cast Out Disease: A History of the International Health Division of the Rockefeller Foundation (1913–1951)* (Oxford: Oxford University Press, 2004), p. 3.
72   ibid., p. 29.
73   ibid., pp. 61–2.

school was supposed to train public health officers for America as a whole, tropical disease experience was clearly an important criterion.[74] The Johns Hopkins school became a model the Rockefeller Foundation exported to the rest of the world. In 1909, for example, the Oriental Education Commission stressed the need for a modern medical school in China, leading to Rockefeller funding and supervision of the Peking Union Medical College in 1915.[75] Rockefeller funding was also crucial in establishing the London School of Hygiene and Tropical Medicine in 1929.

Cilento eventually joined the flow of medical students and personnel through these institutional networks, yet only after he had experienced the tropics himself through Australia's occupation of New Guinea. Cilento recorded in his diary the ferment that gripped the medical school at Adelaide during World War I. 'Feverish activity characterises all', he wrote on 5 August 1914 after the British declaration of war: 'The medical students enthusiastically sang the "National Anthem" in the middle of a practical chem lecture. Excitement prevails.'[76] Cilento was a member of a rifle club at the time and received a notice of mobilisation, yet it was not until 1916 that he enlisted. Medical students were held back until the completion of their studies, however, and he only served for 45 days at a training camp at Murray Bridge, east of Adelaide. He again enlisted after completing his degree in 1918 and was posted as a captain with the Australian Naval and Military Expeditionary Force, a separate volunteer force that had occupied German New Guinea since 1914.[77] Cilento's first work as a qualified medical practitioner was thus as an army medical officer in what was to become an Australian colonial territory.

Cilento's first impressions of New Guinea excited his love of amateur ethnography and the blunt racism that was to shape his dealings with indigenous people in Melanesia and Australia. When Cilento's boat arrived at Rabaul, the German-built capital, in late December 1918, '[h]alf a dozen native boys, some copper coloured boys from New Guinea some jet black Buka boys, came aboard like big monkeys'. He recorded the clothes, the beaded and feathered decorations and hairstyles of these young men with fascination, before writing: 'Their faces are amiably murderous and their

---

74   Farley, *Bilharzia*, pp. 82–3.
75   ibid., pp. 89–91.
76   Cilento, Diary: Medical School, 4 August 1914, UQFL44, Box 11, Item 16.
77   Australian Imperial Force Enlistment Form, 17 June 1918; Australian Imperial Force Enlistment Form, 13 December 1918, NAA: B2455, CILENTO R W.

mental development is about that of a child of 10.'[78] In a fashion typical of New Guinea officials and residents, Cilento represented indigenous people as violent and lacking in Christian sympathy or kindness:

> The natives are disgusting sometimes. This poor sick thing trembling here like a St. Vitus dance victim was an object of joy to the rest who nicknamed her 'gooria' (earthquake) and crowded around mimicking, laughing, pushing or spitefully teasing her.

In another story, a young boy of eight killed his ageing mother because she was a burden, leading Cilento to observe that 'filial love is not very obvious'.[79] His claims about indigenous inferiority thus swung between assertions of intellectual simplicity and inherent capacity for violence.

Violence was an official and casual feature of Australian military occupation in New Guinea, to which Cilento was sympathetic. By the time he arrived, however, officials in Canberra had begun to reform administration of the territory to ensure Australia avoided international censure.[80] Cilento was especially critical of a ban on flogging that took effect in 1919:

> The natives are children of 10 years of age and they do not feel any punishment but a corporal one—the idea of putting them in prison (calaboose) is a farcical one.[81]

All that the ban achieved, he argued, was to drive violence on to the plantations, where planters would flog their employees 'viciously and secretly'.[82] The sanctimony of Australian officials who wished to present an image of enlightened 'native administration' to the world was thus, he claimed, undermining the effective government and development of New Guinea. 'Heaven help New Guinea if we ever get the ruling of it', he wrote. 'Everyone here prays earnestly that any nation from Greenland to Timbuctoo shall get it rather than that Australia shall add it to her museum of wasted opportunities.'[83] For Cilento—developing a belief that was to run through his career—progressive government lay less in recognition and observance of rights than in authoritarian and disciplinary paternalism.

---

78 Raphael Cilento, Diary: New Guinea, 28 December 1918, pp. 9–10, UQFL44, Box 11, Item 17.
79 Cilento, Diary: New Guinea, 23 April 1919, p. 41, UQFL44, Box 11, Item 17.
80 Pedersen, *The Guardians*, pp. 135–6.
81 Cilento, Diary: New Guinea, 22 April 1919, p. 38, UQFL44, Box 11, Item 17.
82 ibid., p. 39.
83 ibid., p. 40.

Besides a handful of Europeans, Rabaul was home to significant Chinese, Japanese and Malay communities. The German New Guinea Company, which administered the colony until the German imperial government took control, had brought the Chinese to the territory as plantation labourers. By the time of the Australian occupation, many had worked as overseers, merchants, restaurateurs or businessmen for over a decade.[84] In colonial discourse, however, 'coloured' people were not all equal. The Ambonese living in the Chinese quarter, Cilento wrote, were 'the best class of coloured people here and are well educated … All are more or less skilled musicians, lighter skinned than the natives and many speak English, German, Dutch and Malay'.[85] Cilento thus assumed, as colonial discourse had elsewhere, racial hierarchies that distinguished between different 'Asiatic' peoples as well as between Europeans and others.

Europeans typically represented Chinese communities as especially unclean, and their bodies, dwellings and businesses as reservoirs of disease. The threat of contagion was often entwined with the degraded morality of opium dens and gambling. In Rabaul, Cilento would sometimes eschew the company of the officers to visit Chinatown. 'Hollow-cheeked and hollow-eyed', the denizens of one such establishment 'lay about inert, only moving now and then to add another particle of the filthy treacle to the flame. The Gov. intends soon to stop the trade'. Asian businesses and social gatherings were not all loathsome, although Cilento took his racism everywhere. On one occasion, he dismissed an officers' social gathering as a 'cask-emptying' stunt and instead visited a Japanese restaurant with a civilian acquaintance. Dinner was followed with a visit to a Malay dance, where the women were free to choose a partner:

> You can easily imagine my feeling then when a black-eyed coquette danced up to me who all unsuspecting was enjoying the fun. Your poor Raphael revolved in the mazy waltz with a brown skinned fling! There was no escape.[86]

The mixed society of a colonial town such as Rabaul was thus both grotesque and fascinating to the young man.

---

84   See Peter Cahill, 'Chinese in Rabaul—1921 to 1942: Normal Practices, or Containing the Yellow Peril?,' *The Journal of Pacific History*, 31(1), 1996, pp. 72–3.

85   Cilento, Diary: New Guinea, 30 December 1918, p. 15, UQFL44, Box 11, Item 17.

86   Cilento, Diary: New Guinea, 31 December 1918, p. 17, UQFL44, Box 11, Item 17.

Cilento's responsibilities as an army medical officer were broad, including hospital work, examination of labourers and routine patrols. On Cilento's first full day, the principal medical officer showed him a few slides of the malaria parasite. For the rest of his stay in Rabaul, Cilento was confined to treating minor ailments in hospital and felt he was missing out on more interesting tropical diseases.[87] In March 1919, however, he was dispatched to Kavieng on New Ireland, which presented a much more interesting environment. At the hospital there, he treated cases of gonorrhoea, granuloma, syphilis, leprosy and goitre. He visited missions and local plantations to inoculate hundreds of indigenous labourers against influenza.[88] Medical officers also accompanied district officers on patrols that allowed some medical surveillance. Cilento noted in March that malaria would intensify and that 'many attempts at sanitation loom in my mental future'.[89] Years later, Cilento would reflect that this first fortuitous experience of working in medicine and public health in the tropics 'had set a pattern that was to govern my whole later life'.[90]

Cilento left New Guinea in 1919 to marry his fiancée, Phyllis McGlew, who had studied medicine in his class at Adelaide. Phyllis later recalled that her aunt had died in the Solomon Islands and that her father, through his connections in the Commonwealth Government, managed to block any immediate return to New Guinea.[91] Cilento's developing taste for tropical health work, however, drove him to try again for a colonial post. He was struggling to maintain a private practice in Adelaide, and both he and Phyllis chafed against the boredom of suburban life. An opportunity to go abroad again soon presented itself. The Federated Malay States was suffering from a shortage of medical officers and advertised positions in *The Lancet* and the *British Medical Journal*. Although imperial postings often provided the beginnings of a career away from the competition of private practice in Britain, colonial officials in Malaya struggled to attract applicants. They thus insisted that advertisements emphasise that medical officers would be in charge of a hospital.[92] The advertisements also specified that applicants must have qualifications from a British medical

---

87   Cilento, Diary: New Guinea, 1–3 January 1919, pp. 18–19, UQFL44, Box 11, Item 17.
88   Cilento, Diary: New Guinea, 5 April 1919, p. 31, UQFL44, Box 11, Item 17.
89   Cilento, Diary: New Guinea, 29 March 1919, p. 30, UQFL44, Box 11, Item 17.
90   Fisher, *Raphael Cilento*, p. 15.
91   Phyllis Cilento, *My Life* (Sydney: Methuen Haynes, 1987), p. 41.
92   L. N. Guillemard, High Commissioner, Malay States, to Secretary of State for the Colonies, 31 March 1920, pp. 1–2, United Kingdom National Archives, CO 717/1.

school and take a course at either the London or the Liverpool school of medicine. By September, however, the colonial government loosened its requirements to offer Cilento, who had no such qualifications, a position as a medical officer at Teluk Anson in Lower Perak.[93]

Cilento's work in Malaya was much the same as it had been in New Guinea. He was responsible for a hospital and for the Malay villages, or *kampongs*, in his district, while the rubber plantations employing indentured Chinese and Indian labourers had their own medical facilities.[94] As in other colonial territories in Asia and Africa, infant mortality was high. In 1921, the rate was 183 deaths per 1,000 births.[95] Malaria was the most significant cause of mortality and, in 1919, made up over 40 per cent of the hospital admissions among indentured labourers.[96] In 1919, the principal medical officer noted a slight reduction in malaria, reporting:

> [I]f we had only enough staff of doctors and engineers to deal with this, the most serious drawback in Malaya, the mortality would have been still less—every effort must be made to get the men required.[97]

The most important causes of mortality besides malaria were pneumonia and tuberculosis—not commonly thought of as colonial diseases. There were, however, occasional outbreaks of infectious diseases more closely associated with tropical Asia. An outbreak of smallpox near Teluk Anson in 1921 reached 76 cases before being 'stamped out' by the 'energetic action of the Medical and Health authorities'.[98]

Aside from the limited supply of medical officers and sanitary inspectors, colonial discourse typically identified the beliefs and habits of indigenous peoples as the greatest obstacle to progress. British authorities blamed the 1921 smallpox outbreak on Malays who 'had managed to avoid vaccination'.[99] The principal medical officer reported that infant mortality was 'chiefly due to the ignorance and carelessness of the native women'.[100]

---

93 High Commissioner of the Malay States to Secretary of State for the Colonies, 10 September 1920, United Kingdom National Archives, CO 717/4.
94 Cilento, *My Life*, p. 48.
95 Federated Malay States, *Medical Report for the Year 1921* (Kuala Lumpur: Federated Malay States, 1922), p. 2.
96 Federated Malay States, *Medical Report for the Year 1919* (Kuala Lumpur: Federated Malay States, 1920), p. 4.
97 ibid., p. 2.
98 Federated Malay States, *Medical Report for the Year 1921*, p. 3.
99 ibid., p. 3.
100 ibid., p. 2.

If medical officers could not associate tuberculosis with the tropics as they could with malaria, they could still blame the supposedly inherent unhygienic behaviour of 'coloured people':

> Overcrowding, ignorance and dirty habits, with complete disregard of the simplest rules of ventilation, are the main causes of this disease. It is not difficult to design well ventilated houses, but it is impossible to prevent people closing their air entrances.[101]

Phyllis Cilento, appointed Lady Medical Officer in 1921, recalled:

> It was difficult persuading these secluded people bound in tradition to accept western medicine in any form and he [Raphael] found that they would rather die than submit to surgery.[102]

While medical expertise had acquired a more prominent place in colonial government and imperial policy, health departments were often chronically understaffed and underfunded and only too aware of the questionable efficacy of their work.

Domestic life in Cilento's hospital compound was a familiar colonial tableau. The Cilentos employed cooks, a head 'houseboy', a driver, an *amah* or nurse and even someone to wave a fan at dinner. Cilento continued to indulge in amateur ethnography and developed a lasting fascination with Malaya, especially the waves of migration shaping its history and culture.[103] As in New Guinea, he tended to avoid the European club and instead wore sarongs or headdresses, learned Malay, listened to elders tell stories and undertook expeditions into the forests in the hope of meeting indigenous Semang people.[104]

A few months before the end of Cilento's appointment, J. S. C. Elkington, now a senior officer in the new CDH, visited him in Malaya with an offer of employment in the Division of Tropical Hygiene. An international study tour, including attendance at conferences and enrolment at the London School of Tropical Medicine, was a condition of accepting the job. Cilento was also to observe public health practices in Asia, North America and Panama that Commonwealth and state agencies could

---

101 ibid., p. 4.
102 Cilento, *My Life*, p. 48. For Phyllis Cilento's appointment, see Federated Malay States, *Medical Report for the Year 1921*, p. 8.
103 Raphael Cilento, 'Malaya,' Address to Constitutional Club, 13 November 1941, Cilento Papers, UQFL44, Box 17, Item 81.
104 Cilento, *My Life*, p. 49.

implement in the development of tropical Australia.[105] The department itself had its origins in the interplay of empire, international organisations and regional interests. The director of the Quarantine Service, J. H. L. Cumpston, had long advocated an enlarged federal health department and it took the 1919 global influenza pandemic to convince the majority of Australian public health officials that a federal health department was necessary. By 1921, the prospect of increased colonial responsibilities in the Pacific Islands had added weight to the proposition. The centralisation of public health had meanwhile become a global trend, with Britain establishing the national Ministry of Health in 1919. Cumpston made explicit calls for such a department at the 1920 Australasian Medical Congress in Brisbane, but international support proved important. Victor Heiser, the IHB's Director of the East, was especially influential, offering the IHB's expert personnel for special disease campaigns and funding for the training of Australian personnel in overseas institutions.[106]

Cilento accepted the position, stopping first on his world tour at the 1921 Congress of the FEATM in Batavia. The FEATM had emerged from a 1908 meeting in Manila, including British, French, Dutch and American colonial medical officers and health officials and academics from China and Japan.[107] The journal *Science* hailed its creation as bringing together 'English-speaking scientific workers' in the region 'for mutual social and scientific improvement'.[108] Unlike some of the intergovernmental health agencies that emerged in the early twentieth century, such as the Office International d'Hygiène Publique (OIHP), the FEATM was meant to create a network of researchers and health officials with specifically regional concerns. Although it was one of the few international organisations that allowed Asian people to participate, the FEATM was, for the most part, an exercise in regional cooperation between colonial administrations.[109]

105 J. H. L. Cumpston, 'The Australian Institute of Tropical Medicine,' *The Medical Journal of Australia*, 1(15), 1923, p. 399.

106 Roe, 'The Establishment of the Australian Department of Health,' p. 180; Anthea Hyslop, 'A Question of Identity: J. H. L. Cumpston and Spanish Influenza, 1918–1919,' *ACH: The Journal of the History of Culture in Australia*, 16, 1997, pp. 60–76.

107 *British Medical Journal*, 1(2470), 1908, p. 1061.

108 *Science*, 31(792), 1910, p. 343.

109 David Arnold, *Tropical Governance: Managing Health in Monsoon Asia, 1908–1938*, Working Paper No. 116 (Singapore: Asia Research Institute Seminar Series, 2009), pp. 12–21; Tomoko Akami, 'A Quest to be Global: The League of Nations Health Organization and Inter-colonial Regional Governing Agendas of the Far Eastern Association of Tropical Medicine 1910–25,' *The International History Review*, 38(1), 2015, pp. 2–3.

At the 1912 meeting in Hong Kong, governor Sir Frederick Lugard described colonies in Asia as 'lands held in trust for civilization'. Colonial development, he argued:

> Can be raised above the sordid level of more material benefit by the recognition of responsibility towards the people of the tropics, to whom in return for material products we should bring higher standards of material comfort, and above all higher standards of morality, and the benefits which science has conferred on humanity.[110]

Lugard, anticipating the language of trusteeship later codified by the League of Nations and the United Nations, shows how international health organisations in the early twentieth century participated in discourses and practices of colonial development in which knowledge was to flow from a collectively 'civilised' portion of the world to an underdeveloped one.

Cilento's professional and intellectual development took shape within this array of institutions, networks and forums of medical research and training. After resigning his post in the Malay States, Cilento toured Malaya for the CDH before leaving for Batavia. Phyllis had given birth to the pair's first child, Raphael Frederic, nicknamed 'Raffles', and returned to Australia.[111] Arriving in London after stopping at Ceylon and Port Said, Cilento joined the School of Tropical Medicine's 68th session, running from January to March 1922. The Rockefeller Foundation had by this time promised funding for a new and more comprehensive London School of Hygiene and Tropical Medicine, into which Patrick Manson's original institution would eventually be absorbed.[112] Cilento, however, studied in the original school, which had been housed in the Endsleigh Palace Hotel in central London, near University College, since 1919. A diverse group of students joined Cilento in his course, including British medical officers from India, West Africa and the Straits Settlements, indigenous members of the Indian and Kashmir medical services, US Army medical officers, missionaries bound for China, West Africa and India, and Japanese and Egyptian public health officials. Most of the students were private practitioners, some of whom had Indian or Egyptian qualifications.[113] Cilento's lecturers included some of the luminaries and notorious figures

---

110 Far Eastern Association of Tropical Medicine, *Transactions of the Second Biennial Congress, Held at Hong Kong, 1912* (Hong Kong: Noronha & Co., 1914), pp. 3–4.
111 Fisher, *Raphael Cilento*, pp. 25–33.
112 Wilkinson and Hardy, *Prevention and Cure*, p. 65; Farley, *To Cast Out Disease*, pp. 217–20.
113 Register No. 7, Records of the London School of Hygiene and Tropical Medicine, pp. 73–90.

of tropical medicine, such as Philip Manson-Bahr, Louis Westenra Sambon, Aldo Castellani and Robert Leiper. Lectures focused heavily on parasitology and zoology, although there were lecture series on sanitation, water purification, waste disposal and quarantine.[114]

Cilento's training in tropical medicine was thus conventional in its primary concern with specific diseases, such as malaria, trypanosomiasis, yellow fever, filariasis, cholera, plague, bilharzia, hookworm and leprosy, and the technical means of controlling them. Several scholars have critically analysed how these biomedical priorities of tropical medicine led to neglect of the social aspects of health and the basic public health benefits of clean water supplies, effective sewerage and town planning.[115] As shown in subsequent chapters, however, these disciplinary preoccupations would not monopolise Cilento's approach to public health, either in New Guinea or in Australia. Indeed, it was New Guinea that shaped his increasingly positive and social approach to health.

World order: Race, empire and civilisation

As Cilento moved through these larger networks, he was at the same time considering Australia's own relationship with an imperial and racialised world order. In a 1922 graduate thesis submitted to the University of Adelaide, he set out an agenda for tropical medicine that foregrounded Australia's postwar responsibilities in New Guinea and the 'intricate problems of international politics' in which it was enmeshed.[116] The most important development in this regard was the League of Nations. Germany's defeat in World War I left in doubt the future of its colonies, including New Guinea. At the Paris Peace Conference, US president Woodrow Wilson—already known for his wartime speeches on self-determination—proposed an international system of trusteeship.[117] Australian prime minister William Morris (Billy) Hughes, on the other hand, pushed for New Guinea's outright annexation as an Australian colony.[118] The eventual compromise, to which the British prime minister

---

114 London School of Tropical Medicine, *Prospectus* (London: E. G. Berryman & Sons, 1921), pp. 13–24.
115 Denoon, *Public Health in Papua New Guinea*, pp. 20–1; Farley, *Bilharzia*, p. 81.
116 Cilento, 'A Correlation of Some Features of Tropical Preventive Medicine,' p. i.
117 Manela, *The Wilsonian Moment*, pp. 19–25.
118 Hermann Hiery, *The Neglected War: The German South Pacific and the Influence of World War I* (Honolulu: University of Hawai'i Press, 1995), pp. 205–6.

Lloyd George acceded, would involve a system of mandates under the authority of the League of Nations.[119] As resolved at the Paris conference, the league assigned a mandate to specific countries to administer former Ottoman and German territories. In principle, this made those countries responsible to the international community for the governance and development of those territories.[120] It seemed that Australia was destined to receive the mandate for New Guinea and, importantly, Japan would receive that of the Marshall, Marianne and Caroline islands.

It was this international development in the imperial world order that preoccupied Cilento in his graduate thesis. 'The war revolutionised our social and political environment', he wrote. The British dominions now expected greater independence and had in fact won recognition as distinct nation-states in the League of Nations General Assembly. Moreover, the league had entrusted Australia with New Guinea—a sign that Australia had 'come of age'.[121] 'A few years ago,' Cilento wrote, 'Australia was a distant outpost of an empire: today she is recognized as a nation with the responsibilities of government, and with colonies and outposts of her own.'[122] The best way for Australia to justify the trust placed in it, Cilento argued, was to make medicine and the protection of indigenous health the foundations of a progressive course of governance. 'The outstanding feature of the responsibility we have accepted', he wrote, 'is the seriousness of the native problem, and our national honour demands that we attack it without delay.'[123] Only in preventing disease and restoring 'physical constitutions' was there any hope, Cilento argued, of avoiding the extinction of these peoples. In 'medicine and a rational education', the Australian administration in New Guinea thus had the ideal 'point of contact' through which it could:

> build up their institutions on our lines to our level, rather than confront them with the impassable gulf that seems to lie between the height of our attainment and the low level of their own.[124]

119 See Kevin Grant, 'Human Rights and Sovereign Abolitions of Slavery, c. 1885–1956,' in Kevin Grant, Philippa Levine and Frank Trentmann (eds), *Beyond Sovereignty: Britain, Empire and Transnationalism, c. 1880–1950* (Basingstoke, UK: Palgrave Macmillan, 2007), p. 87.
120 Susan Pedersen, 'Back to the League of Nations,' *American Historical Review*, 112(4), 2007, p. 1103.
121 Cilento, 'A Correlation of Some Features of Tropical Preventive Medicine,' p. ii.
122 ibid., p. i.
123 ibid., p. vii.
124 ibid., pp. vi–vii.

Cilento was in this regard fairly typical of colonial officials in this period, insisting on gradual social and cultural transformation, the completion of which lay in the very distant future, if ever.[125]

Cilento also saw the larger geopolitical significance of Australia's colonial commitments in the Pacific. His training in tropical medicine had coincided with a renewed anxiety about Asian challenges to white global dominance. For many politicians and academics, World War I had shattered white solidarity and prestige. As biologists and social scientists issued warnings about the dangers of population growth in Asia, a wave of anticolonial uprisings in India, Egypt and China followed the failure of the Paris Peace Conference to support self-determination.[126] Concepts of race and 'civilisation' remained central to the visions of world order expressed in European and settler-colonial societies.[127] Popular and political responses to a Japanese proposal for racial equality clauses in the League of Nations Covenant were deeply hostile in Australia and the United States, putting American and British delegates in Paris in a difficult diplomatic position. The Australian delegation, however, led by Hughes, was unapologetic in its opposition.[128] Key figures in postwar internationalism and the League of Nations also insisted on the preservation of a paternal relationship between the 'civilised' powers and the peoples of colonised territories. Wilson, whose wartime invocation of a universal right to self-determination had raised the hopes of many nationalists in Asia and Africa, ultimately reaffirmed the imperial character of world order.[129]

Fear about the challenge of Asia to 'civilisation' had been around for some time. Charles Pearson's 1893 book, *National Life and Character: A Forecast*, was a particularly influential expression of these concerns and enjoyed a significant readership in the United States and Britain.[130] Pearson pessimistically foretold a time when the peoples of Asia and Africa would muscle white men out of the tropics and threaten refuges of 'white'

---

125 See Anderson, *Colonial Pathologies*, p. 183.
126 Manela, *The Wilsonian Moment*, pp. 6–9.
127 Geulen, 'The Common Grounds of Conflict,' pp. 69–72; Mazower, *No Enchanted Palace*, pp. 13–14.
128 Brawley, *The White Peril*, pp. 12–16; Manela, *The Wilsonian Moment*, pp. 181–2; Lake and Reynolds, *Drawing the Global Colour Line*, pp. 284–97.
129 Manela, *The Wilsonian Moment*, pp. 4–5, 19–25.
130 Lake and Reynolds, *Drawing the Global Colour Line*, pp. 75–7.

civilisation in Australia and the United States. The Australian policy of excluding non-European peoples was not merely a national imperative, but also a global one:

> We know that coloured and white labour cannot exist side by side; we are well aware that China can swamp us with a single year's surplus of population; and we know that if national existence is sacrificed to the working of a few mines and sugar plantations, it is not the Englishmen in Australia alone, but the whole civilised world, that will be the losers.[131]

One could seek to preserve the whiteness of the settler nations, but it was likely, Pearson argued, that the white man would lose his grip on those parts of the world that maintained large indigenous populations, whose elimination neither humanity nor reality could permit:

> The day will come, and perhaps is not far distant, when the European observer will look round to see the globe girdled with a continuous zone of the black and yellow races, no longer too weak for aggression or under tutelage, but independent, or practically so, in government, monopolising the trade of their own regions, and circumscribing the industry of the European.[132]

For Pearson, this was the almost inevitable outcome of European expansion carrying the benefits of civilisation out into the world. Law and order, roads, communication, health and concepts of self-determination had all stirred 'coloured' peoples to challenge white hegemony.

This discourse found its way into Australian discussions of tropical medicine before the war. In his presidential address at the 1911 Australasian Medical Congress in Sydney, Dr F. Antill Pockley spoke of how the great medical discoveries of the past 20 years were:

> threatening not only to revolutionise the practice of medicine, but, within limits which inexorable Nature ever ordains, to profoundly alter the inter-racial relationships of man and influence his distribution on the face of the globe.[133]

---

131 Charles Pearson, *National Life and Character: A Forecast* (London: Macmillan & Co., 1894), p. 17.
132 ibid., p. 89.
133 F. Antill Pockley, 'Presidential Address,' *Transactions of the Australasian Medical Congress*, 9th Session, 1911, p. 83.

The eradication of diseases such as hookworm and malaria, to which could be ascribed much of the perceived lethargy of non-European peoples, would benefit the 'dark races', as well as open up territories to commerce. With greater freedom from disease, the population of these peoples would likely increase faster than that of Europeans and become 'more formidable competitors than heretofore for the possession of their ancestral domains'.[134] At the same session of the congress, Dr A. Wallace Weihen argued that while non–Anglo-Saxon peoples were very well suited to survival, they were not necessarily suited to anything else, such as participation in democracy and the maintenance of the institutions of civilisation: 'In these days of eugenics we must recognise that, apart from education, any attempt to improve race-stocks are limited to two main directions'—namely, internal segregation and 'refusing entrance to undesirables from without'.[135] The national questions of immigration restriction and whether white men could settle the tropics thus always drew their urgency from a larger understanding of a changing world order.[136]

Popular texts that emerged during and after World War I maintained these themes. Madison Grant's *The Passing of the Great Race*, published in 1917, was particularly influential among biologists, geneticists and social scientists agitating for greater immigration restrictions in the 1920s. Grant's book and others were premised on the same themes as those in *National Life and Character*, although they eschewed Pearson's pessimism in favour of an obstinate determination to control any future global transformations. As Lake and Reynolds have shown, a sense of racial kinship and solidarity between Australian and American advocates of immigration restriction persisted into the 1920s.[137] Grant wrote:

> The bitter opposition of the Australians and Californians to the admission of Chinese coolies and Japanese farmers is due primarily to a blind but absolutely justified determination to keep those lands as white man's countries.[138]

---

134 ibid., p. 91.
135 A. Wallace Weihen, 'The Medical Inspection of Immigrants to Australia,' *Transactions of the Australasian Medical Congress*, 9th Session, 1911, p. 635–6.
136 Bashford, *Imperial Hygiene*, pp. 137–40.
137 Lake and Reynolds, *Drawing the Global Colour Line*, pp. 312–14.
138 Madison Grant, *The Passing of the Great Race, or the Racial Basis of European History* (London: G. Bell & Sons, 1917), pp. 70–1.

The exclusion of non-white people was thus, as Pearson had argued, instinctive.

Grant was followed by a number of other academic observers whose popular books were widely read. Lothrop Stoddard, an American political scientist, published *The Rising Tide of Color Against White World-Supremacy* in 1921. Like Pearson, Stoddard noted that European law and sanitation had fostered population growth, especially in Asia: 'Wherever the white man goes he attempts to impose the bases of his ordered civilization.' The increase in population resulting from the cessation of tribal warfare and the prevention of famine and disease in colonised territories could only result in 'a tremendous and steadily augmenting outward thrust of surplus colored men from overcrowded colored homelands'.[139] Where once a white race drawn together internationally by instinct may have been resisted, now the war had torn any solidarity apart.[140]

Stoddard resigned himself to the inevitable loss of white dominance in those countries with large indigenous populations. Asians, he wrote, were 'gifted peoples who have profoundly influenced human progress in the past and who undoubtedly will contribute much to world-civilization'. They were adopting Western methods in the cultivation of a modernist nationalism: 'That this profound Asiatic renaissance will eventually result in the substantial elimination of white political control from Anatolia to the Philippines is as natural as it is inevitable.'[141] In contrast, the white settler communities in Australia, New Zealand, the United States and Canada had to be defended at all costs. The loss of white dominance elsewhere was acceptable since social and biological divisions between races would remain. In a mixed-race society, however, the danger of diluting the blood of the white race would always be present. Race and blood were the foundations of civilised society and its legal and political institutions:

> It is clean, virile, genius-bearing blood, streaming down the ages through the unerring action of heredity, which, in anything like a favourable environment, will multiply itself, solve our problems, and sweep us on to higher and nobler destinies.[142]

---

139 Stoddard, *The Rising Tide of Color Against White World-supremacy*, pp. 8–9.
140 ibid., pp. 198–206.
141 ibid., p. 229.
142 ibid., p. 305.

Prescott Hall was thus correct, Stoddard argued, in stating that immigration restriction was not merely a national project, but also a method of maintaining a 'civilised' world order through 'segregation on a large scale'.[143] The enforcement of segregation would ultimately be one part of a larger program for the gradual transformation of empire that would preserve 'civilisation'.

Cilento's brief for tropical medicine, including his emphasis on the importance of Australia's responsibility for indigenous health and welfare in New Guinea, was shaped by these transnational anxieties about the political and demographic challenges of Asia. If Australia could not prevent the extinction of indigenous people in New Guinea, it would be forced to import indentured labourers from India or China and thus suffer from 'the menace of their politics, the one imbued with the non-cooperation ideas of Ghandi [sic], the other our "yellow peril"'.[144] Besides the 'swarming masses of the Orient', the increasingly ambitious imperial interests of Japan compounded the threat of war in the Pacific. Japan had become 'a menacing figure in the very heart of the Chinese commercial realm, with an organized and powerful government and a highly developed industrial system'.[145] In addition to earlier annexations in Asia, the League of Nations had entrusted Japan with the Marshall, Marianne and Caroline islands—'a belt right across the Pacific'.[146] The league mandates thus became a geopolitical concern in the Pacific. It was vital, Cilento argued, that Australia develop Rabaul, the administrative capital of New Guinea and a 'half-way house' for commerce in the region, into an 'asset to the whole of Australia'. The terms of the mandate for New Guinea forbade fortification of the territory:

> but the necessity to occupy it and develop its resources is obvious, if we wish to retain it, or (which is as important and, indeed equivalent,) to attract the share of tropical trade that is our right.[147]

Ideally, the government would use indigenous labour for this purpose, making the economic development of New Guinea for the benefit of Australia inseparable from the cultivation of industrious habits that was an obligation of enlightened colonial government.

---

143 ibid., p. 259.
144 Cilento, 'A Correlation of Some Features of Tropical Preventive Medicine,' pp. v–vi.
145 ibid., p. ix.
146 ibid., p. x.
147 ibid., p. xi.

Cilento never allowed internationalism to supersede national interests. All the evidence of China's population growth and Japan's territorial expansion pointed to future conflict, which would likely drift towards the underdeveloped Australian tropics. It was therefore crucial that Australia should settle and develop the north in this period of economic competition between nations:

> We have been granted nationhood and it is our bounden duty to accept the proud responsibility and to strengthen our frontiers. Neither arms, nor warships, fortresses, nor squadrons of aeroplanes, can compare in defensive value with the importance of a population rooted in the soil.[148]

In describing nationhood as having been granted to Australia and coinciding with territorial expansion in the Pacific, Cilento's thesis underlines the mutual constitution of the national, the imperial and the global in this period.[149] In Cilento's mind, imperialism and its increasing internationalisation were crucial in defining national problems, priorities and responsibilities.

After gaining his Diploma of Tropical Medicine and Hygiene, Cilento toured the United States and finally visited Panama. By the time he arrived back in Australia to take up his duties with the CDH in October 1922, he had come up with a working ideological framework for tropical medicine that folded together his nationalism and imperialism, as well as some sense of the globalisation of economic and social life. Cilento became part of a global circulation of medical students, public health officials and missionaries. Beyond the official circuits of Anglo-American imperial institutions there were also voluntary and accidental aspects to Cilento's mobility that intersected with them. His posts in occupied New Guinea and British Malaya arose in fortuitous circumstances—a combination of Australian military prerogatives on the one hand and the needs of the British colonial government on the other.

This was an education in empire, but not one in which Cilento simply passed through a global apparatus designed to reproduce and disseminate models of imperial tropical medicine and public health. His graduate thesis invested his formal training in London with national significance drawn from his early experience of Australian imperialism in the Pacific.

---

148 ibid., p. xiii.
149 For liberal versions of this entanglement, see Sluga, *Internationalism in the Age of Nationalism*, pp. 3–17.

Despite initial misgivings, the Commonwealth's new responsibilities in New Guinea became essential to Cilento's agenda for Australian tropical medicine. The nationalist imperatives of racial homogeneity and development were fundamental to the institutionalisation of tropical medicine in Australia, yet they were entangled in imperial ambition.

2

A medico of Melanesia: Colonial medicine in New Guinea, 1924–1928

In a small, unpublished manuscript from 1928 that he entitled 'A Medico of Melanesia', Raphael Cilento proclaimed that 'it has always seemed to me that there was nothing that could compare for interest and charm with medical work among natives'. Unlike the private practitioner in the suburbs, chained miserably to the 'confounded telephone', colonial medical officers were treated to adventure, exotic disease and the full breadth of social work involved in public health.[1] For Cilento, recording birth and death rates, monitoring water supplies and examining housing, nutrition and waste disposal were all vital aspects of health in Australia's tropical territories. From this viewpoint, he concluded that 'the problem of health is the basic problem of government and permeates every subdivision of administration'.[2] The claim that social and economic progress ultimately depended on health was to become a mantra for his work in public health in both New Guinea and Australia. Colonial administration was thus a crucial context for Cilento's fundamental belief that government must make health and hygiene the core elements of governing all populations and their development.

---

1   Raphael Cilento, 'A Medico of Melanesia,' 1928, p. 1, Cilento Papers, UQFL44, Box 13, Item 37.
2   ibid., p. 3.

Cilento hoped that in New Guinea he might replicate the deeds of medical men such as William Gorgas, whose 'war' against mosquitoes and yellow fever in Panama was legendary.[3] In New Guinea, Cilento could embody the type of man for whom:

> the jungle of the present is the city of the future, and with the ear of the Imperialist and the enthusiasm of the pioneer, he hears the hammer of the builder in the crash of every falling tree.[4]

Yet this ideal image of colonial pioneering belies the more complex realities of colonial hygiene. A chronic lack of money frustrated public health projects across the colonial tropics. At the same time, Cilento had to constantly negotiate the authority of medical knowledge. Tropical hygiene had promised greater efficiency in colonial production and reinforced racial segregation of colonial spaces. Yet Cilento also vigorously lobbied a parsimonious New Guinea administration to spend more on health by appealing to an international discourse of paternal responsibility that itself rested on ideas about modernity, civilisation and backwardness.[5]

Cilento's career as director of the Department of Public Health in the mandated Territory of New Guinea highlights the ambiguous place of public health in colonial government. As Heather Bell suggested in her study of Anglo-Egyptian Sudan, it is important to decentre, to an extent, tropical medicine within the study of colonial medicine. Preventive medicine and other social approaches to health could be just as important in local colonial politics as the discipline of tropical medicine, tied as it was to London and Liverpool.[6] With this in mind, it is important that a fresh examination of public health in New Guinea avoids singling out tropical medicine for criticism while valorising the basic principles of preventive medicine that colonial officials supposedly neglected.[7] Clean water supplies, satisfactory nutrition and sanitary living conditions are

---

3   Andrew Balfour, *War Against Tropical Disease: Being Seven Sanitary Sermons Addressed to All Interested in Tropical Hygiene and Administration* (London: Bailliere, Tindall & Cox, 1920), p. 17. See also Stern, 'Yellow Fever Crusade,' pp. 44–6.

4   Cilento, *The White Man in the Tropics*, p. 11.

5   For the discourse on colonial responsibility, see Susan Pedersen, 'Settler Colonialism at the Bar of the League of Nations,' in Caroline Elkins and Susan Pedersen (eds), *Settler Colonialism in the Twentieth Century: Projects, Practices, Legacies* (New York: Routledge, 2005), pp. 113–34; Grant, 'Human Rights and Sovereign Abolitions of Slavery,' p. 84.

6   Bell, *Frontiers of Medicine in the Anglo-Egyptian Sudan*, p. 1. See also Margaret Jones, *Health Policy in Britain's Model Colony: Ceylon (1900–1948)* (New Delhi: Orient Longman, 2004), pp. 109–10.

7   Denoon, *Public Health in Papua New Guinea*, pp. 20–4.

of course important facets of a sound and just public health system. Yet such practices were as deeply enmeshed in colonial government and culture as were the specific interests of tropical medicine.

Health officers were one kind of colonial agent among many, the interests, objectives and ideologies of whom could be complementary, negotiable, tense or incompatible with each other. Cilento's training in the discipline of tropical medicine made him a conduit for public health policies that legitimated racial segregation and offered technologies for surveillance and population management. While some government officials in Rabaul approved of his proposals for complete racial segregation of urban spaces, commercial interests objected to the costs of transporting indentured labourers from their planned compound. Malnutrition and population decline became the focus of Cilento's scathing criticism of the New Guinea administration, which invoked an international discourse of colonial paternalism enshrined in the League of Nations mandates. Cilento's own construction of racial difference and his justification of colonial rule, however, owed as much to the emerging science of nutrition as they did to tropical medicine's claims about uncleanliness and disease reservoirs among indigenous people.

New Guinea

As a member of the Commonwealth Department of Health (CDH), Cilento was part of a milieu concerned both with national development and efficiency and with making Australia a centre of medical research, training and intelligence in the near Pacific Islands. Cilento found an especially kindred spirit in J. S. C. Elkington, the former public health commissioner in Tasmania and Queensland and the head of the Division of Tropical Hygiene in the CDH. Both men shared an evangelical passion for white settlement of the Australian tropics and the application of preventive medicine for national progress. They developed a close friendship in which Cilento took on the role of pupil to Elkington, whom he later addressed as *Tuan* ('Master' in Malay). J. H. L. Cumpston, the director-general of the department, was never as close to Cilento and their relationship would sour in the late 1920s. Yet they certainly shared a passionate belief in preventive medicine, national advancement and the ambition to make Australia the most important force in public health in the South Pacific.[8]

---

8   Fisher, *Raphael Cilento*, pp. 40–1; Anderson, *The Cultivation of Whiteness*, p. 135.

Plate 2.1 Cilento in 1923
Source: John Oxley Library, State Library of Queensland, Neg: 186000.

As director of the Australian Institute of Tropical Medicine (AITM) in Townsville from late in 1922, Cilento oversaw a shift in its focus. In the wake of the 1920 Australasian Medical Congress, the Commonwealth took control of the institute and emphasised the need for more practical public health work. Climate continued to represent a problem in the minds of many local practitioners and observers, but Commonwealth health officials maintained that pathogens were the chief obstacles to tropical development. Disease prevention would require improved local clinical knowledge and detailed epidemiological information on mortality, morbidity and the distribution of disease. Cilento's work in 1923 thus focused on organising surveys of malaria, filariasis and hookworm across Queensland and the Northern Territory from his base in Townsville.[9]

Cilento's fascination with colonial health work continued to tug at him. He would later reflect on how stultifying, pretentious and stubborn Townsville society could be. He and his wife, Phyllis, had urged townsfolk to adopt styles of dress more suited to life and work in the tropics. Cilento later recalled that when he donned a white two-piece suit: 'The conventional were scandalised to think that anyone in my position could be so odd; the lower middle class were, as always, the most condemnatory, and the ultimate imitators.'[10] The ladies of Townsville were similarly affronted when Phyllis suggested to the local Women's Club that they should adopt a Malayan-style sarong and bare midriffs.[11] The couple had evidently developed a self-conscious worldliness, and Cilento kept hoping for a new position in New Guinea that might provide an arena for the pioneering and stimulation that he relished.

An opportunity arrived when Colonel Andrew Honman retired from the New Guinea Department of Public Health in 1923. Cumpston had long desired to place a Commonwealth medical officer in New Guinea in some capacity, and now he was able to put forward Cilento's name as most qualified to direct the health department, stressing in particular

---

9   See Australian Institute of Tropical Medicine, *Collected Papers* (Townsville, QLD: Australian Institute of Tropical Medicine, 1914–30); Australasian Medical Congress, 'Tropical Australia,' *Transactions of the Eleventh Session*, 1920, pp. 40–52; 'Report on the Activities of Division of Tropical Hygiene for the Period March 1921 to December 1925,' p. 2, NAA: A1928, 927/14. See also Parker, 'A "Complete Protective Machinery",' p. 183.

10   Raphael Cilento to Albert Henry Spencer, 17 December 1940, Cilento Papers, UQFL44, Box 4, Item 11.

11   Nikki Henningham, '"Hats Off, Gentlemen, to Our Australian Mothers!" Representations of White Femininity in North Queensland in the Early Twentieth Century,' *Australian Historical Studies*, 32(117), 2001, pp. 319–20.

the importance of his formal training and experience in tropical medicine.[12] The appointment worried the administrator of the territory, Evan Wisdom, who feared resentment from veteran officers denied a chance for advancement.[13] Cilento, however, ultimately impressed the Commonwealth Government and was set to commence his duties in March 1924.

When Cilento steamed into Rabaul Harbour for the second time, he arrived in a territory emblematic of imperial continuity and change. A lasting European presence in New Guinea had begun late in imperial history, when German companies such as Godeffroy of Hamburg and, later, the New Guinea Company, established coastal trading posts in the 1870s. These companies remained the chief agents of German colonialism for some time, with the German Government granting sovereignty to the New Guinea Company over its portion of the islands in 1885. Britain had quashed Queensland's attempt to annex south-eastern New Guinea in 1883, but, after some prompting, declared a protectorate over the same portion of the main island in 1884. The German Government took over control of its portion from the New Guinea Company in 1899, while Australia took control of British New Guinea in 1906. The territorial claims of the 1880s, however, largely fixed the imperial boundaries that lasted until World War I: the Netherlands held western New Guinea, Britain held the south-eastern portion (later named Papua, under Australian control) and the Germans held the north-east and the Bismarck Archipelago.[14]

Colonial influence was everywhere limited and partial, centred on coastal settlements that were the shipping centres for surrounding coconut plantations. Until the discovery of major gold deposits in the 1930s, the production and export of copra—the dried kernel of coconuts— dominated the colonial economy, making up over 90 per cent of the value of exports in the 1920s. Planters produced the copra, which companies such as Burns Philp and W. R. Carpenter shipped from their wharves at major centres such as Kavieng on New Ireland and the capital, Rabaul,

---

12   J. H. L. Cumpston to Secretary of the Prime Minister's Department, 6 October 1921, NAA: A457 (A457/1), 741/2; Cumpston to J. G. McLaren, Secretary of the Department of Home and Territories, 31 December 1923, NAA: A452 (A452/1), 1959/5894.

13   Brigadier-General Evan Wisdom, Administrator, Mandated Territory of New Guinea, to Department of Home and Territories, 7 January 1924, NAA: A452 (A452/1), 1959/5894.

14   *The Official Yearbook of the Commonwealth* (Melbourne: Commonwealth of Australia, 1922), pp. 961–6.

on New Britain.[15] The difficulties of transport and communication over the mountainous terrain left much of the interior and its diverse indigenous groups beyond the reach of colonial administrations. These indigenous groups were not, however, traditionally isolated from each other. For generations, they had fashioned large trading networks and social connections through the exchange of goods, technology, marriage, language and stories.[16] Europeans initially missed these larger connections and communities beyond the level of the village. The belief that these communities had been cut off from the civilising influences of trade and travel that had shaped Europe and Asia became central to colonial representations of diverse Pacific Island cultures as primitive and hostile to outsiders.[17] Indigenous scholars and writers and historians have since sought to challenge these colonial discourses by emphasising the exchange networks that gave Pacific Islanders a connected and dynamic culture and history.[18]

Australia established a civil administration in 1921 after seven years of military occupation, under the umbrella of a League of Nations mandate— one of a new kind of colonial territory. With the mandates, international society as embodied in the league granted the responsibility for governing dependent territories to other countries as trustees. These trustees, which would not enjoy complete sovereignty, were obliged to promote 'to the utmost the material and moral well-being and the social progress' of indigenous people.[19] Article 22 of the League of Nations Covenant in fact described the wellbeing of the subjects of the former German colonies as a 'sacred trust of civilisation'. The league mandates ultimately did little to change colonial practice and many recognised the hollowness of claims about the enlightened reform of imperialism. As Susan Pedersen has argued, however, the mandates did force colonial practices into the glare of international scrutiny and produced an international 'official mind' on colonialism. Unlike late nineteenth-century attempts to reconcile empire

---

15   K. Buckley and K. Klugman, 'The Australian Presence in the Pacific': Burns Philp 1914–1946 (Sydney: George Allen & Unwin, 1983), p. 167; Judith Bennett, 'Holland, Britain and Germany in Melanesia,' in K. R. Howe, Robert C. Kiste and Brij V. Lal (eds), Tides of History: The Pacific Islands in the Twentieth Century (Sydney: George Allen & Unwin, 1994), p. 57; Clive Moore, New Guinea: Crossing Boundaries and History (Honolulu: University of Hawai'i Press, 2003), p. 186.
16   Moore, New Guinea, pp. 10–11.
17   Donald Denoon, with Stewart Firth, Jocelyn Linnekin, Malama Meleisea and Karen Nero (eds), Cambridge History of the Pacific Islanders (Cambridge: Cambridge University Press, 2004), pp. 69–77.
18   Matt Matsuda, 'The Pacific,' American Historical Review, 111(3), 2006, pp. 760–3.
19   The Official Yearbook of the Commonwealth, p. 975.

with liberal ideals of democracy, the League of Nations' mandates, in denying sovereignty to the ruling power, theoretically placed a temporal limit on colonial rule.[20]

The mandate system emerged as a compromise among the great powers over the future of Ottoman territory and German colonies. At the Paris Peace Conference, US president Woodrow Wilson proposed an international system of colonial administration instead of annexation. In a series of famous wartime speeches, Wilson had argued that the equality of nations, a mechanism for international cooperation and the right of self-determination should be the foundations of peaceful international order.[21] Speaking before the US Congress in January 1917, Wilson made it clear that international peace would fail unless there was universal recognition that:

> governments derive all their just powers from the consent of the governed, and that no right anywhere exists to hand peoples about from sovereignty to sovereignty as if they were property.[22]

When it came to the British Empire, however, the fulfilment of these principles faltered. Wilson did not consider the colonial world within his framework and had little interest in challenging the entire imperial world order.[23] Instead, self-determination for colonised societies, which were considered unready for it, would come gradually and through the guidance of advanced countries subject to the expectations of the international community.

This proposition drew Wilson into an increasingly personal confrontation with the British and with Australian prime minister Billy Hughes, who insisted on Australia's right to annex German New Guinea.[24] The compromise that emerged involved the creation of A-, B- and C-class mandates under the League of Nations that set out different limits and conditions of administrative power. It was a classification based on what had become a transnational understanding of 'civilisation' in which societies were assumed to pass through common historical stages

20 Pedersen, 'Settler Colonialism at the Bar of the League of Nations,' pp. 113–14; Pedersen, 'Back to the League of Nations,' pp. 1103–6.
21 Manela, *The Wilsonian Moment*, pp. 22–3.
22 ibid., p. 24.
23 ibid., p. 25.
24 Hiery, *The Neglected War*, pp. 202–5. They also clashed over the racial equality clause that Japan proposed for the League of Nations Covenant; see Manela, *The Wilsonian Moment*, p. 182.

of economic and political organisation.[25] The league assigned C-class mandates to territories whose indigenous peoples it deemed to be at the most primitive stage of this universal development and in greatest need of tutelage. This status satisfied imperialists such as Hughes, since in granting the trustee full control of administration and legislation it provided 'most of the substance of annexation'.[26] Trustees were, however, obligated to enact certain regulations, including banning forced labour and the sale or trade of alcohol, arms and opium to indigenous people, along with the obligation to submit an annual report to the Permanent Mandates Commission of the League of Nations.

Many of these policies and the language of the mandate had clear precedents in late nineteenth-century international relations and diplomacy. As Kevin Grant notes, the General Act of the 1885 Berlin Conference, at Britain's insistence, included a commitment to suppressing slavery, while the signatories of the Act, in a clear echo of the terms of the mandate, pledged to protect the 'moral and material well-being' of indigenous people in Africa. Later documents, such as the 1890 General Act and Declaration of Brussels, addressed the trade in arms and liquor.[27] These policies reflected nineteenth-century discussions about the rehabilitation of empire through the enlightened, paternal guidance of colonised people.[28] As Jeanne Morefield shows, intellectuals such as Gilbert Murray and Alfred Zimmern exemplify how liberal internationalism rested on articulating imperialism as a civilising and paternalistic force. The notion of the 'family of man' in fact emerged as the dominant metaphor helping these thinkers to resolve the tensions between liberalism and the subjugation of other peoples, since it could legitimise empire as a natural order.[29] In other words, a race of natural parents should lead a race of natural children who were not yet ready for self-government.[30] Mark Mazower has convincingly argued that these

---

25   Grant, 'Human Rights and Sovereign Abolitions of Slavery,' p. 84. On the role of notions of universal history in representations of colonial societies, see Uday Singh Mehta, *Liberalism and Empire: A Study in Nineteenth Century British Liberal Thought* (Chicago: University of Chicago Press, 1999), pp. 77–82.

26   J. C. Rookwood Proud, *World Peace, the League and Australia* (Melbourne: Robertson & Mullens, 1936), p. 36. See also Hiery, *The Neglected War*, p. 205.

27   Grant, 'Human Rights and Sovereign Abolitions of Slavery,' pp. 83–4.

28   Mehta, *Liberalism and Empire*, p. 199.

29   Jeanne Morefield, *Covenants without Swords: Idealist Liberalism and the Spirit of Empire* (Princeton, NJ: Princeton University Press, 2005), pp. 105–7, 214–15.

30   Mehta has shown how metaphors of infancy and family pervaded British liberalism. See Mehta, *Liberalism and Empire*, pp. 31–3.

ideas were deeply felt among those who played key roles in framing the character of the League of Nations and liberal internationalism generally, including Zimmern and the South African field marshal and politician Jan Smuts.[31] Indeed, it was Smuts who provided much of the language and ideas that Wilson used to reconcile his internationalist principles with the ongoing exercise of imperial rule.[32]

The language of the mandate system featured prominently in Australian policy debates over the future of New Guinea, especially in the contributions of the lieutenant governor of Papua, Hubert Murray, and public servants such as Edmund Piesse, who took up the discourse of colonial duty in earnest. In his 1925 book, *Papua of To-day*, Murray described Article 22 of the League of Nations Covenant as marking:

> the abandonment of the theory that a colony is to be regarded merely as a business proposition, and the native inhabitants merely as 'assets' to be utilized for the purpose of this business.[33]

Colonial governments everywhere needed to heed this spirit, Murray argued, in which the 'interests of the native are to be regarded as of the first importance'.[34] This rhetoric had provoked prime minister Hughes into trying to marginalise Murray over the future of German New Guinea, which ultimately became a separate territory out of Murray's reach.[35]

Piesse, appointed to head the Pacific branch within the prime minister's department in 1921, read widely on colonial policy and indigenous customs in the hope of pushing official policy on land and labour closer to international norms.[36] Among that collected literature was a speech that John Wear Burton, the head of the Methodist mission in Sydney, gave in Melbourne in July 1921. Drawing on Murray and the prominent British internationalist C. Reginald Enock, Burton's speech articulated neatly with international conversations. The league and its covenant, Burton argued, represented a:

31　Mazower, *No Enchanted Palace*, pp. 14–21.
32　Grant, 'Human Rights and Sovereign Abolitions of Slavery,' pp. 87–8; Manela, *The Wilsonian Moment*, p. 39; Mazower, *No Enchanted Palace*, pp. 40–5.
33　Hubert Murray, *Papua of To-day, or an Australian Colony in the Making* (London: P. S. King & Son, 1925), pp. 210–11.
34　ibid., p. 213.
35　Bennett, 'Holland, Britain and Germany in Melanesia,' pp. 56–7.
36　Edmund Piesse, 'Preparation of a Handbook of the Natives of the Territory of New Guinea,' 29 September 1922, pp. 1–3, Papers of Edmund Leolin Piesse [hereinafter Piesse Papers], MS 882, Series 6, Item 321, NLA.

[d]aring scheme of corporate living which transcends every other attempt in human history to provide an enduring and practical basis for human society. In looking out upon the nations of the earth it sees them as members of one great human family and has for its objective the promotion of true family feeling.

Following the British liberals, Burton argued that 'some members of the family are merely infants'. The imperial powers were obligated to educate and train indigenous people 'in order that they may come to full stature'.[37] This project rested on the rejection of contract labour that bonded indigenous people to plantations and mines and the encouragement of independent indigenous production of export crops. Ultimately, imperialism was cast as a moral mission, aimed at uplifting colonised people through hygienic, spiritual, agricultural and economic instruction.[38]

The league's Permanent Mandates Commission was largely powerless to affect or enforce the terms of the mandate. International media scrutiny exerted the most pressure on the colonial policy of sensitive governments, yet even then had limited impact. South African atrocities in the former German South West Africa colony were condemned, yet there was little change in colonial conduct.[39] As Pedersen has pointed out, the terms of the mandates were also flexible. While Burton argued that following the ideals of the mandate would lead to peasant proprietorship, others, including the head of the Commonwealth Bank in Rabaul, used the terms of the mandate to justify the introduction of forced labour.[40] The government anthropologist in New Guinea, Ernest Chinnery, suggested in 1927 that legislation be introduced that would allow government officers to compel indigenous people to work as carriers on patrols.[41] The territory's annual report for 1926–27 informed the Permanent Mandates Commission that some forced labour of 'a very light nature' had been used for road maintenance.[42]

37   John Wear Burton, 'The Australian Mandate,' Speech delivered to meeting of League of Nations Union, Melbourne, 21 July 1921, pp. 1–2, Piesse Papers, MS 882, Series 6, Item 563-89, NLA.
38   ibid., p. 20.
39   Pedersen, 'Settler Colonialism at the Bar of the League of Nations,' pp. 115–16; Pedersen, 'Back to the League of Nations,' pp. 1104–5.
40   C. I. H. Campbell, 'The Natives of New Guinea. Australia's Responsibility,' 17 November 1920, p. 1, Piesse Papers, MS 882, Series 6, Item 556, NLA.
41   Ernest Chinnery, Government Anthropologist, to Evan Wisdom, 29 November 1927, Papers of Ernest William Pearson Chinnery [hereinafter Chinnery Papers], MS 766, Series 5, Folder 3, NLA.
42   Parliament of the Commonwealth of Australia, *Report to the Council of the League of Nations on the Administration of the Territory of New Guinea from 1st July 1926 to 30th June 1927* [hereinafter *New Guinea Annual Report*] (Melbourne: Government Printer, 1928), p. 26.

The goal of indigenous welfare could be used to support a range of different labour regimes. The administrator, Brigadier-General Evan Wisdom, urged continuation of the contract labour system for the plantation economy that had been more effectively developed in the German territory than in the Territory of Papua:

> If the policy is such as to enable the native with his small wants to loaf and live on the production of others, the ruin of the country economically is sure, and with it all hope of the moral and material uplifting of the native. If the native is to be uplifted, it must be done in conjunction with the progress of the country, and progress is only possible with abundance of native labour.[43]

The protection of indigenous land tenure in Fiji, he claimed, had entrenched an Indian labouring class at the expense of indigenous communities. This had created a situation in which the government would be forced to grant Indians 'full rights' or cease economic activity by repatriating them, either of which was an unpalatable outcome.[44] The best solution, therefore, in the interests of indigenous welfare and the economic progress of New Guinea, was contract labour:

> We must, therefore, lay down the principle that any policy should, whilst ensuring that the terms of the Mandate, as regards forced labor are observed, avoid making it more difficult to obtain and use to as full an extent as possible, the native labor.[45]

Piesse challenged this insistence on indentured plantation labour, drawing on anthropological literature on indigenous land use to make a case for alternatives. In particular, Piesse argued the importance of encouraging indigenous communities to produce cash crops on their own land, as Papua had done.[46]

---

43 Evan Wisdom to Secretary of the Prime Minister's Department, 3 August 1921, p. 2, Piesse Papers, MS 882, Series 6, Item 174-8, NLA.
44 ibid., p. 1. On the tensions between the White Australia Policy and the mobility of British imperial subjects, see Lake and Reynolds, *Drawing the Global Colour Line*, p. 20; McKeown, *Melancholy Order*, p. 185.
45 Evan Wisdom to Secretary of the Prime Minister's Department, 3 August 1921, p. 3, Piesse Papers, MS 882, Series 6, Item 174-8, NLA.
46 Edmund Piesse, 'Territory of New Guinea—Land Policy as it Affects the Welfare of the Natives,' 19 August 1921, p. 4, Piesse Papers, MS 882/6/195-203, NLA.

Piesse warned the Commonwealth Government about the 'scrutiny and criticism' Australia would face from the League of Nations, Germany and the International Board of Missions.[47] His influence was limited, however, and almost all authority over legislation and policy rested with Wisdom, who rejected most of Piesse's proposals.[48] The number of indentured labour contracts climbed from just over 27,000 in 1921–22 to more than 40,000 by the onset of World War II.[49] Wages were kept at 5 shillings a month, with a maximum of 10 shillings, which Cilento later pointed out was much lower than the average wages of 10 and 20 shillings in Papua and the British Solomon Islands, respectively.[50] The administration defended its low pay by reminding critics that 'the wants of the native are few, and that he might not make wise use of a larger wage'.[51] Wages were also withheld until the expiration of the three-year contracts. Exploitation could thus be explained away as inculcating industrious habits and discipline. Encouraging manual labour, including handicrafts, was part of the government's responsibility for the 'welfare of the natives', argued the secretary of the prime minister's department, who also noted that admitting Indian workers 'who are culturally far above them' would place indigenous people at a serious disadvantage.[52] The government thus deployed the language of the 'sacred trust' to justify extending racial immigration restrictions to New Guinea and thus preserve indigenous populations as a source of labour.

Reconciling indigenous welfare and colonial economic development had become an important trope of imperial discourse by the 1920s. Frederick Lugard's notion of the 'dual mandate' was the most famous of these formulations, in which railways, health measures, trade and employment would increase wealth, check disease and encourage industrious habits. Economic development for the benefit of colonising countries and indigenous welfare could be made 'reciprocal'.[53] The framing of labour

47 ibid., pp. 8–9.
48 Roger Thompson, 'Making a Mandate: The Formation of Australia's New Guinea Policies 1919–1925,' *The Journal of Pacific History*, 25(1), 1990, pp. 71–3.
49 Bennett, 'Holland, Britain and Germany in Melanesia,' p. 57; Moore, *New Guinea*, p. 186.
50 Raphael Cilento to Harold Page, Government Secretary, 21 September 1925, NAA, A1 (A1/15), 1925/24149.
51 *New Guinea Annual Report 1921–22*, 1923, p. 52. The justification of low pay on the basis of the supposedly simple life of non-European peoples was persistent; see H. Ian Hogbin and Camilla Wedgwood, *Development and Welfare in the Western Pacific* (Sydney: Australian Institute of International Affairs, 1943), p. 8.
52 Secretary of the Prime Minister's Department to Secretary of the Governor-General's Department, 31 May 1921, p. 2, Piesse Papers, MS 882, Series 6, Item 101, NLA.
53 Frederick Lugard, *The Dual Mandate in British Tropical Africa* (Edinburgh & London: William Blackwood & Sons, 1926), p. 617.

in New Guinea similarly made indigenous and colonial interests two sides of the same coin. As Patricia O'Brien puts it, measures to protect indigenous people were 'entwined with economic growth and preservation of a labour supply'.[54] Despite the prevalence of an international discourse that made indigenous welfare and progress the primary concerns of empire, the hope for Australian profits from plantation copra exports remained central to the social and political order of Australian New Guinea between the wars.

Hubert Murray's apparently progressive rhetoric in Papua belied the racist paternalism and violence that informed government in both Papua and New Guinea. Echoing Cilento's description of the 'gulf' between colonisers and colonised, Murray claimed:

> The Papuan, on the arrival of the white man, is confronted with an entirely new civilization, and is invited to step over a gap which the wisest and most gifted races have hardly crossed in twenty centuries.[55]

The government was thus obliged to protect the welfare of the people in the face of this supposed cultural shock by protecting indigenous health and inculcating 'habits of industry'.[56] One Papuan regulation, for example, compelled Papuan villagers to maintain coconut groves. As Penelope Edmonds has shown, Murray framed this policy as inculcating the value of regular labour and peasant proprietorship yet also designed it to augment government revenue.[57] Such policies were necessary, Murray explained, because of the 'ignorance of the natives and their weakness and the backwardness of their civilization'.[58] Australian government must also transform indigenous society by sweeping away the 'superstitious terrors which haunt the darker side of Papuan life' and remake them in a European image.[59] The writings of Murray, once considered a 'progressive' colonial administrator, are thus typical of colonial disdain for 'savage' and 'primitive' customs and the vain determination to erase them.

---

54   Patricia O'Brien, 'Remaking Australia's Colonial Culture? White Australia and its Papuan Frontier 1901–1940,' *Australian Historical Studies*, 40(1), 2009, p. 103.
55   Murray, *Papua of To-day*, p. 220.
56   ibid., p. 253.
57   Penelope Edmonds, 'Dual Mandate, Double Work: Land, Labour and the Transformation of Native Subjectivity, 1908–1940,' in Patricia Grimshaw and Russell McGregor (eds), *Collisions of Culture and Identities: Settlers and Indigenous People* (Melbourne: Melbourne University Press, 2006), pp. 127–37.
58   Murray, *Papua of To-day*, pp. 252–3.
59   ibid., p. 224.

The violence and brute force of Australian colonial rule also undermined any progressive image that Australian colonialism might have once enjoyed.[60] George le Hunte and Australian-born Christopher Robinson—successive governors of British New Guinea in the early years of the twentieth century—presided over massacres that together killed more than 150 indigenous people at Gaoribari Island.[61] Murray's police were known to fire on Papuans who resisted.[62] Under pressure from public criticism and constant reports of illegal flogging in the press, the Commonwealth Government invited Colonel John Ainsworth, a former native commissioner in Kenya, to investigate indigenous welfare in the mandated territory in 1924. Ainsworth's report suggested that this kind of violence was common, yet Wisdom ignored it.[63] Aside from covert brutality, official punitive expeditions were not uncommon. Cilento himself participated in such expeditions, including once during the military occupation when reports of attacks on villages along the Sepik River prompted the dispatch of a force comprising two machine guns, a three-pound cannon and 80 indigenous police.[64] In 1927, Cilento volunteered for another expedition, in response to the killing of four European miners in the Nakanai District of New Britain. The Permanent Mandates Commission questioned the Australian High Commissioner in London over the Nakanai expedition, which killed 18 indigenous people, but little was made of the incident.[65]

Indigenous resistance in New Guinea never achieved the sustained and collective anticolonial demands for autonomy that had arisen in Samoa.[66] The vast array of communities and languages and the complete lack of colonial influence in many areas made large-scale rebellion or protest difficult or unnecessary. Villagers occasionally assaulted or killed Europeans, such as the miners mentioned above, often as retaliation

---

60   Brij V. Lal, 'The Passage Out,' in K. R. Howe, Robert C. Kiste and Brij V. Lal (eds), *Tides of History: The Pacific Islands in the Twentieth Century* (Sydney: Allen & George Unwin, 1994), pp. 442–3.

61   Roger Thompson, *Australia and the Pacific Islands in the 20th Century* (Melbourne: Australian Scholarly Publishing, 1998), p. 5; O'Brien, 'Remaking Australia's Colonial Culture,' pp. 101–2.

62   Edward P. Wolfers, *Race Relations and Colonial Rule in Papua New Guinea* (Sydney: Australia and New Zealand Book Company, 1975), p. 16.

63   ibid., pp. 92–3; Thompson, 'Making a Mandate,' pp. 74–80.

64   Raphael Cilento, Diary: Sepik River Expedition, 20 February – 10 March 1919, Cilento Papers, UQFL44, Box 11, Item 18.

65   Permanent Mandates Commission, *Minutes of the 11th Session*, 1927, pp. 43–4.

66   Hiery, *The Neglected War*, pp. 192–200; Peter Hempenstall, 'Releasing the Voices: Historicizing Colonial Encounters in the Pacific,' in Robert Borofsky (ed.), *Remembrance of Pacific Pasts: An Invitation to Remake History* (Honolulu: University of Hawai'i Press, 2000), pp. 50–1.

against the indigenous police who accompanied European officers.[67] When the government seized valuable land for a new hospital, local people harassed the survey party and removed pegs marking out the site.[68] The major exception to localised resistance was the Rabaul maritime strike of 1929, led by sailors and police who earned more than ordinary indentured labourers, who assembled at the Catholic and Methodist missions outside Rabaul after stopping work. The industrial action soon fell apart when the missionaries told the strikers to return to work, but the response of colonial authorities was harsh. Many of the leaders were sentenced to three years' confinement and colonists vocally resisted attempts to provide better education for indigenous people in the wake of the strike. As Bennett suggests, this reaction speaks to the insecurity of the European elite and their desire to retain New Guineans as a subservient labour force.[69]

Cilento's somewhat turbulent time as the Director of Public Health in New Guinea took shape at this intersection of imperial capital, colonial violence and international discourses on indigenous welfare. Medicine was in many ways tied to the project of imperial conquest and development, providing options for maintaining labour supplies and enforcing colonial order. Yet medical knowledge could also be in tension with colonial policy and practice and provide a platform from which to critique other priorities and interests. Nutrition, in particular—a research field that emerged within imperial contexts and encouraged social perspectives on health and sickness—became an important platform from which Cilento criticised the colonial government.

Public health, labour and policing a territory

Cilento's first task as Director of Public Health was to conduct a full review of medical services in the territory. At the time, these were divided between the administration and the Expropriations Board that maintained former German property and employed hundreds of indentured labourers and demanded more. Prefacing his report by stressing that it was not meant to be contentious, Cilento nevertheless bluntly claimed, 'It may be

67   Ernest Chinnery to Harold Page, 19 April 1928, pp. 1–2, Chinnery Papers, MS 766, Series 5, Folder 15, NLA.
68   *Sydney Morning Herald*, 15 October 1938, p. 12.
69   Bennett, 'Holland, Britain, and Germany in Melanesia,' pp. 57–8.

said that *there is little, if any, progress being made in medicine or sanitation throughout the Territory*, noting in particular that nearly every aspect of preventive medicine he or his predecessors pursued had been undermined by crippling financial stringency.[70]

Tropical medicine has come in for special criticism in studies of health and medicine in New Guinea. It was a specialty founded on assumptions about the profound environmental and racial differences of the tropics as a colonial world. Tropical rainfall, humidity and ecological fecundity had produced alien pathogens that ravaged European communities. European science also comprehended the tropics as having produced races characterised by physical and mental lethargy. With the discovery of germs carried in the bloodstream or digestive tract and communicated by insect vectors or contaminated soil, medical knowledge increasingly depicted the indigenous peoples of the tropics as a threat to Europeans and therefore to governance, productivity and commerce. For Donald Denoon, this tendency to pathologise whole racial groups dominated the medical policy of New Guinea. Denoon understood tropical medicine— by neglecting nutrition, clean water and other basic aspects of applied public health, and in hopelessly obsessing over the elimination of specific diseases—as having condemned New Guineans to generations of sickness and suffering.[71] Tropical medicine is thus contrasted with a more virtuous preventive medicine.

Cilento's public health policies certainly rested on racist logic. Yet Cilento clearly favoured a broadly preventive approach to medical services that included the protection of water supplies and the disposal of waste. 'The infinitely greater aspect of the subject is preventive medicine,' he wrote in his report, 'upon which depends the increase or decrease of endemic and epidemic diseases, and, practically every essential problem of public health.'[72] One of Cilento's great frustrations was the difficulty of obtaining funds for an incinerator in Rabaul, the purchase of water tanks and the mosquito-proofing of these and other water sources in the town.[73] The design and construction of sanitary latrines were also major priorities. Cilento concluded his report with a scathing accusation:

70   Raphael Cilento, 'Medical Progress and Policy in the Territory of New Guinea,' January 1925, p. 1, NAA: A518, F832/1/3. Cilento's emphasis.
71   Denoon, *Public Health in Papua New Guinea*, pp. 21–2.
72   Cilento, 'Medical Progress and Policy in the Territory of New Guinea,' pp. 7–8.
73   ibid., p. 4.

<u>No criticism of the policy could be so severe as this intrinsic condemnation. Prevention is the whole basis of public health administration and this policy aims not at it but at the multiplication of hospitals and personnel. In other words the whole policy is directed towards combating effects with a total disregard of the causes, which produce them.</u>[74]

The point here is not to absolve tropical medicine or to suggest that public health in New Guinea was indeed progressive, but to show that the distinction between tropical hygiene and preventive medicine was not as sharp as some have suggested. Prevention was an important concept in imperial tropical hygiene, while laudable aspects of public health— such as ensuring clean water supplies, effective waste disposal and good nutrition—were equally enmeshed in the politics, discourse and finances of colonial administration.[75]

Australian colonial officials did not receive Cilento's report well. Writing from neighbouring Papua, Hubert Murray supposed that:

> most medical men would like to spend almost the whole of a limited revenue on medical services, just as most agriculturalists would spend it on agriculture, and engineers on works.[76]

In Rabaul, Evan Wisdom complained of the severity of Cilento's report and suggested that he was seeking personal glory:

> It must be kept in mind that Dr. Cilento is an enthusiast given an opportunity to do a big work and sees everything through the glasses of his idealism. To him the whole horizon is medical and everything else must give way.[77]

Cilento had indeed asserted this in his report:

> All well established tropical administrations recognise in fact that all other problems are subservient to those of health, since if a country can be made healthy it can survive even poor administration; while if it remain[s] unhealthy no government however conscientious or well-intentioned in other respects, can secure permanent progress.[78]

74 ibid., p. 59. Cilento's emphasis.
75 For similar connections between colonial and metropolitan preventive medicine in the British Empire, see Jones, *Health Policy in Britain's Model Colony*, pp. 109–22.
76 J. H. P. Murray to J. G. McLaren, 20 March 1925, NAA: A518, F832/1/3.
77 Evan Wisdom to J. G. McLaren, 27 October 1925, p. 1, NAA: A518, F832/1/3.
78 Cilento, 'Medical Progress and Policy in the Territory of New Guinea,' p. 4.

This insistence on expanding the remit of medicine in New Guinea inevitably provoked resistance from the government. In Cilento's mind, water, housing, labour laws and town planning were all the purview of applied public health in the tropics. Yet these were aspects of administration that he would have to wrest from other departments that were responsible for them. The purchase and mosquito-proofing of water tanks in Rabaul, for example, put him in conflict with the Department of Public Works.[79] As elsewhere in the Pacific and Asia, in New Guinea, the scarcity of funding and the conflicting priorities of medical men, district officers, engineers and the central government made for a complicated relationship between medicine and government.

Malaria in New Guinea was a chronic infection for many indigenous people outside the Highlands and a lethal danger for Europeans. Prolonged exposure to malaria can confer a degree of resistance to specific strains of the *Plasmodium* parasites in individuals and to larger communities that enjoy a stable set of social and economic relationships. This does not prevent infection, but lessens the severity of the disease and can be lost if time is spent away from the ecological context that gives rise to it.[80] The various *Anopheline* mosquito species, whose bites introduce parasites to the human bloodstream, reproduce in different types of aquatic environments.[81] Epidemics and outbreaks of the disease thus usually followed changes in the distribution or flow of water, which in turn changed the number and distribution of mosquitoes, or after the introduction of new strains of the parasite through migration. Agricultural or infrastructure development and population movements associated with migrant labour or refugees were very often at the heart of these ecological changes. The intensive development of commercial plantation agriculture in the colonial tropics—which involved significant land clearing, labour migration and a range of effects on nutrition—meant that malaria persisted as an endemic disease far longer in Africa, Asia and Latin America than in Europe and North America.[82]

Cilento described the *Plasmodium* parasite as having shaped the body of indigenous society, reporting: 'Malaria, in a native territory such as New Guinea, passes beyond the stage of a prevalent disease to become

---

79   ibid., p. 8.
80   Randall Packard, *The Making of a Tropical Disease: A Short History of Malaria* (Baltimore: The Johns Hopkins University Press, 2007), pp. 28–9.
81   ibid., p. 7.
82   ibid., pp. 84–95.

practically a normal circumstance in native environments.'[83] His approach nevertheless reflected an increasing emphasis in tropical medicine on the ecological and social aspects of the disease.[84] Malaria, Cilento argued, could not be stamped out once and for all by a 'violent crusade':

> Time, agriculture, and the gradual evolution of more sanitary methods of living, coupled with the steady repulse of the jungle, must be regarded as the all essential lines of the offensive throughout the main mass of the native-owned land.[85]

If sanitation reform across the territory seemed a long-term project, intensive effort at least promised to control malaria in the towns and outstations where the disease persistently threatened European health.[86] Malaria outbreaks were most common in Rabaul between May and June when the *Anopheles* mosquito population that carried the disease increased dramatically. The local *Anopheles punctulatus* mosquitoes bred in bodies of still water such as swamps, rainwater puddles, ditches and permanent pools.[87] Although one study dismissed the possibility of mosquitoes breeding in discarded tins and coconut shells, routine measures continued to collect them.[88] Control thus focused on the periodic destruction of larvae and eliminating breeding places by filling holes, oiling water tanks, collecting bottles and treating wells with lime.[89]

Hookworm and yaws, or framboesia, were also common diseases targeted in mass treatment and eradication campaigns.[90] Historians have justly critiqued such specific disease campaigns, which were explicitly linked to the expansion of colonial authority and influence.[91] Officials hoped that mass treatment, which was often dramatically effective, would convince indigenous people of the effectiveness of Australian medicine. Routine

83 *New Guinea Annual Report 1924–25*, 1926, pp. 15–16.
84 Anderson, *Colonial Pathologies*, pp. 208–15.
85 Cilento, 'Medical Progress and Policy in the Territory of New Guinea,' pp. 24–5.
86 *New Guinea Annual Report 1924–25*, 1926, p. 15; *New Guinea Annual Report 1926–27*, 1928, p. 128.
87 G. A. M. Heydon, 'Malaria at Rabaul,' *The Medical Journal of Australia*, II(24), 15 December 1923, p. 626.
88 ibid., p. 626.
89 *New Guinea Annual Report 1925–26*, 1927, pp. 71–2.
90 *New Guinea Annual Report 1924–25*, 1926, pp. 16–17.
91 Denoon, *Public Health in Papua New Guinea*, p. 51; Randall Packard, 'Visions of Postwar Health and their Impact on Public Health Interventions in the Developing World,' in Frederick Cooper and Randall Packard (eds), *International Development and the Social Sciences: Essays on the History and Politics of Knowledge* (Berkeley: University of California Press, 1997), p. 95.

patrols treated yaws en masse with injections of the arsenical drug Novarsenobillon, which usually cleared major lesions. In his 1925 report, Cilento claimed that the injections were the:

> ideal weapon for penetration work among suspicious and timid native groups. In the experience of the writer nothing contributes so towards popularising and assisting the advance of Australian medicine and prestige as a successful framboesial drive.[92]

Evidence suggests that European medicine actually had very limited influence on indigenous attitudes. Annie Stuart, for example, has argued that instead of simply transmitting Western knowledge, such encounters between indigenous people and Western medical men produced hybrid meanings.[93] Yet for some colonial officials, medicine was a potential spearhead for extending government influence across the territory.

The New Guinea administration similarly saw hookworm treatment campaigns as 'a means of penetrating into country little touched by the Administration and establishing relations with the natives in the best way possible'.[94] Officials were also concerned with the way hookworm impaired the fitness of labourers and reduced resistance to tuberculosis and pneumonia, which were the principle causes of disease mortality among labourers.[95] Victor Heiser, the Director of the East for the International Health Board (IHB), had visited Australia, Papua and Fiji in 1916, and subsequently proposed an anti-hookworm campaign in Papua, New Guinea and northern Australia modelled on the programs the IHB had developed in other tropical regions.[96] That type of program was ultimately deemed unsuitable for New Guinea, yet hookworm remained a special target of health work in the territory.[97] At a 1921 meeting of administration officials, business representatives and Sylvester Lambert

---

92   Cilento, 'Medical Progress and Policy in the Territory of New Guinea,' p. 27.

93   Annie Stuart, 'We Are All Hybrid Here: The Rockefeller Foundation, Sylvester Lambert, and Health Work in the Colonial South Pacific,' *Health and History*, 8(1), 2006, pp. 56–79.

94   Evan Wisdom to Secretary, Department of Home and Territories, 4 August 1921, NAA: A457 (A457/1), 741/2.

95   'Minutes of Second Meeting of Hookworm Committee of the Territory of New Guinea,' 19 July 1921, pp. 1–2, NAA: A457 (A457/1), 741/2; *New Guinea Annual Report 1924–25*, 1926, pp. 17–18.

96   James Gillespie, 'The Rockefeller Foundation, the Hookworm Campaign and a National Health Policy in Australia, 1911–1930,' in Roy MacLeod and Donald Denoon (eds), *Health and Healing in Tropical Australia and Papua New Guinea 1911–1930* (Townsville, QLD: James Cook University, 1991), pp. 71–2.

97   Donald Denoon, 'The Idea of Tropical Medicine and its Influence in Papua New Guinea,' in Roy MacLeod and Donald Denoon (eds), *Health and Healing in Tropical Australia and Papua New Guinea 1911–1930* (Townsville, QLD: James Cook University, 1991), p. 16.

(an IHB officer who was to become an important figure in the Pacific Islands) it was suggested that Lambert and the Commissioner for Native Affairs, Captain H. C. Cardew, draft a labour ordinance requiring that employers examine indigenous workers and provide treatment when they signed on and every six months.[98] Wisdom later informed the Department of Home and Territories that the hookworm campaign would treat 32,000 indentured labourers and a total of 197,000 indigenous people.[99]

Tuberculosis and pneumonia—diseases not usually associated with the tropics—dominated statistics on mortality. A series of postmortem examinations of indigenous people in Rabaul attributed one-third of all deaths to tuberculosis alone.[100] In another report, Cilento described pneumonia as the 'most prolific cause of death in the Territory'.[101] In the 1920s, British colonial health officials began recognising that the living conditions of migrant workers in mines and plantations in Africa were leading to high levels of mortality and morbidity from diseases associated with overcrowding and malnutrition rather than with tropical environments.[102] Cilento similarly noted that bringing indigenous people to work around Rabaul caused significant social dislocation, while their living conditions in town and on plantations were conducive to respiratory infections. One sanitary inspector reported that quarters for labourers contracted to the administration had been constructed from rusty kerosene tins, galvanised iron and grass. Strict regulations were frequently breached, making it easy to understand 'why there is so much sickness among the native labourers'.[103] Cilento and members of his team of medical officers and sanitary inspectors thus asserted the need for stronger government action on indigenous sickness and to some extent recognised that structures of colonial rule impacted on indigenous health.

---

98 'Minutes of Second Meeting of Hookworm Committee of the Territory of New Guinea,' p. 4.
99 Evan Wisdom to Secretary, Department of Home and Territories, 4 August 1921, NAA: A457 (A457/1), 741/2.
100 *New Guinea Annual Report 1925–26*, 1927, p. 77. See also Cilento, 'Medical Progress and Policy in the Territory of New Guinea,' p. 28.
101 Cilento, 'Medical Progress and Policy in the Territory of New Guinea,' p. 29.
102 Joseph Morgan Hodge, *Triumph of the Expert: Agrarian Doctrines of Development and the Legacies of British Colonialism* (Athens, OH: Ohio University Press, 2007), pp. 121–3.
103 Cilento, 'Medical Progress and Policy in the Territory of New Guinea,' pp. 40–2.

Health became an important aspect of attempts to reform conditions of colonial labour in the first decades of the twentieth century.[104] The territory's annual report for 1921–22 acknowledged criticism of the social disruption and health risks involved, but insisted that populations were increasing in recruitment areas and medical examination at the expiration of contracts prevented the spread of disease. Ultimately, the administration argued, 'the native must be induced to work'.[105] The Native Labour Ordinances of 1922 required that employers provide a sick ward or, where there were more than 100 employees, a separate hospital building. Where there were over 500 workers, employees had to provide a qualified medical practitioner and in all cases there must be a store of prescribed drugs, bandages and other treatment materials. Employers were required to send seriously ill employees to the nearest government hospital and cover charges for inpatient and outpatient treatment.[106]

Public health in many respects revolved around managing indigenous mobility, while the limitations of disease surveillance and control over the territory often brought colonial anxiety to the surface. In August 1921, rumours heard from indigenous people suggested an outbreak in Dutch New Guinea of a disease resembling smallpox, which the administration associated with Asia and was desperate to exclude from the territory. The Dutch resident informed the outstation at Vanimo that smallpox had indeed broken out, advancing more than 30 kilometres towards the border in 10 days. There was an urgency, even panic, in the correspondence between Rabaul and Melbourne. 'Terror-stricken' Malays from the Dutch side were said to be streaming towards Australian territory, requiring urgent quarantine action by police and medical officers.[107] Without adequate personnel, Wisdom feared an epidemic might be unavoidable: 'If cannot stop epidemic through inability to obtain medical advisers requested, it is my wish to be absolved from responsibility.'[108] A shortage of personnel and the lack of real control over the territory struck fear into the heart of the colonial government.

---

104 See C. F. Andrews, *Indian Indentured Labour in Fiji* (Perth: The Colortype Press, 1918); Christine Weir, 'An Accidental Biographer? On Encountering, Yet Again, the Ideas and Actions of J. W. Burton,' in Brij V. Lal and Vicki Luker (eds), *Telling Pacific Lives: Prisms of Process* (Canberra: ANU E Press, 2008), pp. 215–25.

105 *New Guinea Annual Report 1921–22*, 1923, p. 52.

106 ibid., pp. 172–3.

107 Rabaul to Prime Minister's Department, 13 August 1921, NAA: A457 (A457/1), 741/1.

108 Evan Wisdom to Prime Minister's Department, 12 August 1921, NAA: A457 (A457/1), 741/1.

Anxiety over such threats prompted efforts to extend epidemiological surveillance and control movement across the territory. The 1921 Quarantine Ordinance gave the administrator authority to declare quarantine areas in response to epidemics.[109] Severe epidemics of dysentery, whooping cough or pneumonia occasionally struck rural districts, prompting efforts to restrict movement in or out of the quarantined areas.[110] Following a 1927 meeting with government officials, including Cilento and government anthropologist Chinnery, infectious disease regulations included Christian missions and schools in the collection of vital statistics and epidemiological information.[111] 'We want to have a hundred eyes, and we want an eye in every village', Cilento told the missionaries.[112] Systematic government patrols collected vital statistics and data on diseases, food and water supplies, housing, the disposal of waste and topography on standardised forms and maps.[113] In this way, Cilento wanted to make all the hidden spaces of New Guinea visible and legible to the public health gaze.

The indentured labour system exacerbated fears about the movement of pathogens. One outbreak of gonorrhoea soon after Cilento's arrival illustrates the contradictions and failures of attempts to regulate this movement. In 1924, government hospitals in Rabaul and Kavieng were swamped by 300 or so cases of the disease. In Wisdom's absence, Cilento decided that treatment—in any case difficult—was futile given the scale of the problem. Instead, he opted to release a substantial number of patients with certificates that stated 'Gonorrhoea—no facilities for treatment'. Having required that employers send cases of venereal disease to government hospitals under the Native Labour Ordinances, this was an acute embarrassment. Wisdom also recognised, however, that contradicting Cilento and stopping the practice he instituted would 'have a disastrous effect on business and domestic matters generally, and would land us with a horde of natives with whom we are unable to deal ... effectively'.[114]

109 *New Guinea Annual Report 1921–22*, 1923, p. 31.
110 *New Guinea Annual Report 1926–27*, 1928, pp. 121–3.
111 *New Guinea Gazette*, 1 July 1927, p. 2.
112 *Mission Government Conference Proceedings*, 21 June 1927, p. 6, Chinnery Papers, MS 766, Series 5, Folder 13, NLA.
113 *New Guinea Annual Report 1925–26*, 1927, pp. 66–7.
114 Evan Wisdom to Secretary, Department of Home and Territories, 29 October 1925, NAA: A1, 1926/19358.

At the same time, the prospect of time-expired workers spreading disease when they returned to their home districts continued to unsettle colonial medical officials, as it did in other colonies.[115] Cilento noted:

> Areas of gonorrhoea have been found in most distant districts recently opened up, where one or two returning labourers (perhaps the only ones who have been outside the tribal area) had brought the disease back with them.

One village in Talasea district, which patrols had visited only twice, had an 80 per cent infection rate.[116]

Cilento responded by establishing depots for isolating and treating off-contract labourers on Vulcan Island, in Rabaul Harbour, and on Nago Island, in Kavieng District, New Ireland. When the major outbreak of gonorrhoea occurred in the first half of 1925, many patients were kept in temporary compounds on these islands. Cilento complained, however, that the indigenous police assigned to guard the 6 kilometres of coast, besides some of them being themselves infected, were 'refractory and incompetent' and made little attempt to hinder 'deserters'. The buildings in the compound were made from local bush materials and Cilento noted that when repairs were needed, 'the coastal natives acting apparently in concert have refused to allow any further bush timber to be cut'.[117] So although colonial officials dreamt of effectively controlling the spread of disease through surveillance and detention, practical attempts to do so faltered on limited resources and indigenous resistance. Such examples highlight the general weakness and unease of colonial governance in New Guinea, which at different times found expression in punitive violence, panic or resignation.

Public health, town space and colonial social order

If medical knowledge and public health practices had limited impacts on governance in New Guinea, they certainly played a role in planning colonial order. In particular, tropical medicine helped construct colonial

---

115 Maryinez Lyons, *The Colonial Disease: A Social History of Sleeping Sickness in Northern Zaire, 1900–1940* (Cambridge: Cambridge University Press, 1992), pp. 26–8.
116 *New Guinea Annual Report 1925–26*, 1927, p. 82.
117 Cilento, 'Medical Progress and Policy in the Territory of New Guinea,' p. 31.

subjects as dangerous and provided one rationale for racial segregation, especially through the concept of the 'reservoir'.[118] The increasing dominance of bacteriology and parasitology in the knowledge and practice of medicine had a corollary in the idea that some human communities, in long association with their environment, could develop resistance or even immunity to diseases. This would allow them to carry the infection without suffering from obvious or debilitating symptoms.[119] Colonial health personnel could thus represent whole populations as practically permanent reserves of pathogens posing a grave threat to planters, traders and government officials. Beyond immunity, medical discourse also pathologised non-Europeans in sanitary terms. Certain races, it was assumed, lacked modern understandings of hygiene and continually created insanitary conditions through habits and customs relating to housing, waste disposal, cleanliness and food preparation. Racial segregation within urban and institutional spaces thus became a central principle of tropical medicine and of colonial government generally in the first decades of the twentieth century.[120]

Rabaul was an ethnically diverse and very masculine place, with a small European population and a larger, predominantly male indigenous population living throughout the town near their places of work.[121] The German Government had introduced a significant Chinese labour force that, by the time of Cilento's appointment, had become a prominent community of hoteliers, restaurateurs and traders.[122] Cilento noted in one report that racial segregation had been important in the original plans for Rabaul:

> The demands of hygiene, racial inclination, and variations in the standards of living, all emphasize the desirability of some such subdivision, and the Department of Public Health has endeavoured to continue and develop this policy of racial segregation.[123]

118 Farley, *Bilharzia*, p. 18; Harrison, *Public Health in British India*, p. 163; Anderson, *The Cultivation of Whiteness*, p. 146; Anderson, *Colonial Pathologies*, p. 92.
119 Anderson, *Colonial Pathologies*, p. 88.
120 Lugard, *The Dual Mandate*, p. 148; Yarwood, 'Sir Raphael Cilento and *The White Man in the Tropics*,' p. 52; Vaughan, *Curing their Ills*, p. 150; Stern, 'Yellow Fever Crusade,' p. 50; Anderson, *Colonial Pathologies*, pp. 210–4.
121 Amirah Inglis, *The White Women's Protection Ordinance: Sexual Anxiety and Politics in Papua* (London: Sussex University Press, 1974), pp. 25–8.
122 Peter Cahill, 'Chinese in Rabaul, 1921 to 1942: Normal Practices, or Containing the Yellow Peril?' *The Journal of Pacific History*, 31(1), 1996, pp. 72–4.
123 *New Guinea Annual Report 1925–26*, 1927, p. 73.

In another report, he stressed:

> The native population represents a constant reservoir of disease, and it is believed that the removal of the natives from the township area will do much to minimize the risk of transference of all parasitical and protozoal diseases.[124]

But Cilento also criticised lapses in sanitation in Chinese parts of the township, pointing to the closure of one restaurant and the demolition of nine residences as evidence of positive health policies. He reported:

> The Chinese houses that have been removed represented a continual menace to the inmates of the neighbouring European buildings in this important section of the township, and several cases of bacillary dysentery had been traced to them.[125]

Indigenous and Chinese communities were thus represented as persistent sources of disease because the characteristics that supposedly made them so were assumed to have a racial basis. This construction of non-Europeans as inherently pathogenic demanded the erection and maintenance of racially structured social boundaries.

The long, tortuous process of planning and building a new hospital and housing compound for labourers at Rapindik, just outside Rabaul's town limits, demonstrates, however, the limits of hygiene logic in shaping a racialised social order. Cilento's predecessor had condemned the old 'native' hospital as a 'grave danger to the health of the white community' two years before Cilento arrived.[126] Scarce funds delayed attempts to move the hospital or upgrade its facilities, although Cilento continued to stress that its patients and latrines posed a threat to European residents. Following the gonorrhoea crisis at Vulcan Island, he asked for funds to build a new lock hospital to detain patients, but anticipated that it would become a new general hospital for indigenous people. Venereal disease control was ultimately kept on Vulcan Island, however, and new buildings at Rapindik were instead expanded with the aid of an annual grant of £10,000 intended for 'native welfare'.[127] The hospital was finally finished in late 1928, after Cilento had returned to Australia.[128]

---

124 *New Guinea Annual Report 1926–27*, 1928, p. 127.
125 *New Guinea Annual Report 1925–26*, 1927, p. 73.
126 Evan Wisdom to Secretary of Prime Minister's Department, 11 October 1922, p. 2, NAA: A518 (A518/1), R832/1/3.
127 J. G. McLaren, Secretary of Department of Home and Territories, to Evan Wisdom, 24 January 1925; Grant Expenditure, 1927–28; Grant Expenditure, 1928–29, NAA: A518 (A518/1), D822/1/3.
128 *New Guinea Annual Report 1927–28*, 1929, p. 87.

The new hospital was in fact part of a larger plan to more thoroughly segregate indigenous people from the township. In a memo to the secretary of the prime minister's department, Wisdom noted that segregation rested on more than medical logic:

> It is the universal practice to have the white and coloured communities kept entirely separate. At present, the white, asiatic and native communities are all grouped together in the same area and practically mixed up with each other.[129]

In his annual report for 1926–27, Cilento explained that the planning of the new hospital had been carried out in conjunction with construction of a police barracks, prison and housing compound, in which the entire indentured labour force employed around Rabaul was to be permanently housed. Officials planned the Rapindik compound as three blocks of housing, a central playground or park and walls, with one boundary formed by the shoreline.[130] The experience of other colonial administrations was here influential. When discussing the hygiene of labourers' compounds in his book *The White Man in the Tropics*, Cilento drew extensively on the work of A. Pearson and R. Mouchet, who worked as medical officers for the mining company Union Miniere in the Belgian Congo.[131] In 1930, when officials were still discussing the compound, the Commissioner for Native Affairs reminded a meeting of the New Guinea Advisory Council: 'We have something to go on in the fact that they have compounds in Africa and other native countries. We are not experimenting.'[132]

Public health discourse may have provided a powerful rationale for segregation, but the demand for a native compound reflected the influence of broader representations of indigenous people and the threat they apparently posed to social order.[133] Cilento noted that the compound would help prevent petty crimes and other social problems in Rabaul,

129 Evan Wisdom to Secretary of Prime Minister's Department, 11 October 1922, p. 1, NAA: A518 (A518/1), R832/1/3.
130 *New Guinea Annual Report 1926–27*, 1928, pp. 126–7.
131 A. Pearson and R. Mouchet, *The Practical Hygiene of Native Compounds in Tropical Africa: Being Notes from the Experience of the First Eighteen Years of European Work in the Katanga* (London: Bailliere, Tindall & Cox, 1923); Cilento, *The White Man in the Tropics*, pp. 145–6, 168. See also Cilento, 'Medical Progress and Policy in the Territory of New Guinea,' p. 45.
132 'Minute Paper of the Advisory Council of New Guinea,' 4 July 1930, NAA: A518, S840/1/3.
133 Harriet Deacon has also questioned whether medical knowledge had a determining role in shaping racial segregation in the context of nineteenth-century Cape Town. See Harriet Deacon, 'Racism and Medical Science in South Africa's Cape Colony in the Mid to Late Nineteenth Century,' *Osiris*, 15, 2000, pp. 203–5.

which 'doubtless flourish owing to the fact that natives reside within the limits of the European area, and constantly have the opportunity for misdemeanours'.[134] At a 1930 meeting of the Advisory Council, the district inspector argued that housing indigenous people in one area would simplify policing.[135] Two years earlier, Chinnery described how:

> [u]ntil recently there was no street lighting system in Rabaul and in the complete darkness … one might brush into prowling natives at all hours of the night without being able to see them.

Officials highlighted the sexual threat that indigenous men posed to European women. 'There is scarcely a European woman in the Town', wrote Chinnery, 'who is free from the fear that she might be molested at night. Many sleep with loaded revolvers near them.' Even in broad daylight, 'European women have been accosted and insulted by natives on the walks in the public gardens and in lonely parts of the principle roads'. The native compound, Chinnery argued—along with street lighting, banning football, establishing night patrols and other policing measures—was a vital part of preventing a 'contemptuous indifference' that, if not dealt with, could lead to a 'nasty native problem'.[136] Indeed, it was contact between indigenous people and Europeans, Chinnery argued, that had led to racial problems in Rabaul:

> The lack of systematic and intelligent method and the isolated cases of foolish intimacy, mutilation of the dead, treachery and other manifestations of incompetence, produced re-actions from which the native has not yet recovered.[137]

Segregation was thus a vital element in the creation of the social order necessary for fulfilling the 'ideals of progress laid down in our policy of native administration', reflecting the wider commitment to segregation in the British Empire.[138]

---

134 *New Guinea Annual Report 1926–27*, 1928, p. 127.

135 'Summary of Minutes of Advisory Council Meeting,' 29 May 1930, p. 2, NAA: A518 (A518/1), S840/1/3.

136 Ernest Chinnery to Harold Page, 5 April 1928, pp. 1–9, Chinnery Papers, MS 766, Series 5, Folder 4, NLA. For this racist sexual anxiety and legislation, including restrictions on dancing, drumming and singing in Papua and New Guinea, see Wolfers, *Race Relations and Colonial Rule in Papua New Guinea*, pp. 93–7.

137 Ernest Chinnery to Harold Page, 5 April 1928, p. 3, Chinnery Papers, MS 766, Series 5, Folder 4, NLA.

138 ibid., p. 2. See Lugard, *The Dual Mandate*, pp. 148–9.

Colonial authorities could at times be ambivalent about the maintenance of strict racial boundaries, which was evident in Cilento's attitude to the prohibition on indigenous people wearing European clothing. The government required that indigenous people wear only a lap-lap, a kind of skirt-cum-loincloth, which was supposed to approximate traditional dress. Indigenous people, it was said, did not know how to wear European clothes and would let shirts get dirty and sodden to the point where they became a health risk. This was a fairly common concern across the colonial world and part of a discourse that implicated the trappings of European 'civilisation' in the decline of indigenous society.[139] Other colonial authorities instead argued that clothes were a convenient way of bridging the gulf between the colonisers and the colonised. In Papua, Hubert Murray suggested European clothes might 'foster a sense of dignity' among indigenous people, who, with the proper permit, may receive official recognition as 'a man of prudence and intelligence beyond the ordinary run of his fellows'.[140] Cilento similarly claimed that where the 'better class native' increasingly desires European marks of social status, 'clothing is a great civilizing factor'. After quoting the Filipino nationalist José Rizal on the importance of dignity, Cilento asserted:

> An absolute prohibition against clothing would be recognized by the natives as a barrier that places them definitely and finally in a position of obvious inferiority. Inferiority there doubtless is, but its ostentation, however unintentional, is harmful and unnecessary.[141]

Colonial discourse could thus be condescending and contradictory in its assertions of social inequity and the possibilities of indigenous improvement.

---

139 John Wear Burton, *Our Task in Papua* (London: The Epworth Press, 1926), p. 55. Clothes were one suggested factor in Fijian depopulation; see Margaret Jolly, 'Infertile States: Person and Collectivity, Region and Nation in the Rhetoric of Pacific Population,' in Margaret Jolly and Kalpana Ram (eds), *Borders of Being: Citizenship, Fertility, and Sexuality in Asia and the Pacific* (Ann Arbor: University of Michigan Press, 2001), p. 277. See also Randall Packard, 'The "Healthy Reserve" and the "Dressed Native": Discourses on Black Health and the Language of Legitimation in South Africa,' *American Ethnologist*, 16(4), 1989, pp. 686–703; Rani Kerin, '"Natives Allowed to Remain Naked": An Unorthodox Approach to Medical Work at Ernabella Mission,' *Health and History*, 8(1), 2006, pp. 80–99.
140 Murray, *Papua of To-day*, p. 256.
141 *New Guinea Annual Report 1925–26*, 1927, p. 78.

The indigenous compound reflected multiple rationales of colonial government, but it later became a contested site in colonial politics as debate surrounded its planning well into the 1930s. Business interests in Rabaul objected most, particularly the larger companies such as Burns Philp and W. R. Carpenter & Co., which were either building or maintaining copra wharves and stores just outside the official town boundaries. In May 1930, both companies officially requested that they be exempt from any requirement to house labourers in the planned compound. Burns Philp employed about 500 indentured labourers and claimed to have spent £4,000 developing housing and medical facilities on land leased from the government inside the township. W. R. Carpenter had also developed facilities to house labourers on its land, at Toboi, outside the township. The Rabaul manager for Burns Philp claimed that transport would take over three hours from the 10-hour working day, adding: 'It seems practically certain that natives will not willingly take to the restriction of life in a compound.'[142] W. R. Carpenter similarly argued: 'If we were compelled to occupy quarters at Rapindik the transport of our labour each morning would entail heavy cost and serious loss of time.'[143] The immediate priorities of reducing costs and squeezing as much labour as possible out of its employees thus brought business into conflict with the official policy of racial segregation.

The principles of tropical medicine thus had to compete with other interests in shaping colonial social order. Cilento saw medical knowledge and public health as the central principles of governance in a way that led to his alienation from the rest of the administration. Cilento's successors as Director of Public Health would prove to be less demanding. Indeed, when Burns Philp and W. R. Carpenter asked for their exemptions, the Acting Director of Public Health noted: 'I would say that the last thing we want is to cause Burns Philp any embarrassment.'[144] Medicine was not therefore simply a tool of colonial government and conquest. Rather, it provided ways of imagining and enforcing a colonial social order, its authority always negotiated and contested in the context of financial parsimony and the dictates of imperial capitalism.

142 P. Coote, Rabaul Manager of Burns Philp, to Evan Wisdom, 12 May 1930, NAA: A518, S840/1/3.
143 J. A. Carpenter, Managing Director of W. R. Carpenter and Co., to Evan Wisdom, 2 May 1930, NAA: A518, S840/1/3.
144 'Minutes of Advisory Council Meeting,' 29 May 1930, NAA: A518, S840/1/3.

Population, diet and the colonial future

Tropical medicine and the imperatives of imperial rule clearly shaped Cilento's work as the Director of Public Health in New Guinea. Yet he did have medical and social concerns beyond his formal training in tropical medicine and, indeed, beyond the interests and expectations of the central administration in New Guinea. Cilento often framed health and sickness within a historical narrative of colonialism and its social impacts, rather than simply appealing to inherent racial characteristics of indigenous or 'Asiatic' peoples. Cilento's work in New Guinea roughly coincided with a flurry of anthropological reflections on the European impact on culture and society in the Pacific, which focused especially on population decline.

Cilento's ambivalent relationship to this discourse was clearest in his deepening preoccupation with diet and its relationship to health and society. He had early on questioned the quality and quantity of rations for indentured labourers in government employment across New Guinea. In his review of medical services, Cilento suggested: 'The question of native food is possibly the most important factor connected with conditions of indentured labour.' After a tour of the territory to inspect living and working conditions, he claimed that 54 per cent of New Guinean police, labourers and prisoners at the government station at Manus suffered from 'incipient' beriberi, a condition of vitamin B deficiency causing weight loss and weakness.[145] The issue later became Cilento's most important conflict with the administration, as diet moved to the heart of his broad medical *and* social vision for New Guinea and its future. Diet and nutrition, in other words, became Cilento's chief means of constructing the past and present of indigenous people, and a future for them under the guidance of 'civilised' peoples.

Modern knowledge of human nutrition had roots in colonial laboratories and fieldwork and fed back into discussions of public health across the world. In this way it is an illuminating example of the complicated 'networked' routes that ideas and practices have taken across imperial space.[146] Robert McCarrison conducted comparative studies of diets in the

145 Cilento, 'Medical Progress and Policy in the Territory of New Guinea,' p. 45.
146 Michael Worboys, 'The Discovery of Colonial Malnutrition between the Wars,' in David Arnold (ed.), *Imperial Medicine and Indigenous Societies* (Manchester: Manchester University Press, 1988), pp. 208–25; Anne Hardy, 'Beriberi, Vitamin B1 and World Food Policy, 1925–1970,' *Medical History*, 39, 1995, pp. 61–77; Amrith, *Decolonizing International Health*, p. 28.

mid-1920s and advised the Indian Government of the influence of vitamin deficiencies on disease resistance. John Boyd Orr carried out comparative analyses of diets and health among African tribes that seemed to suggest the superiority of protein over carbohydrates in protecting health. Earlier research in the late nineteenth and early twentieth centuries in the Dutch East Indies and the Federated Malay States produced a wealth of results linking beriberi to a deficiency of vitamin B brought about by a reliance on polished rice in the diet of prisoners.[147] By the mid-1930s, the League of Nations had established committees to investigate and synthesise current knowledge of the physiological, economic and social aspects of diet on a global scale.

Cilento tried to bring this research to bear on New Guinea health policy. Drawing on Elmer McCollum and Nina Simmond's *Newer Knowledge of Nutrition* (largely based on McCollum's research at Johns Hopkins), Cilento stressed that health was not just the absence of disease, but also a positive quality that a multitude of factors, continually operating on the body throughout one's life, could cultivate or undermine.[148] Poor nutrition, he wrote, affected 'the relative muscular power, physical endowment, degree of endurance, resistance to disease, and even the place to which a tribe or race has won in manliness, energy, and soldierly instincts'.[149] When Cilento pushed the administration on dietary reform, he pointed to examples from Northern Rhodesia, South Africa and other African colonies as guides to policy in New Guinea.[150] The international literature and the policies of other territories, in other words, became resources for Cilento's efforts to reform workers' rations.

Cilento at first concentrated on the immediate problem of the diet of indentured labourers employed by the government, particularly those on outstations. Their food rations consisted mainly of tinned meat and polished rice, which had been stripped of its vitamin and nutrient-rich

---

147 Robert McCarrison and Hugh M. Sinclair, *The Work of Sir Robert McCarrison* (London: Faber & Faber, 1953), pp. 261–81; J. L. Gilks and J. B. Orr, 'The Nutritional Condition of the East African Native,' *The Lancet*, 12 March 1927, pp. 560–2; Worboys, 'Discovery of Colonial Malnutrition between the Wars,' p. 214; Ken De Bevoise, *Agents of Apocalypse: Epidemic Disease in the Colonial Philippines* (Princeton, NJ: Princeton University Press, 1995), p. 119; Stephen Toth, *Beyond Papillon: The French Overseas Penal Colonies, 1854–1952* (Lincoln: University of Nebraska Press, 2006), p. 91.
148 Raphael Cilento, *The Causes of the Depopulation of the Western Islands of the Territory of New Guinea* (Canberra: Government Printer, 1928), p. 18.
149 Raphael Cilento, 'Report on Diet Deficiencies in the Territory of New Guinea,' n.d., p. 1, NAA: A1, 1925/24149.
150 Raphael Cilento to Evan Wisdom, 8 August 1925, NAA: A1, 1925/24149.

husk and other outer layers during processing. By the time Cilento was appointed director of public health in New Guinea, most health officials recognised that consumption of polished rice was the cause of beriberi among colonised peoples in the tropics. Moreover, medical authorities also understood that vitamin deficiencies undermined resistance to diseases, including tuberculosis, pneumonia and malaria. Anne Hardy has noted that nutritional researchers in the late 1920s and early 1930s, such as Wallace Aykroyd and Benjamin Platt, resisted nutritional reform that emphasised the replacement of vitamins lost through processing. Instead, they took a holistic approach that recommended increasing the variety and quantity of food, so providing a healthy foundational diet.[151]

Cilento began from a similar perspective, suggesting that colonial policy should reflect the knowledge that the whole diet of indigenous people shaped their health in a broad sense. After raising the issue, Cilento criticised Wisdom's suggestion of importing red rice from Asia as a useless measure. Instead, rations needed to reflect the more complete traditional local diets of villagers. In October 1925, he wrote to Wisdom:

> I state deliberately and emphatically that the diet supplied to labourers is grossly inferior to that used by them even in their own villages and that the death rate from food deficiency has a direct and indirect relation to the total mortality and the depopulation of this country.[152]

The rations Cilento developed, although a compromise, were designed to provide a more complete diet that mimicked the village diet while also increasing the consumption of animal protein. Eventually included in the Native Labour Ordinance in 1927, the rations included 5 lb (2.3 kg) of either taro or breadfruit, along with dried beans or lentils, wholemeal barley or wheat and fresh meat or fish.[153]

For Cilento, the pace of change was frustratingly slow. He had been pressing the administration to adopt new dietary standards since 1924, but the administration argued it would be too costly and prevaricated with assertions that natives did not need the 9 oz (255 g) of meat Cilento originally prescribed. In September 1925, government secretary H. Page relayed Wisdom's statement that he thought it 'most undesirable that

---

151 Hardy, 'Beriberi, Vitamin B1 and World Food Policy,' p. 68.
152 Raphael Cilento to Evan Wisdom, quoted in Cilento to J. H. L. Cumpston, 8 September 1927, p. 3, NAA: A452, 1959/5894.
153 *New Guinea Annual Report 1926–27*, 1928, pp. 101–7.

we should compulsorily increase the cost of the native diet to the extent indicated'.[154] Cilento replied by pointing out how low the wages in New Guinea were compared with those in Papua and the Solomon Islands: 'There is no country in the world where so little money is expended by the planter for the safeguarding of the native.' In an excoriating indictment of the administration, Cilento wrote:

> I now state deliberately that the Administration, with the facts established by me before it, is faced with the question of either improving the diet obligatory for natives or of being party to the deliberate destruction of the race to whose moral and social welfare it has pledged itself.[155]

For Cilento, medical knowledge, his professional identity and the language of the mandate gave him a position from which he felt he could criticise the colonial administration in strong terms.

The tension between Cilento and the administration snapped when beriberi broke out among labourers on the recently opened goldfields at Bulolo and Edie Creek in the Waria River area. The rush of prospectors began in earnest in 1926 and 1927, which worried the administration. In October 1927, Wisdom sent Chinnery to the area to address the increasingly tense situation between miners, indigenous police and local communities.[156] Prospectors had already gone into areas where there had been little contact and no government control.[157] Cilento had advised that they observe the ration scales outlined in the labour ordinance, but the miners failed to implement them for their contracted labourers. The outbreak of beriberi on the goldfields confirmed for Cilento that the administration lacked progressive spirit. He wrote to Wisdom in May 1927:

> I am persuaded to take this step in final recognition of the futility of my attempting, as matters are, to establish in this Territory an efficient and effective medical service.

---

154 Harold Page to Raphael Cilento, 19 September 1925, NAA: A1 (A1/15), 1925/24149.
155 Raphael Cilento to Harold Page, 21 September 1925, NAA: A1 (A1/15), 1925/24149.
156 Ernest Chinnery to Harold Page, 19 April 1928, Chinnery Papers, MS 766, Series 5, Folder 15, NLA; Ernest Chinnery, Diary: 20 August – 21 November 1927, Chinnery Papers, MS 766, Series 30, Folder 5, NLA.
157 Ernest Chinnery to Leahy and Extone, 24 October 1927, Chinnery Papers, MS 766, Series 5, Folder 15, NLA.

He stressed that he would not accept responsibility for:

> [the] epidemic of beri-beri at present gathering way at Idi [sic] Creek, where roughly a thousand natives shew marked evidences of malnutrition, several hundred have definite beri-beri, scurvy or ulcerative stomatitis and many have died.[158]

Cilento felt his 'personal and professional reputation' was under threat and asked Cumpston whether he could return to Australia early.[159]

Anne Hardy has noted that many nutrition researchers in the late 1920s and early 1930s—such as McCarrison in India, Wallace Aykroyd in Newfoundland and Benjamin Platt in China—began to see illness as a structural problem of income and living conditions in both the metropolitan and the colonial worlds.[160] This was not a new idea, but knowledge of nutrition could provide new ways to understand that connection. Cilento similarly linked diet and health in New Guinea to social and economic conditions. Beyond workers' rations, nutrition was at the centre of a narrative in which Cilento traced the sickness of indigenous people to the social and economic changes that followed colonisation. At the same time, however, nutrition helped represent racial difference in new ways that justified ongoing colonial rule.

Acute humanitarian and economic anxieties about declining indigenous populations had marked colonial discourse in the Pacific Islands since the late nineteenth century.[161] Distant metropolitan observers, as Margaret Jolly has shown, tended to portray indigenous women as the antithesis of idealised middle-class European mothers and blamed high infant mortality on 'faulty' feeding methods and 'insouciance' towards children.[162] W. H. R. Rivers, a Cambridge University psychologist-cum-anthropologist, published an edited collection of Essays on Depopulation in 1922, including contributions from missionaries, anthropologists and his own paper on 'The Psychological Factor'.[163] George Henry Lane-Fox

158 Raphael Cilento to Evan Wisdom, 21 May 1927, NAA: A452, 1959/5894.
159 Raphael Cilento to J. H. L. Cumpston, 28 May 1927, NAA: A452, 1959/5894.
160 Hardy, 'Beriberi, Vitamin B1 and World Food Policy,' p. 63.
161 Jolly, 'Infertile States,' pp. 274–7.
162 Margaret Jolly, 'Other Mothers: Maternal "Insouciance" and the Depopulation Debate in Fiji and Vanuatu 1890–1930,' in Kalpana Ram and Margaret Jolly (eds), Maternities and Modernities: Colonial and Postcolonial Experiences in Asia and the Pacific (Chicago: University of Chicago Press, 1998), pp. 182–3.
163 W. H. R. Rivers, 'The Psychological Factor,' in W. H. R. Rivers (ed.), Essays on the Depopulation of Melanesia (Cambridge: Cambridge University Press, 1922), pp. 84–114.

Pitt-Rivers' *The Clash of Cultures* and Stephen Roberts' *Population Problems of the Pacific* showed the influence of Rivers' text.[164] While acknowledging the impact of introduced diseases, these works emphasised psychological explanations for depopulation. Put in its simplest form, the disruption of headhunting, dancing and other customs created an environment in which 'the native', deprived of the rituals and activities that created his universe and provided meaning for his existence, fell into a listless despair. Noting Rivers' claim regarding 'the enormous influence of the mind upon the body among lowly peoples', Roberts argued that the coming of European civilisation had left indigenous people 'suspended as it were, in mid air'; 'the native, making up his mind to die, forces his body to keep pace with his mental pessimism, and dies'.[165] In this strange and fantastic rendering of 'native' fragility, indigenous people were prone to physical collapse when cultural contact undermined the spiritual, symbolic and customary world they inhabited.

Cilento shared a deep concern about depopulation but engaged critically with prevailing thought. In February 1927, he undertook a health and population survey of the Western Islands of the Bismarck Archipelago. In his report, he criticised Rivers and Pitt-Rivers for overemphasising psychology, arguing that they had mistaken effect for cause.[166] In all the island groups Cilento visited, he found high rates of malaria, as was common in most communities in New Guinea except the Highlands. At Auna, on the island of Matti (Wuvulu), Cilento claimed that 68 per cent of males under the age of 14 showed signs of malarial infection, while the disease also accounted for a significant proportion of infant mortality.[167] Other introduced diseases, such as tuberculosis and pneumonia, also contributed significantly to total mortality, just as they did in the rest of the territory. In one village on an island in the Ninigo Group, Cilento claimed that malaria accounted for the deaths of 66 per cent of children in the 20 years before his study.[168]

164 George Henry Lane-Fox Pitt-Rivers, *The Clash of Cultures: An Anthropological and Psychological Study of the Laws of Racial Adaptability* (London: George Routledge & Sons, 1927).

165 Stephen Roberts, *Population Problems of the Pacific* (London: George Routledge & Sons, 1927), pp. 73–4.

166 Cilento, *The Causes of the Depopulation of the Western Islands of the Territory of New Guinea*, p. 37.

167 ibid., p. 12.

168 ibid., p. 26.

Cilento emphasised how diseases interacted with malnutrition among the indigenous people of these islands. He rejected the notion that they had lived in a kind of languid paradise, arguing that the predominantly carbohydrate diet of precolonial life would at times have left them in a state of starvation for significant periods. Yet he also rejected the idea that Pacific Island populations were already in irreversible decline before colonisation: 'We cannot, we fear, lay such flattering unction to our souls.'[169] For Cilento, the way European cash cropping had undermined indigenous agriculture was the greater cause of sickness and depopulation in the islands. Planters and governments had taken the best land, separating indigenous people from their social foundations:

> Land was obtained by purchase, by force or by fraud, foreign labourers and foreign diseases were introduced, and the natives were soon driven from their ancestral properties to a common concentration depot on some inferior island or set of islets.[170]

Loss of agricultural land had led to reliance on imported rice, sometimes supplemented with coconut and fish, which was 'no basis for progress or initiative'.[171] The resulting malnutrition had lowered resistance to malaria, leading to the very high mortality Cilento observed. Malaria and vitamin A deficiency in turn made indigenous people more vulnerable to tuberculosis and pneumonia. Dental defects were also common.[172] Disease, moreover, had led to high rates of uterine defects that directly affected fertility.[173] Cilento wrote of the island of Matti:

> One can only deplore the unfortunate fact, that ignorance of the true condition of affairs permitted the alienation, a generation ago, of practically the whole of the valuable land, destroying, as an unforeseen consequence, the social organization and the institutions of the natives in favour of a company, and reducing an artistic and intelligent people from a high plane of potential development to the lowly status of dependence on the bounty of foreign intruders.[174]

---

169 ibid., p. 21.
170 ibid., p. 9.
171 ibid., p. 26.
172 ibid., p. 17.
173 ibid., pp. 19–20.
174 ibid., p. 6.

In his analysis of diet and health, Cilento did not therefore entirely blame sickness on indigenous people, and in fact suggested that patterns of dispossession and economic transformation involved in colonisation were responsible for much of the sickness suffered across the territory.

If Cilento traced sickness and depopulation back to the impacts of colonisation, nutrition was an important part of how he conceived of racial difference and a justification of paternalistic administration. Cilento built up around diet and nutrition an 'anti-conquest' narrative of the kind that Mary Louise Pratt has described for the eighteenth century. In these stories, imperial agents 'seek to secure their innocence in the same moment as they assert European hegemony'.[175] Cilento asserted that the predominance of carbohydrates in New Guinean diets had historically shaped indigenous people as weaker and less creative than European peoples:

> The character of the carbohydrate eater is opposed to the character of the races which include in their diet an adequate proportion of animal protein, in that it is deficient in the qualities of energy, initiative, and progress, though it possibly surpasses the latter in the power of endurance at monotonous physical tasks. Such nations are hewers of wood and the drawers of water for the more vigorous nations. They make ideal porters and pack carriers, and apparently they do not desire to be otherwise.[176]

In this account, diet had made some non-European peoples an ideal labour force for the economic development of tropical countries. So, while nutrition had allowed a critique of colonisation and exploitation, it simultaneously asserted the superiority of European peoples and justified colonial rule founded on paternal guidance.[177]

In paying such close attention to nutrition, Cilento constructed racial difference within a narrative of environmental and social history rather than heredity alone. Diet shaped embodied subjects as contingent products of history, culture and the environment. Indeed, colonial discourse and law tended to incorporate a range of cultural attributes in the idea of

---

175 Mary Louise Pratt, *Imperial Eyes: Travel Writing and Transculturation* (London: Routledge, 1992), p. 7: Neil Smith, *American Empire: Geography and the Prelude to Globalization* (Berkeley: University of California Press, 2003), pp. 79–80.

176 Cilento, *The White Man in the Tropics*, pp. 154–5.

177 On the place of nutrition in representations of racial difference in the 1920s, see Nick Cullather, 'Foreign Policy of the Calorie,' *American Historical Review*, 112(2), 2007, pp. 354–9.

race rather than reduce it to hereditary biology.[178] Cilento's discussion of depopulation similarly framed race in terms of lost or declining forms material production, customs, stories and art. The inhabitants of the Western Islands had once been an 'active and capable race', responsible for stonework of a 'high order of excellence'. The islands had been part of a thriving trading network supporting vital communities:

> Decorated earthenware, pottery and such like evidences of handicraft and progressive culture were traded, native legends, dances and songs, with the mythology they illustrated were exchanged, and a considerable intercourse aided the social development of all parties. This has now entirely disappeared, such fragments of pottery, &c., as do remain being jealously hoarded by the natives as belonging to the 'time before'.[179]

On the other hand, Cilento often drew on ethnography to suggest an underlying instinct towards the consumption of meat. Assertions concerning widespread cannibalism in the past and the high social value of protein-rich shark livers across Melanesia suggested to Cilento an instinctive recognition of nutritional value.[180] In this way, knowledge of diet and nutrition constructed racial difference in terms of the cultural and environmental constraints of place, while also positing a universal instinct towards an ideally balanced diet. It was on this basis that Cilento claimed there was a need for intervention in the 'social development' of indigenous people.[181]

If reformers believed that peasant proprietorship could uplift colonised peoples from barbarism to membership of international society and commerce, Cilento presented it as the most meaningful and lasting safeguard for the health of indigenous people. In Cilento's account, the people of Unia (Unea) Island had maintained their customs and institutions and 'remain true peasant proprietors', cultivating traditional

---

178 Ann Laura Stoler, *Carnal Knowledge and Imperial Power: Race and the Intimate in Colonial Rule* (Berkeley: University of California Press, 2002), p. 97; Geulen, 'The Common Grounds of Conflict,' p. 70. On the idea of carbohydrate or rice eaters as a category, see Maria Letitia Galluzzi Bizzo, 'Postponing Equality: From Colonial to International Nutritional Standards, 1932–1950,' in Veronika Lipphardt and Alexandra Widmer (eds), *Health and Difference: Rendering Human Variation in Colonial Engagements* (New York: Berghahn Books, 2016), pp. 129–48.
179 Cilento, *The Causes of the Depopulation of the Western Islands of the Territory of New Guinea*, p. 10.
180 Raphael Cilento to Evan Wisdom, 15 October 1925, p. 4, NAA: A1 (A1/15), 1925/24149; Raphael Cilento, 'The Value of Medical Services in Relation to Problems of Depopulation,' *The Medical Journal of Australia*, II(16), 15 October 1932, p. 482.
181 Cilento, *The Causes of the Depopulation of the Western Islands of the Territory of New Guinea*, p. 10.

staple crops on land that they largely owned.[182] Cilento suggested setting up communal gardens that could emulate this supply of a varied and traditional diet; the surplus of such gardens could be sold for profit. Cilento's plan, however, reserved for senior medical assistants the authority to approve or disapprove indigenous requests for purchases using money from an administration trust fund to which 50 per cent of annual receipts would go.[183]

Nothing came of these proposals, but Cilento's pursuit of indigenous dietary reform illustrates conflicting agendas in colonial government and the contradictions and ambivalence within colonial discourses on social development. It is clear that Cilento attributed much disease and sickness among indigenous communities to the social and economic consequences of colonisation. Malnutrition, he argued—deriving from both poor rations and the alienation of land for commercial agriculture—underpinned the vast majority of illness and deaths among indigenous labourers in New Guinea.[184] The colonial economy was thus an important structural factor in indigenous sickness and disease, in his view. Yet nutrition also served as a way to represent racial difference, not in terms of heredity per se, but through a narrative of environmental and social history. Poor nutrition thus lay at the heart of the indigenous lethargy that seemed apparent to the colonial eye:

> It is protein deficiency at the present day which makes the native the undeveloped, dull and indolent creature that he is and that contributes to his excessive tendency to tuberculosis, his ready surrender to disease and his heavy death rate.[185]

Nutrition thus allowed Cilento to criticise colonial policies while representing difference in a way that justified supervision of the social transformation of indigenous people as they were drawn into a tightening net of global economic relations.

Cilento's career in New Guinea illustrates the ambiguous position of medicine and public health in colonial governance. Rather than a simple tool, it was always complicit and contentious, authoritative and marginal. With the establishment of schools of tropical medicine in Britain and the

---

182 ibid., p. 11.
183 ibid., p. 50.
184 Raphael Cilento to Harold Page, 28 May 1927, NAA: A452 (A452/1), 1959/5894.
185 Raphael Cilento to Evan Wisdom, 15 October 1925, p. 4, NAA: A1 (A1/15), 1925/24149.

United States, the medical profession acquired new influence on imperial policy and practice. Beyond protecting the health of European officials, medical officials were by the 1920s claiming responsibility for the efficiency of the whole colonial enterprise. Cilento was certainly a conduit for the disciplinary practice of colonial hygiene. Racial segregation and control of specific infectious diseases such as malaria and hookworm were central aspects of the activities of Cilento's Department of Health. Programs for the mass treatment of hookworm and gonorrhoea, and the attempt to expunge mosquitoes and their larvae from pools, puddles and water-filled tin cans, were central aspects of the routine work of Cilento's department. Yet Cilento brought basic principles of public health to New Guinea, including protection of water supplies, sanitary disposal of waste and the provision of an adequate diet. He was often forced to contest what was considered the domain of medicine as he developed a strong conception of the broad role of public health in government that was, on occasion, in conflict with imperial capitalism.

3

Coordinating empires: Nationhood, Australian imperialism and international health in the Pacific Islands, 1925–1929

The first International Pacific Health Conference, held in Melbourne in 1926, brought together senior health officials from the Pacific Islands, as well as from the League of Nations, the Philippines, Japan, French Indochina and Britain. On the agenda was the creation of a local variant of international health regimes recently appearing elsewhere in the world: standardised quarantine, regional training programs, the exchange of research and an epidemiological intelligence service using telegraph and wireless networks. Since the mid-nineteenth century, a series of international sanitation conferences had negotiated uniform quarantine codes intended to prevent more of the plague and cholera epidemics that had struck Europe prior to the 1850s. By the 1920s, several new international organisations—particularly the League of Nations Health Organization (LNHO) and the International Health Board (IHB) of the Rockefeller Foundation—collectively administered a much wider repertoire of activities of the kind that were considered in Melbourne. The LNHO had already established an epidemiological bureau in Singapore, which would later coordinate study tours, courses in malariology and epidemiological studies and treatment campaigns at the request of various national and colonial governments across Asia. In the 1930s, the LNHO became involved in nutrition surveys and social medicine and on one occasion participated in the wholesale reorganisation of national public health administrations.[1]

Although the participants shared concerns about the transmission of epidemic disease and population decline, the conference in Melbourne was also part of an Australian project in empire and security. The geography of the Pacific Islands was a constant source of worry for health officials. Their archipelagic nature seemed to make it easier for shipborne diseases to pass between territories undetected in an era of increasingly rapid and extensive commerce with Asia. Cumpston, Elkington and Cilento saw the islands—administered by chronically underfunded governments often lacking in personnel and quarantine infrastructure—as ready soil for new foci of smallpox, cholera and plague. The CDH produced a map for the conference of the 'Austral-Pacific Regional Zone', which incorporated the island groups of Near and Remote Oceania and would be centred on a bureau and training centre somewhere in Australia. The map of the 'Austral-Pacific' was thus a representation of what Commonwealth health officials considered a sphere of informal authority over health services across the islands. In establishing such dominance over colonial medicine and 'native administration', they sought not only to safeguard the Commonwealth, but also to fulfil dreams of Australian hegemony in the Pacific Islands.[2]

The League of Nations responded to a request for assistance in the report of the conference by initiating the Pacific Health Mission, which aimed to investigate epidemiology, nutrition, health services and population decline in the islands. When the time came to carry out this inquiry, it was Cilento, along with French colonial officer Paul Hermant, who travelled through Fiji, New Caledonia, the New Hebrides, Papua, New Guinea and the Solomon Islands. This brief experience of other social, economic and political regimes of the Pacific—especially the variety of indigenous

1   Dimitra Giannuli, '"Repeated Disappointment": The Rockefeller Foundation and the Reform of the Greek Public Health System,' *Bulletin of the History of Medicine*, 72(1), 1998, pp. 47–72. For the history of international health in the nineteenth century, see Harrison, 'Disease, Diplomacy and International Commerce,' pp. 197–217. For the history of international health conferences and organisations generally, see Paul Weindling, 'Introduction: Constructing International Health between the Wars,' in Paul Weindling (ed.), *International Health Organisations and Movements, 1918–1939* (Cambridge: Cambridge University Press, 1995), pp. 1–16; Dubin, 'The League of Nations Health Organisation,' pp. 59–60; Bashford, *Imperial Hygiene*, pp. 133–5.
2   'Native administration' referred to the special government of indigenous people. Sir Arthur Gordon's Fijian administration used the term in the 1870s. See Bennett, 'Holland, Britain, and Germany in Melanesia,' p. 42.

and migrant populations—reaffirmed Cilento's ideological commitment to racial and cultural homogeneity as a general principle of world order. In letters from Fiji, he dwelt on how Indian indentured labourers had displaced indigenous cultivators, precluding the peasant proprietorship he had advocated in New Guinea. As he toured the colonial Pacific, Cilento elaborated on his claims that health rested on national social homogeneity and environmental equilibrium. Moreover, the connections he made in New Guinea between health, nationhood, homogeneity, agriculture and nutrition would equally underpin his contributions to public health reform in Australia.

Steamships and conferences: Quarantine, epidemiological intelligence and international health in the interwar years

Medical officials in the South-West Pacific, particularly those within the CDH, worried about the epidemiological implications of closer commercial ties with Asia. They also worried about the underdevelopment of and lack of coordination in preventive medicine in the region. From the 1880s, as Bashford has shown, such concerns played a powerful role in defining the boundaries of a potential Australian nation. As commercial shipping between the Australian colonies and India, Ceylon, the Straits Settlements, French Indochina, China and the Dutch East Indies became more rapid and frequent, Australia appeared ever more vulnerable to cholera, plague, smallpox and other diseases associated with Asia. Where once the sea had seemed to provide a natural barrier—as the time taken to cross it allowed disease symptoms to appear among an inbound vessel's passengers—modern steamships made the distance between Australia and Asia seem uncomfortably close. Quarantine in the Australian colonies and in the post-Federation Commonwealth thus provided ways to imagine Australia as a 'clean' island nation.[3]

Quarantine also became part of the Australian imperial imagination. Public health within colonial territories revolved around combating the supposed 'backwardness' of indigenous subjects. International cooperation in quarantine instead spoke to fear about the effect on indigenous populations of their integration with a modern world economy, with all

---

3   Bashford, *Imperial Hygiene*, pp. 123–31.

its varied exchanges of disease, goods, ideas and customs. At the second Pan-Pacific Science Congress, held in Australia in 1923, Cumpston spoke of the need for 'conservation of the native races' and called for greater cooperation between island health authorities in preventing epidemics and improving indigenous health.[4] In 1925, the Australian Government, responding to frustration among copra planters in New Guinea, dropped a provision from the Navigation Act that forced ships carrying their produce to pass through Sydney en route to their destination. Cilento noted that ships coming directly from Hong Kong would now take only eight days to arrive in Rabaul. This interval, he pointed out, was about six days shorter than the incubation period for smallpox, raising the possibility that it might escape the gaze of quarantine officers.[5]

The International Pacific Health Conference, convened by the Commonwealth in Melbourne in December 1926, was the federal government's first significant international involvement in regional public health. The 1884 Australasian Sanitary Conference had included the Chief Medical Officer of Fiji in debates over the efficacy of quarantine and vaccination.[6] However, while the 1880s had been marked by the question of whether Fiji and New Zealand would be included in an Australian federation, the 1920s conference was clearly oriented towards a larger consideration of the Pacific Islands as a region. The conference included chief medical officers from most of the Pacific Island administrations, including Cilento (New Guinea), Walter Strong (Papua), Aubrey Montague (Fiji), T. Russell Ritchie (Samoa) and H. B. Hetherington (Solomon Islands), as well as M. H. Watt from New Zealand. Participants also came from further afield, including Eusebio Aguilar (the Philippines), Paul Hermant (French Indochina), Genzo Katoh (Japan), A. R. Wellington (the Straits Settlements), Sir George Buchanan (the United Kingdom) and F. Norman White from the League of Nations. Delegates from the Dutch East Indies were invited but were unable to send a representative. The composition of the conference thus reflected a focus on improving preventive health in the island groups of the South-West Pacific and a secondary concern with the way a Pacific Islands health regime might be articulated within the larger regional and global apparatuses of international health that had been developing since the beginning of the twentieth century.

---

4   J. H. L. Cumpston, 'Depopulation of the Pacific,' *Proceedings of the Pan-Pacific Science Congress*, 2(4), 1923, p. 1394.
5   *The Age*, [Melbourne], 19 November 1925, n.p., NAA: A1928 (A1928/1), 705/11.
6   Bashford, *Imperial Hygiene*, pp. 25–8.

Participants presented papers on disease conditions in their territories, existing public health measures and—always wary of committing their governments—guarded commentary on the agenda and proposals of the conference. Contributions to the conference varied in depth and detail. Strong and Cilento presented papers with considerable geographic and ethnographic information, as they sought to emphasise the challenges faced by medical authorities in territories with limited financial resources, difficult terrain and the responsibility of governing 'primitive' races.[7] Cilento explained the waves of migration that had shaped the populations of South-East Asia and the Pacific Islands in racial terms. At one point he emphasised how the first 'negrito' peoples of Melanesia had 'moiled' and 'mixed' with the successive waves of migrating races from Asia. Despite this 'blending' of 'stock', however, Cilento related how 'four great racial variants'—namely, the Malays, Malayoids, Papuo-Melanesians and Polynesians—had emerged with 'fixed characters, fixed customs, fixed boundaries, and all speaking, with innumerable mutations, the Oceanic tongue'. With no unity or 'common patriotism' among these peoples, Cilento asserted, colonial powers had established themselves with borders coinciding neatly with racial boundaries.[8] In reality, colonial borders not only cut across networks of commerce and cultural exchange, but also contained extremely diverse and dynamic archipelagic cultures.[9]

Constructing domains of governance was an important theme of the conference. Aguilar presented extensive information on the epidemiology and public health practices of the Philippines, with regard to leprosy, cholera, smallpox and plague, many of which did not occur significantly or at all in the Pacific Islands further east. Cilento in fact tried to delineate epidemiological boundaries that he felt should shape international administrative arrangements. As Sunil Amrith has shown, tropical medicine did much to define 'Asia' as a region with a common set of problems and thus as a distinct area for the 'government of life and welfare'.[10] Racial and political divisions also corresponded, Cilento argued, to differences in disease distribution that gave added resolution to regional distinctions. While Malaysia had the 'problems associated with Asia, including the presence of plague, small-pox, and other dangerous quarantinable diseases', the absence of these diseases in Melanesia and

---

7   Commonwealth of Australia, 'Report of the International Pacific Health Conference,' *Commonwealth Parliamentary Papers*, 5, 1926, pp. 826–32.

8   ibid., p. 832.

9   See Moore, *New Guinea*, pp. 3–6.

10   Amrith, *Decolonizing International Health*, p. 76.

Polynesia presented a different epidemiological terrain that included 'endemic depressive' diseases such as hookworm and local epidemics of bacillary dysentery. Polynesia was further differentiated from Melanesia by the absence of *Anopheles* mosquitoes and thus malaria.[11]

Plate 3.1 The first International Pacific Health Conference, 1926
Source: National Archives of Australia: AA1969, A9.

The rhetoric of responsibility for indigenous welfare that had risen to international prominence ran through this conference as well.[12] In lofty opening remarks, acting prime minister and former surgeon Earle Page declared that 'the efforts of the last 50 years to introduce the material benefits of civilization have been directed by peaceful and humane ideals'.[13] Page highlighted the impact of diseases such as measles, influenza and hookworm, urging: '[W]e should seek to help each other in our common task of securing and improving the health and happiness of these people for whom we are responsible.'[14] A global conversation about the impacts of cultural and economic contact and the need to accept 'uplift' as the central project of civilised imperial nations was thus a significant aspect of the International Pacific Health Conference.

---

11 Commonwealth of Australia, 'Report of the International Pacific Health Conference,' p. 836.
12 Pedersen, 'Settler Colonialism at the Bar of the League of Nations,' pp. 113–14.
13 Commonwealth of Australia, 'Report of the International Pacific Health Conference,' p. 821.
14 ibid., p. 822.

While the emphasis in other contexts may have centred on indigenous rights or political and economic tutelage, in the Pacific Islands the very survival of indigenous peoples was often foremost in the minds of colonial officials. The 1896 report of the Fijian Commission did much to establish the causes of population decline in colonial discourse in the Pacific. These ranged from introduced disease and malnutrition and European clothing to indigenous customs and habits such as headhunting, polygamy, narcotics use, communality, improvidence and infanticide.[15] Often these factors were seen to overlap, especially in the work of anthropologically inclined observers such as W. H. R. Rivers and Stephen Roberts.[16] In such representations of indigenous motherhood, officials attributed careless feeding, harmful practices and neglect to racial attributes, yet also worried that colonisation produced a psychological malaise among indigenous people.[17] Colonial anxiety about population manifested in census taking and more deliberate health interventions. In this way, authorities, often with the support of an indigenous male elite, sought to realise a concept of population that, as Margaret Jolly puts it, 'connected native bodies to the state'.[18] Colonial governments thus sought to extend and secure knowledge and control of indigenous populations as assets for development.[19]

The International Pacific Health Conference made colonial depopulation a subject of international cooperation. A history of devastating epidemics loomed large in the minds of medical men in the Pacific. Page, Elkington, Ritchie and Cumpston referred throughout the conference to the 1875 measles outbreak that had killed an estimated 25 per cent of the indigenous population of Fiji, as well as to the impact of influenza in Samoa and Tonga in 1918–19.[20] At the time of the conference, narratives about the impact of epidemic diseases on population could not be disentangled from representations of the primitive status of Pacific Islanders.[21] Ritchie told the conference that, as the Chief Medical Officer of Samoa, he was fortunate to be working with 'a more advanced race', which could be

15   Colony of Fiji, *Report of the Commission Appointed to Inquire into the Decrease of the Native Population* (Suva: Colony of Fiji, 1897), pp. 5–7. See also Nicholas Thomas, *Colonialism's Culture: Anthropology, Travel and Government* (Cambridge: Polity Press, 1994), p. 112.
16   See Chapter 2, this volume.
17   Jolly, 'Other Mothers,' pp. 182–7.
18   Jolly, 'Infertile States,' p. 277.
19   Jolly, 'Other Mothers,' p. 179.
20   Commonwealth of Australia, 'Report of the International Pacific Health Conference,' pp. 822, 839, 871.
21   Matsuda, 'The Pacific,' pp. 771–2.

taught to react properly to the influx of influenza.[22] Others, however, argued that an almost universal 'native mind' was a crucial element shaping medical work in the Pacific Islands. Cilento in particular stressed the extent to which 'that inelasticity of mentality which curses the whole of the native races' hampered preventive health measures in the Pacific.[23] Indeed, Cilento frequently described the vulnerability of islanders in terms of their 'inelasticity' to changes in the availability of food and the introduction of diseases.[24]

Many scholars have stressed the importance of accounting for the place of disease in the demographic past in the Pacific Islands without reinscribing old colonial representations. It is all very well, they argue, to overcome narratives that diminish indigenous agency, but it is hard to ignore the tragic impact of disease on some Pacific Island societies.[25] This study returns to the place of disease in depopulation, but in a way that connects these to regional geopolitics. International health in the Pacific Islands illustrates the way empires in the twentieth century became entangled and, in particular, the way in which international organisations became involved in coordinating imperial governance.[26]

Beyond moral responsibility for indigenous welfare, colonial health authorities at the conference were practically concerned with the preservation and management of an indigenous labouring population. Ernest Chinnery, the Government Anthropologist in New Guinea, spoke of the need to develop 'scientific control of native labour'—both for its economic value and for the larger 'progress of the indigenous races'. Cilento informed the conference about long-term campaigns in the Dutch East Indies against yaws and hookworm that had increased the proportion of 'first-class' labourers from 35 per cent to 90 per cent.[27] He emphasised the need to look beyond introduced epidemic diseases and focus on the continuing impact of tuberculosis, pneumonia, dysentery and malaria

---

22   ibid., p. 839.
23   ibid., p. 872.
24   Cilento, 'The Value of Medical Services in Relation to Problems of Depopulation,' p. 480; Raphael Cilento, 'Some Problems of Racial Pressure in the Pacific,' p. 45.
25   Lal, 'The Passage Out,' pp. 440–1; David Chappell, 'Active Agents versus Passive Victims: Decolonized Historiography or Problematic Paradigm,' *The Contemporary Pacific*, 7(2), 1995, p. 316; Jolly, 'Infertile States,' p. 275; Matsuda, 'The Pacific,' pp. 770–2.
26   Paul Kramer and John Plotz, 'Pairing Empires: Britain and the United States, 1857–1947,' *Journal of Colonialism and Colonial History*, 2(1), 2001, p. 2.
27   Commonwealth of Australia, 'Report of the International Pacific Health Conference,' pp. 836, 886.

on indigenous populations.[28] The time devoted to discussing labour at the conference underscores Sunil Amrith's argument that international health was less the initiative of a 'vanguard of cosmopolitan doctors' and more an 'inexorable process of governmentalization, itself a response to the challenge of governing growing populations increasingly integrated into the world economy'.[29] Colonial health officials in the Pacific were attracted to cooperation in international health because it offered the means to manage the impacts of economic integration on indigenous peoples, whose labour was vital for that integration.

Preserving and cultivating populations in the Pacific Islands, 'from a humanitarian and a commercial stand-point', were thus the chief objects of cooperation in the Pacific Islands.[30] Elkington, the Director of the Division of Tropical Hygiene of the CDH, reiterated the problems of preventive medicine in the Pacific in his opening address, noting that the speed of ships was increasing annually, removing distance as a factor in the defence of invasion from germs.[31] Cumpston, the conference president, declared:

> [T]he Pacific Ocean … has, within recent years, become a field of international maritime commerce, and the problems essentially involved in such a development are constantly being brought to our notice.[32]

Elkington reminded the conference that a New Zealand vessel had carried the influenza that had wrought devastation in Samoa in 1918, while blackbirding ships from Queensland had been responsible for outbreaks of measles in the islands in the 1860s.[33]

A lack of coordination in quarantine and epidemiological information compounded these problems. Dr Aubrey Montague told the conference that 'each State has its own idea of what diseases are quarantinable'.[34] One health authority might take little action against malaria on board a ship, endangering any malaria-free territories, such as Fiji, which may be its next port of call. Information sharing between the islands was rudimentary and intermittent; medical officers complained of being

---

28   ibid., p. 833.
29   Amrith, *Decolonizing International Health*, p. 11.
30   Felix Speiser, quoted in Cumpston, 'Depopulation of the Pacific,' p. 1390.
31   Commonwealth of Australia, 'Report of the International Pacific Health Conference,' p. 824.
32   ibid., p. 823.
33   ibid., p. 825.
34   ibid., p. 840.

blind to conditions in the ports and islands from which commercial and passenger vessels had embarked. Ritchie pointed out that traffic between the islands carrying 'those diseases which are looked upon in civilized communities as being childish complaints' was as great a problem as contact with disease foci in Asia. The use of bills of health in the Pacific Islands was a 'farce', he argued, as they failed to provide useful information on the important local diseases that might be present in the port or territory from which ships arrived:

> What would be of more importance than a bill of health would be that when a boat sails from a port a wireless message should be sent to the port to which the vessel is proceeding, telling, in addition, any diseases that may be present on the vessel, as well as what diseases are prevalent in the country in the vicinity of the port from which the vessel has departed.[35]

Ritchie was echoing the Commonwealth's own agenda for the conference. The first proposal concerned quarantine measures, including a model bill of health and the standardisation of inspection procedures for diseases such as measles, influenza, dysentery, cerebral spinal meningitis, hookworm, malaria and others of an epidemic or chronically debilitating nature. Under the resolutions of the conference, governments were to declare first ports of entry at which all incoming ships must call and post a fully qualified medical officer as a quarantine officer in each of these. After a medical inspection of all persons on board, the quarantine officer would then request a health report from the master of each vessel, including a record of where the vessel hailed from and its ports of call, the notifiable diseases at those ports, communication with infected vessels and any previous medical inspection. Once satisfied, the quarantine officer could then grant the vessel pratique. The second proposal concerned the establishment of an epidemiological bureau at the Australian Institute of Tropical Medicine (AITM) in Townsville, which had been established in 1910 to study the physiology of the 'white race' in tropical Queensland.[36] Now Cumpston suggested that it could serve as a centre for the regular collection and distribution of epidemiological data across the region, orchestrated by wireless and telegraph from Australia.

These proposals were essentially for local versions of established international health practices. In the wake of major cholera epidemics in the nineteenth century, European medical men worried about how steamships seemed

---

35   ibid., p. 840.
36   Anderson, *The Cultivation of Whiteness*, pp. 102–18.

to open a Mediterranean gateway to the fundamentally diseased centres of the 'Orient', while the Panama Canal would later threaten to spread yellow fever to Asia from the Americas.[37] In 1907, the Treaty of Rome established the Office International d'Hygiène Publique (OIHP) in Paris, which began collecting and disseminating epidemiological information. It was not, however, until the establishment of the LNHO in 1921 that the development of international health, as a set of specific and accepted practices, gathered speed. With a large part of its finances provided by the Rockefeller Foundation, the LNHO expanded personnel exchanges and arranged research projects at the request of governments.[38]

The creation of the League of Nations' Eastern Bureau in Singapore in 1925 represented perhaps its most significant contribution. The Singapore bureau was by 1931 receiving weekly telegraph and wireless messages from 135 ports across an area stretching from the east coast of Africa to India and South-East Asia, and to Oceania and Japan.[39] These data were also transmitted to the OIHP, which issued global summaries. The bureau also coordinated research in the region, arranged study tours and offered training in malariology for sanitation officials.[40] Gilbert Brookes, the port health officer at Singapore, described the bureau as an 'incalculable boon'. Alison Bashford has argued that, in creating a huge web of new lines of communication, the bureau worked to shift spatial conceptions of the globe 'from a national–imperial axis to a regional–world axis'.[41] At the very least, the bureau outlined a region with what Patrick Zylberman might call common 'geo-epidemiological realities' based on commerce, which were countered with conventional sanitary measures and international coordination of information.[42]

Australia, New Zealand and the Pacific Islands all took advantage of and appreciated the services of the Singapore bureau, yet all felt that the data failed to address the disease threats specific to those Melanesian

---

37   Patrick Zylberman, 'Civilizing the State: Borders, Weak States and International Health in Modern Europe,' in Alison Bashford (ed.), Medicine at the Border: Disease, Globalization and Security, 1850 to the Present (Basingstoke, UK: Palgrave Macmillan, 2006), p. 25; Stern, 'Yellow Fever Crusade,' p. 41.

38   Dubin, 'The League of Nations Health Organisation,' pp. 67–72.

39   Manderson, 'Wireless Wars in the Eastern Arena,' p. 120.

40   ibid., p. 109.

41   Straits Settlements, Annual Report of the Medical Department for the Year 1927 (Singapore: Government Printer, 1928), p. 13; Alison Bashford, 'Global Biopolitics and the History of World Health,' History of the Human Sciences, 19(1), 2006, p. 72.

42   Zylberman, 'Civilizing the State,' p. 25.

and Polynesian island groups that were the focus of the Melbourne conference. Watt told the conference that while the bureau provided useful information on the status of cholera, yellow fever, plague and other diseases in foreign ports, it had shortcomings:

> In relation to the South Pacific … there is a sort of hiatus, because we have to consider the minor infectious diseases, such as measles, influenza, &c., which are generally not taken into cognizance by the Ministry of Health and the Singapore Bureau.[43]

Cumpston and Montague noted that locally important information had been shared only occasionally, such as when the Governor of New Caledonia had alerted Australia to the arrival of a ship carrying cerebral spinal meningitis. Cumpston reminded the conference of the Australian proposal in the draft document provided to the participants:

> For the better prevention of the spread of epidemic diseases, and for the improvement of public health measures generally, it is desirable to establish a special system of intelligence between the health administrations of islands in the Pacific, situated south of the equator and between longitude 140 deg. E. and 140 deg. W.[44]

This region was dubbed the 'Austral-Pacific Regional Zone' and included New Guinea, Papua, the Solomon Islands, New Caledonia, the New Hebrides, the Gilbert and Ellice Islands, Fiji, Western and Eastern Samoa, the Cook Islands, the Marquesas Islands and Tonga. Australia was offering to host and administer an epidemiological bureau that would function in a similar way to the one in Singapore yet adapted to the specific needs of the region.

Cilento framed the local development of such a system as the extension of the colonial surveillance practices established across territories such as New Guinea. He told the International Pacific Health Conference that on his office wall in New Guinea he had a map on to which he could place all the data gathered through the missions, patrols and district medical officers. Vital statistics, epidemiological data and information on sanitation and hygiene could all be plotted on the map, producing a 'perfect graphic record of the health state of the whole area'.[45] The territorially defined state was, however, increasingly integrated into regions and the world

---

43 Commonwealth of Australia, 'Report of the International Pacific Health Conference,' p. 851.
44 ibid., p. 850.
45 ibid., p. 834.

as a whole, suggesting that the problems of managing the health of populations could be divided into two branches: domestic administration and medical services on one hand, and the international measures of quarantine and research on the other. In this way, Cilento conceptualised international health as the meshing of colonial public health measures with international networks of surveillance and regulation of disease.[46] In this sense, he was suggesting that the governance of colonised populations become more thoroughly international.

For those representing Asian territories and international organisations, the proposal for a local epidemiological intelligence service was a source of some concern. White, the LNHO representative, confessed to confusion over Australia's proposal to host a bureau. While admitting that the information provided by Singapore seemed to be insufficient, White assumed that the proposed bureau would be integrated into the existing framework of international health:

> If you decide to create an organization out here, under the authority of the League of Nations, I can assure you … that the health organization of the League will only be too pleased to give you every possible assistance.[47]

Buchanan, a senior official of the British Ministry of Health, pointed out that Australia's proposal was more informal, involving a new centre within the CDH aimed at collecting and disseminating data on diseases not covered by the Singapore bureau. This regional service would send summaries to the Eastern Bureau, but it would ultimately be run by Australia as an independent bureau for the Pacific. Wellington, the representative of the Straits Settlements, continued to query the concept, asking:

> In other words, the scheme reduces the importance of the Singapore Bureau by cutting off its relations with the islands, and substitutes an independent centre, which will cooperate with the Singapore Bureau, but which will not be in any way under it. Am I correct?[48]

Cumpston was somewhat mystified by this unease and tried to assure the representatives that the Commonwealth did not intend to cut off the region from the main stream of international health. L. N. Guillemard, the High Commissioner of the Federated Malay States, told the Australian

---

46 ibid., pp. 836–7.
47 ibid., p. 848.
48 ibid., p. 851.

Government that his administration would not adopt the resolutions of the International Pacific Health Conference, writing that the 'rigid Australian system' of quarantine had 'been framed to meet the needs of the Austral-Pacific administrations'.[49] There was thus no neat articulation with a singular global structure of public health surveillance, reflecting not only a sense of distinct Pacific epidemiology, political economy and culture, but also the imperial ambitions of Commonwealth health officials, especially Cilento.

The Austral-Pacific Regional Zone: Security and empire

Commonwealth officials included a map of the 'Austral-Pacific' in the report of the International Pacific Health Conference and in the *Epidemiological Record* that it distributed throughout the Pacific Islands until 1941. The map encompassed the eastern half of Australia, Papua and New Guinea, New Zealand, Nauru, Tahiti and everything in between. Lines crossing the map indicated the distance between Sydney, Suva, Rabaul, Wellington, Thursday Island, Townsville, Noumea and many other ports. International health elsewhere had developed on an international basis—through the funding of the IHB of the Rockefeller Foundation, the authority of the League of Nations and the direction of international committees and advisory councils. In the Pacific Islands, the development of the same instruments of international health was largely the initiative of Australian Commonwealth officials. In mapping the islands, the CDH was outlining not just an administrative region, but also one in which Australia must exercise informal authority over public health.

---

49   L. N. Guillemard to Governor-General, Australia, 28 January 1928, NAA: A518/1, D832/1/3.

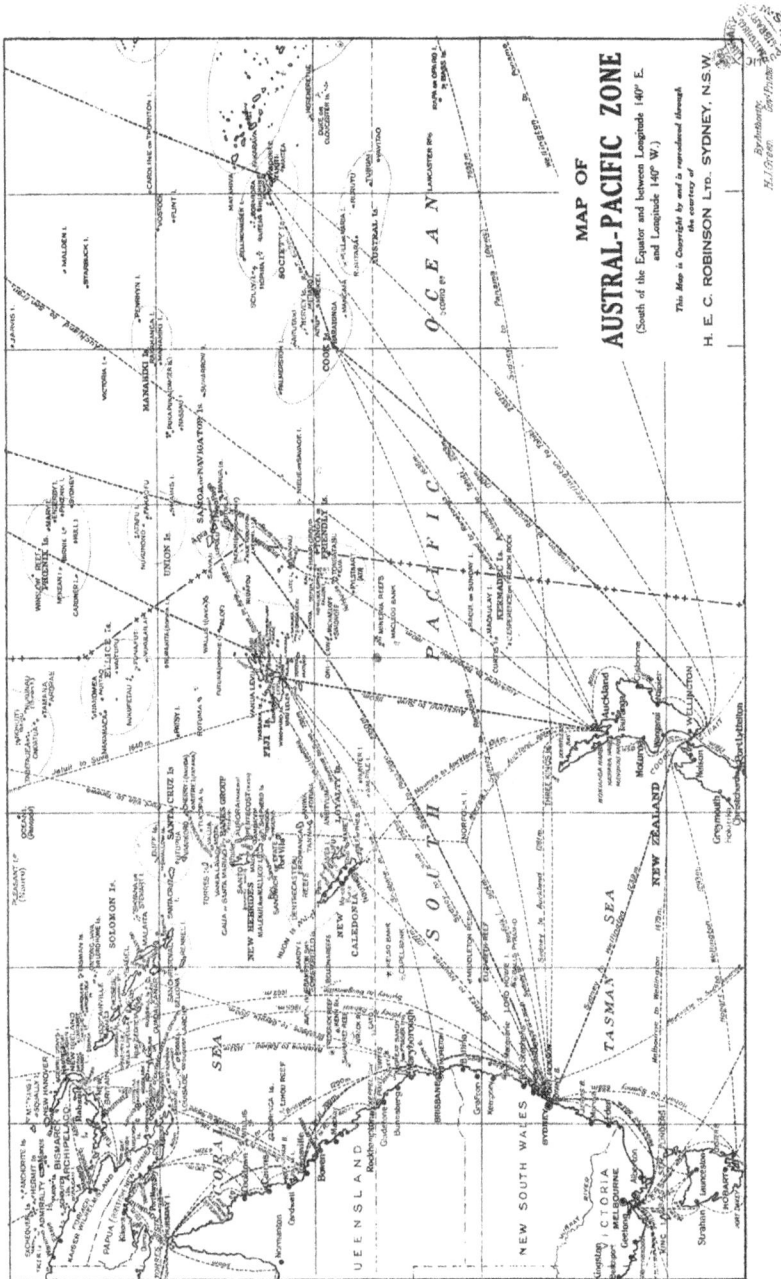

Map 3.1 Map of the 'Austral-Pacific Regional Zone'

Source: *Epidemiological Record of the Austral-Pacific Zone for the Year 1928* (Canberra: Government Printer, 1929), State Library of New South Wales, Q614.4906/A.

Governments had earlier mapped and intervened in the health administration of regions. Patrick Zylberman has examined how European doctors, in the wake of the 1865 cholera epidemic, identified the Mediterranean as a 'door to the Orient'. The Ottoman Empire, which oversaw quarantine during the Muslim pilgrimage, was, they argued, a weak state, justifying European intervention in its public health affairs.[50] In the late nineteenth and twentieth centuries, American doctors similarly mapped Latin America as a biomedical threat to the United States, especially after the construction of the Panama Canal. For many, this threat justified military intervention in Cuba and Puerto Rico in 1898 and control of Panamanian public health in the first decades of the twentieth century. It also led to the 'mental' mapping of Latin America, particularly through the Rockefeller Foundation's Yellow Fever Commission, which Stern has argued was part of 'expanding US scientific and cultural hemispheric dominance'.[51]

Australia similarly mapped the Pacific Islands as a collection of underfunded and underdeveloped imperial territories that were vulnerable to introduced diseases. The circulation of diseases around the region threatened these islands, which therefore became immediate threats to Australia itself. A national security imperative thus underpinned Australian intervention in the region. At the International Pacific Health Conference, Elkington told participants that, given Australia's geographical and commercial relationship with the Pacific Islands, 'very obvious risks would accrue to us in the event of the implantation of any of the great epidemic diseases in any of these island groups', which would become 'stepping-stones' to Australia.[52] There is a clear sense, then, that Australia, in extending its quarantine line out from its own political boundaries, was still acting to maintain an imagined cleanliness against contamination. Australian officials were at the same time deeply concerned about the geopolitical consequences of indigenous population decline. While visiting the United States in 1924, Cumpston conferred with Victor Heiser and other IHB officials to discuss 'saving the indigent races of the South Pacific Islands'. Cumpston noted that if French colonies in the Pacific continued to replace a declining indigenous people with

---

50 Zylberman, 'Civilizing the State,' p. 26.
51 Stern, 'Yellow Fever Crusade,' p. 41–2.
52 Commonwealth of Australia, 'Report of the International Pacific Health Conference,' p. 824.

Chinese and Japanese labour, later 'domination' by these communities 'would mean just that much more territory lost to the whites, and would be most serious for Australia and the British Empire'.[53]

Intervention in international health was also an attempt to fulfil Australians' own imagined imperial destiny. The Australian constitution had excluded the Commonwealth from domestic public health, limiting federal responsibilities to the administration of quarantine regulations. Australia's assumption of colonial administration in New Guinea thus became a potent argument that Cumpston used to support the establishment of a federal health department.[54] In this sense, the CDH owed its existence to Australian imperialism. Yet Cilento, Elkington and, to a lesser extent, Cumpston saw the wider Pacific Islands as an Australian sphere of influence. At the International Pacific Health Conference, the Acting Director of the AITM, Dr Alec Hutcheson Baldwin, suggested that, in addition to its role as an intelligence bureau, the Institute could offer three-month courses in tropical medicine to students from across the Pacific. It could, moreover, function as a clearing-house for technical information and as a research and diagnostic centre.[55] For Cilento, the institute's role as a regional centre for training was vital for encouraging:

> [a] continually rising standard of efficiency among the medical personnel of each and all colonial or territorial services, with … the final objective of the production throughout the Pacific of a group of medical services of maximum capability and worldwide recognition.[56]

Commonwealth officials thus hoped to make the courses offered at the institute the standard for the training of personnel throughout the region.

Cilento in particular embraced a tradition of seeing an imperial destiny in the national history of Australia. Roger Thompson has noted that, although concerns about German and French activities dominated debates over Pacific expansion, Federation invigorated another strand of Australian imperialism. An editorial in the Adelaide *Advertiser* asserted that, with Federation:

53 'Memorandum re Conference with Cumpston, Vincent, Russell, Heiser,' p. 1, 19 August 1924, Victor Heiser Papers [hereinafter Heiser Papers], American Philosophical Society, Series 4, Box 68, Folder 4.
54 Roe, 'The Establishment of the Australian Department of Health,' pp. 189–90.
55 Commonwealth of Australia, 'Report of the International Pacific Health Conference,' p. 892.
56 ibid., p. 837.

We may expect to find attention once again turned towards the numberless islands that dot the huge watery waste around us, and which—whatever allegiance they may now own—we still regard as ... preordained, at however remote a date, to be our heritage.[57]

This culture of associating nationhood with imperial status informed Cilento's thinking especially. Reflecting a strongly gendered conception of nationhood, he asserted in a 1925 speech to the Rotary Club that the indigenous peoples of Papua and New Guinea 'were placed under control of the Commonwealth when Australia won manhood status, and every Australian should be sympathetic to the charge laid upon the nation'.[58] In a contribution to the 1931 report of the Federal Health Council, he wrote:

Australia's aspirations towards nationhood brought about the annexation of British New Guinea [the Territory of Papua] in 1883–84—a gesture that found its complete expression only after federation had become a fact, and Australia's national feeling had made a lusty growth during the Great War of 1914–18.[59]

The gradual acquisition of Papua and New Guinea was in this narrative the fulfilment of Australia's growth towards nationhood.

At a time when further imperial ambition in Australia had become more ambivalent in the face of financial stringency and political uncertainty, Cilento and Elkington hoped to cultivate an informal empire in the Pacific.[60] After the International Pacific Health Conference, Cilento wrote to Brigadier-General Evan Wisdom, the administrator in New Guinea, telling him that, as a result of the conference:

The whole of the island groups of importance in the Pacific south of the equator are drawn into relationship with Australia which will enormously enhance the prestige of Australia and will make her a country to which practically the whole of such islands will look for guidance in matters of medicine, sanitation, hygiene, and in fact, native administrations in a sociological sense.[61]

57   Roger Thompson, *Australian Imperialism in the Pacific: The Expansionist Era 1820–1920* (Melbourne: Melbourne University Press, 1980), p. 158.
58   *The Argus*, [Melbourne], 19 November 1925, p. 14. See Marilyn Lake, '"The Brightness of Eyes and Quiet Assurance Which Seems to Say American": Alfred Deakin's Identification with Republican Manhood,' *Australian Historical Studies*, 38(129), 2007, pp. 32–6.
59   Raphael Cilento, 'Review of the Position of Tropical Medicine and Hygiene in Australia,' *Report of the Federal Health Council of Australia*, 5, 1931, p. 33.
60   Thompson, *Australia and the Pacific Islands in the 20th Century*, pp. 88–90.
61   Raphael Cilento to Brigadier-General Evan Wisdom, 7 February 1927, NAA: A518/1, D832/1/3.

The map of the 'Austral-Pacific' was therefore an expression of the imperial ambitions of officials within the CDH. In contrast to other maps that defined Australia as a 'clean' island nation isolated against an outside teeming with contaminating germs and people, the 'Austral-Pacific' map made Australia part of a region. It expressed a desire to reorient the Pacific Island administrations away from Paris and London towards Australia and a region centered on it. In place of formal empire, Commonwealth health officials worked to establish Australian pre-eminence in the knowledge and practice of tropical medicine and the governance of indigenous people.

Despite financial constraints, all the CDH's proposals were implemented in some form, although these ambitions were ultimately frustrated. Donald Denoon and Warwick Anderson have argued that the CDH retreated from the tropics in the mid-1920s and the Pacific health network had little substance. The closure of the AITM in 1930 and the incorporation of its functions into the School of Public Health and Tropical Medicine at the University of Sydney were emblematic of a shift in focus towards health in urban centres.[62] Cumpston certainly lost much of his interest in the tropics. He warned Cilento against continuing to evangelise on the topic of settling northern Australia and, in the early 1930s—citing financial constraints—he significantly curtailed the activities of Cilento's Division of Tropical Hygiene.[63]

Yet the departure from the pursuit of regional interests was neither complete nor clean, as the conference led to lingering interaction. Cumpston and the CDH continued to envision the School of Public Health and Tropical Medicine, which took over the teaching functions of the AITM, as serving the Pacific region. At a meeting of the Advisory Council for the school in November 1929, Cumpston noted recent developments in Australia's relationship to the 'Oceanic or Australasian section of the Pacific Ocean' and stated: 'It is felt that the teaching of medical graduates in T. M. and H. [Tropical Medicine and Hygiene] could well be undertaken for this area by the Sydney School.'[64] Australian officials thus hoped the school

---

62   Denoon, *Public Health in Papua New Guinea*, p. 44; Anderson, *The Cultivation of Whiteness*, pp. 151–2.
63   J. H. L. Cumpston to Raphael Cilento, 18 July 1932, Cilento Papers, UQFL44, Box 24, Item 177; J. H. L. Cumpston to C. H. E. Lawes, 23 November 1933, Papers of John Howard Lidgett Cumpston, MS 613, Box 13, NLA.
64   'Report of the Meeting of Advisory Council,' *Minute Book*, 28 November 1929, p. 14, NAA: C1942, Box 1.

would act as a training centre for British colonial officials en route to Fiji and the Solomon Islands. At a meeting of the Advisory Council in early 1933, Cumpston drew attention to a letter from the British Secretary of State for Dominions that indicated that the Sydney school would be listed as an institution approved for the training of British medical officials in the Western Pacific.[65] The CDH, and particularly Cilento, thus hoped to use the teaching and intelligence functions of the School of Public Health and Tropical Medicine to spread models of colonial public health.

This vision of Australian dominance over the way medical services developed across the region never quite eventuated. While the occasional candidate for the Diploma of Tropical Medicine came from the Solomon Islands, Ocean Island or the British Phosphate Commission on Nauru, most students undertaking the course came from the Australian dependencies and New South Wales.[66] The school's research activity was also limited to the Australian tropics, Papua, New Guinea and Norfolk Island. Australia continued to supply intelligence to the region until 1941, but the teaching and research roles of its institutions of tropical medicine were never as developed or as extensive as originally imagined. If this truncation of the Australian presence in the Pacific was for Cumpston a necessary strategic step, it was for Cilento a bitter disappointment. Writing to Phyllis in 1929, he cursed the 'bad ministers' and 'selfseeking parliamentary mountebanks' for tying 'Australia hand and foot at the moment that chance summonses her to dominance throughout the whole of Melanesia'.[67] Cilento thus laid the blame for the failure of Australian imperial ambitions at the feet of political hesitation and self-interest, rather than geopolitical and economic constraints.

A year after the conference, the Senior Medical Officer of the Solomon Islands told the Resident Commissioner that resources were not available for a quarantine station and modern bacteriological lab. He argued that it would be difficult to have a qualified medical officer stationed at every port of entry, noting that Faisi and Vanikoro lacked fully qualified staff for most of the year. In fact, the medical officer at Vanikoro was the doctor of the Vanikoro Timber Company.[68] The Solomon Islands Government

---

65   'Report of the Meeting of Advisory Council,' *Minute Book*, 4 March 1933, p. 71, NAA: C1942, Box 1.
66   'Annual Report for the Year 1933,' *Minute Book*, p. 102, NAA: C1942, Box 1.
67   Raphael Cilento to Phyllis Cilento, 2 July 1929, Cilento Papers, UQFL44, Box 11, Item 21.
68   Senior Medical Officer to Resident Commissioner, Solomon Islands Protectorate, 16 June 1927, NAA: A518 (A518/1), D832/1/3.

did construct a quarantine station in 1928, but it remained idle for most of the 1930s.[69] Indeed, in his annual report for 1927, the Senior Medical Officer in the Solomon Islands questioned the wisdom of strict quarantine after recalling mild measles outbreaks introduced from the New Hebrides, confessing: 'I am doubtful of the wisdom of attempting to exclude measles by rigid quarantine measures and so producing or attempting to produce and maintain a non-immune population.'[70] Tonga said it had a quarantine station, but regretted that research would be too costly.[71]

Competing models of medical development also challenged Australian claims to control over international health in the Pacific. Initially providing financial support to campaigns against hookworm and other parasitic diseases in the British Empire, the IHB later initiated yellow fever eradication programs in Latin America and supplied much of the funding of the LNHO.[72] The IHB had a presence in Australia and the Pacific, although mostly in the form of Sylvester Lambert, an independently minded American doctor who had worked on the aborted hookworm campaign in Papua in 1917 and in north Queensland during the Australian Hookworm Campaign of the early 1920s.[73] Lambert was later based at Suva, carrying out surveys and treatment campaigns in Fiji, the Solomon Islands and the Cook Islands.[74] His expansion of indigenous medical education through the Central Medical School, established in Suva in 1929, was arguably his more significant work. Lambert hoped that training indigenous students from across the Pacific Islands at this school would be an effective solution to chronic shortages of staff in the region.[75] After a four-year course, students graduated with the title of 'Native Medical Practitioner' and a status just below that of a fully qualified European medical officer.

---

69 British Solomon Islands Protectorate, *Annual Medical and Sanitary Report* (Suva: Government Printer, 1928), p. 31; British Solomon Islands Protectorate, *Annual Medical and Sanitary Report* (Suva: Government Printer, 1935), p. 4.

70 British Solomon Islands Protectorate, *Annual Medical and Sanitary Report* (Suva: Government Printer, 1927), p. 3.

71 Premier of Tonga to J. S. Neill, 24 June 1927, NAA: A518 (A518/1), D832/1/3.

72 Farley, *To Cast Out Disease*, Chs 4, 6; Stern, 'Yellow Fever Crusade,' p. 53.

73 Gillespie, 'The Rockefeller Foundation, the Hookworm Campaign and a National Health Policy in Australia,' p. 73.

74 British Solomon Islands Protectorate, *Annual Medical and Sanitary Report*, (1928), p. 10; Commonwealth of Australia, 'Report of the International Pacific Health Conference,' p. 838.

75 Annie Stuart, 'Contradictions and Complexities in an Indigenous Medical Service: The Case of Mesulame Taveta,' *The Journal of Pacific History*, 41(2), 2006, p. 126.

These graduates, Lambert hoped, would go back to their islands and contribute to the development of medical services as colonial intermediaries. The scheme enjoyed broad support among the island administrations and New Zealand sent students from the Cook Islands. According to Annie Stuart, the school attempted to maintain what it believed were indigenous identities and culture, such as through its requirement that students wear traditional dress. Complete control was not possible and Europeanised students wearing shoes and trousers often confounded attempts to manage cultural exchange. Once in service, especially outside Fiji, practitioners faced ambiguity in status and a lack of support.[76]

Australia was singular in its refusal to participate in Lambert's scheme and in the end devised its own medical training scheme for Papuan students beyond the existing rudimentary instruction in first aid. The report of Cilento and Hermant's tour for the League of Nations declared: 'The Papuan native has not yet reached the stage at which it is considered that he is fit for education as a native medical practitioner.'[77] The annual report of the School of Public Health and Tropical Medicine for 1932 announced that a scheme for training Papuan 'native medical assistants' was planned, under the influence of Walter Strong, and asserted: 'An attempt is not being made to turn out fully fledged trained practitioners as in Fiji.'[78] At a meeting of the school's Advisory Council in 1934, a more complete set of reasons was offered:

> The facilities at the Sydney Medical School and the School of Public Health and Tropical Medicine, the relative proximity of Sydney, the satisfactory arrangements for the care and supervision of the students, their relative primitive character and limited education, and, above all, the responsibility of Australia for Australian territory, decided against Fiji.[79]

Australia's refusal thus rested on racism and reiteration of the special Australian responsibility for Papuans. Many years later, Lambert criticised the Commonwealth in his memoirs:

76   ibid., pp. 132–4.
77   Raphael Cilento and Paul Hermant, 'Report of the Health Mission to the Pacific of the League of Nations,' October 1928 – April 1929, p. 18, Cilento Papers, UQFL44, Box 18, Item 112.
78   'Annual Report for the Year 1932,' *Minute Book*, p. 90, NAA: C1942, Box 1.
79   'Minutes of meeting of Advisory Council,' *Minute Book*, 24 April 1934, p. 100, NAA: C1942, Box 1.

The Canberra Government was standing pat on White Man's Australia, and the 'black fellow' was not supposed to have a head on his shoulders. Papuan and New Guinea natives, they said, were not adequately prepared for higher education. I knew better, for I had seen those boys, and worked with them … According to Australia's yardstick, students from the New Hebrides and the Solomons were also inadequately prepared; but they were entering our first class.[80]

Indigenous responses to these schemes are in fact difficult to gauge. Attitudes to European medicine generally ranged from pragmatic enthusiasm to ambivalence or indifference. Responses to imperial rule itself varied across the Pacific. The more dispersed social and political character of Papua and New Guinea made organised responses to colonial rule rare in the first half of the twentieth century, whereas calls for autonomy from Samoan elites were persistent and determined.[81] The voices of graduates from the school in Suva are largely absent from records, although it is clear that, despite the distinguished careers of some of these men, life for others was unsettled.[82] Occasionally indigenous voices can be heard directly, if somewhat opaquely. Lahui Ako, a Papuan native medical assistant, spoke at the second International Pacific Health Conference, in 1935. Ako's paper outlined his duties, including record keeping and treatments, which included injections and the dressing of ulcers. Ako wrote: 'We give out much treatment for "Levo", which doctors call "Tinea imbricate".'[83] In privileging an indigenous name for the disease, there is a sense of some pattern of accommodation in the education of Papuan medical assistants. Yet there is little evidence of resistance to specific schemes for regional health. Assistants would occasionally record births and deaths so that, Ako explained, the Chief Medical Officer could 'tell in which districts the population is increasing and in which it is decreasing'.[84] Through this provision of vital statistics, Papuan graduates from Sydney became part of the apparatus of colonial government.

Lambert's plan was different from Cilento's vision of an expanding and improving colonial medical service in the Pacific. Lambert tried to get Australia involved in his medical education program, but later suggested

---

80 Sylvester Lambert, *A Doctor in Paradise* (Melbourne: Georgian House, 1941), p. 287.
81 Hiery, *The Neglected War*, pp. 183–200; Hempenstall, 'Releasing the Voices,' pp. 47–51.
82 Stuart, 'Contradictions and Complexities in an Indigenous Medical Service,' pp. 138–42.
83 'Report of the Second International Pacific Health Conference,' 1935, p. 58, NAA: A518, D832/1/3.
84 ibid., p. 58.

that 'Australia was jealous of little Fiji's rise as a medical centre'.[85] When Heiser met Cumpston and Cilento in Australia in 1934, he noted their racial arguments against the program, but also suggested: 'Australia could not bear to have it said that Fiji was training its personnel; at present they are only making messengers out of them to report to the nearest white man.'[86] Cilento, in a letter to Phyllis, asserted that the aim of the Suva school was to establish a 'South Pacific medical service with Fiji as its centre and Lambert as its head', a scheme that 'Australia cannot afford to tolerate'.[87] The Central Medical School thus established Suva as the locus of an alternative scheme for medical development that—however colonial and racist in its own right—conflicted with the harder racism and imperial ambitions of Commonwealth medical officials.

Race, nationhood and migration: Cilento's Pacific Island health mission

Among the resolutions of the International Pacific Health Conference was one requesting assistance from the League of Nations, the OIHP and any other international organisations that could help. Australia sent the report to Geneva, where the 11th session of the health committee recommended a two-man survey of the Pacific Islands, which 'would yield results of international interest and importance'.[88] Although a representative of French Indochina, Paul Hermant, participated in the expedition, its planning was left almost entirely to Cilento. The route would take the two through Fiji, New Caledonia and the New Hebrides in a first leg and Papua, New Guinea and the Solomon Islands in a second, between October 1928 and April 1929. Its program in each island group was the inspection of every hospital and public health institution and the condition of labourers. It was a league activity in name only, as Cilento and Hermant, for whom Cilento had high regard, let their colonial interests shape their schedule. Cilento wrote to Phyllis:

85   Lambert, *A Doctor in Paradise*, p. 288.
86   Heiser Diary, 9 March 1934, RG 12, Box 217, 1932–33, Folder 2, Rockefeller Archives Center.
87   Raphael Cilento to Phyllis Cilento, 20 November 1928, Cilento Papers, UQFL44, Box 11, Item 20.
88   Cilento and Hermant, 'Report of the Health Mission to the Pacific,' pp. 1–2.

He [Hermant] was relying on me entirely for [the] programme as I hoped, but has two or three side issues up his sleeve, especially the question of the conditions of his Annamite and Tokinese labourers in New Caledonia.[89]

Cilento made sure that nutrition and population were major objects of study for the journey. When Cilento and Hermant reached Fiji, however, governor Eyre Huston and chief medical officer Aubrey Montague expressed their complete ignorance of the whole mission. The Pacific Mission was clearly on the fringes of international health when one compares it with the extensive exchanges in personnel being organised by the League of Nations elsewhere.

In the interwar years, the league played an important role in mobilising public health officials across colonial borders. In 1930, for example, the Malaria Commission sent Ludwik Anigstein, a medical officer in British Malaya, to carry out a survey of malaria and mosquitoes in Siam.[90] The LNHO also arranged for collective study tours, including one to India in 1928 involving 15 medical officers from Australia, Ceylon, New Zealand, the Dutch East Indies, the Philippines, Egypt and elsewhere. This group examined water supplies and sewage disposal, yet it was also given the opportunity to study 'the prevention of tuberculosis, child welfare, medical research work and other subjects which are of interest and importance to every country, wherever situated'.[91] Plans were also made for a study tour of rural hygiene in May of the same year. The medical director wrote: 'In every country visited the participants will study the governmental machinery designed to provide public health protection for rural districts.'[92] They were to visit public welfare agencies and agricultural schools, while paying attention to the work of cooperative associations, health insurance funds and other organisations. There were, in addition, a number of individual health missions organised for the same year. While tropical medicine retained a focus on specific local environments, the league was at the same time interested in how the knowledge and practices of broad-based preventive medicine and rural hygiene could be developed and applied in a range of places.[93]

---

89   Raphael Cilento to Phyllis Cilento, 23 October 1928, Cilento Papers, UQFL44, Box 11, Item 20.
90   Ludwik Anigstein, 'Malaria and *Anopheles* in Siam: Report on a Study Tour,' *Quarterly Bulletin of the Health Organisation of the League of Nations*, 1(2), 1932, pp. 233–308.
91   League of Nations Health Organization [hereinafter LNHO], 'Report by the Medical Director on the Work of the Health Organisation Since October 1927' (Geneva: League of Nations, 1928), p. 3.
92   ibid., p. 4.
93   ibid., pp. 3–5.

Cilento and Hermant arrived in Suva in November 1928. Overall, the town disappointed Cilento. Photos of the place had given him the impression that Suva was an 'up to date town' and a 'brisk, capable and most progressive community'.[94] What Cilento found was the worst nightmare of an Australian imperialist steeped in racist conceptions of urban space and progress. 'Shops of wood stretched, cheek by jowl, along [the streets],' he wrote to Phyllis, 'with no attempt at racial discrimination so that the backyards were a babel of sound, and the front windows a study in contrasts.'[95] Racial boundaries were also lacking in public space. 'Whites, yellows, browns and no-colours jostled one another in the streets', while at the bank counter, 'a couple of dirty Chinese, a … Tamil or two, a half-caste and an American tourist fought for preference'.[96] Clothes, bearing and other signs also failed to mark clear racial distinctions: '[A] white man in dirty khaki and a native in a clean white shirt and black sulu dragged a small cart by hand along the main street.'[97] The streets themselves were strikingly cosmopolitan and full of hybrid colonial subjects:

> Bobbed harried female clerks of all types, white and yellow Samoans, Tongans, half-castes, with brown or black Fijians and Indians all dressed in European clothes, chic costumes and short skirts, all arch or smug, bold or demure, minced along the pavement.[98]

On the streets, '[e]very lamppost was held up by half a dozen coloured, discoloured or slack loafers. The white man's prestige was not obvious'.[99] Cilento's descriptions of Suva are striking examples of tension between imperial anxiety about white status and the transgression of racial boundaries made possible in colonial towns in the Pacific.

As Cilento and Hermant went out from Suva to the agricultural districts, the local medical services did little to impress. Public health infrastructure was a mixture of government facilities and those provided by the Australian Colonial Sugar Refining Company (CSR), which dominated the plantation economy. The CSR hospital in the village of Ba and the general hospital at Nailaga were well built and maintained but mostly

---

94 Raphael Cilento to Phyllis Cilento, 2 November 1928, Cilento Papers, UQFL44, Box 11, Item 20.
95 Raphael Cilento to Phyllis Cilento, 14 November 1928, Cilento Papers, UQFL 44, Box 11, Item 20.
96 ibid.
97 ibid.
98 ibid.
99 ibid.

empty.[100] Decent hospitals seemed to abound, but with indentured labour long discontinued and Fijians apparently confining themselves to their villages, they were left idle most of the time.[101] Doctors were apparently losing faith and indigenous medical practitioners and nurses, as in the village of Nandi, were 'very lacking in efficiency and initiative'.[102] Writing to Cumpston, Cilento noted that quarantine at Suva was 'purely nominal': 'Kanakas roamed about the wharf within the barriers and chatted amiably among themselves and to the passengers.'[103] In Cilento's view, medical services in Fiji were broken into 'self-contained, self-complacent and inept fragments', which failed in particular to serve indigenous people.[104]

As Cilento and Hermant toured Fiji visiting hospitals, sugar plantations and mills, the social context of health and its historical origins were what preoccupied the Australian. The relationship between diet, health and fertility he had studied in New Guinea became the lens through which he understood the Fijian situation. Wondering at the absence of indigenous Fijians in the hospitals, he visited villages in the hills and valleys. At Vitongo, near the CSR town of Lautoka, Cilento sat in the *bure*, or men's house, and talked about diet and fertility with the chief and other men. According to Cilento, the villagers spoke of how they had in years past fed on plentiful greens, especially the young, vitamin-rich shoots of taro. Now, they told him, they leased land to Indian peasant proprietors and lived on food bought from stores. 'The people are no longer fertile', Cilento wrote: 'The women have one or two children when they are young and then in spite of their using no contraceptives they seem to lose their fertility.'[105] Cilento was here reciting a familiar narrative about reproduction and population decline in the Pacific from his discussion with the chief.[106] For Cilento, the tinned meat and polished rice from the company store were no substitute

---

100 Raphael Cilento to Phyllis Cilento, 17 November 1928, Cilento Papers, UQFL44, Box 11, Item 20.

101 Raphael Cilento to Phyllis Cilento, 19 November 1928, Cilento Papers, UQFL44, Box 11, Item 20.

102 ibid.

103 Raphael Cilento to J. H. L. Cumpston, 2 November 1928, Cilento Papers, UQFL44, Box 11, Item 20.

104 Raphael Cilento to Phyllis Cilento, 20 November 1928, Cilento Papers, UQFL44, Box 11, Item 20.

105 Raphael Cilento to Phyllis Cilento, 19 November 1928, Cilento Papers, UQFL44, Box 11, Item 20.

106 ibid. See also Christine M. Dureau, 'Mutual Goals? Family Planning on Simbo, Western Solomon Islands,' in Margaret Jolly and Kalpana Ram (eds), *Borders of Being: Citizenship, Fertility, and Sexuality in Asia and the Pacific* (Ann Arbor: University of Michigan Press, 2001), pp. 236–7; Jolly, 'Infertile States,' pp. 274–5.

for traditional foods such as taro and yams. In the Fijian context, however, the presence of a large community of Indian peasant farmers gave the issue of diet added social and political dimensions.

When the British established a Crown Colony in Fiji in 1875, governor Arthur Gordon pursued a land policy that ensured indigenous title and sought to protect indigenous communities from recruitment as plantation labourers. The law did not completely prevent recruitment, yet land largely remained in the hands of indigenous Fijians.[107] Between 1879 and 1916, more than 60,000 indentured workers from southern India provided the bulk of labour on the sugar plantations, through a system with which Gordon was familiar from his governorship in Trinidad. In this version of indirect rule—in which governors delegated authority to a reorganised hierarchy of chiefs—the colonial governors imagined they were protecting Fijians, who were supposed to carry on their traditional social and economic customs.[108] Under pressure from the Indian Government and Indian nationalists, the system of indentured migrant labour ceased in 1916, while all remaining contracts were cancelled in 1920. With the cessation of the indenture system, many Indian families settled on land leased from Fijians or the CSR. Small-scale Indian cane growers thus became important in supplying the CSR mills.[109] Lal notes that by 1930 almost half of the sugar cane in Fiji was grown on land leased from indigenous owners. Indentured Indian workers had experienced an autocratic regime on the plantations, yet post-indenture society involved continuing hardship for Indian farmers.[110] Leasing land from Fijian communities was a tortuous process and agricultural unions contested exploitative practices for many years after the end of indenture. CSR officials could evict Indian families for reasons that were not always clear to those on the receiving end of their apparent caprice.[111]

---

107 See 'Atu Bain, 'A Protective Labour Policy? An Alternative Interpretation of Early Colonial Labour Policy in Fiji,' *The Journal of Pacific History*, 23(2), 1988, pp. 119–36.
108 Denoon et al., *The Cambridge History of the Pacific Islanders*, pp. 179, 267; Lawrence Brown, 'Inter-colonial Migration and Refashioning of Indentured Labour: Arthur Gordon in Trinidad, Mauritius and Fiji (1866–1880),' in Alan Lester and David Lambert (eds), *Colonial Lives Across the British Empire: Imperial Careering in the Long Nineteenth Century* (Cambridge: Cambridge University Press, 2006), pp. 204–27.
109 Brij V. Lal, '*Girmit*, History, Memory,' in Brij V. Lal (ed.), *Bittersweet: the Indo-Fijian Experience* (Canberra: Pandanus Books, 2004), p. 5.
110 Denoon et al., *The Cambridge History of the Pacific Islanders*, p. 231.
111 Brij V. Lal, *Broken Waves: A History of the Fiji Islands in the Twentieth Century* (Honolulu: University of Hawai'i Press, 1992), pp. 99–100; Rajendra Prasad, *Tears in Paradise: A Personal and Historical Journey, 1879–2004* (Auckland: Glade Publishers, 2004), pp. 154–9.

The writings of missionaries such as John Wear Burton and Charles Freer Andrews provided much of the ammunition for international criticism of indentured labour. Both described the deplorable material conditions in which Indian workers lived, but, as missionaries, they gave special emphasis to the perceived moral and spiritual decay that indenture seemed to bring about. In 1910, Burton claimed: 'The difference between the state he now finds himself in and absolute slavery is merely in the name and terms of years.'[112] Workers were crammed into cubicles measuring 3.1 × 2.1 metres and had low fixed wages and poor food. They lived in 'indescribable and disgusting filth', so that '[i]t is small wonder that sickness and disease hold carnival, and such places are a disgrace to civilization and a stain upon commerce'.[113] Worst of all, since neither the government nor the planters provided 'elevating influences', the 'coolie' lines led to moral degradation:

> Wickedness flaunts itself unshamedly [sic]. Loose, evil-faced women throw their jibes at criminal-looking men, or else quarrel with each other in high, strident voices made emphatic by wild, angry gestures. The beholder turns away striving to discover whether pity or disgust is uppermost in his mind.[114]

Here Burton echoes Cilento's colonial anxiety about public behaviour, as immorality and private space spill out into public view. Andrews similarly described Indian communities in Fiji as immoral and violent, claiming that plantations had established a 'regulated prostitution' in which women were assigned to five men. Fathers would sometimes sell their daughters to multiple men so that:

> by far the most terrible fact which met us on every side, like a great blight or devastation, was the loss of any idea of the sanctity of marriage and the consequent sexual immorality that was rampant on every side.

Violence was rife, including among the very high-caste men, who 'even in their first and second years begin committing suicide and stabbing and murdering their fellows'. Indenture was thus a dislocation that produced violence and moral malaise.[115]

---

112 John Wear Burton, *The Fiji of To-day* (London: Charles H. Kelly, 1910), p. 271.
113 ibid., pp. 272–3.
114 ibid., pp. 273–4.
115 Andrews, *Indian Indentured Labour in Fiji*, pp. 29–33.

Burton noted the irony of the approaching extinction of the indigenous people just as missionaries were becoming more successful in converting them. Although Burton asserted that the church could not neglect them, he also suggested that this decline was ordained:

> The laws that are bringing about the extinction of the Fijian, or at least his diminution, are the surest warrant we have that the highest moral interests of the human race are not looked upon indifferently by the Creator.[116]

Burton certainly acknowledged some of the other causes examined by the 1896 commission. Communal life, the 'murderer of healthy ambition, and the parent of shiftlessness and improvidence', had choked individual will—the driving force of strong, progressive societies.[117] His view—ubiquitous in discussion of Pacific population decline—was that, with the destruction of indigenous social organisation, 'they have been crammed with the indigestible matter of European civilization'.[118] Yet Burton clearly resigned himself to Fijian extinction and the rise of Indian society in the group. Drawing on an Arabian parable of the camel who only wanted to put its nose in the tent before eventually forcing the man out, Burton wrote: '[A]s we need this particular camel very much, we cannot say him nay at this time.'[119] Capital and the growth of Asian populations were irresistible forces—part of the Zeitgeist. He explained:

> The lazy, shiftless islander must go. The remnant that is left of his breed must by industry and effort coalesce with the more vigorous peoples who will plough the almost virgin lands of his forefathers. Such peoples there are in plenty, and their eyes are turned in this direction. The Pacific is the natural outlet for the pent-up pressure of human life. It is the line of least resistance, and in human history, as well as in mechanics, force moves thither-wards.[120]

Missionary discourse on Indian immigration, from which came the majority of writing on Indian migration, thus blended concerns with the moral and spiritual degeneracy of colonised people, the welfare of British imperial subjects and a sense of resignation to the forces of capitalism and population pressure. 'The orientalization of the Pacific', Burton wrote, although a challenge to 'the West', represented an 'alteration

---

116 Burton, *The Fiji of To-day*, pp. 193–4.
117 ibid., p. 205.
118 ibid., p. 209.
119 ibid., p. 265.
120 ibid., p. 261.

in the world's affairs' that could not be ignored.[121] Although tragic, the extinction of certain peoples under the weight of the world had a measure of inevitability.

Cilento's letters, in contrast, championed the 'autochthones', whose status as the healthy and progressive workers of the land had been sacrificed to the immediate needs of the corporate giant, embodied in CSR. As Cilento moved through the country, his criticism intensified, seeing in depressed indigenous health and fertility the fruits of colonial policy on land and labour. Because of the influence of CSR and a weak colonial government, the Fijian 'retreats to the hills':

> In the neighbourhood of Indian villages, which are springing up like mushrooms everywhere, he lets his lands and lives on his rents, on store food. As a result his grasp is feebler and feebler.[122]

The problems of health, fertility and depopulation, Cilento argued, arose from the way in which commercial and government support for a migrant labour system had divorced indigenous people from working their own land. Cilento's criticism reflected a broader discourse that linked sovereignty, ownership and national vitality to the occupation and use of agricultural land. In 1921, for example, Lothrop Stoddard expressed relief that non-white immigrants settled primarily in the cities, claiming as a 'solemn truth that those who *work* the land will ultimately *own* the land'.[123] As noted earlier, Cilento followed Stoddard in his 1922 thesis by framing white occupation of Australia as dependent on 'a population rooted in the soil'.[124] Cilento's assessment of colonial Fijian society was thus based on settler-colonial constructions of sovereignty and title. In other words, settler-colonial anxiety about the white occupation of land in the midst of increasing migration also provided a lens through which Cilento critically assessed Fijian colonial society.

Cilento's account of Fiji shared Burton's belief in the mutual incompatibility and hostility of indigenous and Indian communities. His sympathies, however, lay with indigenous people and he even considered violence towards Indian migrants a natural expression of national feeling. Cilento's encounter with a senior Fijian minister named Asere, as they steamed

---

121 ibid., pp. 257–8.
122 Raphael Cilento to Phyllis Cilento, 17 November 1928, Cilento Papers, UQFL44, Box 11, Item 20.
123 Stoddard, *The Rising Tide of Color Against White World-supremacy*, p. 294.
124 Cilento, 'A Correlation of Some Features of Tropical Preventive Medicine,' p. xiii.

around the coast, is illuminating. Cilento wrote that he was beginning to understand indigenous resentment towards Indians, 'who were eating up their lands', and the 'white men who have and are permitting it'.[125] He noted that some Fijians advocated organised violence against the government:

> One leader is at present serving a sentence of some years imprisonment in distant ROTU-MAH, because he advocated one great stand to wipe out the English. 'We have no aeroplane, no cannon', he had said, 'We will all perish on the rebound, but let us die like man [sic], and not by slow starvation, landless and hungry men!'[126]

Cilento was told that Indian taxi drivers would 'try to entice away FIJIAN girls at night', leading to violent reprisals.[127] In Cilento's telling, the Fijian voice seethes with resentment at the encroachment of a foreign race and the debasement of Fijian society. Cilento asked Asere about:

> the cause of the Fijians decline from a warrior race that met invading spear and club with spear and club, and that now sat brooding in sloth while a foreign race ate up the country.

Asere, in Cilento's ventriloquist paraphrasing, claimed that 'it was because they had departed from the simple life of their fathers and followed the white man's customs and the white man's food'.[128] Cilento then invoked the same parable as Burton had earlier, in which a travelling Arab slowly gives up space in his tent to a camel trying to escape a sandstorm. For Cilento, in contrast to Burton, this had to be resisted. In fact, he offered another parable in which Indians became a mass of black spears rushing up out of the sea, which 'could only be met by a forest of similar spears spreading from the hills to the water + driving the invaders back'.[129] Cilento's imagery opposed ideals of kinship, belonging and nationhood as being destructive to mixed societies. Cilento imagined Fiji as an incipient nation defined broadly by race, cultural uniformity and belonging to land. In this exchange, Cilento represents himself as a sympathetic character, one who understands the primordial desire of indigenous people to defend their land, maintain their social order and assert their status. He wrote in his

---

125 Raphael Cilento to Phyllis Cilento, 20 November 1928, Cilento Papers, UQFL44, Box 11, Item 20.
126 ibid.
127 ibid.
128 ibid.
129 ibid.

letters that Asere, in stressing the role of Christianity and traditional ways of life in maintaining the health of the community, echoed the message coming from many of the pulpits in Australia.[130]

The deep and abiding antagonism in Fiji between indigenous and foreign invaders that Cilento constructed in his letters reflected his imperial discourses about race and nationhood, as well as his own Australian anxieties about settler-colonial occupation. The reality of Fijian history and society was, and is, far more complex than a clash between 'native' and foreigner. Like Cilento, the report of the 1896 population commission claimed: 'The two races regard one another with undisguised contempt.'[131] Indian immigration under British colonial rule has of course led to a complex, sometimes violent, postcolonial politics. The four coups that have partly derived from and exacerbated tense ethnic politics over the past century have led to frequent representations of deep social divisions.[132] Yet social divisions were never as fundamental as Cilento represents. Kenneth Gillion suggests that, although social interaction was minimal, it was not nonexistent. Indian bus and taxi drivers and shopkeepers met and talked with Fijians. Some in both communities learned the other's language and exchanged cultures of food and drink and there was little overt violence.[133]

In his parables and metaphors, Cilento constructed Fijians as natural and deeply tethered 'natives', once isolated and now struggling to preserve their status in the face of foreign encroachment. Meanwhile, Pacific scholarship has contrasted the colonial trope of island isolation to the complexity and dynamism of Oceanic history, including the importance of seafaring, economic and cultural exchange and forms of political suzerainty and tribute between archipelagic societies.[134] Multicultural relations in Fiji have been represented from a perspective that sees identity and relations as 'not the natural outcomes of autochthony or migration, of certainties flowing from precedence in dwelling', but as active 'articulations of

130 ibid.
131 Colony of Fiji, Report of the Commission Appointed to Inquire into the Decrease of the Native Population, p. 185. See also K. L. Gillion, *The Fiji Indians: Challenge to European Dominance 1920–1946* (Canberra: Australian National University Press, 1977), p. 6.
132 Elfriede Hermann and Wolfgang Kempf, 'Introduction to Relations in Multicultural Fiji: The Dynamics of Articulations, Transformations and Positionings,' *Oceania*, 75(4), 2005, p. 309. See also Martha Kaplan, *Neither Cargo nor Cult: Ritual Politics and the Colonial Imagination* (Durham, NC: Duke University Press, 1995), p. 11.
133 Gillion, *The Fiji Indians*, pp. 15–16.
134 Matsuda, 'The Pacific,' p. 770.

creative subjects'.[135] Fijian songs, stories and *yaqona* rituals celebrate migration, rupture and transformation in Oceanic history, contrasting with ultranationalist narratives of 'primordial autochthony'.[136] Elfriede Hermann and Wolfgang Kempf argue that postcolonial nationalist politics is a legacy of colonial alliances between the British and the Fijian elite that served to maintain the power of chiefs and keep the Indian community—prone to industrial and anticolonial agitation—in check.[137] Cilento's representation of territory and people—both given and mutually constituting each other as a natural and fixed polity—thus reflected British colonial transformations of chiefly power and identity that have shaped contemporary ethnic nationalism among the Fijian elite.[138]

Cilento's representation of Fijian autochthony and Indian foreignness reflected British rhetoric about their duty to protect primitive and vulnerable indigenous Fijians, but it had little in common with actual colonial policy. Indian strikes in the 1920s led to changes in land tenure rules that allowed Indians to become smallholders and the backbone of the sugarcane economy. Cilento argued that the colonial government should have repatriated Indian labourers after the end of the indenture system, but this was politically impossible to contemplate. The British depended on Indian farmers for the economy and settled on maintaining racial division as their chief instrument of rule.[139] In contrast, Cilento continued to argue that multiracial society was doomed to failure. The Indian was a foreign race whose presence was degrading and destabilising to European rule and the civilising mission:

> Fiji is well on the way to becoming an Indian colony, just as Malaya is becoming a Chinese one, and all because of the pull of several big companies and the inevitable stupidity of the English. It is always the same—once you introduce a population of intermediate status it is only a matter of time before it is fatal to white man and native people alike.

135 Margaret Jolly, 'Epilogue: Multicultural Relations in Fiji—Between Despair and Hope,' *Oceania*, 75(4), 2005, p. 418.
136 ibid., pp. 419–20. *Yaqona*, ground and infused kava root, is a ceremonial drink, the use of which has changed over time. See Kaplan, *Neither Cargo nor Cult*, p. 107.
137 Hermann and Kempf, 'Introduction to Relations in Multicultural Fiji,' p. 311. See also Kaplan, *Neither Cargo nor Cult*, pp. 15–16; Jolly, 'Epilogue,' p. 422.
138 John D. Kelly and Martha Kaplan, *Represented Communities: Fiji and World Decolonization* (Chicago: University of Chicago Press, 2001), pp. 126–30.
139 ibid., pp. 129–30.

Siding with those planters who felt they ought to have more access to the land and employ indigenous labourers if Fiji was to progress, Cilento lamented their exclusion. He wrote:

> For a momentary advantage to one or two capitalists who are totally uninterested in the country or its autochthones, the race is pacified and the region forever lost to the white man.[140]

Cilento represented sovereignty and nationhood as inhering in a racial and cultural social body imagined as distinct and possessing overriding claims to indigeneity, but the global social and economic pressures on places such as Fiji required the enlightened and scientific guidance of white men. Cilento thus portrayed empire as a social project designed to ease vulnerable people into an increasingly integrated world economy and so ameliorate the impacts of a capitalist order. The labour migration encouraged by nineteenth-century imperial capitalism was, for Cilento, emblematic of the failure of British indirect rule and of the kind of strictly isolationist paternalism associated with Arthur Gordon and other Fijian governors.[141]

Beyond humanitarian elegies for dying races, the migration of Chinese and South-East Asian peoples to the Pacific Islands caused considerable anxiety on the part of Australian officials. Not all shared this anxiety. Business interests had been particularly vocal and effective in forcing changes to policy in Samoa. Edward Knox, the Director of CSR, and European planters in Fiji continued to lobby for migrant labour years after migration had ceased in 1916, particularly during the 1921 strike by Indian workers.[142] Stephen Roberts criticised the New Guinea administration for enforcing the Immigration Restriction Act and relying on indigenous labour, pointing to successes with 'Asiatic' workers in Hawai'i, New Caledonia, the New Hebrides and Samoa. Some argued that Indian migrants would be a civilising influence on indigenous people, while Indian public opinion—'embittered' by Australia's exclusion of migrants—might drive India towards closer ties with Japan.[143] Professor L. F. Rushbrook Williams, the Director of Public Information for the Government of India, wrote in his report for 1922–23:

---

140 Raphael Cilento to Phyllis Cilento, 17 November 1928, Cilento Papers, UQFL44, Box 11, Item 20.

141 Denoon et al., *The Cambridge History of the Pacific Islanders*, pp. 193–4; Brown, 'Inter-colonial Migration and Refashioning of Indentured Labour,' p. 208.

142 Thompson, *Australia and the Pacific Islands*, p. 78.

143 Stephen Roberts, 'Racial and Labour Problems,' in F. W. Eggleston (ed.), *The Australian Mandate for New Guinea: Record of Round Table Discussion* (Melbourne: Macmillan & Co., 1928), pp. 83–4.

It must be frankly admitted that in the past, and to a large degree at the moment of writing, the treatment accorded to Indians in certain of the self governing Dominions and in the Colonies is not such as befits the nationals of a country whose destiny has been solemnly recognised by His Majesty's Government to be Dominion status, and equal partnership in the Britannic Commonwealth.[144]

Admitting Indians to New Guinea, where they could take up land and contribute to the development of the territory, would thus strengthen the empire in the Pacific. One author declared:

An act of friendliness to India in its present stage and status, such as free consultation between Australia and India, as between two Dominions of the British Commonwealth, would be a graceful recognition on Australia's part of India's new status.[145]

Such appeals to the free movement of British imperial subjects were, however, very much echoes of a past era. Barriers to regulate and restrict migration had, as Adam McKeown points out, divided the world into separate zones of migration that in turn subdivided the British Empire.[146] The White Australia Policy had been a key legislative element in this partition and remained political orthodoxy. Commonwealth health officials such as Cumpston, Elkington and Cilento could not countenance migration to the Pacific Islands from India, China or South-East Asia. At the 1923 Pan-Pacific Science Congress, Cumpston claimed that, without an effort to develop medical services, the indigenous people of the islands would die out, allowing repopulation by 'varying breeds of Asiatic coolies'. He then warned: 'The next phase will be the introduction of the higher types of the same races, and the final phase, not overdistant, will be serious international conflict, diplomatic or military.'[147] In his 1922 thesis, Cilento had argued that, if the indigenous people of New Guinea were to become extinct, Tamil or Chinese 'coolies' would replace them, bringing the 'menace of their politics, the one imbued with the non-cooperation ideas of Gandhi, the other our "yellow peril"'.[148] In a 1932 article on the role of medical services in depopulation, Cilento wrote that, in the event of the extinction of native Pacific Islanders, 'they can only be replaced, if at

144 Quoted in unknown author, 'Immigration Policy in the Territory of New Guinea,' n.d., p. 5, Chinnery Papers , MS 766, Series 5, Folder 9, NLA.
145 ibid, p. 9.
146 McKeown, *Melancholy Order*, p. 185.
147 Cumpston, 'Depopulation of the Pacific,' p. 1389.
148 Cilento, 'A Correlation of Some Features of Tropical Preventive Medicine,' pp. v–vi.

all, by races bringing with them economic, social and political obligations of a very grave character'.[149] Depopulation was, therefore, 'the greatest question in the Pacific as far as Australia is concerned'.[150] The interest of Commonwealth health officials in the Pacific thus rested on anxiety about the geopolitical consequences of the mobility of Asian peoples in the region.

The tour of the Pacific Islands demonstrated to Cilento the importance of extending racial immigration restrictions to form a grid over the whole world. Scholarship on the history of immigration restriction has rightly focused on settler colonies as connected political and social spaces in which distinctly white racial identities arose in the context of nineteenth-century mass migration.[151] The construction of the independent, self-determining, rights-bearing white male subject from the 1840s onwards depended on the construction of the increasingly visible Chinese migrant as servile, collectivist and therefore unfit for participation in liberal democracy.[152] Non-European immigrants, especially Chinese and Melanesian men, were also seen as morally and pathologically corrupting.[153] Cilento, for example, insisted that introduction of foreign 'natives' to Australia would threaten to 'pollute our children and debase our social order'.[154] Yet he also applied these ideas to defend the racial and cultural integrity he imagined in Pacific Island societies. CSR had betrayed Fijians by opposing repatriation of Indian labourers and thus, in Cilento's view, risked the closure of Fiji to progressive white men.[155] Again, Stoddard had emphasised the need to restrict Asian migration not only to 'white race-areas', but also to Latin America and Africa.[156] Immigration restriction, in other words, represented more to Cilento than a 'colour line' to protect a white Australia; it was a principle shaping an imperial world order. In Cilento's vision of this world order, colonial territories that had cut across cultural affinities and contained diverse societies became incipient nations indefinitely bound to the coordinated guidance of 'civilised' societies.[157]

149 Cilento, 'The Value of Medical Services in Relation to Problems of Depopulation,' p. 480.
150 ibid., p. 480.
151 Lake, 'White Man's Country,' pp. 354–6.
152 Lake and Reynolds, *Drawing the Global Colour Line*, p. 27.
153 Bashford, *Imperial Hygiene*, pp. 88, 110–11.
154 Raphael Cilento to Phyllis Cilento, 14 July 1929, Cilento Papers, UQFL44, Box 11, Item 21.
155 Raphael Cilento to Phyllis Cilento, 17 November 1928, Cilento Papers, UQFL44, Box 11, Item 20.
156 Stoddard, *The Rising Tide of Color Against White World-supremacy*, pp. 231–2.
157 On the relationship between colonial territories, nation-states and decolonisation, see Tracey Banivanua-Mar, *Decolonisation and the Pacific: Indigenous Globalisation and the Ends of Empire* (Cambridge: Cambridge University Press, 2016).

This internationalising impulse was clear during a visit to the Fijian village of Vitongo. After a *yaqona* ceremony, villagers presented Cilento and Hermant with a whale's tooth—a gift usually presented to visiting chiefs as a welcome or a call to an alliance.[158] In return, Cilento and Hermant gave a stick to the chief, who had it inscribed with a phrase that Cilento had translated as 'To the King (prince) of Vitongo, as a gift from the two doctors from the League of Nations'. Cilento made a speech in which he spoke of the common medical problems across a politically fragmented region:

> The whole body needed to act as one, and since it was necessary that any infant, or any new born thing should learn before walking, and equally that any convalescent who was beginning after a serious illness to get about, should be supported by a stick or guided by a nurse, the League of Nations was willing to be the nurse or the prop.[159]

Cilento's vision of world order was thus founded on the international governance of 'backward' peoples. This international coordination of empire must take as its primary aim the progressive social reform of indigenous societies, through means that were more often coercive than persuasive. Cilento's paternalism thus represented an attempt to reconcile the contradiction between segregation on a global scale and his participation in colonial rule, which had at its heart the objective of incorporating the labour and resources of the Pacific into the industrial world economy.

International health in the Pacific Islands was a complex mix of Australia's imperial ambition, mutual anxieties over the movement of people and pathogens and the increasingly dense webs of international exchange and governance. As the movement of ships intensified commercial contact between Asia and the Pacific Islands, anxiety arose concerning the policing of people and pathogens. On one level, interventions in regional health were therefore a matter of security. Not only might pathogens pass unnoticed through this archipelagic space, but also epidemic disease might transform the Pacific Islands into an Asian society that threatened white settler societies in other ways. In the mind of Australian officials, the resolutions of the International Pacific Health Conference also reconstituted the Pacific Islands as an Australian sphere of influence.

---

158 Kaplan, *Neither Cargo nor Cult*, pp. 47, 58; Kelly and Kaplan, *Represented Communities*, p. 127.
159 Raphael Cilento to Phyllis Cilento, 19 November 1928, Cilento Papers, UQFL44, Box 11, Item 20.

The map of the 'Austral-Pacific' charted this ambition to direct the development of health and medical services in the Pacific and accrue prestige on an international stage.

Although few of these ambitions came to pass, Cilento was the most zealously imperial voice and foremost in enthusiasm for Australia's role in cooperating with the LNHO and colonial authorities within a regional administrative framework. The 'Austral-Pacific' was a spatial imaginary infused with imperial ambition. Yet the way in which Cilento framed health and sickness in Fiji simultaneously involved a vision of world order. Indeed, it was his social perspective on health that encouraged Cilento to attribute sickness and population decline to the effects of Asian migration in the Pacific. Controlling disease and cultivating health depended on regulating this movement of people and enforcing racial homogeneity on a global scale. For Cilento, international health in the Pacific Islands was the coordination of colonial governance across a new imperial space. Colonial health officers insisted that regional networks of modern communications and regulatory mechanisms could achieve this end. International health in the Pacific, especially Cilento's conception of it, thus spoke to the tension between protecting 'native' societies from modernity and the colonial exploitation of indigenous labour and tropical resources.

4

Colonialism and Indigenous health in Queensland, 1923–1945

Raphael Cilento designed the medal that bears his name shortly before he was knighted in 1935. A sketch in one of his notebooks depicts a winged sphinx spanning the tropical north of Australia and the territories of Papua and New Guinea. Next to the drawing, Cilento wrote: 'The "Cilento" Medal—For Advancing the Knowledge of Tropical Hygiene and Native Welfare Work in Areas Under Australian Control.'[1] Around the edge of the finished design was a Greek inscription asking: 'Can you unravel this riddle?'[2] In covering the announcement of the medal, *The Courier-Mail* recounted the story of the Greek sphinx that sat astride the road putting riddles to travellers, who forfeited their lives if they could not answer. In evoking this story, the newspaper suggested, the medal resonated with the problems facing the nation:

> If Australia is unable to provide an adequate reply to the riddle that has been set her in tropical Australia and the neighbouring islands, her national survival as a white country is undoubtedly threatened.[3]

---

1   Raphael Cilento, Diary: 15 March 1934 – August 1942, Cilento Papers, UQFL44, Box 11, Item 24. Recipients of the Cilento Medal included Francis E. Williams, the government anthropologist in Papua (1935); Cecil Cook, the Chief Medical Officer and Chief Protector of Aborigines in the Northern Territory (1936); Thomas Clunie, a medical officer in Fiji and founder of the journal *Native Medical Practitioner* (1937); E. H. Derrick, Director of the Laboratory of Microbiology and Pathology, Queensland Health Department, with Frank Macfarlane Burnet, at the Walter and Eliza Hall Institute (1939); and Edward G. Sayers, a former medical officer of a mission hospital in the British Solomon Islands (1940).
2   *The Courier-Mail*, [Brisbane], 21 February 1935, p. 14.
3   ibid., p. 14.

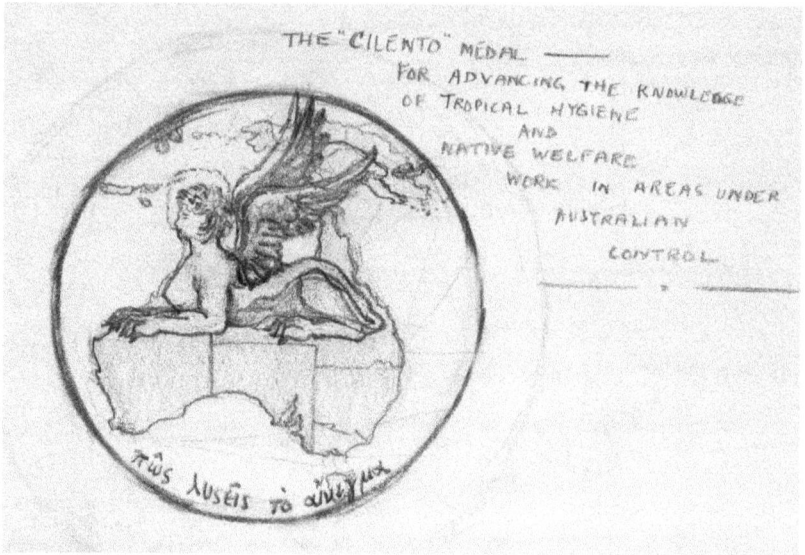

Plate 4.1 Sketch of the Cilento Medal

Source: Diary 1934–42, Papers of Sir Raphael Cilento, UQFL44, Box 11, Item 24, Fryer Library, University of Queensland Library. Reproduced with permission of the Cilento family.

The medal illustrates how Cilento viewed Pacific imperialism and tropical hygiene in northern Australia within a single frame. Settling and developing the Australian tropics were ongoing colonial projects that had different meanings and material dimensions than colonial rule in Melanesia. Australia was to be a white man's country—unlike New Guinea, where indigenous people, in principle, retained their sovereignty.[4] Nevertheless, these colonial projects were never completely distinct. As previously shown, a white Australia seemed to depend on good government in Papua and New Guinea. Cilento went further by trying to bring discourses and practices concerning race and hygiene in the Pacific to bear on state intervention in Aboriginal health and welfare in north Queensland. Of course, the system of Aboriginal 'protection' through state intervention in labour, wages, marriage, forced removals to institutions and the separation of parents and children led to patterns of control and punishment in Aboriginal life distinct from New Guinean communities. Yet historians have begun to understand Aboriginal 'protection' regimes in Queensland in the context of transcolonial migration and the growth of mixed-descent communities

---

4   Cilento, *The White Man in the Tropics*, p. 5.

of Aboriginal, Torres Strait Islander, Pacific Islander and Asian peoples.[5] Cilento shared typical anxieties about this many-sided blurring of racial boundaries, which seemed to be obliterating distinctions between tropical Australia and colonies in the Pacific and Asia. In light of this, Cilento tried to apply discourses and practices of tropical hygiene and colonial governance from Asia and the Pacific to the settler-colonial context of Queensland, often in contradictory ways.

There have been several studies of state intervention in Australian tropical hygiene and Aboriginal health that have focused on the local situation. Gordon Briscoe and Meg Parsons have produced detailed and insightful studies of government attempts to act against disease in Aboriginal populations and remake Aboriginal people as hygienic subjects. Parsons in particular has exposed discursive and practical contradictions in health interventions within the system of institutions that essentially incarcerated thousands of Aboriginal people in Queensland. She has also highlighted the psychological and cultural impact of these practices on Aboriginal communities today.[6] At the same time, historians have been drawn to Cilento's preoccupation with white settlement of the tropics, especially the kinds of climatic adaptations it would require.[7] Parsons did trace the global circulation of ideas and practices regarding leprosy while also insisting on the importance of local factors and a microhistorical approach to institutions. Yet the nation remains the primary frame of analysis in most of these studies of Australian tropical medicine and Aboriginal health.[8]

5   See, for example, Ann McGrath, 'The Golden Thread of Kinship: Mixed Marriages between Asians and Aboriginal Women during Australia's Federation Era,' in Penny Edwards and Shen Yuanfang (eds), *Lost in the Whitewash: Aboriginal–Asian Encounters in Australia, 1901–2001* (Canberra: ANU Humanities Research Centre, 2003), pp. 37–58; Regina Ganter, 'Coloured People: A Challenge to Racial Stereotypes,' in Anna Shnukal, Guy Ramsey and Yuriko Nagata (eds), *Navigating Boundaries: The Asian Diaspora in Torres Strait* (Canberra: Pandanus Books, 2004), p. 221. On Indigenous and Asian connections generally, see Julia Martinez and Adrian Vickers, *The Pearl Frontier: Indonesian Labor and Indigenous Encounters in Australia's Northern Trading Network* (Honolulu: University of Hawai'i Press, 2015).
6   Briscoe, *Counting, Health and Identity*; Meg Parsons, 'Spaces of Disease'.
7   Yarwood, 'Sir Raphael Cilento and *The White Man in the Tropics*,' pp. 47–63; Walker, 'Climate, Civilization and Character in Australia,' pp. 90–1; Walker, *Anxious Nation*, p. 150; Bashford, '"Is White Australia Possible?",' pp. 248–71; Dixon, *Prosthetic Gods*, pp. 38–46; Anderson, *The Cultivation of Whiteness*, pp. 135–52.
8   Parsons, 'Spaces of Disease,' p. 30.

Focusing on Cilento means having to situate these interventions in wider colonial relationships more thoroughly. Warwick Anderson has noted the influence of New Guinea on Cilento's approach to Aboriginal health, although only in passing.[9] Robert Dixon, analysing many of the same texts as does this chapter, has further demonstrated how the ambitious modern state used tropical hygiene to subject both 'native' and white settlers to 'pedagogic' and normalising regimes of surveillance, tutelage and discipline.[10] Around the world, knowledge of the microbial causes of disease and modes of transmission through waste and 'dirt' maintained an emphasis on personal cleanliness and hygienic responsibility, especially in the domestic sphere.[11] In the tropics, behaviour was further scrutinised in the context of socioeconomic conditions and the climatic factors that most believed would still affect white settlers in distinct ways.[12]

Examining white and Indigenous sickness within one colonial field complicates the picture of how public health officials thought about disease, health, compulsion and the state. This is not to argue that the ways in which the state acted on the health and sickness of white colonists, Aboriginal people and New Guineans were equivalent. They certainly were not. State governments and the Commonwealth subjected Aborigines to draconian control and surveillance, while indigenous people in New Guinea never experienced the same kind of dispossession. It is, however, to suggest that Cilento, on one hand, marked all these people as populations requiring disciplinary and protective interventions by the state, while on the other, conceived of Aboriginal governance within the wider frame of imperial and international practices and obligations. Cilento considered his own involvement in Aboriginal health to be an extension of his Pacific expertise and the international body of knowledge of tropical hygiene that circulated the globe in the first half of the twentieth century.

---

9   Anderson, *The Cultivation of Whiteness*, pp. 146–7.
10   Dixon, *Prosthetic Gods*, pp. 24–7.
11   Kerreen Reiger, *The Disenchantment of the Home: Modernizing the Australian Family 1880–1940* (Melbourne: Oxford University Press, 1985), p. 2; Nancy Tomes, *The Gospel of Germs: Men, Women and the Microbe in American Life* (Cambridge, MA: Harvard University Press, 1998), Chs 6, 10; Anderson, *Colonial Pathologies*, p. 161.
12   Anderson, *The Cultivation of Whiteness*, pp. 138–9.

Colonising the nation

Even as he pursued Australia's imperial destiny in the Pacific Islands, Cilento continued to oversee and promote colonisation of the Australian tropics. When he was appointed Director of the Australian Institute of Tropical Medicine (AITM) in Townsville in 1922—by then under the control of the Commonwealth Department of Health (CDH)—many continued to question whether white settlement of the north was possible. Others conceded that the tropics were tenuously occupied, but forcefully argued that white men could secure them with greater effort. The controversial senior ophthalmologist James Barrett declared in 1918:

> The people of Australia are … realising that the proper use of their northern possessions is vital to national existence, since we are quite unable to keep a valuable part of the earth's surface idle.[13]

Seven years later, Barrett continued to combat scepticism, arguing in *The Margin* that, with proper sanitation and intelligent adaptation to climate, 'there is nothing whatever to prevent the peopling of tropical Australia with a healthy and vigorous white race'.[14] White settlement and economic development, however, had never kept pace with dreams of prosperity.[15]

In the Northern Territory and the Torres Strait Islands, the European community was often a minority among a large Indigenous population as well as Chinese, Japanese, Malay, Javanese, Papuan and Filipino people working as merchants, cooks, carpenters, market gardeners, pearl divers and fishermen. Chinese communities in Queensland had been important to the economic and social life of northern towns since the gold rush and minorities of Melanesian, Indian, Italian and various other European, African and Asian peoples were also facts of life.[16] Aboriginal people, moreover, were vital workers across the north, especially in the pastoral industry.[17] As discussed in Chapter 1, doubts about the ability of white

---

13   Barrett, *The Twin Ideals*, p. 283.
14   James W. Barrett, 'Can Tropical Australia be Peopled by a White Race?,' *The Margin*, 1, 1925, p. 30.
15   Walker, *Anxious Nation*, pp. 113–16.
16   The Australian Hookworm Campaign developed shorthand for a wide range of different racial and national categories. See 'Race Classification,' n.d., NAA: SP1061/1, 83/2. See also Henry Reynolds, *North of Capricorn: The Untold Story of Australia's North* (Sydney: Allen & Unwin, 2003), pp. 61–82; Anna Shnukal, Guy Ramsey and Yuriko Nagata, 'Introduction,' in Anna Shnukal, Guy Ramsey and Yuriko Nagata (eds), *Navigating Boundaries: The Asian Diaspora in Torres Strait* (Canberra: Pandanus Books, 2004); Ganter, *Mixed Relations*.
17   Ann McGrath, *Born in the Cattle: Aborigines in Cattle Country* (Sydney: Allen & Unwin, 1987); Henry Reynolds and Dawn May, 'Queensland,' in Ann McGrath (ed.), *Contested Ground: Australian Aborigines under the British Crown* (Sydney: Allen & Unwin, 1995), p. 179.

men of British or Northern European 'stock' to live and work in the tropics had always shadowed hopes for settlement. Indeed, these doubts, expressed especially by older residents and employers, continued to haunt the White Australia Policy well after the 1920 Australasian Medical Congress had declared that climate did not represent an insuperable barrier to white settlement in the tropics.[18]

As the Director of the AITM in Townsville, Cilento inherited from Elkington the mantle of chief public advocate of white settlement in the tropics. Throughout the 1920s and into the 1930s, he wrote and spoke often on the subject in articles, papers and public lectures.[19] He railed against misinformation circulating among the political and social elite in the southern states, while also lamenting a lack of civic feeling among opportunists who came to the north only to leave once they had exploited what they could.[20] The production of propaganda on the question of whether a 'working white race' could settle and develop resources in the tropics was ongoing. In 1923, the Townsville Chamber of Commerce asked Cilento, in his capacity as AITM director, to assist in producing a pamphlet on the question of climate and health in the tropics to be distributed to the southern states and the British Empire Exhibition in London in 1924.[21]

In 1926, the CDH published parts of this pamphlet and other papers as *The White Man in the Tropics*—perhaps Cilento's most well-studied work. In it, he echoed Elkington's criticisms of myths and exaggerations about 'rank and steaming forests'.[22] The climate of Queensland—far from conforming to the imagination—was varied and mild.[23] It was thus

---

18   Russell McGregor notes that, in the Northern Territory, doubts persisted into the late 1930s. See Russell McGregor, *Imagined Destinies: Aboriginal Australians and the Doomed Race Theory, 1880–1939* (Melbourne: Melbourne University Press, 1997), pp. 88–9; McGregor, 'Drawing the Local Colour Line,' pp. 329–46.

19   Raphael Cilento, 'Preventive Medicine and Hygiene in the Tropical Territories under Australian Control,' *Report of the Sixteenth Meeting of the Australasian Association for the Advancement of Science*, 1924, pp. 672–84; Raphael Cilento, 'Observations on the Working White Population of Tropical Queensland,' *Health*, 4(1, 3), 1926, pp. 5–14; Raphael Cilento, 'The White Settlement of Tropical Australia,' in P. D. Phillips and G. L. Wood (eds), *The Peopling of Australia* (Melbourne: Macmillan & Co., 1928), pp. 222–45; Raphael Cilento, 'The Future of Tropical Settlement,' *Church of England College Annual (Brisbane Diocese)*, 1931, pp. 41–4; Raphael Cilento, 'Australia's Orientation,' *Health Bulletin*, 35–6, 1933, pp. 1039–65.

20   Cilento, *The White Man in the Tropics*, pp. 11–12.

21   N. B. Marks to Raphael Cilento, 12 October 1923, NAA: SP1061/1, 341.

22   Cilento, *The White Man in the Tropics*, p. 7.

23   ibid., p. 8.

possible—with suitable clothing, moderate exercise, a sensible diet and minimal alcohol—to live comfortably in northern Australia.[24] The people settled along the coast of north Queensland were:

> The largest mass of a population purely white settled in any part of the tropical world, and represent a huge, unconscious experiment in acclimatization, for here the white settler is … simply a working man, carrying out every occupation from the most laborious tasks to the higher grades of mental effort.[25]

Cilento was thus a prominent figure in a project Anderson has described as a 'remapping' of the Australian tropics as a zone that disciplined and dutiful white citizens could settle and incorporate into the imagined body of the nation.[26]

But if it was simply a fact that a healthy population of white working people had settled the Australian tropics 'in defiance of every previously accepted theory', individuals still required disciplined hygienic conduct to maintain their health in such an environment.[27] *The White Man in the Tropics* collected information for a reading public on types of clothing, house designs, working hours and patterns of food consumption that would shield white people from the debilitating effects of the tropical climate. In prescribing the minutiae of personal conduct, tropical medicine maintained a tension between asserting the possibility of permanent white settlement and perpetuating the sense that white bodies in the tropics were out of place. To survive in the tropics, in other words, white men had to put material and behavioural barriers between themselves and the environment.[28]

Despite new confidence about white settlement, there was still talk, including from Cilento, about the emergence of a new type of white physiology and exertion in the tropics, which again emphasised the foreignness of white bodies in the region.[29] This type was 'tall and rangy', but strong:

---

24   ibid., p. 10.
25   ibid., p. 9.
26   Anderson, 'Geography, Race and Nation,' p. 463; Anderson, *The Cultivation of Whiteness*, pp. 138–9.
27   Cilento, 'The White Settlement of Tropical Australia,' p. 224.
28   Anderson, *The Cultivation of Whiteness*, p. 138; Bashford, *Imperial Hygiene*, pp. 158–63.
29   Bashford, '"Is White Australia Possible?",' pp. 262–3; Anderson, *The Cultivation of Whiteness*, pp. 137–8.

One can pick him out in the streets by the fact that … he walks more deliberately. In the women this becomes a gracefulness of movement that reminds one of those nations of the East that live in similar environments.

In fact, Cilento claimed, 'the race is in a transition stage', as a 'distinct tropical type' slowly emerged in Queensland.[30] He was also interested in the social and cultural aspects of adaptation that were 'racial or national'—aimed at producing equilibrium between European bodies and their new environment.[31] The norms of clothing, housing, consumption and leisure that had become traditional in temperate climes would not do in the tropics:

> Our greatest enemy here is not climate, but tradition, in that we have to fight for a white population which has absorbed for generations a traditional life routine until it has come to accept habit as its conscience.[32]

Cilento's wife, Phyllis, campaigned publicly in Townsville for changes in the way women dressed in the Australia tropics, including the adoption of more loosely fitting clothes that mimicked Indian or Malay styles of dress.[33] At the 1924 meeting of the Australasian Association for the Advancement of Science, Cilento similarly argued that white settlers in the Australian tropics must adopt some of the lifestyles of Asian peoples, such as working early in the day and resting in the afternoon.[34]

While the state should provide a sanitary environment, Cilento asserted, it was also important for white subjects to act as citizens responsible for their own health. As Anderson notes, the white embodied subject became the object of 'unremitting surveillance, discipline, and mobilisation'.[35] Cilento initiated a sociological investigation in which nurse Ada Gorman surveyed living conditions and domestic knowledge and practices among housewives in north Queensland. Her report ranked residents in Townsville according to knowledge of hygiene and concluded that 27 per cent had no such knowledge. Allowing pollution of soil with human waste and failing to protect food from flies were thus relatively common. Almost half had moderate knowledge, but failed 'in such

30 Cilento, *The White Man in the Tropics*, p. 74.
31 ibid., p. 9.
32 Raphael Cilento to C. M. Wenyon, London, 17 January 1924, NAA: SP1061/1, 300.
33 Henningham, '"Hats Off, Gentlemen, to Our Australian Mothers!",' pp. 319–20.
34 Cilento, 'Preventive Medicine and Hygiene in the Tropical Territories under Australian Control,' pp. 678–9.
35 Anderson, *The Cultivation of Whiteness*, p. 139.

matters as leaving the lids off garbage tins or closet pans'.[36] At the same time, by highlighting the conditions under which many working people lived in north Queensland—often lacking piped water, ice chests or water closets—nurse Gorman's study implied that life in the tropics could also be improved with more modern amenities.[37]

Although the Commonwealth continued to issue propaganda on the question of climate, in the 1920s, the focus of public health practice in the tropics turned to diseases such as hookworm and malaria. Victor Heiser, the Director of the East for the International Health Board (IHB) of the Rockefeller Foundation, visited the AITM in Townsville shortly after the Commonwealth takeover and recommended that it shift away from pure research on climate and physiology towards routine diagnostic services, epidemiological study and some clinical research.[38] As shown in previous chapters, it was common in colonial public health discourse to represent indigenous and other non-European communities as persistent reservoirs of infection, either as asymptomatic carriers of disease or as habitually insanitary individuals and communities. In seeking to rehabilitate the tropics for white settlement, many medical authorities sought to minimise aboriginal populations.[39] James Barrett claimed: 'The strength of the position in Australia is the absence of a large native population, acting as a reservoir of disease.'[40] In *The White Man in the Tropics*, Cilento similarly claimed: 'The tropical areas of Australia are unique in that they have no teeming native population, riddled with disease.'[41] The emphasis instead fell, as Anderson argues, on the need to cultivate a body of reformed and disciplined white citizens, protected from sickness and degeneration by their own hygienic behaviour.[42] As this chapter will show, however, Cilento and other health officials continuously contradicted these claims by insisting on the hygienic importance of racial segregation across northern Australia.

Malaria, filariasis and leprosy were major subjects of epidemiological study in Queensland, but it was hookworm disease that attracted the most sustained attention in the 1920s—from survey to treatment and prevention. Hookworm was rarely fatal in white communities in the early

---

36   Cilento, 'Observations on the Working White Population of Tropical Queensland,' p. 9.
37   ibid., pp. 6–12.
38   'Report on March 1921 – December 1925,' 22 February 1925, p. 3, NAA: A1928, 927/14; Parker, 'A "Complete Protective Machinery",' p. 183; Anderson, *The Cultivation of Whiteness*, p. 136.
39   Anderson, 'Geography, Race and Nation,' p. 463.
40   Barrett, 'Can Tropical Australia be Peopled by a White Race?,' p. 28.
41   Cilento, *The White Man in the Tropics*, p. 9.
42   Anderson, *The Cultivation of Whiteness*, p. 139.

twentieth century, and low levels of infestation often left no symptoms. Following a series of investigations in Europe, Latin America and the southern United States, however, the hookworm parasite became known as the 'germ of laziness'—blamed for anaemia and fatigue among miners, agricultural workers and 'poor whites'.[43] It was not a serious public health problem in Australia, but in light of its supposed effects on the physical and mental development of children, it helped to maintain the notion that the tropical environment would in some way lead to racial degeneration.[44]

The knowledge of hookworm's lifecycle and the relative ease of treatment suggested that a campaign might prove an effective popular demonstration of the value of modern hygiene. Its presence in several states and colonial territories also strengthened the case for a federal health department.[45] It was well known that the parasite anchored itself to the gut, giving rise to a range of symptoms, including anaemia. The ova were passed with faecal matter, potentially contaminating damp, porous soils where sanitation facilities were rudimentary or where individuals defaecated on the ground. Infection occurred when larvae that hatched in contaminated soil entered human hosts through bare feet. Campaigns against hookworm thus tended to focus on insanitary habits, the design of privies and water closets and the disposal of waste. Hookworm programs thus also focused on encouraging local authorities to improve sanitation facilities and educate individuals and communities in hygiene.[46]

In 1916, the Commonwealth Government invited the IHB to conduct a campaign modelled on those it had supported elsewhere in the British Empire. After initial surveys of Papua and Australia, officials decided to focus a full-scale campaign, using American expertise, on Queensland and northern New South Wales, beginning in 1919. Intensive surveys of districts in north Queensland, including schools, established the prevalence of hookworm. Sanitation teams went door-to-door, distributing tin containers for households to fill with faecal samples and return to the AITM in Townsville.[47] Propaganda activities, including lectures

---

43   Matt Wray, *Not Quite White: White Trash and the Boundaries of Whiteness* (Durham, NC: Duke University Press, 2006), pp. 96–105.
44   Anderson, *The Cultivation of Whiteness*, p. 144.
45   Gillespie, 'The Rockefeller Foundation, the Hookworm Campaign and a National Health Policy in Australia,' pp. 66–72; Anderson, *The Cultivation of Whiteness*, pp. 143–4.
46   Farley, *To Cast Out Disease*, pp. 28–9.
47   Sylvester Lambert, *Completed Area Report No. 1: The Control of Hookworm Disease in the Bowen District, Queensland* (Brisbane: Hookworm Campaign, 1920), pp. 3–6.

and exhibitions for schools and the general public, aimed to energise local sanitation and cultivate habits of personal cleanliness, and drew enthusiastic public participation in the early stages of the campaign.[48] Surveys were followed by intensive treatment, involving a series of purges of worms and eggs using oil of Chenopodium and, later, carbon tetrachloride.[49] By 1923, the IHB began passing control of the campaign to local officials and Cilento became its director in north Queensland.[50] With the withdrawal of American funding and personnel, the campaign persisted under Commonwealth and state control into the 1930s.

If its primary concern was sanitation and hygiene in the white settler community, the Hookworm Campaign also pathologised Aboriginal people. Whether Aborigines were a source of hookworm infection in white communities was officially an unanswered question at the time and the campaign endeavoured to collect evidence. Survey units always examined Aboriginal communities in camps, government settlements and missions in their districts and frequently recorded infestation rates of between 50 and 90 per cent.[51] Anderson has suggested that, in hookworm among Aborigines, Cilento had found his 'reservoir' of disease.[52] Parsons, however, has argued that the long-serving Chief Protector of Aborigines in Queensland J. W. Bleakley was less concerned with Aboriginal people as sources of infection. While local residents may have pathologised Aboriginal people, Parsons argues, scientific investigations at state and federal levels were preoccupied with the white and male embodied subject.[53] It is quite clear that hookworm campaign personnel did consider Indigenous people to be sources of hookworm infestation in white communities in northern New South Wales and Queensland. In 1923, Noel Charlton reported on the Cairns area, including Yarrabah Mission on Cape Grafton, where infestation rates had once reached 85.7 per cent. The mission was built on swampy soil, Charlton noted, making it fertile

---

48   ibid., pp. 13–14.
49   Noel B. Charlton, *Completed Area Report No. 18: The Control of Hookworm Disease in Cairns and Vicinity and in the Yarrabah and Mona Mona Aboriginal Missions, North Queensland* (Brisbane: Hookworm Campaign, 1923), p. 9.
50   Attached report, n.d., p. 2, J. S. C. Elkington to Raphael Cilento, 10 December 1923, NAA: SP1061/1, 350.
51   G. H. Burnell and John McKee, *Survey Report No. 12: A Hookworm Survey of the South-eastern Part of the Rockhampton District* (Brisbane: Hookworm Campaign, 1921), p. 37; Charlton, *Completed Area Report No. 18*, p. 15; Noel B. Charlton, *Completed Area Report No. 19: The Control of Hookworm Disease in the Cooktown Area of North Queensland, Including a Special Report on the Cape Bedford Mission Station* (Brisbane: Hookworm Campaign, 1923), pp. 3–10.
52   Anderson, *The Cultivation of Whiteness*, p. 145.
53   Parsons, 'Spaces of Disease,' pp. 121–3.

ground for hookworm: '[W]hen to this is added the usual insanitary habits of the natives it is evident that the place is a particularly favourable one for the spread of hookworm disease.'[54] A biweekly boat service from the mission to Cairns only emphasised the potential for Aborigines travelling for work to contaminate the area.[55]

Representing Aboriginal communities as a potential source of hookworm, however, did not necessarily mean the construction of a racial binary between clean, contained white bodies and the open, promiscuous bodies of Indigenous people. In Australia, the imperative to reform white embodied subjects often accompanied the construction of the unhygienic 'native'.[56] In his 1926 survey of the Atherton area, near Cairns, H. Pearson noted that the majority of the hookworm infestation among the white population could be traced to 'promiscuous defaecation' among whites themselves, rather than 'their (slightly, as regards sanitation) more primitive dark brethren'.[57] Pearson noted that infestation rates among Aborigines were high in northern New South Wales, but the disease was not spread to white communities 'by contiguity'. Rather, Aboriginal people, 'whose habits are dangerous', contaminated ground that was now occupied by white people:

> It appears highly probable, but remains unproven, that under such conditions existing as described hookworm infestation is acquired by whites from the blacks, and by the existence of privy and other conditions favourable for spread amongst the whites, persistent and spreading infestation is favoured.[58]

In other words, Aboriginal people might contaminate the soil, but 'primitive' insanitary conditions and the habits of working-class white communities were also crucial to the persistence of endemic hookworm disease. Cilento and others meanwhile linked the introduction and persistence of hookworm infestation in Queensland to the history of Melanesian indentured labour and the living conditions of Italian workers.[59]

---

54   Charlton, *Completed Area Report No. 18*, p. 15.
55   ibid., p. 21.
56   Anderson, *Colonial Pathologies*, pp. 105–7.
57   H. Pearson, *An Investigation into the Epidemiology of Hookworm Disease in the Atherton Area, N.Q.* (Brisbane: Hookworm Campaign, 1926), p. 2.
58   H. Pearson, *Activities of Hookworm Campaign Unit No. 1 in the Northern Rivers District of New South Wales, 1926* (Brisbane: Hookworm Campaign, 1926), p. 418.
59   See Charlton, *Completed Area Report No. 18*, p. 8; Cilento, 'The Future of Tropical Settlement,' p. 42.

Tropical colonisation thus drew 'white', Aboriginal, Southern European and Pacific Islander people into relationships of management and tutelage by the state. On some occasions, resistance among white communities even seemed to justify coercive examination and treatment that were usually reserved for Aborigines.[60] Cilento wrote in 1923 to the American director of the campaign, W. C. Sweet, concerning passive resistance among poor white communities in Townsville. People were increasingly failing to return faecal samples for examination. 'These individuals believe', Cilento claimed, 'that the examination is simply a "capitalistic" ruse, to determine which among them are most healthy, with a view to employing them alone; and similarly absurd things'.[61] Their ignorance, he argued, was such that 'no amount of education will affect' them to cooperate:

> The particular locality in which Hookworm Disease is rife, is, as one would expect, among the low class waterside workers immune to any form of argument short of force. It is to be regretted that one cannot quarantine the whole area and subject them by compulsion to routine examination, though of course, this policy would be impracticable.[62]

Philippa Levine has noted how colonial medical discourse represented indigenous peoples, in their refusal of Western medicine, as obstacles to modernity.[63] The resistance to facts and reason Cilento complained of in Townsville similarly marked working-class white communities as bottlenecks to rational scientific governance, providing an in-principle justification for coercive state intervention. Ideas about scientific reason, the role of the state and both the necessity of and the capacity for the participation of communities in public health thus connected Cilento's representations of class and race in colonial north Queensland. Hookworm personnel likewise made racial distinctions between white and Aboriginal people while conflating them within a broad notion of backwardness. Cilento's attitudes towards race and class thus reflected and prompted a similar logic in which rights and liberty were subordinate to the interests of the state and the social prescriptions of modern scientific knowledge.

---

60   A. H. Baldwin to Raphael Cilento, 7 June 1929, NAA: SP1061/1, 83/2.
61   Raphael Cilento to W. C. Sweet, 10 April 1923, pp. 1–2, NAA: SP1061/1, 93/1.
62   ibid., p. 2.
63   Philippa Levine, *Prostitution, Race, and Politics: Policing Venereal Disease in the British Empire* (New York: Routledge, 2003), p. 9.

White and Indigenous people in north Queensland were not treated alike in practice. Matt Wray has discussed how, during the hookworm campaigns in the southern United States, health personnel could find it hard to distinguish poor whites from black southerners. Yet they also thought of treatment of poor whites as a kind of racial whitening, or a clarification of racial difference, since civilised qualities were coded as white.[64] Modern liberal states in this period reserved the right to deal with problematic populations by compulsion, including white people suffering from leprosy and other diseases.[65] While Cilento may have wished for coercive treatment of obstinate white communities, he recognised the political and logistical impossibility in this particular context. More importantly, Cilento was deeply committed to a colonial ideology that figured non-European peoples as racially inferior. Compulsory examination and treatment of white subjects was limited to isolation of subjects suffering leprosy, venereal disease and mental illness. In contrast, Aboriginal people were already subjected to radically more intrusive and punitive governmental controls that rested on a wider array of racial anxieties and ideologies and that structured interventions in their health.

Medicine and Indigenous health in Australian colonial space

When Cilento returned to Australia after his time in the colonial Pacific, he involved himself more directly in Indigenous health than he had as the Director of the AITM. At first, this was opportunistic since Cilento, as a Commonwealth official, had no formal role in Aboriginal health policy and administration. By the late 1920s, the effect of climate on white tropical settlement was a less pressing issue than it once had been.[66] Health concerns had refocused on venereal disease and leprosy—the latter a deeply stigmatised disease that had acquired new meanings as racial degeneracy and contamination since colonial encounters in the Pacific and Asia in the mid-nineteenth century.[67] Cecil Cook, who worked as

---

64 Wray, *Not Quite White*, pp. 120–2.
65 Alison Bashford and Carolyn Strange, 'Isolation and Exclusion in a Modern World: An Introductory Essay,' in Alison Bashford and Carolyn Strange (eds), *Isolation: Places and Practices of Exclusion* (London: Routledge, 2003), p. 22.
66 Anderson, *The Cultivation of Whiteness*, p. 152.
67 Zachary Gussow, *Leprosy, Racism, and Public Health: Social Policy in Chronic Disease Control* (Boulder, CO: Westview Press, 1989), pp. 19–20; Bashford, *Imperial Hygiene*, p. 83.

a medical officer on the Hookworm Campaign before becoming Chief Medical Officer and Chief Protector of Aborigines in the Northern Territory, published a major epidemiological study of leprosy in Australia in 1927. The newly established Federal Health Council subsequently adopted leprosy as one of its concerns, partly at the urging of Cilento.[68]

Cilento in fact took a special interest in leprosy and pressed constantly for permanent surveillance of Aboriginal communities and reform of the way the disease was managed throughout the 1930s.[69] As a Commonwealth official, he did what little he could. During a 1931 inspection tour of northern Queensland, Cilento coopted a local police sergeant to search for cases of leprosy among Aboriginal camps around Gordonvale, south of Cairns. He later confessed to Phyllis: 'Everything I did was unauthorised, not to say illegal, and it all went along like a song!'[70] Yet his sense of satisfaction did nothing to change the fact that Cilento had no authority over Aboriginal health in the tropics.

Official interventions in Aboriginal sickness and health in Queensland in the twentieth century occurred within a larger system governing Indigenous people that emerged with the *Aboriginals Protection and Restriction of the Sale of Opium Act 1897*. Drawing too sharp a line between phases in the relationship between Aboriginal people and European invaders obscures how violence and 'protection' coexisted in the nineteenth and twentieth centuries. As Tim Rowse and others suggest, however, one can discern a broad historical shift in which the frontier violence of the nineteenth century gave way to systems of control and exploitation in the twentieth century.[71]

The Act was the first legal sanction of official state control of Indigenous people in Queensland, and came as a response to mounting humanitarian criticism of widespread abuse and exploitation of Aboriginal communities that had grown around most towns in the 1880s. Aboriginal people in Queensland were tired and depleted after decades of brutal frontier

---

68   Cecil Cook, *The Epidemiology of Leprosy in Australia* (Melbourne: Government Printer, 1927); *Report of the Federal Health Council of Australia*, 1st Session, 1927, p. 6.
69   Raphael Cilento, 'Brief Review of Leprosy in Australia and its Dependencies,' in *Report of the Federal Health Council*, 7th Session, 1934, pp. 19–23.
70   Raphael Cilento to Phyllis Cilento, 25 September 1931, Cilento Papers, UQFL44, Box 11, Item 21.
71   Tim Rowse, *White Flour, White Power: From Rations to Citizenship in Central Australia* (Cambridge: Cambridge University Press, 1998), p. 7; Anna Haebich, *Broken Circles: Fragmenting Indigenous Families 1800–2000* (Fremantle, WA: Fremantle Arts Centre Press, 2000), pp. 131–2.

conflict with settlers and the Native Mounted Police.[72] Many now opted for life in the camps that developed on the outskirts of rural towns. Besides whatever hunting or fishing they could still manage, many found work in the pastoral industry or employment with townspeople. They were paid in food, tobacco, clothes, opium or not at all.[73] White townspeople were ambivalent about the camps. They were pools of cheap labour and sexual gratification, but others saw them as a material and moral threat. Many towns established curfews, resulting in a daily ritual in which the police drove Aboriginal people beyond the town limits at sunset.[74]

Under mounting humanitarian pressure in the mid-1890s, the Queensland Government commissioned Archibald Meston, a journalist, politician and self-professed Aboriginal expert, to survey race relations and the living conditions of Aboriginal people in the north of the state. In his 1896 *Report on the Aboriginals of Queensland*, Meston highlighted the arbitrary violence perpetrated against Aborigines and the kidnapping and rape of women by white men. Meston argued for strict institutional segregation:

> There is no prospect of any satisfactory or permanent good without the creation of suitable reserves, the establishment of 'Aboriginal Settlements,' chiefly, if not altogether, self-supporting, and *absolute isolation* from contact with whites except those specially appointed to guide them.[75]

Reserves were there to not simply protect, Meston argued, but also gradually transform Indigenous people from nomadic hunters into settled farmers. They must be established on good land to allow for agriculture and livestock. Residents were to cultivate their own patch of land for food, while '[h]abits of cleanliness and industry would be taught regularly, and enforced when necessary'.[76] Villages would be laid out in an orderly fashion, with sanitation provisions and adequate water supplies. The whole life of people on the reserves—including work, leisure and

72 Noel Loos, *Invasion and Resistance: Aboriginal–European Relations on the North Queensland Frontier 1861–1897* (Canberra: Australian National University Press, 1982), pp. 22–3; Reynolds and May, 'Queensland,' pp. 172–3.
73 Reynolds and May, 'Queensland,' pp. 179–81.
74 ibid., p. 181.
75 Archibald Meston, *Report on the Aboriginals of Queensland* (Brisbane: Government Printer, 1896), p. 13, Meston's emphasis; Raymond Evans, Kay Saunders and Kathryn Cronin, *Race Relations in Colonial Queensland: A History of Exclusion, Exploitation and Extermination* (Brisbane: University of Queensland Press, 1988), pp. 85–91; McGregor, *Imagined Destinies*, pp. 60–1; Haebich, *Broken Circles*, pp. 138–41.
76 Archibald Meston, *Queensland Aboriginals: Proposed System for their Improvement and Preservation* (Brisbane: Government of Queensland, 1895), p. 26.

sleep—must be regulated in the interests of social harmony and progress: 'The whole community must be governed by a fixed code of laws, sternly enforced at all hazards when necessary.'[77] The reserves would eventually produce fit and capable workers to replace Pacific Islanders on the sugar plantations, going out to work before returning at the end of the season.[78]

Meston's recommendations were the basis for the Aboriginals Protection Act, which established a range of measures that ostensibly sought to prevent abuse and exploitation. It empowered the home secretary to establish government reserves and to remove any Aboriginal person to or between those reserves. He was also mandated to proclaim any regulation relating to the mode of removal, the administration of reserves, the duties of protectors, the care and custody of children and the maintenance of discipline and order on reserves. The Act furthermore allowed for the control of Aboriginal employment, requiring that officials be present in the negotiation of contracts. The legislation led in 1904 to the appointment of a Chief Protector of Aborigines within the home secretary's department, in addition to a network of local protectors.

This system quickly became a means to control and exploit Aboriginal people.[79] The authority to remove Aboriginal people to government settlements and missions became a punitive measure, frequently used to banish undesirable people from the vicinity of anxious white townships.[80] With no provision for magisterial review or any legal recourse, individuals could be removed for any reason a protector or the home secretary wished, including attempts to acquire alcohol, seeking to organise Aboriginal labour against exploitation or protesting the system itself.[81] Attempts to enrol children in local schools were often met with local panic and threats of removal by local protectors, who were usually also police officers.[82] The government also used the settlement network to extend the prison sentences of some Aboriginal men or even incarcerate suspects whom the

---

77   ibid., p. 26.
78   ibid., p. 27.
79   Reynolds and May, 'Queensland,' p. 182.
80   Thom Blake, 'Deported … At the Sweet Will of the Government: The Removal of Aborigines to Reserves in Queensland 1897–1939,' *Aboriginal History*, 22, 1998, p. 53.
81   Reynolds and May, 'Queensland,' pp. 187–8; Haebich, *Broken Circles*, pp. 160–3.
82   Haebich, *Broken Circles*, pp. 177–8. This process was not restricted to Queensland; see Anna Haebich, '"Clearing the Wheat Belt": Erasing the Indigenous Presence in the Southwest of Western Australia,' in A. Dirk Moses (ed.), *Genocide and Settler Society: Frontier Violence and Stolen Indigenous Children in Australian History* (New York: Berghahn Books, 2007), p. 273.

courts had acquitted.[83] The 1901 amendments to the Act provided the chief protector with the authority to approve or forbid marriages. Just the threat of removal to settlements—increasingly notorious as places of separation and punishment among Aboriginal families—proved an effective way of ensuring compliance with orders, according to some historians.[84]

Settlement life was a strict regimen of work and obedience. The dormitory system isolated children from their families and subjected them to a daily regimen of cleaning, inspection and schooling.[85] Children were escorted to school by an Aboriginal guard and inmates could have their heads shaved or be sent to jail for being late to inspection parades. Authorities banned Aboriginal languages and the government could prohibit whatever Indigenous customs it decided were harmful to the order of the reserve. In the 1920s, chief protector Bleakley oversaw the expansion of a more regulated dormitory system in reserves such as Barambah (later Cherbourg). Aboriginal children and young women had been separated in dormitories for some time. Bleakley's reforms, including the construction of new and larger girls' homes, increased the dormitory population dramatically and took on a more reformative purpose.[86] Bleakley also oversaw construction of weatherboard cottages at Barambah intended to inculcate domestic habits and pride. The establishment of Aboriginal villages on settlements became a general ideal. In this way, settlement design and practice sought to discipline Aboriginal people and transform them into moral subjects within European-style nuclear family units.[87]

In reality, official neglect turned settlements into incubators of disease instead of refuges, undermining the paternalistic ideals with which some had invested the Act. The rations provided to inmates were poor in both calories and nutritional value, consisting mainly of flour, sugar and tea,

83   Blake, 'Deported … At the Sweet Will of the Government,' pp. 56–7.
84   Joanne Watson, 'Becoming Bwgcolman: Exile and Survival on Palm Island Reserve, 1918 to the Present' (PhD Thesis, University of Queensland, 1993), p. 58, and p. 64 on the 1901 amendments; Fiona Probyn-Rapsey, '"Uplifting" White Men: Marriage, Maintenance and Whiteness in Queensland, 1900–1910,' *Postcolonial Studies*, 12(1), 2009, pp. 89–106.
85   Watson, 'Becoming Bwgcolman,' pp. 91, 108, 350–1; Thom Blake, *A Dumping Ground: A History of the Cherbourg Settlement* (Brisbane: University of Queensland Press, 2001), pp. 73–5; Parsons, 'Spaces of Disease,' pp. 203–6.
86   Parsons, 'Spaces of Disease,' pp. 190–206.
87   David King and Malcolm Vick, 'Keeping 'Em Down: Education on Palm Island under Queensland's Aboriginal Acts,' *History of Education Review*, 23(1), 1994, pp. 6–12. This rhetoric and practice accelerated in the 1930s on settlements such as Barambah; see Parsons, 'Spaces of Disease,' pp. 207–11.

while meat supplies were mostly bone and sometimes arrived spoiled. Overcrowding and poor housing encouraged persistently high levels of morbidity and mortality from infectious diseases. As Parsons shows, mortality at Barambah reached an annual average of 13 per cent during the first 15 years of control by the protection office. Rates declined in the 1920s and 1930s, but they remained triple the national average.[88] Children were often forced to steal from food supplies reserved for the European staff and escape attempts were frequent.[89] By the 1940s, conditions were as bad as ever as the size of the reserve system increasingly outstripped the capacity of the renamed Department of Native Affairs to administer it.[90]

The settlements functioned in part as reservoirs of labour for rural industries and domestic service.[91] Girls were usually sent out to work as domestic servants at the age of 14, while boys worked as stockmen or loggers. The Act did not govern the settlements alone, however, and provided the government with power to intervene in the working lives and intimate relationships of Aboriginal people across the state. In 1919, the state government set a minimum wage for Aboriginal workers at two-thirds that of white workers. The Act had always provided for the control of Aboriginal wages, however, and despite political rhetoric, it was accepted practice for the government to take the majority of Aboriginal earnings and place them in a combination of individual trust accounts and provident funds. This money made up the bulk of the budget for the chief protector's office and was reinvested in the upkeep of reserves.[92]

Hygiene was one consideration among several in the spatial management of race. Expert medical knowledge, moreover, could be a basis for criticism of Aboriginal policies and their administration. Parsons and Rosalind Kidd have uncovered the tensions and competing agendas among multiple actors that shaped this administration.[93] In many ways, their approach reflects larger trends in colonial studies that have emphasised how a range of colonial actors—including officials, planters and missionaries—sought to rework the aims of colonial rule and the social categories involved in

---

88 Parsons, 'Spaces of Disease,' pp. 154–5.
89 Blake, *A Dumping Ground*, pp. 105–10; Parsons, 'Spaces of Disease,' p. 200.
90 Parsons, 'Spaces of Disease,' p. 71.
91 Blake, *A Dumping Ground*, p. 65; Parsons, 'Spaces of Disease,' pp. 180–1.
92 Raymond Evans, '"Fallen among Thieves": Aboriginal Labour and State Control in Inter-war Queensland,' *Labour History*, 69, 1995, p. 127; Jackie Huggins, 'White Aprons, Black Hands: Aboriginal Domestic Servants in Queensland,' *Labour History*, 69, 1995, pp. 188–95.
93 Rosalind Kidd, 'Regulating Bodies: Administrations and Aborigines in Queensland 1840–1988' (PhD Thesis, Griffith University, 1994), pp. 4–10; Parsons, 'Spaces of Disease,' pp. 27–9.

government.[94] Kidd and Parsons have analysed these dynamics at a very local level, seeking the distinctive tensions around policy and practice in Queensland. Their work, however, also reflects an understanding of this history as part of a national settler-colonial project. Yet colonial projects in this period often connected to others across national boundaries, as soldiers, missionaries, doctors and policymakers moved along circuits carrying ideas and practices between different French, British, American and Dutch colonial sites.[95]

Cilento's career provides an opportunity to examine relationships between colonial medicine in north Queensland and elsewhere in the Pacific and Asia in greater detail. He certainly did not conflate white settlement of Australia with colonialism in the Pacific Islands. In fact, Cilento defined the settler-colonial project as a reinforcement of the racial and epidemiological boundaries between Australia and the Pacific. Health problems in Queensland, he wrote, could be traced to Melanesian indentured labourers 'bequeathing their diseases to their masters'.[96] For Cilento, Australian tropical hygiene thus consisted of clearing up the legacies of Queensland's past exchanges with the Pacific Islands. By the time he became directly involved in Aboriginal health in the late 1920s, Cilento also had extensive experience of colonial hygiene in South-East Asia and the Pacific and he remained fascinated with 'native' and tropical life and disease in general. When Cilento wrote or spoke about Aboriginal health and tropical hygiene, he related it to his broader colonial experience and Australia's responsibilities in the Pacific. In turning his attention to Aboriginal health, he drew on principles and practices of public health that could be redeployed in various colonial sites that fell within a larger Australian imperial space incorporating northern Australia, the Torres Strait Islands and the territories of Papua and New Guinea.

As a young medical student, Cilento was once called on to visit an Aboriginal camp and remove the afterbirth from a new mother. Cilento and his biographer, Fedora Fisher, described a crowd of Aboriginal eyes intent on the young medical man performing his work in an environment that crystallised the hardships that Indigenous people faced in the first decades of the twentieth century. Years later, Cilento wrote of how 'that

94   Ann Laura Stoler and Frederick Cooper, 'Between Metropole and Colony: Rethinking a Research Agenda,' in Frederick Cooper and Ann Laura Stoler (eds), *Tensions of Empire: Colonial Cultures in a Bourgeois World* (Berkeley: University of California Press, 1997), pp. 19–22.
95   ibid., p. 28.
96   ibid., p. 226.

one experience set me on the road to a life-long interest in their complex situation in relation to our after-coming race that had dispossessed them'.[97] In fact, Cilento often acknowledged that Europeans had violently dispossessed Aboriginal people, and he generally framed Indigenous health within an account of the culpability of settler colonialism for Aboriginal poverty and sickness. He had read the 1837 report of the British Select Committee on Aborigines, and sometimes echoed its conclusions about the historical disregard for 'the territorial rights of the natives' and their welfare.[98] After his attempt to find suspected cases of leprosy around Gordonvale in 1931, he wrote to his wife: 'Their medical condition was a shame and a reflection on the whites who have dispossessed them.'[99] A few years later, he commented that, in mainland Queensland, 'only rapidly declining tribal remnants remain' outside the reserves. Such communities were forced to live on worthless land—'a standing reflection upon the civilisation that permits the conditions producing this situation'.[100]

Such admissions were fairly commonplace among politicians and officials. In 1929, Bleakley argued that white settlers were obliged to provide aid to older Aborigines 'who have been deprived of their natural means of subsistence by the usurpation of their tribal hunting grounds'.[101] A Queensland government pamphlet in the late 1930s asked: 'HAVE you ever stopped to consider the fate of the 20,000 odd aboriginals in Queensland, remnants of the race from whom we took this country?'[102] This was also the kind of language that permeated the literature of humanitarian organisations, such as the Aborigines' Protection League and the Association for the Protection of Native Races, which began campaigning in the early 1930s for greater protection of the rights of Aborigines as Indigenous people.[103] The way in which Cilento framed Indigenous health thus reflected established narratives of Australian colonisation.

---

97 Cilento quoted in Fisher, *Raphael Cilento*, p. 14.
98 *Report of the Select Committee on Aborigines (British Settlements)* (Cape Town: C. Struik, 1966), p. 10. Cilento transcribed sections of the report in a notebook: Raphael Cilento, Diary: 15 March 1934 – August 1942, Cilento Papers, UQFL44, Box 11, Item 24.
99 Raphael Cilento to Phyllis Cilento, 25 September 1931, Cilento Papers, UQFL44, Box 11, Item 21.
100 Raphael Cilento, 'Report of A Partial Survey of Aboriginal Natives of North Queensland,' p. 5, NAA: A1928, 4/5 SECTION 1.
101 J. W. Bleakley, 'The Aboriginals and Half-castes of Central Australia and North Australia,' *Commonwealth Parliamentary Papers*, 2, 1929, p. 1167.
102 'What is their Destiny?,' n.d., p. 2, Queensland State Archives [hereinafter QSA], Series 12355, Item 8887.
103 Bain Attwood, *Rights for Aborigines* (Sydney: Allen & Unwin, 2003), pp. 85–6.

As in New Guinea and Fiji, Cilento articulated such sympathies within assumptions of racial difference and the inferiority of Aboriginal people.[104] As Tim Rowse observes in the case of biologist and Northern Territory administrator W. Baldwin Spencer, understandings of Aboriginal inferiority often framed expressions of sympathy or the acknowledgement of dispossession and murder.[105] In an account of his search for cases of leprosy around Gordonvale, Cilento described the first man, who was armed with a knife, who emerged from the huts to confront him and his police companion:

> Truculent and sullen he asked sharply what we wanted and who we were and straightened himself up eye to eye with a fine show of defiance and bravado but below his lean and muscular ribs his telltale heart fluttered the skin like a captive bird. I felt a curious little pang of pity and remorse.[106]

In this representation, there is an echo of former nobility, brave yet fearful, wavering and defeated in the face of the white man. Cilento thus reiterated representations of Aboriginal people as broken and pitiable 'remnants' that cultural contact had left rudderless and vulnerable.[107] The animal simile is also telling. In *Triumph in the Tropics*, Cilento argued that Aboriginal people were 'creatures of impulse' who, when faced by something outside their experience, succumbed to 'shivering immobility'. These reactions were like those of 'feral jungle creatures'.[108] Elsewhere, he attributed Aboriginal distrust of European medicine to a 'blind and unreasoning fear of anything outside his experience'.[109] The evident suspicion of the man had more to do with the threat of removal to Palm Island, as Cilento acknowledged.[110] Yet, as in earlier settler-colonial discourse, Cilento's sympathy and sense of responsibility for Aboriginal people positioned them as an instinctive and superstitious people who could not withstand the impact of superior European settlers possessed of reason.

---

104 ibid., p. 85.

105 Rowse, *White Flour, White Power*, p. 15.

106 Raphael Cilento to Phyllis Cilento, 25 September 1931, Cilento Papers, UQFL44, Box 11, Item 21.

107 Rowse, *White Flour, White Power*, p. 32.

108 Raphael Cilento and Clem Lack, *Triumph in the Tropics: An Historical Sketch of Queensland* (Brisbane: Smith & Paterson, 1959), p. 179.

109 Cilento, 'Brief Review of Leprosy in Australia and its Dependencies,' p. 21.

110 Raphael Cilento to Phyllis Cilento, 25 September 1931, Cilento Papers, UQFL44, Box 11, Item 21.

By the time Cilento became more directly and extensively involved in Aboriginal health, the range of his experience and perspective encompassed a larger colonial field that included and related to Aboriginal people in Queensland, Torres Strait Islanders and New Guineans. In fact, as a Commonwealth medical officer, he often worked in parts of north Queensland that had been sites of colonial connections between the Pacific and Asia for many decades. While conducting an inspection tour of quarantine stations and hospitals in 1929, Cilento discovered a case of malaria in a boy from the village of Poid, on Banks (Moa) Island, in the Torres Strait. Writing to Phyllis, he said he was 'thrilled to the core'.[111] Cilento also examined Indigenous patients on Thursday Island with old skin lesions and learned of high rates of granuloma. He wrote to Phyllis:

I am interested in this place more than in any of the other stations—I suppose it is the native element and the native diseases that attract me. It is difficult to cast off the old love.

During his visit, the veteran pearler Reg Hocking took Cilento on a trip to the mouth of the Jardine River with his 'splendid Malay crew'. Cilento also gave a lecture at Thursday Island on 'Medical Problems of the Pacific', in which he spoke of 'invasions and migrations of the various peoples, their disease problems, the coming of the white man with the dread triad of war–pestilence–famine'.[112] Cilento thus recognised in the Torres Strait Islands points of contact, or a zone of overlap, between the Australian tropics and the Pacific and Asian colonies he had experienced.

As many scholars have noted, even after Queensland had annexed all the Torres Strait Islands by 1879, Thursday Island remained a node connecting goods, people and cultures that have continued to blur Australia's territorial, social and cultural boundaries.[113] Cilento hated this cosmopolitan hybridity, and described Thursday Island in much the same terms as he had used for Suva: 'The place reeks with all kinds of coloured and dis-coloured natives, halfcaste mixtures—"liquourice allsorts"!' Thursday Island was 'a very battered front door Australia presents to the world—wants repainting badly—the old colours have "run" badly!' Cilento dreamt of a time when the enforcement of racial segregation and

---

111 Raphael Cilento to Phyllis Cilento, 23 July 1929, Cilento Papers, UQFL44, Box 11, Item 21.
112 Raphael Cilento to Phyllis Cilento, 14 July 1929, Cilento Papers, UQFL44, Box 11, Item 21.
113 Paul Battersby, 'Mapping Australasia: Reflections on the Permeability of Australia's Northern Maritime Borders,' in Anna Shnukal, Guy Ramsey and Yuriko Nagata (eds), *Navigating Boundaries: The Asian Diaspora in Torres Strait* (Canberra: Pandanus Books, 2004), pp. 13–14.

sanitation regulations might transform Thursday Island into a 'second MIAMI, for Australia's FLORIDA'.[114] Cilento could obviously see the professional continuities between his work in New Guinea and Thursday Island, but he was ultimately hoping to replace the legacies of a much more open movement of people and culture around the region with an Australian colonial order that would reinforce racial segregation and control across northern Queensland, the Torres Strait and New Guinea.

The Queensland Government invited Cilento to conduct a series of clinical surveys of Aborigines in fringe camps, government settlements and missions in the early 1930s. Besides Cecil Cook's leprosy survey, there had been little systematic collection of broad and detailed medical information about Indigenous communities in Queensland. Cilento's first survey, from October to November 1932, included communities around Cardwell, Innisfail, Cairns and a number of other towns, as well as Mona Mona Mission and the government settlement on Palm Island. A second, hastily arranged survey in 1933 included Cooktown and Coen, the Yarrabah, Cape Bedford and Lockhart River missions and a number of fringe camps associated with other towns. As in the case of Cook's earlier leprosy survey, Cilento's methods and documentation expressed a claim to dominance of embodied subjects, especially on those occasions when he ordered Aboriginal people to line up and strip completely naked for clinical examination.[115] The surveys reflected a desire for synoptic knowledge of subject Indigenous populations that had marked Cilento's time in the Pacific Islands. Much of his effort in New Guinea had aimed to provide the colonial state with knowledge of the pathological status and movements of people who were deemed both a threat to white health and a useful source of labour.[116] The Queensland reports produced pages of data on individuals, including age, sex and clinical and social observations.

When Cilento submitted his first report to the Queensland Government, he attached a copy of his article on depopulation in the Pacific Islands from *The Medical Journal of Australia*.[117] Cilento had acquired a reputation for his expertise in the Pacific and the way it related to Aboriginal health. In a memo to the Queensland home secretary Edward Hanlon, Bleakley

---

114 Raphael Cilento to Phyllis Cilento, 14 July 1929, Cilento Papers, UQFL44, Box 11, Item 21.
115 Raphael Cilento to Phyllis Cilento, 28 October 1932, Cilento Papers, UQFL44, Box 11, Item 22. See also Cecil Cook to A. H. Baldwin, 15 February 1926, NAA: SP1061/1, 94/2.
116 See Chapters 2 and 3, this volume.
117 Cilento, 'The Value of Medical Services in Relation to Problems of Depopulation,' pp. 480–3.

noted that Cilento possessed both a 'keen interest in the aboriginal conditions' and 'wide experience in other lands with native races'.[118] *The Mail* reported in 1933:

> Probably no man, medical or otherwise, knows more about the habits and customs of the aborigines of Queensland and the nearer islands of the Pacific than does Dr. R. W. Cilento.[119]

Some historians have argued that colonial agents invented 'the native' as a universal non-European figure sharing childlike, fearful and unhygienic qualities, and lacking in the virtues of initiative and thrift.[120] Cilento certainly participated in this broad colonial discourse, believing that his knowledge of indigenous peoples, essentialised as the impulsive and dirty 'native', could then be brought to bear on Queensland.

The settler-colonial context of Queensland led to a structure of spatial management and social intervention that differed markedly from that in New Guinea, where villages were far from the centres of white settlement and power. As discussed in Chapter 2, segregation in New Guinea was deemed necessary only in the urban context of Rabaul, where the authorities nevertheless failed to implement longstanding plans for a compound for indentured labourers. Little attempt was made to intrude in indigenous culture, except where European sensibilities considered local cultural practices repugnant.[121] In contrast, colonisation in Queensland was a more thorough dispossession. In the early 1930s, Aboriginal fringe camps swelled with families after many men lost work in the pastoral industry during the economic depression.[122] Cilento's report echoed typical white anxieties about the threat posed by these communities: 'The mainland native resident in relation to the larger towns is considerably worse off and more a menace than any other.'[123] Despite the pervasive powers of the Aboriginals Protection Act, Cilento highlighted the 'minimal restrictions' placed on many mainland Indigenous populations, even as the proportion of Queensland Aborigines incarcerated in government settlements such as Barambah (Cherbourg) and Palm Island increased.[124]

---

118 J. W. Bleakley to E. M. Hanlon, Home Secretary, 10 April 1933, p. 7, QSA, Series 4356, Item 716952.

119 *The Mail*, [Brisbane], 22 October 1933, NAA: A1928, 4/5 SECTION 1.

120 Denoon et al., *The Cambridge History of the Pacific Islanders*, p. 262; Geoffrey Gray, *A Cautious Silence: The Politics of Australian Anthropology* (Canberra: Aboriginal Studies Press, 2007), pp. 34–5.

121 *The Official Yearbook of the Commonwealth*, p. 971.

122 Briscoe, *Counting, Health and Identity*, pp. 307–8.

123 Cilento, 'Report of A Partial Survey of Aboriginal Natives of North Queensland,' p. 2.

124 ibid., p. 1.

Queensland's system of government and mission settlements provided a ready structure for the medical segregation of Aboriginal people from the white community. Cilento's reports are peppered with recommendations for removals under the existing Aboriginals Protection Act, in which moral and medical concerns overlapped. In his first report, Cilento recommended that one 16-year-old girl, who suffered from gonorrhoea and was 'said to be promiscuous in her habits', be removed to Palm Island.[125] Such anxieties over venereal disease and the control of female Aboriginal sexuality had been central to debates over the isolation and employment of girls and young women in domestic service.[126] In his second report, he recommended that a number of individuals and even entire fringe camps be 'eliminated' and dispersed to different reserves. At Helensvale, he noted there were several girls whose 'associations are undesirable' and for whom removal to Yarrabah Mission would be beneficial. He recommended that the whole camp at Bloomfield be broken up and sent to different settlements.[127] Indigenous people did not accept these interventions passively. At Atherton, Cilento described a young woman from nearby Mareeba as:

> a flash half-caste gin in the employ of a local lawyer, who is apparently very jealous of her rights. It was only after waiting two hours that this young lady indignantly put in an appearance.[128]

Even in a document that functioned as part of the system of policing and control, Aboriginal people could thus force into view a defiant assertion of their rights and freedom from state interference. This incident shows that while Cilento's reports acknowledged a history of dispossession, he was ultimately less concerned with underlying causes of disease than with identification and removal of Aboriginal people and communities that he considered a threat to white settlers. Australian tropical hygiene was thus joined neatly to the existing moral norms and policing imperatives of the Queensland system of protection.

---

125 ibid., p. 6. Local protectors had already ordered the removal to Palm Island of some of the individuals whom Cilento had recommended when his report reached the chief protector; J. W. Bleakley to E. M. Hanlon, 10 April 1933, p. 1, QSA, Series 4356, Item 716952.
126 Parsons, 'Spaces of Disease,' pp. 188–9.
127 Cilento, 'Interim Report on Aboriginals,' pp. 38–9, NAA: A1928, 4/5 SECTION 1.
128 Cilento, 'Report of a Partial Survey of Aboriginal Natives of North Queensland, Appendix A,' p. 15, NAA: A1928, 4/5 SECTION 1.

It is nevertheless important to contextualise Cilento's participation in this system within his Pacific colonialism, including the way he framed problems of health in tropical Australia as products of Pacific and Asian connection and exchange. 'The health problems of tropical Australia and her dependencies', he wrote in 1931, 'corresponds very closely to the health problem of the Malay States'.[129] In fact, he would frequently compare northern Australian health issues with examples from the Pacific as well—not just as parallels, but also as connected places. Australian scholars, especially Regina Ganter, have argued for the interpretation of histories of Aboriginal protection in the context of north Queensland's communities of mixed Indigenous, Asian and Pacific people. A history of Asian and Pacific migration to north Queensland and intermarriage with Aboriginal and Torres Strait Islanders had produced communities that fell outside the categories of Aboriginal and 'half-caste' as defined in the 1897 Aboriginals Protection Act and were thus outside the authority of the bureaucracy. Without new legislation, Queensland protectors often stepped beyond their authority, which led in turn to repeated challenges from these people, families and communities.[130]

Cilento shared official concerns about miscegenation and the rising population of 'half-castes' of Asian and Pacific descent living around the towns of north Queensland.[131] In his 1932 report to the Queensland Government, he described the fringe dwellers around Cairns as 'an almost insoluble problem, which is further complicated by the presence of numbers of natives, half-castes, Malays, South Sea Islanders, and others, outside any jurisdiction, ignorant, dirty, and arrogant'.[132] Cilento added biomedical significance to the moral concerns about these communities, while likening them to places such as Rabaul and Suva. The 'intermediate coloured person' lived in:

> sordid surroundings indistinguishable from those of native communities in the Pacific Islands, and invariably centres for infection with hookworm disease, to which is added venereal disease, and occasionally filariasis and malaria.

---

129 Raphael Cilento, 'Review of the Position of Tropical Medicine and Hygiene in Australia,' *Report of the Federal Health Council of Australia*, 5, 1931, p. 33.
130 Ganter, 'Coloured People,' pp. 219–45. See also McGrath, 'The Golden Thread of Kinship,' pp. 37–58.
131 Haebich, *Broken Circles*, p. 134; Parsons, 'Spaces of Disease,' pp. 187–8.
132 Cilento, 'Report of A Partial Survey of Aboriginal Natives of North Queensland,' p. 7.

Cilento stated generally:

> It is emphatically my opinion that the coloured groups, both aboriginal
> and other, in the neighbourhood of towns, should be eliminated, either
> by absorption of the better elements into the general community, or by
> the transfer of the aboriginals to Aboriginal Settlements.[133]

Cilento noted that mixed-descent communities in Cairns with
Melanesian, Asian and Aboriginal heritage largely escaped state control
due to limitations in the existing legislation:

> Many of these cannot under any circumstances be said to live other than
> as natives, though they are housed within the town, and on some such
> quibble [are] regarded as independent citizens.[134]

Cilento's dismissal of their rights as a quibble reflects the authoritarian
paternalism that ran through his approach to government. His emphasis
on living conditions and habits in these passages suggests that precise
racial classification in law meant less to him than enlarging state authority
over all such people. Cilento, in other words, represented these groups as
dangerous because of their 'native' character—little different from people
under colonial governance in the Pacific—which speaks to the wider
colonial frame of reference with which he worked.

*The Aboriginals Protection and Restriction of the Sale of Opium Acts
Amendments Act 1934* widened the powers of the Act to encompass
people of Asian and Pacific descent who had previously been exempt from
its provisions. These included all 'half-castes' regardless of whether they
associated with Aborigines, as well as the children of Aboriginal and non-
white, non-Aboriginal people.[135] Concern about 'coloured' people who
lived free from the Act was longstanding. In 1915, William Lee-Bryce, the
local protector for the Somerset Aboriginal District, which included part
of Cape York Peninsula and the Torres Strait Islands, urged the government
to '[b]ring all South Sea, Manila, Malay, and other coloured men married
to, or associating with, aboriginals within the definition of aboriginal'.[136]
It is possible Cilento's arguments about health provided some new impetus

133 ibid., p. 3.
134 ibid., pp. 7–8.
135 Reynolds and May, 'Queensland,' p. 193; Henry Reynolds, *Nowhere People* (Melbourne: Viking, 2005), pp. 139–49.
136 Lee Bryce, 'Memorandum Relative to Administration of the Somerset Aboriginal District,' 13 December 1915, p. 13, QSA, Series 4356, Item 716946.

to legislation. Bleakley reported in 1934 that his department had known people of mixed Aboriginal and 'alien' descent carried infectious diseases but were powerless to control these people.[137] He also wrote to Hanlon about Cilento's first report, repeating concerns about the 'crossbreeds' of Aborigines, Pacific Islanders and Malays who had 'all the privileges of any white citizen'. Bleakley noted that, on occasion, his department had stretched the powers of the existing Act and advised: 'Any extension of this Department's powers to embrace the, at present, free coloured people … would require fresh legislation.'[138] Once that legislation passed, Bleakley could issue instructions to local police protectors to compile a list of the names and locations of people who would now fall under the Act. This would help, as Bleakley wrote, to 'facilitate the discovery and treatment of disease'.[139] Public health imperatives in Queensland thus played an influential role in redefining categories of Aboriginal and 'coloured' and extending state authority. Cilento saw these people and communities in terms of a broadly 'native' character, connected conceptually, socially and biologically to the populations of colonial spaces in the Pacific and South-East Asia.

Hygiene, governance and the cultivation of populations

Despite articulating a policy of segregation and the importance of protecting white communities from 'native' diseases, Cilento's interest in the 'Aboriginal problem' went beyond exile. In 1934, he left the CDH to take up the new office of Director-General of Health and Medical Services in Queensland. He had hoped to gain executive powers over all health matters, including medical services, nutrition and medical staffing on Aboriginal reserves.[140] Cilento had to settle, however, for the position of 'professional' head of the health division of the Department of Health and Home Affairs, with a largely advisory role.[141] This provided him with

---

137 J. W. Bleakley, 'Report of the Aboriginal Department for 1934,' *Queensland Parliamentary Papers*, 1, 1935, p. 976.
138 J. W. Bleakley to E. M. Hanlon, 10 April 1933, p. 3, QSA, Series 4356, Item 716952.
139 See Kidd, *The Way We Civilise*, pp. 108–10.
140 Raphael Cilento, 'Preliminary Report on the Re-organisation of the Home Department to Provide for the Separate Existence or Co-existence of a Ministry of Health,' 10 December 1934, pp. 3–15, QSA, Series 5263, Item 848707.
141 Ross Patrick, *A History of Health and Medicine in Queensland 1824–1960* (Brisbane: University of Queensland Press, 1987), p. 104.

opportunities to carry out inspections of the network of state reserves and mission stations. In this position, he often called for reforms to Aboriginal reserves that would place the cultivation of health, conceived in broad terms, at the centre of the governance of Indigenous people.

In seeking to understand the role of medicine and public health in shaping the repression and exploitation of Aboriginal people in Australian history, many scholars have looked to strategies of isolation employed in cases of leprosy and venereal disease. The continued use of strategies of isolation for Aborigines suffering from leprosy long after experts in the British Empire had abandoned such practices seemed to reflect deeper fears of racial contamination and hybridity pervading public health discourse in Australia.[142] Especially in the case of Queensland, the emphasis has thus been on the ways in which medical intervention in Australia focused on rigid segregation. The aim here is not to challenge but to complement this detailed and particular work with an analysis of some of the larger colonial logics involved. The nearly exclusive focus on institutional isolation of specific diseases misses the way knowledge of health could be ambivalent, even contradictory, over questions of race, culture, the state and the future. This is not to highlight discrepancies between central policy and its local implementation in the way Kidd and Parsons have done, but to emphasise the deeper tensions and contradictions of colonialism and medicine.[143]

Cilento's first inspections of Aboriginal government and mission settlements during his surveys in 1932 and 1933 prompted pointed criticism—of Palm Island, in particular.

He wrote:

> A visitor would be tempted to ask whether the system is not merely one for the convenience of the white population, and based on the acceptance of the extinction of the colored in due course.[144]

---

142 Saunders, 'Isolation,' pp. 168–81; Alison Bashford and Maria Nugent, 'Leprosy and the Management of Race, Sexuality and Nation in Tropical Australia,' in Alison Bashford and Claire Hooker (eds), *Contagion: Epidemics, History and Culture from Smallpox to Anthrax* (Sydney: Pluto Press, 2002), pp. 106–28; Briscoe, *Counting, Health and Identity*, pp. 315–18; Bashford, *Imperial Hygiene*, pp. 83–113; Parsons, 'Spaces of Disease,' Chs 6, 7; Parsons, 'Fantome Island Lock Hospital and Aboriginal Venereal Disease Sufferers 1928–45,' pp. 41–62.
143 Kidd, 'Regulating Bodies,' pp. 4–10; Parsons, 'Spaces of Disease,' p. 23.
144 Cilento, 'Report of A Partial Survey of Aboriginal Natives of North Queensland,' p. 4.

Without a clear plan, detention in a settlement became 'merely a period of imprisonment', doing nothing for the 'social and material benefit' of Aboriginal people.[145] For all the education and training received in Aboriginal institutions, the inmates were for the most part doomed to a life of tedium and inactivity:

> It is frequently objected that it is impossible to inspire the aboriginal to active and purposive work. I have no hesitation, after a long experience of many kinds of colored people, in directly denying this suggestion. There is a certain lethargy found in most native peoples living under stereotyped conditions, but this is almost invariably because the conditions are faulty.[146]

Again, Cilento appealed to the ideals and practices of colonial governance elsewhere. Indeed, his references to population decline, 'extinction' and the potential of state intervention clearly echoed his earlier commentary on New Guinea and Fiji. Australian authorities, he argued, could learn much about the management of Indigenous populations by recognising that they would respond to active government investment in their health and development.

This emphasis on investment in Aboriginal development reflected longstanding rhetoric about protection and contemporary international discourses of trusteeship. Meston and other protectors in Queensland and the Northern Territory had emphasised that reserves—through education, training and religious instruction—should seek the material and moral 'uplift' of Aboriginal people.[147] By the 1930s, however, calls for reform often placed Australian policy and practice in the context of international discourse on colonial trusteeship. A. P. Elkin, the Chair of Anthropology at the University of Sydney, published papers calling for the abandonment of 'negative' protection in favour of a 'positive policy of giving the natives new interests and training in stock-work, agriculture and various crafts' on the government and mission settlements.[148] Elkin suggested that New Guinea might serve as a model, not only for its administrative arrangements, but also because 'we are morally bound to aid the development of the primitive race in our own continent just as in

---

145 ibid., p. 20.
146 ibid., p. 20.
147 Meston, *Queensland Aboriginals*, pp. 26–7; Bryce, 'Memorandum Relative to Administration of the Somerset Aboriginal District,' pp. 9–11, QSA, Series 4356, Item 716946. See also McGregor, *Imagined Destinies*, pp. 60–74; Gray, *A Cautious Silence*, p. 37.
148 A. P. Elkin, 'A Policy for the Aborigines,' *The Morpeth Review*, 3(25), October 1933, p. 33.

New Guinea'.[149] At the same time, feminist advocates of protection, such as Mary Bennett and Edith Jones, used the League of Nations Covenant and the league's work against the trafficking of women and children as standards against which to assess Aboriginal policy across Australia.[150]

In contrast to the reformed protectionism of Elkin and others, an increasing population of mixed-descent people in this period prompted some to advocate policies of biological absorption into the white race. In the late 1920s, Cecil Cook, the Chief Protector of Aboriginals and Chief Medical Officer in the Northern Territory, and A. O. Neville, the chief protector in Western Australia, similarly envisioned programs in which states would facilitate the marriage of young mixed-descent women to white men. Drawing on an assumption that Aboriginal people were racially akin to Europeans, they hoped this process would gradually 'breed out' Aboriginality.[151] By 1937, when chief protectors and representatives of protection boards met at a conference on Aboriginal welfare, most states had adopted policies of biological absorption. For Cook and Neville, uncontrolled miscegenation represented, in the short term, a moral and racial deterioration that threatened public order and tropical development. The increasing half-caste population, Cook argued, could not adequately be employed in the underdeveloped north, unless white men were displaced and transformed into supervisors. This proposal conflicted fundamentally with the cherished ideal of complete white settlement. Denying work to such a growing population would, however, lead to resentment among mixed-descent men and 'racial conflict which may be serious'.[152] Violence and disorder thus seemed to be the inevitable results of racial mixing. Neville asked the conference rhetorically:

> What is to be the limit? Are we going to have a population of 1,000,000 blacks in the Commonwealth, or are we going to merge them into our white community and eventually forget that there ever were any Aborigines in Australia?[153]

---

149 ibid., p. 34.
150 Fiona Paisley, *Loving Protection? Australian Feminism and Aboriginal Women's Rights, 1919–1939* (Melbourne: Melbourne University Press, 2000), pp. 11–13; Attwood, *Rights for Aborigines*, pp. 87–93.
151 Commonwealth of Australia, *Aboriginal Welfare: Initial Conference of Commonwealth and State Aboriginal Authorities held at Canberra, 21st to 23rd April 1937* (Canberra: Government Printer, 1937), pp. 10–11. See also Anderson, *The Cultivation of Whiteness*, pp. 214–38; Reynolds, *Nowhere People*, pp. 167–9.
152 Commonwealth of Australia, *Aboriginal Welfare*, p. 13; Reynolds, *Nowhere People*, p. 166.
153 Commonwealth of Australia, *Aboriginal Welfare*, p. 12.

Neville and Cook thus framed their projects not as serving Indigenous welfare, but as clarifying racial boundaries that had been dangerously blurred.[154]

This policy had many critics, including Elkin, humanitarian societies and feminist activists such as Bennett.[155] In their view, Aborigines possessed a unique and valuable culture, had special rights as original owners of the land and ought to be protected against exploitation and cruelty, while being actively encouraged to adopt European religion and domesticity.[156] Queensland also stood out as a dissenting state government, but for different reasons. Bleakley argued that the high proportion of mixed-descent people with Asian or Pacific Islander heritage in Queensland precluded the possibility of any half-caste marriage scheme.[157] Bleakley had advised the Commonwealth in 1929 that while mixed-descent children should continue to be 'rescued' from camps and educated in reserves, they would be 'happier if raised to this civilization in company with the young aboriginals of his own generation'.[158] Bleakley thus advocated traditional policies of 'upliftment'. Governments should cultivate health, encourage village life and provide practical education and training through settlements, subsidised religious missions and a planned industrial colony for mixed-descent boys.[159]

While these officials and activists debated the future of Aboriginal people, Cilento sought to foreground an expansive conception of health within the 'native administration' of Queensland that owed much to his experience in New Guinea. The first task in Queensland, he wrote in his 1932 report, was 'cleaning up the aboriginals from the point of

---

154 Anderson, *The Cultivation of Whiteness*, p. 236; Patrick Wolfe, 'Settler Colonialism and the Elimination of the Native,' *Journal of Genocide Research*, 8(4), 2006, p. 388.

155 Paisley, *Loving Protection?*, pp. 26–7; Russell McGregor, 'Governance, Not Genocide: Aboriginal Assimilation in the Postwar Era,' in A. Dirk Moses (ed.), *Genocide and Settler Society: Frontier Violence and Stolen Indigenous Children in History* (New York: Berghahn Books, 2007), pp. 294–5.

156 Paisley, *Loving Protection?*, pp. 13–18, 83.

157 Reynolds, *Nowhere People*, pp. 140–1; Katherine Ellinghaus, *Taking Assimilation to Heart: Marriages of White Women and Indigenous Men in the United States and Australia* (Lincoln: University of Nebraska Press, 2006), pp. 205–6.

158 Bleakley, 'The Aboriginals and Half-castes of Central Australia and North Australia,' p. 1186. See also Tony Austin, *Never Trust a Government Man: Northern Territory Aboriginal Policy 1911–1939* (Darwin: Northern Territory University Press, 1997), pp. 299–300; Anderson, *The Cultivation of Whiteness*, p. 239. Cilento later told Cumpston that Bleakley resented Cecil Cook's dismissal of his recommendations; Raphael Cilento to J. H. L. Cumpston, 26 June 1933, NAA: A1928, 4/5 SECTION 1.

159 Commonwealth of Australia, *Aboriginal Welfare*, pp. 6–9.

view of health'.[160] Cilento had argued in New Guinea that indigenous sickness and population decline had roots in the depressing influence of malnutrition and disease. Health should be measured not by the presence or absence of infectious diseases alone, but also by the cumulative effects of diet and environment on fitness, energy and stamina. The wider problems of 'native administration'—including labour, productivity, education, village life and the general 'progress' of Indigenous people— thus depended on the improvement of health in a positive sense.

Cilento continued to privilege medicine in this way when making policy recommendations to the Queensland Government. Soon after taking up his position as Director-General of Health and Medical Services, Cilento advised his minister, Edward Hanlon:

> The aboriginal problem is almost entirely one of health. It has been proved, for example, that 90 per cent of the natives need health attention in some way or other, and the whole problem of their survival depends upon whether or not they can be made healthy and can be kept that way.[161]

In his 1932 report to Bleakley, Cilento had declared that, without a 'more liberal food issue' for Aboriginal people in Queensland, 'they are merely doomed to extinction, in a way that reflects little credit upon the community'.[162] A few years later, he told Hanlon that, with regard to settlements:

> [T]he idea behind the routine seemed to be that time would solve the problem by the elimination of the native race ... [and] an active policy to establish the native as a self-respecting social unit was the only thing that would save him from extinction.[163]

In appealing to 'extinction' and the responsibility to preserve Indigenous peoples, Cilento echoed old discourses of protection, but was also relating medical interventions in Queensland to problems of population decline and colonial obligations across the Pacific.

This continuity of colonial medical knowledge and practice is evident in the broad concept of health that Cilento brought to bear on Indigenous health in Queensland. After an inspection of Palm Island and the Yarrabah

---

160 Cilento, 'Report of a Partial Survey of Aboriginal Natives of North Queensland,' p. 4.
161 Raphael Cilento to E. M. Hanlon, 1 October 1935, p. 4, QSA, Series 12355, Item 8904.
162 Cilento, 'Report of A Partial Survey of Aboriginal Natives of North Queensland,' p. 3.
163 Cilento, 'Visit of Inspection to Palm Island, Yarrabah, and Monamona Aboriginal Settlements,' February–March 1937, p. 11, QSA, Series 4356, Item 717183.

and Mona Mona missions in 1937, Cilento reported to Hanlon that 'work among natives is to a very great extent a medical problem, that wide term including all aspects of welfare from diet to working hours and working conditions'.[164] Diet remained the most important of these social factors. In 1932, Cilento had reported to Bleakley:

> It has been my experience in New Guinea and elsewhere that an absence of protein in an assimilable form is marked by a tendency to chest and bowel troubles, skin diseases, and a very distinct loss of energy and initiative.[165]

Former inmates of Palm Island and Cherbourg have testified that persistently inadequate and poor-quality food at Aboriginal settlements— consisting of flour, sugar, tea and poor-quality cuts of meat or bones— aggravated disease and left children constantly hungry.[166] After his 1937 inspection, Cilento expressed dismay at the inadequate quantity and quality of the rations provided at the settlements and the lack of interest and expertise in agriculture on Palm Island. 'The native problem in Queensland is purely a medical problem', he advised, 'and the medical side includes the question of feeding'.[167] This included the expert selection of crops, provision of cultivation areas and cooking.[168] A year later, he again told Hanlon:

> The medical problem of the aboriginal is at present his only problem. No measure of improvement is of any value if he is to die of malnutrition, and any plan for his future can only begin once his health is stabilised.[169]

Although he and Cilento shared only limited correspondence, Elkin expressed the same view in 1944: '[P]eople need to feel fit and strong before they can take a positive and active interest in cultural advance and change, and in new forms of work and thought.'[170] A healthy diet, based on meat and a range of vitamin-rich foods, was for Cilento the basis of both health and the larger success of efforts to shape the future of Indigenous people.

---

164 Raphael Cilento to E. M. Hanlon, 23 March 1937, QSA, Series 4356, Item 717183.
165 Cilento, 'Report of a Partial Survey of Aboriginal Natives of North Queensland,' p. 9.
166 Marnie Kennedy, *Born a Half-caste* (Canberra: Australian Institute of Aboriginal Studies, 1985), p. 16; Blake, *A Dumping Ground*, pp. 105–10; Parsons, 'Spaces of Disease,' p. 228.
167 Cilento, 'Visit of Inspection to Palm Island, Yarrabah, and Monamona Aboriginal Settlements,' p. 3.
168 ibid., p. 3.
169 Raphael Cilento to E. M. Hanlon, 10 October 1938, QSA, Series 505, Item 506596.
170 A. P. Elkin, *Citizenship for the Aborigines: A National Aboriginal Policy* (Sydney: Australasian Publishing Co., 1944), p. 23.

Cilento frequently recommended increasing the amount of meat, fresh vegetables, milk and eggs in the rations supplied at settlements and mission stations, to increase the intake of vitamins and minerals.[171] Administrative inertia and competing ideologies, however, led to persistent failure in making such improvements. Cilento reported deficiencies in the rations provided to Aboriginal people in his 1932 report, but Bleakley responded by stressing that 'the aim has been to avoid pauperisation and only supplement the efforts of the inmate to raise his home consumption needs'.[172] Cilento made further recommendations as the new Director-General of Health and Medical Services in 1934. Bleakley's priority, however, was to minimise costs and he made little effort to implement changes.[173]

In 1937, Cilento reported that the diet at Mona Mona Mission still fell far short of the minimum requirements set down by the League of Nations' International Committee on Nutrition.[174] At Yarrabah Mission, rations were even more inadequate and were the root of many diseases. The diet of flour, tea and sugar was 'entirely lacking in vitamin of any kind whatever' and would endanger 'healthy development'.[175] Inmates on Palm Island complained directly to Cilento about the old and 'withered' vegetables supplied to them.[176] A. Jefferis Turner, the Queensland Director of Infant Welfare, and the American nutrition specialist Weston Price joined Cilento in condemning the handling of settlement nutrition.[177] Rations at Mona Mona were still inadequate in 1946, demonstrating Cilento's lack of effective influence on the administration of reserves.[178] Yet his emphasis on physical development demonstrates that Cilento saw state intervention as seeking the cultivation of health in a positive sense, rather than the mere removal of dangerous infectious diseases. Settlements, in his

---

171 Cilento, 'Visit of Inspection,' p. 24.
172 J. W. Bleakley to E. M. Hanlon, 10 April 1933, QSA, Series 4356, Item 716952, p. 5.
173 J. W. Bleakley to Herberton Protector, 18 July 1934, QSA, Series 8767, Item 282688. See also Kidd, *The Way We Civilise*, p. 112.
174 Cilento, 'Visit of Inspection,' p. 24.
175 ibid., p. 14.
176 ibid., pp. 2–3.
177 Blake, *A Dumping Ground*, pp. 112–13. Ironically, Bleakley referred to dietary deficiencies as an instance of neglect in J. W. Bleakley, *The Aborigines of Australia: Their History, Their Habits, Their Assimilation* (Brisbane: The Jacaranda Press, 1961), pp. 179–80.
178 Director of Native Affairs to Superintendent, Mona Mona Mission, 10 January 1946, QSA, Series 505, Item 506596.

view, were supposed to be spaces for the active encouragement of health, with trained and qualified medical staff following modern international standards and practices.

For Cilento, this meant an ambitious program of paternalistic control involving reorganisation of the entire settlement network as a system for sorting and treating sickness in the whole Aboriginal population in Queensland. During his 1932 survey, Cilento suggested that, given high rates of gonorrhoea on Palm Island, where the disease was unsatisfactorily treated, the government should institute a program in which 'all natives might be worked through Fantome [Island] + back to Gt Palm (except incurables) + the permanent station at Gt. Palm kept absolutely clean'.[179] In his first report that year, he went into further detail, writing that it was vital first to separate the 'medically fit from the unfit'. This would be accomplished by the 'transfer through the Palm Islands Settlement of all available aboriginal natives by a deliberate policy of collecting the natives from locality after locality'. A grading scheme, using index cards, would sort cases into the healthy, the young and curable, the acute but curable and various categories of incurable. Those who were healthy or cured would be moved from Fantome Island to Palm Island or mainland settlements, where they would continue with their education and training in trades or domestic skills:

> If it be suggested that this converts Palm Island into no more than a clearing station for the health of natives, it may be pointed out that, in effect, the care of natives is essentially a matter of constant medical supervision—a supervision that goes all the way from actual disease control to the control of adequate food supplies and suitable working conditions, and methods of recreation and educational improvement.[180]

The scheme Cilento outlined thus made the whole Palm Island group a medical complex with the purpose of collecting, categorising and sorting the Aboriginal population of Queensland.

---

179 Raphael Cilento to J. W. Bleakley, 31 October 1932, Cilento Papers, UQFL44, Box 11, Item 21.
180 Cilento, 'Report of A Partial Survey of Aboriginal Natives of North Queensland,' pp. 21–2.

For many Aboriginal people, this process meant exile. Cilento, Cook, Bleakley and other officials across Australia regarded leprosy and venereal disease in Aboriginal people—in light of their assumptions about Indigenous culture and sexuality—as requiring permanent isolation from the white community. In the nineteenth century, leprosy had increased in prevalence in the tropical colonial world, where public health officials reframed it as a disease of non-European peoples.[181] As white doctors increasingly associated the disease with the supposed moral and physical inferiority of other races, transmission of the disease from 'coloured' to white communities came to represent more than mere pathological communication. In Australia, a narrative of transmission from Chinese men, through Aboriginal women to white men implied the contamination of white manhood with the racial matter of others.[182] Compulsory isolation re-emerged in the 1860s as leprosy marked colonised people as an unclean and immoral population threatening the degeneration of Europeans in the tropics.[183] By the 1920s, however, many experts— particularly Sir Leonard Rogers, whose work in Calcutta had made him an internationally recognised authority—argued that strict isolation had failed to control the disease. Loosening provisions for segregation would reduce fear of separation from family and thus encourage sufferers to present themselves. This would facilitate early detection when the disease could be treated more effectively and make regular examination of contacts easier.[184]

Australian authorities respectfully rejected Rogers' specific criticisms of their insistence on maintaining strict segregation of all leprosy patients. The hygiene habits of Aboriginal people and the practical difficulties of surveillance of suspected contacts among those communities, they argued, made compulsory isolation absolutely necessary. In a paper presented to the 1934 meeting of the Federal Health Council, Cilento stated that the problem of tracing contacts among people whose exact kinship relations were difficult to ascertain and who feared European medicine 'renders it utterly impossible to contemplate any system other than segregation'

---

181 Gussow, *Leprosy, Racism, and Public Health*, pp. 19–20; Bashford, *Imperial Hygiene*, p. 83.
182 Bashford, *Imperial Hygiene*, p. 110.
183 Rod Edmond, *Leprosy and Empire: A Medical and Cultural History* (Cambridge: Cambridge University Press, 2006), Ch. 4. See also Deacon, 'Racism and Medical Science in South Africa's Cape Colony,' p. 204; Bashford, *Imperial Hygiene*, p. 88.
184 Leonard Rogers to Andrew Balfour, 4 April 1926, Papers of Sir Leonard Rogers [hereinafter Rogers Papers], PP/ROG/C.13/725, Wellcome Library, London; Leonard Rogers to P. E. Deane, 29 April 1925, Rogers Papers, PP/ROG/C.13/534; Bashford, *Imperial Hygiene*, pp. 89–90.

for Aboriginal cases.[185] In the mid-1920s, Cook reported that '[t]he complete neglect of hygiene in a tribal camp and the filthy habits of the natives themselves', as well as the 'practice of sleeping three or more together between fires', had predisposed Aboriginal people to inherit the disease from equally unhygienic Chinese migrants.[186] Bleakley similarly commented on the 'ignorance of the simplest rules of health' among Aboriginal communities.[187] Officials thus represented Aboriginal people as incapable of the kind of hygienic conduct that a modern white citizenry might be taught to practice outside institutions.

Most cases of leprosy in Queensland—including white, Chinese and Aboriginal patients—were segregated on Peel Island between 1907 and 1940. Officials had established racial segregation on Peel Island alongside gender segregation of the European inmates.[188] Towards the end of the 1930s, however, as doctors on Palm Island were faced with an increasing number of leprosy patients and more cases emerged at Mona Mona Mission, Cilento and Palm Island medical staff began to agitate for more thorough racial separation.[189] Since 1937, Cilento had overseen ongoing investigation of leprosy in Queensland with funding from the National Health and Medical Research Council (NHMRC). Part of this funding had been put aside to finance construction of a separate Aboriginal leprosarium on Fantome Island in the Palm Island group.[190] The Aboriginal inmates of Peel Island were transferred to the new leprosarium in 1940, when construction was only partially complete and supplies of food and water remained a serious problem.[191] Visiting Peel Island in 1931, Cilento felt both pity and revulsion for those white inmates who faced a 'blank parade of endless days'.[192] Yet his disgust was hard to suppress: 'The long

---

185 Cilento, 'Brief Review of Leprosy in Australia and its Dependencies,' p. 21.

186 Cook, *The Epidemiology of Leprosy in Australia*, pp. 17–18. See also Bashford, *Imperial Hygiene*, p. 100; Parsons, 'Spaces of Disease,' p. 331.

187 Bleakley, 'The Aboriginals and Half-castes of Central Australia and North Australia,' p. 1169.

188 Parsons, 'Spaces of Disease,' pp. 270–1. On racial segregation in institutions, see Harriet Deacon, 'Racial Segregation and Medical Discourse in Nineteenth-century Cape Town,' *Journal of Southern African Studies*, 22(2), 1996, pp. 287–308.

189 J. W. Bleakley to Under-Secretary, Department of Health and Home Affairs, 30 September 1938, QSA, Series 4356, Item 717182; Geoffrey Courtney to J. W. Bleakley, 6 January 1939, QSA, Series 4356, Item 717182; Raphael Cilento to Under-Secretary, 19 July 1938, p. 2, QSA, Series 8400, Item 279841.

190 Raphael Cilento to J. H. L. Cumpston, 28 October 1938, NAA: A1928, 690/8/106; *Report of the National Health and Medical Research Council*, 5th Session (Canberra: Government Printer, 1938), p. 6.

191 D. W. Johnson to Raphael Cilento, 26 March 1940, QSA, Series 4356, Item 717220. See Parsons, 'Spaces of Disease,' p. 343.

192 Raphael Cilento to Phyllis Cilento, 31 August 1931, Cilento Papers, UQFL44, Box 11, Item 21.

hours in intimate contact with them … gradually produced a revulsion of feeling that made me anxious to leave the home of misery.'[193] Cilento, however, never reserved any such sympathy for Aboriginal people with the disease:

> I should add that <u>cure</u> is hardly to be expected amongst native lepers: the disease is only arrested in any case, and to return to their homes in such circumstances merely means the revival of the disease, and the possibilities of greater spread. It is anticipated, therefore, that most natives admitted to Fantome as proven lepers will remain there till they die.[194]

The control of leprosy, as a chronic disease for which there was no truly effective cure, depended on close surveillance and the hygienic discipline of dutiful citizens. These capacities and expectations of the state were precisely what officials felt were unattainable in light of the ways in which they constructed Indigenous people. Of course, when Aboriginal people hid from police and doctors, they were fleeing from those who had time and again broken up and incarcerated families.[195] As mentioned above, local protectors in Queensland were also local police. Cilento himself orchestrated raids on Aboriginal communities and recommended many individuals for removal to institutions. In evading protectors and health officials, Indigenous people were practising a form of resistance to a carceral regime. For Australian officials such as Cilento, this non-cooperation instead demonstrated an inability to participate in the progressive work of the state. His representations of Aboriginal people as both unhygienic and incapable of modern citizenship combined to entrench segregation as the only policy he could contemplate for controlling leprosy.[196]

Despite this emphasis on medical policing and segregation, some of Cilento's reports express a contradictory range of ideas about assimilation and segregation. Like Bleakley, Cilento rejected Cook's plan to 'eliminate' Aboriginal people through biological absorption. Visiting the Northern Territory and western Queensland in 1933, he dismissed the project as hopeless given the calibre of the white men in the area—'the most useless, feckless + and helpless of people'.[197] It was far better for young

193 ibid.
194 Raphael Cilento to Under-Secretary, Department of Health and Home Affairs, 2 September 1941, QSA, Series 12355, Item 8883. Cilento's emphasis.
195 Saunders, 'Isolation,' p. 171; Parsons, 'Spaces of Disease,' p. 328.
196 Bashford and Nugent, 'Leprosy and the Management of Race, Sexuality and Nation,' p. 114.
197 Raphael Cilento, Diary: Northern Territory/Cape York Peninsula Survey, 29 July 1933, Cilento Papers, UQFL44, Box 11, Item 23.

Aboriginal women to 'get back into [the] tribe' than marry such physically degraded and morally dissolute white men.[198] Instead, Cilento found himself agreeing with Bleakley on the need for a 'temporary programme of paternalism' within the system of reserves.[199] Meg Parsons has examined how Bleakley sought to turn Cherbourg into a model reforming settlement, in which a regimen of instruction and training in hygiene and domesticity might produce responsible mothers, workers and nuclear families. Queensland authorities assumed the need for strict disciplinary and punitive measures, yet poor living conditions, impoverished rations and inadequate education laid bare the hollowness of this policy.[200]

Throughout the 1930s, Cilento invoked similar policy ideas as a criticism of Bleakley's administration, yet they rang just as hollow. His inspection reports are peppered with comments about discipline, training and domesticity—all of which he reimagined as the domain of medical experts. He praised the sewing work of the women and girls on Palm Island, although he lamented that so little was done.[201] Cilento concurred with an earlier report on Mona Mona that praised the superintendent, the Seventh-Day Adventist missionary Reverend L. A. Borgas: 'The native population, particularly the halfcaste women display keen interest in their home life which reflects credit on the Mission for the training that has been given the girls.'[202] Cilento himself praised the housing of young married couples at Mona Mona 'in what is actually the nucleus of a native town'.[203] Training imparted discipline: 'It is useless to talk about the girls being troublesome so long as so little sewing is done.'[204] On Palm Island, he criticised an alleged ban on tennis as 'a reactionary attitude suggesting that the settlements are penitentiaries rather than areas for the development and social education of a backward race of unfortunate people'.[205] Settlements and missions were, for Cilento, spaces that ought to facilitate the paternal remaking of Indigenous people into villagers. His emphasis on diet and hygiene reform thus underscores the simultaneously racist and technocratic nature of his approach.

---

198 ibid.
199 Cilento, 'Report of a Partial Survey of Aboriginal Natives of North Queensland,' p. 2.
200 Parsons, 'Spaces of Disease,' Ch. 5.
201 Cilento, 'Visit of Inspection,' p. 5.
202 ibid., p. 22.
203 Cilento, 'Report of a Partial Survey of Aboriginal Natives of North Queensland,' p. 8.
204 Cilento, 'Visit of Inspection,' p. 5.
205 ibid., p. 4.

There were strong continuities here between colonial visions in New Guinea and in Queensland. As Anderson has suggested, there are distinct parallels in the way Cilento sought to make Indigenous people productive workers in both colonial settings.[206] In his 1932 report to Bleakley, Cilento wrote positively on the work of the settlements, which promised hope for the Aborigine as 'an individual, and as an economic asset to Australia'.[207] A very deliberate attempt, he argued, should be made at 'assimilating these tribes into the population as useful and economic units'.[208] He advised that the settlements adopt a system of index cards used in New Guinea, which would designate inmates according to health, age and education. These categories included young and healthy (white A1 card); healthy but uneducated and middle aged (A2 card); young, healthy and previously under treatment (yellow B1 card); acutely diseased but curable (red C1 card); young, chronic and incurable (red C2 card); and a few others.[209] Cilento went so far as to 'suggest that the whole aboriginal problem, from the point of view of Settlements, be regarded as an indenture system, with the State as protector'.[210] By the 1920s, international consensus regarded systems of indentured labour as morally unacceptable, especially in their most migratory forms, yet Australia remained committed to them as essential to both economic development and Indigenous improvement.[211] The project of cultivating the health of the Aboriginal population thus sought the creation of an expanded pool of labour that was vital to the economic development of the tropics, while at the same time satisfying, from an Australian point of view, the moral demand for the uplift of Indigenous people that ran through the notion of imperial trusteeship.

Cilento's proposals for Aboriginal policy could be deeply ambiguous and contradictory. Despite a reputation for his commitment to segregation and medical policing, he at times spoke confidently of the possibility of 'assimilation'.[212] The settler-colonial context of Queensland, where tropical development and the fulfilment of the White Australia Policy were paramount, suggested to Cilento the desirability of an assimilation

---

206 Anderson, *The Cultivation of Whiteness*, pp. 146–7.
207 Cilento, 'Report of a Partial Survey of Aboriginal Natives of North Queensland,' p. 22.
208 ibid., p. 4.
209 ibid., p. 21.
210 ibid., p. 22.
211 See Chapter Three, this volume.
212 Anderson, *The Cultivation of Whiteness*, p. 213; Briscoe, *Counting, Health and Identity*, p. 333.

project that veered between the socioeconomic and the biological. Aboriginal people would respond to paternalism at first, Cilento argued, but in the future:

> that moiety of the natives able to measure up to the accepted economic standards of the day would reach their adequate stature of development, with subsequent return to life among the white community.[213]

At one point, he wrote that the ultimate hope of Aboriginal people in settlements should be 'freedom from supervision, with transfer back to the mainland, and elimination by absorption into the general body of the white race'.[214] The emphasis on 'elimination' and 'absorption' demonstrates a tension in Cilento's thought about the future of Indigenous people. Elsewhere, he suggested a socioeconomic version of assimilation, writing of Aborigines' future 'social absorption into pursuits of value to the country'.[215] In some ways, Cilento's plan resembled that of Elkin, who in 1944 suggested that reserves and settlements should be conceived of as 'preparation bases', readying Aboriginal people for social and economic assimilation.[216]

Cilento shared little of Elkin's ostensible humanitarianism or respect for Aboriginal custom and identity. In the Pacific Islands, anthropologists tended to attribute population decline to cultural loss and crisis.[217] In arguing that malnutrition and disease were far more significant in causing high levels of mortality, infertility and infanticide, Cilento turned this anthropological account on its head. Indeed, he claimed, there was no correlation between the collapse of Indigenous customs and population decline.[218] In Queensland, Cilento similarly distinguished between culture and bodies at the expense of Indigenous social relations, custom and language. Like many other commentators, Cilento represented Aboriginal people as 'remnants'—a broken people who had experienced profound cultural loss.[219] In place of the preservation of culture, Cilento argued for a focus on the deliberate transformation of Aboriginal people:

---

213 Cilento, 'Report of a Partial Survey of Aboriginal Natives of North Queensland,' p. 22.
214 ibid., p. 21.
215 Cilento, 'Interim Report on Aboriginals,' p. 65.
216 Elkin, *Citizenship for the Aborigines*, pp. 37–8.
217 Rivers, 'The Psychological Factor,' pp. 84–114; Pitt-Rivers, *The Clash of Cultures*, pp. 69–70; Roberts, *Population Problems of the Pacific*, pp. 65–75.
218 See Chapter 2, this volume.
219 Rowse, *White Flour, White Power*, p. 32; Gray, *A Cautious Silence*, p. 32.

> It must be recognised that for all practical purposes natives in contact with whites have already lost all semblance of their original social organisation or folk-lore, and must be treated not as museum pieces, but as an element in the community which will have whatever future the white race deliberately chooses to give it. [220]

The only alternative to the passive permission of extinction was to intervene 'deliberately and intimately, to superimpose upon his forgotten usages the social and industrial requirements that his contact with white men makes inevitable'.[221] The dangers of breaking down cultures were 'hypothetical', functioning as excuses for a 'laissez faire' attitude and 'tacit acceptance' of inevitable extinction.[222] It was the task of the state, in other words, to actively transform Aboriginal people so as to adapt them to the economic and social realities of cultural contact and allow them to participate in 'progressive life'.[223]

Cilento's early enthusiasm for such 'progressive' reform of Indigenous people gave way in later years to pessimism. The settlements were strained and Cilento warned of the lack of an 'outlet for the talents and energies that are being built up in the native race under white tuition'.[224] While Cook, Neville, J. B. Cleland and other authorities at the Canberra welfare conference resolved that Aboriginal policy should work towards biological absorption, Cilento suggested segregation on a large scale through the creation of a 'native state':

> The development scheme put forward some years ago by which it was proposed that a native state should be built up on the Torres Straits, Cape York Peninsula, Palm Island axis, with gradual centralisation towards this axis of true native stocks, and gradual dispersal from it of near white stocks, is the only solution that is a progressive one.[225]

Although these decisions were beyond his purview, Cilento reported that his 'experience in New Guinea and Papua' had convinced him that such a territory for a 'native community' was the only way to 'give aboriginal policy a definite and attainable purpose in this State'.[226] In an

220 Cilento, 'Interim Report on Aboriginals,' p. 65.
221 ibid., p. 65.
222 ibid., p. 66.
223 ibid., p. 66. This resonated with Elkin's language, which suggested the policy of protection on inviolable reserves savoured 'much of "laissez faire"'. See Elkin, 'A Policy for the Aborigines,' p. 29.
224 Cilento, 'Visit of Inspection,' p. 25.
225 ibid., p. 25.
226 Raphael Cilento to E. M. Hanlon, 23 March 1937, QSA, Series 4356, Item 717183.

earlier proposal for a model Aboriginal state, the Aborigines Protection League in South Australia had called for the recognition of sovereignty and respect for Indigenous self-determination.[227] As Bain Attwood has argued, the white Australian humanitarians who made proposals of this kind were wedded to an anthropological view of Aborigines as primitive and deserving of special rights to inviolable reserves and special courts.[228]

Cilento's proposal was premised less on rights and culture than on racial difference and the imperatives of hygiene and social order. If he had once hoped to transform Queensland's settlements into model villages preparing Aboriginal people for assimilation, he now suggested the creation of a separate territory for them in north Queensland:

> [T]here appears no possibility of solving the native problem in a way that will be to the advantage of the native, and at the same time, will prevent social conflict between white labourers and coloured.[229]

When some of the 'better class natives' on Palm Island brought a written complaint to Cilento regarding the failure of the minister to act on a promised 'native council', he reported a 'dangerous temper among many of the natives'.[230] This resentment at the lack of good faith on the part of the minister was understandable, Cilento argued, yet it also meant that disillusioned Indigenous leaders might now fail to correct growing 'immorality, drunkenness, stealing and gambling'.[231] Cilento fundamentally assumed the need for colonial supervision of Aboriginal people, with his confidence about 'uplift' giving way to complete isolation of Indigenous populations from white society.

In many ways, Cilento's visions of education, independence and racial progress for Indigenous people were facile dreams that evaded the real issues of dispossession, racism and poverty. Medicine and public health were in many respects subordinate to the broader goal of segregating Aboriginal people. Cilento himself had few real administrative responsibilities and was busy with reforming mainstream public health services that excluded Aboriginal people.[232] He had no real clout when

---

227 Kevin Blackburn, 'White Agitation for an Aboriginal State in Australia (1925–1929),' *Australian Journal of Politics and History*, 45(2), 1999, pp. 161–2; Attwood, *Rights for Aborigines*, p. 65.
228 Attwood, *Rights for Aborigines*, p. 100.
229 Cilento, 'Visit of Inspection,' p. 25.
230 ibid., p. 10.
231 ibid., pp. 7–10. See also Watson, 'Becoming Bwgcolman,' pp. 225–6.
232 Parsons, 'Spaces of Disease,' p. 112.

it came to wider Aboriginal policy and the changes he wanted were not radical. Incarceration in settlements—where discipline was brutal, wages were stolen and rights were denied—remained the norm into the 1970s.[233] Meg Parsons has shown that the policy rhetoric of the government belied the reality of settlement life. Poor housing undermined the public aim of cultivating healthy individuals adjusted to white domestic and economic life.[234] The continued use of Aboriginal labour outside reserves made a mockery of the notion of 'protection', while there were several instances of corruption among white staff who skimmed off wages before they went into trust accounts.[235] Morbidity and mortality on reserves also remained high, while the incompetence of administration, diagnosis and treatment at the Aboriginal medical institutions on Fantome Island led to their complete failure to isolate or ameliorate the diseases they were meant to control. Rather than fulfilling government fantasies of precise isolation, these institutions incarcerated indiscriminately.[236]

The aim of this chapter has been to explore the broader colonial logics and strategies of medical interventions against Indigenous people in Queensland. While it is important to remain attuned to the local specificities of place and people and to avoid conflating policy and the vagaries of practice, as Parsons has stressed, this should not preclude a wider examination of colonial cultures and technologies of rule.[237] In his engagement with Indigenous health, Cilento overlaid a commitment to segregation with a shifting rhetoric about progress and uplift that drew heavily from the ideological and epistemological frameworks that had shaped his work in New Guinea. In this sense, Cilento's contributions reflected his colonial sensibilities in two ways. On one level, he sought to implement general objectives and strategies of 'native' health and administration in Queensland of the kind that could be transposed between colonial sites while still adjusting to different political and social contexts. Cilento of course recognised the fundamental distinction between New Guinea and the settler-colonial context of Queensland. Yet his approach

---

233 Note the brutal crackdown against the 1957 strike on Palm Island. Watson, 'Becoming Bwgcolman,' pp. 15–16; Kidd, *The Way We Civilise*, pp. 245–8.
234 Parsons, 'Spaces of Disease,' pp. 211–12.
235 ibid., p. 51. Public service inspectors D. W. Johnson and C. D. O'Brien reported that white staff at Palm Island had defrauded Aboriginal inmates of wages: 'Report No. 1—On the Sub-Department of Native Affairs and in Particular the Administration of the Palm Island Settlement and of the Lock Hospital and Lazaret at Fantome Island,' 9 December 1941, pp. 4–6, QSA, Series 12355, Item 8883.
236 See Parsons, 'Spaces of Disease,' Chs 6–7; Parsons, 'Fantome Island Lock Hospital,' pp. 41–62.
237 Parsons, 'Spaces of Disease,' pp. 28–31.

to Indigenous health in Queensland consciously drew on his experience in New Guinea and the increasingly international corpus of knowledge of colonial medicine. In particular, the aspiration to selectively classify, treat and cultivate efficient workers from among indigenous populations was common to Cilento's work in New Guinea and Queensland. On another level, Cilento framed the state's role in indigenous health in the Australian tropics, the Torres Strait Islands and New Guinea as part of the same domain of colonial responsibility.

Indigenous health in the colonial spaces of New Guinea, Malaya, Queensland and the Torres Strait was where Cilento worked out and elaborated some of the shared objectives, logics and strategies of public health. Parsons has argued that Aboriginal health in Queensland was merely a 'sideline' interest for Cilento.[238] Yet it is important to see his efforts in Indigenous health and mainstream public health as part of a singular colonial quest for efficiency. These diverse spaces of colonial government were where Cilento developed concepts of health that were social and holistic, constructed populations through the expansion of official surveillance, sought to orient public health to social reform and economic development and promoted health as the domain and guiding principle of the work of the modern state. The next chapter will show that, in Cilento's contributions to public health reform in Australia, colonial medicine provided important knowledge and practice, while colonial discourse and imperial visions of world order were also important in constructing the populations that public health sought to shape and improve.

---

238 ibid., p. 112.

5

'Blueprint for the Health of a Nation': Cultivating the mind and body of the race, 1929–1945

One of the difficulties in a democracy is the fact that it is impossible to institute reforms by order, however well recognised the necessity for reform may be. The one thing in which the Australian worker will not tolerate dictation is in the matter of his breakfast table.

— Raphael Cilento, 1936[1]

In 1937, Raphael Cilento, now a Knight Bachelor and the Director-General of Health and Medical Services for the State of Queensland, wrote a short review of Archibald Joseph Cronin's novel *The Citadel*, which told the story of a young doctor starting his life as a practitioner in a Welsh mining town.[2] In his review, Cilento noted that Cronin's own bitter experience of academia and private practice had shaped the novel's negative portrayal of the medical profession. Quoting the observation of Henry E. Sigerist, the prominent Johns Hopkins University historian of medicine, that society determines the influence and status of doctors, Cilento added the assertion that 'every degraded or venal type in medicine, as elsewhere, answers a direct demand from the public, and can only exist while it answers that direct demand'. Cilento was a vocal advocate of social medicine and state coordination of medical practice in Australia throughout the 1930s and 1940s, and drew deeply on the work of European and American

---

1   Raphael Cilento to F. Kemp, 4 September 1936, QSA, Series 14769, Item 86221.
2   Archibald J. Cronin, *The Citadel* (London: Victor Gollancz, 1939).

reformers. His professional elitism was akin to that of social hygienists of the late nineteenth century who saw doctors as leaders, especially when they dedicated themselves to public health. Samuel Johnson had it right, Cilento suggested, when he observed 'the utterly undeserving nature of the public, and its incapacity to appreciate work done in its interests, or done as the best expression of the personality of the doctor'. Cronin therefore, in subjecting the profession to accusations of greed and self-interest, while expressing half-truths about private practice, was playing to a 'vulgar trait' inherent to the 'great public'.[3]

As the Director-General of Health and Medical Services in Queensland from 1934 to 1945, Cilento was at the heart of the politics of health reform in Australia. Like other Australian doctors and public health officials—such as J. H. L. Cumpston, the Director-General of the Commonwealth Department of Health (CDH), and E. Sydney Morris, the Director-General of Public Health in New South Wales—he was part of an international movement to enlarge the role of the state in providing a complete health service to all members of the community. He drew on American, British and European debates about the relationship between the state, the medical profession and the community. Public health officials increasingly identified housing, diet, working conditions and forms of leisure as determinants of disease, of poor physical development among children and of the health of workers. The state should address these through teaching and publicity, by opening up access to and controlling medical services and by using baby clinics, home visits, school health and workplace inspections to enable expert surveillance of the life of individuals from birth to adulthood. A desire to improve populations as a productive citizenry able to defend the nation was often at the heart of these social medical discourses. As Gillespie notes, this meant that social medicine had support across the political spectrum, from socialism to fascism.[4]

Cilento's contributions to social medicine and public health reform also had an important relationship to his own colonialism and colonial experience in the Pacific Islands. Diet occupied a central place in social medicine and it was in the context of colonial government in New Guinea

---

3   Raphael Cilento to C. E. Sligo, 23 September 1937, Cilento Papers, UQFL44, Box 4, Item 11. See Henry Sigerist, 'The Physician's Profession Through the Ages,' *Bulletin of the New York Academy of Medicine*, 9(12), 1933, p. 676.
4   Gillespie, *The Price of Health*, p. 51.

that Cilento became convinced of its importance in fostering health and fitness in a broad sense. If a balanced national diet was vital for saving the indigenous peoples of New Guinea and Fiji from extinction, it was just as essential for cultivating the health, security and future of a white Australia. This colonial 'discovery' of nutrition also reintroduced a global frame of reference to Cilento's increasing number of public lectures and articles.[5] In these contributions to professional and public discourse, he reflected on the relationship between nutrition and the rise and fall of civilisations. He would ultimately link sickness and social decline among 'the Papuan' and the 'city dweller' through modern industrial food production and consumption. Diet, health, fertility and population were all globally interconnected, incorporating Europeans, Japanese and Pacific Islanders within a shared historical process. The version of social medicine that Cilento developed thus rested on a global historical imagination that had its roots in empire.

The lily of progress

Returning from his survey of the Pacific Islands in 1929, Cilento spent six more years as an officer in the CDH. His responsibilities and influence shrank as the department itself contracted—first, with the states' rejection of national health reforms proposed in the 1925 Royal Commission on Health and, then, with the beginning of the Depression.[6] When Elkington retired in 1928, Cilento became the Director of the Division of Tropical Hygiene.[7] Between 1929 and 1934, Cilento did odd jobs that the constitutionally limited powers of the department allowed. From his base in Brisbane, he travelled regularly up and down the length of Queensland. Besides inspecting the quarantine stations and laboratories that were the Commonwealth's direct responsibility, he also met with Queensland health officials, including John Coffey, the Public Health Commissioner after 1929, and Leslie St Vincent-Welch, the Chief Medical Officer for Schools. He also organised surveys of malaria, rat leprosy and hookworm—tropical diseases that transgressed state borders and gave the Commonwealth scope for intervention.[8]

---

5   Worboys, 'The Discovery of Colonial Malnutrition between the Wars,' pp. 208–25.
6   Gillespie, *The Price of Health*, pp. 44–7.
7   Raphael Cilento to A. H. Baldwin, 4 July 1928, NAA: SP1061/1, 336.
8   Raphael Cilento to Phyllis Cilento, 5 July 1929, Cilento Papers, UQFL44, Box 11, Item 21.

Financial pressure led to the closure of the tropical hygiene division in 1933 and, the following year, Cilento moved to Canberra—a departure the Brisbane press noted with regret.[9] Phyllis stayed in Brisbane while Cilento looked for a house, but his eldest son, Raphael, later joined him in Canberra. The capital quickly became a 'penitentiary', 'boring to the verge of nausea'.[10] He remained pugnacious, especially in his increasingly fractious relationship with Cumpston. Cracks had appeared between them in 1929, although Cilento remained loyal.[11] Cumpston kept Cilento busy with the Australian tropics, the Pacific Islands and the emerging problem of aerial quarantine. A few years later, Cilento began to feel the department slipping into a gloomy paralysis and, by 1934, his relationship with Cumpston—who isolated himself and 'is letting the office go to ruin in its minor branches'—reached a nadir.[12] Cilento in fact felt that Cumpston was trying to put him in situations that would discredit him. In 1934, Cumpston asked Cilento to present a paper to a conference of administrators from Australia's external territories, which instantly made Cilento 'public enemy no. 1' in Melanesia. This was especially disappointing given the fact that, in recent years, Cilento had hoped to return to New Guinea in some capacity. Yet he also won concessions, including support from the Federal Health Council for his Aboriginal leprosy program, a revival in 1935 of the International Pacific Health Conference and Australian representation at the 1934 congress of the Far Eastern Association of Tropical Medicine (FEATM) in Nanking. He was, he told his wife, 'bubbling with fight'. He also looked forward to visiting 'the East again', where practical experts in tropical medicine studied local problems with which academics in London and Liverpool were, in his view, so out of touch.[13] Over the next few months, however, these gains evaporated. Cumpston cancelled Cilento's trip to China, which Cilento described as the price for being allowed leave to take his bar examination in Brisbane.[14] His hopes of returning to New Guinea

---

9   *The Courier-Mail*, [Brisbane], 19 February 1934, p. 10.

10   Raphael Cilento to Phyllis Cilento, 9 March 1934; Raphael Cilento to Phyllis Cilento, 14 March 1934, Cilento Papers, UQFL44, Box 11, Item 21.

11   Raphael Cilento to Phyllis Cilento, 12 July 1929, Cilento Papers, UQFL44, Box 11, Item 21. In another letter, Cilento noted that Neville Howse, the Minister for Health and Repatriation, and Home and Territories, was supposed to dislike him, which he thought might explain Cumpston's attitude to Cilento. Raphael Cilento to Phyllis Cilento, 2 July 1929, Cilento Papers, UQFL44, Box 11, Item 21.

12   Raphael Cilento to Phyllis Cilento, 1 March 1934, Cilento Papers, UQFL44, Box 11, Item 21.

13   Raphael Cilento to Phyllis Cilento, 19 March 1934; Raphael Cilento to Phyllis Cilento, 30 March 1934, Cilento Papers, UQFL44, Box 11, Item 21.

14   Raphael Cilento to Phyllis Cilento, 15 April 1934, Cilento Papers, UQFL44, Box 11, Item 21.

were dashed with the appointment of Sir Harry Lawson as Minister for External Territories, who looked set to continue the government's policy of favouring ex-servicemen for appointments.[15]

These years were reflective ones for Cilento, as he witnessed the effects of the Depression and ran his eye over Australian society. The dominance of agriculture in Queensland reduced the impact of the Depression, yet unemployment was still severe.[16] Cilento's letters to Phyllis during his tours of north Queensland are full of concern for the future alongside a passionate progressive belief in work and collective service. 'I am on fire to do something for Australia,' he wrote to Phyllis from Cairns, 'something especially that will teach our own people that work and discipline, not piracy and mendicancy are the only things that can make a nation great.'[17] In north Queensland, he lamented failing industries, writing that, in some places, 'the whole country is dead'.[18] He laid the blame at the feet of migratory entrepreneurs who returned none of their profits to the 'permanent progress' of tropical Australia. White settlement and development of the tropics remained the keystones of his racist vision of Australia's future. In Cairns, he listened to a Sydney businessman who 'ranted for half an hour on the delights (to the bosses) of a 'Black Australia' (strictly limited by indentures etc. etc., + all the utter rubbish + futility by which corporations seek to stifle conscience)'.[19]

Cilento's sense of social stagnation in Australia thus associated racial decline partly with the social indifference of liberal capitalism, reflecting his growing distaste for the political mainstream.[20]

Decadence and degeneration were central themes of Cilento's correspondence. One letter expressed his concerns in especially strong terms and is worth quoting at length:

---

15 Raphael Cilento to Phyllis Cilento, 21 April 1934, Cilento Papers, UQFL44, Box 11, Item 21.
16 Ross Fitzgerald, *From 1915 to the Early 1980s: A History of Queensland* (Brisbane: University of Queensland Press, 1984), pp. 166–8.
17 Raphael Cilento to Phyllis Cilento, 14 November 1933, Cilento Papers, UQFL44, Box 11, Item 21.
18 Raphael Cilento to Phyllis Cilento, 3 April 1930, Cilento Papers, UQFL44, Box 11, Item 21.
19 Raphael Cilento to Phyllis Cilento, 14 November 1933, Cilento Papers, UQFL44, Box 11, Item 21.
20 Raphael Cilento to Phyllis Cilento, 4 November 1933, Cilento Papers, UQFL44, Box 11, Item 21.

It is sad to see this country so young and yet so old with the age-stamp of its parents, a poor marasmic morsel of humanity as pathetic as a wizened little congenital syphilitic waiting for cure and yet indifferent to it—with life all ahead of it and its eyes fixed only on a paper boat in a slum gutter. Its girls pluck their eyebrows and paint their lips glaring purple in a thickly powdered face to orientalise their features as definitely as their clothes— their pyjamas, kimonos, slacks, shorts and so on. How old Father Time remembering Rome and looking at the patient trousered drudges of China the descendants of just such undeserving heirs of all previous ages, must shake with mirthless laughter. Is it worth attempting anything for so dumb-witted a race of thriftless human waste?[21]

Here Cilento brought together strands of reflection on history, modernity, race and decline, anticipating the themes that he and others would discuss in articles and lectures in the 1930s and 1940s.[22] The above passage illustrates the interplay of ideas about health, race and gender in interwar discourses of modernity. The crisis of Australian society is here not merely economic, but also one of racial deterioration from the potential youthful vigour that Cilento communicates through the syphilis metaphor. This further betrays the importance of sex and gender in this discourse. Girls adopting Asian fashions here represents cultural decline born of the global exchange of images and texts. Like Cilento's other commentary on young women in this period, here the girls are concerned with consumption and display, instead of progress and civic duty. In another letter, he described a crowd of 'flappers' at the Leichhardt Hotel in Rockhampton:

Their talk is all of the eligibles of each sex; every woman watches her neighbours' chances jealously and every pair of girls or mother and daughter squabbles and is at odds over varying points of view. There is not an idea of value or a progressive action among the whole cargo.[23]

The figures who surround Cilento in his letters frequently appear superficial, pretentious or petty, and his arrogant elitism is palpable. Vanity and apathy, Cilento complained, plagued Australian society, especially in its middle and upper echelons, bleeding vitality and initiative.

These social observations, which Cilento imbued with portentous meanings, fed into his politics. He increasingly expressed his alienation from mainstream politics and the dominance of the major parties. 'I get

---

21   Raphael Cilento to Phyllis Cilento, 21 April 1934, Cilento Papers, UQFL44, Box 11, Item 21.
22   See, for example, John Bostock and L. Jarvis Nye, *Whither Away? A Study of Race Psychology and the Factors Leading to Australia's National Decline*, 2nd edn (Sydney: Angus & Robertson, 1936).
23   Raphael Cilento to Phyllis Cilento, 13 July 1933, Cilento Papers, UQFL44, Box 11, Item 21.

tired of all this little dirty political squabbling and sordid mess from which one tries to pick the lily of progress and service', he confessed to Phyllis in a letter from Townsville.[24] He criticised the Labor Party for supporting the White Australia Policy but only in the interests of the 'the lowest-grade white', while attacking the National Party for sacrificing 'the interests of any who stand in the way of their own easy opulence'. Ultimately: 'Corruption and self-interest destroy any possible ideal of patriotism.'[25] Labour militancy in Queensland in the late 1920s and 1930s was, for Cilento, especially degrading:

> The cane-cutter holds a pistol to the head of the grower, extorts exorbitant wages, spends them in an orgy of booze and filth and 6 weeks after the cutting season demands the dole. The decent cutter whose savings go perhaps by the sudden sickness of his wife or some unforseen [sic] accident is debarred from help because the thrifty scoundrel has dared to purchase his own house![26]

He criticised workers for 'drivelling the futilities of class-warfare' to their children rather than encouraging thrift and service to the nation.[27] Communism was an especially menacing influence and he would later warn the Queensland Government of its growing popularity among sugarcane cutters in northern Australia.[28]

Frustrated at the apparent inability of the Australian public to accept self-discipline and national service, Cilento voiced frankly authoritarian views that many of his professional colleagues and contemporaries were shy of expressing.[29] In a 1936 lecture read in his absence in Brisbane, he argued: 'The fundamental theoretical right of the mass to choose its own representatives remains pure theory, and often farcical theory at that.'[30] Universal suffrage debased politics by handing power to the 'mob' and the opportunistic politicians and media willing to manipulate them.[31] To 'put the highest possible value on every human life, however worthless', was

---

24 Raphael Cilento to Phyllis Cilento, 19 July 1933, Cilento Papers, UQFL44, Box 11, Item 21.
25 Raphael Cilento to Phyllis Cilento, 14 November 1933, Cilento Papers, UQFL44, Box 11, Item 21.
26 ibid.
27 ibid.
28 Raphael Cilento to E. M. Hanlon, Minister for Health and Home Affairs, 22 January 1937, Cilento Papers, UQFL44, Box 4, Item 11.
29 Gillespie, *The Price of Health*, pp. 34–6.
30 Raphael Cilento, 'Historical Parallels,' 9 June 1936, p. 13, Cilento Papers, UQFL44, Box 17, Item 80.
31 ibid., p. 6.

the worst example of 'sentimentality', Cilento argued, insisting that liberty had to be more than 'license'.[32] There was thus in Cilento's view a social hierarchy of worth and character, in which some would lead and others would follow.

There was in these social and political observations a strong kinship with many themes of fascist ideologies. The difficulty of defining fascism as a body of ideas or concepts has been a refrain of fascism studies. While Michel Dobry has recently given up on theories of 'generic fascism', other scholars have sought to define not a distinct political category, but an abstract conceptual device that would assist in the analysis of historical far-right movements and regimes.[33] It is not the purpose here to fall in with any of the various historiographical camps. It is clear, however, that Cilento held a number of social and political views that aligned strongly with much that was present in various fascist movements in Europe. His emphasis on national holism and service, national racial fitness and vital energy, the need for action and wilful progress over economic or social determination; his appeals to elite leadership and related distrust of the principles and institutions of liberal democracy; and his critique of liberalism, socialism and conservatism—all were prominent features of far-right movements in Europe in this period.[34]

Cilento's ideological affinities did lead to several intersections with fascist leaders and officials. After hearing a radio address by Eric Campbell, the leader of the Sydney-based right-wing paramilitary group The New Guard, Cilento 'realized how infinitely better I could do it myself!'.[35] In one

---

32 ibid., pp. 6–7.
33 Roger Griffin, *The Nature of Fascism* (London: Routledge, 1993), p. 1; Stanley G. Payne, *A History of Fascism, 1914–1945* (Madison: University of Wisconsin Press, 1995), pp. 3–6; Michel Dobry, 'Desperately Seeking "Generic Fascism": Some Discordant Thoughts on the Academic Recycling of Indigenous Categories,' in Antonio Costas Pinto (ed.), *Rethinking Fascism: Comparative Perspectives* (Basingstoke, UK: Palgrave Macmillan, 2011), pp. 53–84; Roger Eatwell, 'Ideology, Propaganda, Violence and the Rise of Fascism,' in Antonio Costa Pinto (ed.), *Rethinking the Nature of Fascism: Comparative Perspectives* (Basingstoke, UK: Palgrave Macmillan, 2011), pp. 165–8.
34 Roger Eatwell, *Fascism: A History* (London: Chatto & Windus, 1995), pp. 6–12; Payne, *A History of Fascism*, pp. 8–14; Adrian Lyttelton, *The Seizure of Power: Fascism in Italy 1919–1929*, 3rd edn (London: Routledge, 2004), pp. 42–52.
35 Raphael Cilento to Phyllis Cilento, 18 February 1932, Cilento Papers, UQFL44, Box 11, Item 21. On the New Guard, see Keith Amos, *The New Guard Movement 1931–1935* (Melbourne: Melbourne University Press, 1976); Andrew Moore, *The Secret Army and the Premier: Conservative Paramilitary Organisations in New South Wales 1930–32* (Sydney: UNSW Press, 1989); Macintyre, *A Concise History of Australia*, pp. 179–80; Andrew Moore, 'The New Guard and the Labour Movement, 1931–35,' *Labour History*, 89, 2005, pp. 55–72; Richard Evans, '"A Menace to this Realm": The New Guard and the New South Wales Police, 1931–32,' *History Australia*, 5(3), 2008, pp. 76.1–76.20.

patriotic paroxysm, Cilento proclaimed: 'Italy shews what a new "Augustan Age" age it might be with leadership and inspiration.'[36] In 1935, he wrote a letter of introduction for the West Australian Director of Infant Welfare and School Hygiene, Dr Ethel Stang, who was travelling to Germany to study the Hitler Youth Movement and other programs designed to foster the strength and discipline of young people.[37] In 1939, he wrote to the German consul in Brisbane asking for a subscription to an Axis publication.[38] And, in 1938, Cilento became the inaugural President of the Dante Alighieri Society, sharing membership of this primarily cultural Italian group with openly fascist members.[39] During World War II, many of these Brisbane fascists were interned, leading federal security personnel to investigate Cilento's loyalties.[40]

Attempting to precisely categorise Cilento as a 'fascist' is less interesting, however, than placing him in the larger context of the progressive and racist nationalism out of which fascist movements arose. As Michael Roe has shown, fascism grew out of broad intellectual and political currents in the late nineteenth century that also influenced some left-wing movements and progressive nationalism in the United States, Britain and Australia. Eschewing Hegelian and Marxist notions of social structure, internal conflict and determinism, progressives invoked individual will and collective national vitality.[41] Instead of parliament and law, it was left to an energetic and professional elite to push society towards an ideally ordered social future. This emphasis on elite leadership and social unity as the primary driving forces of history was an important feature of twentieth-century progressivism that manifested as much in some articulations of socialism as in the professed admiration for fascist leaders that can be found in some progressive texts.[42] Cilento, for example,

---

36 Raphael Cilento to Phyllis Cilento, 21 April 1934, Cilento Papers, UQFL44, Box 11, Item 21.
37 Raphael Cilento to Minister of Education, Berlin, 30 October 1935, Cilento Papers, UQFL44, Box 4, Item 11.
38 Raphael Cilento to O. H. Witte, German Consul, 7 August 1939, Cilento Papers, UQFL44, Box 4, Item 11.
39 David Brown, '"Before Everything, Remain Italian": Fascism and the Italian Population of Queensland 1910–1945' (PhD Thesis, University of Queensland, 2008), pp. 183–4. On fascism in the Queensland community, see also, Gianfranco Cresciani, *Fascism, Anti-fascism and Italians in Australia, 1922–1945* (Canberra: Australian National University Press, 1980).
40 Field Security Police Reports, NAA: A6119, 229/REFEREE COPY.
41 Roe, *Nine Australian Progressives*, pp. 1–2.
42 ibid., pp. 6–7.

acknowledged that Soviet ideology reflected some of his own beliefs about the relationship of the individual to the nation: '"Service for us" or "Service for the State" is the question of the day', he wrote to Phyllis:

> Italy and Russia answer the latter two ways, but not essentially in different ways. 'Service for ourselves' is a paltry and spineless thing in comparison but it seems our national aspiration.[43]

Although the point of contact between Cilento and fascism was the broader nationalist movement towards harnessing science for improving populations and racial fitness, he clearly identified most closely with the aspirations and methods of fascist regimes. In his 1936 lecture series *Nutrition and Numbers*, Cilento noted that Italy, Germany and the Soviet Union were the only nations 'with their 250,000,000 white people' that had maintained or increased their birth rate. It was vital that Australia imitate these 'authoritarian states' in an effort to apply the best science towards the aim of national 'self-sufficiency'. In Germany and Italy, Cilento noted:

> The 'Youth' movements, the 'Land-Year,' and all other actual and psychological aids are being co-ordinated with the new necessities of the country, and the eyes of their rising youth are being deliberately deflected from the defeatism and decline associated with every ageing civilisation to a new future of hope and achievement.[44]

These sorts of programs were vital in a world that was fundamentally, Cilento argued, one of competition and conflict:

> Italy and Germany realise that the ideal of immediate universal reconciliation between nations and races so unequally endowed with culture and material goods as the units of our civilisation are, begins with a wistful dream and ends by 'no man lifting a finger so long as misfortune touches only his neighbour'.[45]

There is a clear connection here again with Cilento's longstanding concern about the status of the Australian tropics. 'The constant sneers of our newspapers at Italy', Cilento noted, 'came oddly from a country which is

---

43   Raphael Cilento to Phyllis Cilento, 14 November 1933, Cilento Papers, UQFL44, Box 11, Item 21. Cilento's emphasis.
44   Raphael Cilento, *Nutrition and Numbers: The Livingstone Lectures* (Sydney: Camden College, 1936), pp. 68–9.
45   ibid., p. 69.

almost half undeveloped'.[46] Australia should instead, Cilento argued, try to emulate Italy for its efforts in reclaiming land and constructing towns on the Pontine Marshes—in other words, to apply science for its own national progress. All members of society, Cilento asserted, should thus perform their appropriate roles in the service of national efficiency, with the authority of expert scientific knowledge as a guide.[47]

Public health was one field in which progressive nationalism manifested strongly. Cilento closely resembles the figure of the 'progressive' that Roe has described: he was a qualified professional, confident in his technical expertise, who saw in the combination of scientific knowledge and the initiative of elite individuals the hope for a decisive intervention in society and its development.[48] Paul Weindling and Dorothy Porter have noted that nineteenth- and twentieth-century physicians, as self-consciously elite professionals, increasingly sought to prescribe social transformation on the basis of their scientific knowledge.[49] This in turn drew on emerging social theory in the nineteenth century that stressed the need for scientists to positively engineer social progress and order.[50] In making his contribution to the reform of public health in Australia, Cilento drew mostly on Anglo-American traditions of preventive medicine, and worked closely with a Labor government already committed to government control of health and medical services. Thus, while Cilento's authoritarian predilections and explicit fascist sympathies were pronounced, understanding his contributions to public health in Australia requires a wider lens that can catch the several international and colonial contexts of his reform agenda.

Cultivating the health of the nation: Social medicine and public health governance

In September 1934, Edward Hanlon, the home secretary in Queensland, offered Cilento the temporary position of Director-General of Health and Medical Services, in which his chief task was to reorganise public health and medical services within a single ministry. Cilento accepted and,

---

46   ibid., p. 69.
47   Gillespie, *The Price of Health*, pp. 35–7.
48   Roe, *Nine Australian Progressives*, pp. 6–10.
49   Weindling, *Health, Race and German Politics between National Unification and Nazism*, p. 1; Porter, 'Introduction,' p. 2.
50   Porter, *Health, Civilization and the State*, pp. 74–5.

in 1935, the job, as the professional head of the Department of Public Health, was made a permanent one, which he held until 1946. Freed from the constraints of a subordinate position in the Commonwealth department, he now had a greater say in public health reform in Australia, both in Queensland and as a state representative to federal health bodies. Prior to his appointment, several public medical services were spread across separate government departments. The Department of Home Affairs managed basic public health and sanitation under the authority of the Public Health Commissioner, John Coffey. School medical services were the responsibility of the Department of Public Instruction, while the Department of Labour administered health regulations for factories. Cilento pressed early for the collection of all these health services in one ministry, including hospitals, maternal and infant welfare, school hygiene, industrial hygiene, 'mental hygiene', wards of the state, research and sanitary engineering.[51]

Proposals for such a consolidation had been around since 1909.[52] Coffey had complained in 1931 of conflicts between inspectors of the health and labour departments over the application of the Workers' Accommodation Act, and recommended that its sanitation provisions be included in the Health Act.[53] Consolidation of health services within a single ministry had also been common practice internationally for some time.[54] Cilento noted this international trend towards public responsibility for health and emphasised to Hanlon that a new Health Bill (1937) would centralise coordination of all health and medical services under the government.[55] He reported:

> It is being universally acknowledged that the health of the individual (and therefore the sanitary and medical care of every person in the community) is not only his personal affair, but the concern and responsibility of the whole community.[56]

---

51 Raphael Cilento, 'Preliminary Report on the Re-organisation of the Home Department to Provide for the Separate Existence or Co-existence of a Ministry of Health,' 10 December 1934, pp. 6–8, QSA, Series 5263, Item 848707.
52 Patrick, *A History of Health and Medicine in Queensland*, p. 99.
53 John Coffey to Assistant Under-secretary, 5 January 1931, QSA, Series 12355, Item 8904.
54 Porter, *Health, Civilization and the State*, p. 182.
55 Cilento, 'Preliminary Report on the Re-organisation of the Home Department,' p. 23. See also Raphael Cilento to E. M. Hanlon, 10 July 1935; Memorandum for Hanlon, 1 October 1935, p. 2, QSA, Series 12355, Item 8904.
56 Cilento, 'Preliminary Report on the Re-organisation of the Home Department,' p. 6.

The state also had a responsibility to make its health services 'universally available'. This included a measure of government control over medical personnel—at first over a full-time paid hospital staff and eventually over the whole medical profession.[57]

The Labor Party, which dominated government in Queensland between 1915 and 1957, except for three years at the height of the Depression, had already developed a culture of public health reform by the time Cilento arrived. It had also found allies in the public service, especially in its continued efforts to bring hospitals under government control. *The Hospitals Act of 1923* provided for the creation of hospital districts. A single nine-member board—composed equally of representatives from the government, local councils and contributors—would be responsible for running all the hospitals in that district. The Act initially established the Brisbane and South Coast Hospitals Board (BSCHB), under the chairmanship of Charles Chuter. Chuter, who had entered the Queensland public service in 1898, became the assistant undersecretary of the home department in 1922 and the undersecretary in 1934. Hanlon and Chuter made it their mission to wrest control of hospitals away from local authorities, contributors and the private practitioners who served as honorary staff. In the honorary system, hospitals drew the bulk of their medical and surgical staff from among local private practitioners, who attended outpatient clinics for about three hours twice a week.[58] By the 1930s, many health administrators, hospital board members and medical practitioners regarded the honorary system as an anachronism from a time when hospitals were primarily charitable institutions serving the poor. Now, they argued, perfunctory consultations and long waiting times showed that this system was failing to cope with massive increases in attendance at outpatient clinics in major metropolitan hospitals.[59]

Reorganisation of hospital staffing and administration in Queensland began in earnest in 1937 when a delegation of the honorary staff of the Brisbane Hospital approached the BSCHB with a proposal that would employ visiting staff on a paid basis. Chuter had become deputy chairman of the board, and his views, along with those of some of his fellow board

---

57   Memorandum for E. M. Hanlon, 1 October 1935, p. 3, QSA, Series 12355, Item 8904.

58   Brisbane and South Coast Hospitals Board, *Chairman's Report*, Appendix 2, n.d., p. 48, QSA 8241, Item 278510.

59   Cilento cited statistics indicating that outpatient attendance had increased by 212 per cent in the decade before 1937. Raphael Cilento to E. M. Hanlon, 6 December 1937, p. 2, QSA, Series 8241, Item 278510.

members, diverged from those of the new chairman, T. L. Jones. Chuter wanted internal reorganisation to go beyond paying current honorary staff and insisted on a full-time resident staff for hospitals. Chuter resigned from the board in 1938, telling A. C. Russell, the Secretary of the Royal North Shore Hospital in Sydney, that he had been forced out after attacking the honorary scheme and bringing a 'heap of wrath upon my head'.[60]

Cilento took advantage of this split in the board to become more directly involved. He threw his support behind a plan for a system of part full-time and part part-time employment for physicians and surgeons, which was less radical than Chuter's proposals. He told Hanlon the honorary system was obsolete, but he sided with the BSCHB and the general medical superintendent, Dr Aubrey Pye, in advising against the immediate appointment of permanent full-time staff. Hanlon appointed an advisory committee in 1938 that elected Cilento as its chairman. The committee's report, over which Cilento exercised the greatest influence, outlined a more complete scheme for reorganisation. Besides the institution of a paid visiting staff in place of honorary staff, Cilento—drawing on American precedence and citing the importance of teamwork in modern medicine—suggested a regular review of clinical work by the medical staff in the interests of maintaining standards.[61] Like Chuter, he recommended that the resident superintendent be the supreme authority in the hospital, but that a hospital standing committee also be instituted to maintain 'self-discipline' and esprit de corps.[62] Again pointing to foreign experience, he recommended instituting a compulsory hospital year for the medical graduates who would soon be flowing from the recently established medical faculty at the University of Queensland. This would have the dual benefits of improving the skills of all medical graduates before they were allowed to practice privately, as well as producing new generations of doctors who might be willing to give themselves to public hospital service.[63] In this way, some of the problems of staff shortages would be

---

60   C. E. Chuter to A. C. Russell, 9 September 1938, QSA, Series 8241, Item 278509.
61   'Report of the Advisory Committee on Reorganisation, Brisbane and South Coast Hospitals Board,' May 1938, p. 11, QSA, Series 8241, Item 278509. In a memo to Hanlon, Cilento had stressed the importance of learning from developments in hospital management in the United States, including principles of teamwork and auditing. Raphael Cilento to E. M. Hanlon, 6 December 1937, p. 7, QSA, Series 8241, Item 278510.
62   'Report of the Advisory Committee on Reorganisation,' p. 9.
63   ibid., pp. 4–5. The report proposed making registration of doctors conditional on this hospital year.

solved in the long term. Perhaps most importantly, Cilento suggested the establishment of a network of suburban outpatient clinics within hospital districts designed to relieve pressure on major hospitals, which would be left to concentrate on high-quality specialist and surgical services.[64] Such an internally organised and disciplined hospital network with a well-trained staff under the control of the government was to be open to all sections of society.

Cilento would ultimately advocate a more comprehensive coordination of the medical profession under the state.[65] Much was said and written at the time about the high fees of private practitioners and the charity criteria that denied the middle classes and 'respectable' workers access to high-quality medical care.[66] Cilento himself spoke about the way private practice 'fleeces the worker and the middle classes' and, in 1929, he described private practitioners in north Queensland as 'fee-chasing tradesmen'.[67] He consistently emphasised that greater government control of medical services must have the primary aim of making them freely available to everyone.[68] Such concerns continued into the 1940s when political conflicts over Commonwealth control of all medical services—and particularly the establishment of a salaried medical service—came to a head.[69] M. Foy, a fruit merchant in Melbourne, in 1942 told the Commonwealth Minister for Health, E. J. Holloway, that 'fee loving Medicos' perversely benefited from the perpetuation of sickness and disease under the fee system, while the press often dwelt on the exclusion of the 'middle-income' group from high-quality medical care.[70]

If the Labor Party's aim of improving access to hospitals reflected a political preoccupation with equitable access and social justice, the motives behind Cilento's involvement in hospitals reflected his concern with national

---

64   ibid., pp. 13–18.
65   Raphael Cilento to E. M. Hanlon, 6 December 1937, pp. 8–10, QSA, Series 8241, Item 278510.
66   Gillespie, *The Price of Health*, p. 3.
67   Raphael Cilento to E. M. Hanlon, 1 October 1935, p. 4, QSA, Series 12355, Item 8904. The American statistician Edgar Sydenstricker referred to doctors as 'expensively trained entrepreneurs' in his 'Medical Practice and Public Needs,' in *The Medical Profession and the Public: Currents and Counter-currents* (Philadelphia: The American Academy of Political and Social Science, 1934), p. 24.
68   Raphael Cilento to E. M. Hanlon, 6 December 1937, p. 3, QSA, Series 8241, Item 278510; Raphael Cilento, 'Queensland's Plan for Hospital Co-ordination,' *The Courier-Mail*, [Brisbane], 17 December 1937, QSA, Series 8241, Item 278509.
69   Gillespie, *The Price of Health*, pp. 130–1.
70   M. Foy to E. J. Holloway, Minister of Health, 9 December 1942, NAA: A1928, 690/39 SECTION 3; *Sydney Morning Herald*, 27 May 1943, p. 7.

efficiency. 'The productive capacity of the worker', Cilento told Hanlon, 'is the axle on which the wheels of State prosperity turn'. The role of the hospital was thus:

> to take workers or potential workers whose health is lowering their productive capacity, to recondition them thoroughly, and to return them to the work of productive labour with the least possible delay.[71]

Hospital reform should thus be part of the expansion and coordination of a wide range of health services under the state. Cilento's preliminary report to Hanlon on the reorganisation of the health department made this clear:

> It is for effective work we want our children well-born, carefully nurtured in childhood, educated in school, and developed in brain and brawn both. At their highest point of development they provide the State with good work, sure defence, and profitable parenthood. Physical culture, preventive medicine, hospital treatment, specialised services, rest and recreation, all turn in the last analysis upon the worker and his ability to produce and serve.[72]

All medical services, including prenatal care, baby clinics, school medical services, industrial hygiene and other preventive work, needed to be unified in one government department to achieve 'positive development to the full of every individual's mental and physical powers, in order that the State may profit to the full by the exercise of both in their excellence'.[73] Hospitals had to fit into this wider program of preventive medicine and 'positive' health, which Cilento increasingly discussed in the terms of 'social medicine'.

Cilento was appointed Honorary Professor of Social and Tropical Medicine at the University of Queensland in 1937, several years before John Ryle at Oxford and Francis Crew at Edinburgh established social medicine as an academic discipline in the United Kingdom, in the 1940s.[74] Doctors and public health authorities in Europe and America, however, had long promoted 'social medicine' as an array of public health perspectives and practices. Dorothy Porter identifies a long twentieth-century history of

---

71   Raphael Cilento to E. M. Hanlon, 6 December 1937, p. 1, QSA, Series 8241, Item 278510. Cilento's emphasis.
72   Cilento, 'Preliminary Report on the Re-organisation of the Home Department,' p. 21.
73   ibid., p. 20. Cilento's emphasis.
74   Porter, 'Introduction,' p. 1.

medicine and science aspiring to progressive social planning.[75] German social hygienists, especially Alfred Grotjahn, had, from the late nineteenth century, urged doctors to look beyond clinical medicine. By examining the social, economic and biological factors shaping health, they could take a leading role in shaping the future of the nation and the race. It was thus necessary to add to medical practice the collection of data on nutrition, housing, income and occupation.[76] This work became influential for later advocates, including Andrija Stampar, who wrote on social medicine as a medical student in 1911 and became an international leader in public health while in Zagreb, China and elsewhere.[77]

It was not until after World War I that social medicine began to spread and inform public health administration and research.[78] As it developed in the interwar years, it began to shed an earlier emphasis on heredity among social hygienists such as Grotjahn.[79] In the Soviet Union and among liberal reformers in Europe and the United States, a growing understanding of the social and economic conditions of health shaped the reorganisation of health services and the institutionalisation of social medicine. Malnutrition, for example, led to abnormal development of bones and muscles in infants and children, while chronic vitamin deficiencies in adult workers lowered resistance to disease across the life of the individual. Chemicals, dust and other aspects of industrial workplaces could also harm the health of workers, while poor housing and domestic hygiene might lead to disease and other health problems for women and children.[80] Rene Sand, the Chief Public Health Officer in Belgium, wrote in 1919 that '[a]lmost every medical question ends in a social question', including not just the provision of clean water, but also a good home, balanced nutrition and recreation.[81] Since many of these factors operated

---

75   ibid., pp. 2–3.
76   Weindling, *Health, Race and German Politics between National Unification and Nazism*, pp. 214–21; Porter, *Health, Civilization and the State*, pp. 192–3.
77   Andrija Stampar, *Serving the Cause of Public Health: Selected Papers of Andrija Stampar*, ed. M. D. Grmek (Zagreb: University of Zagreb, 1966), pp. 53–7; Patrick Zylberman, 'Fewer Parallels than Antitheses: Rene Sand and Andrija Stampar on Social Medicine, 1919–1955,' *Social History of Medicine*, 17(1), 2004, p. 82.
78   Weindling, 'Social Medicine at the League of Nations Health Organisation and the International Labour Office Compared,' pp. 134–5.
79   Weindling, *Health, Race and German Politics between National Unification and Nazism*, pp. 184–5; Weindling, 'Social Medicine at the League of Nations Health Organisation and the International Labour Office Compared,' p. 146.
80   Porter, *Health, Civilization and the State*, pp. 291–5.
81   Rene Sand, 'The Rise of Social Medicine,' *Modern Medicine*, 1, 1919, p. 190.

all the time away from the hospital and the general practitioner's clinic, it became clear that health and medical provision must change if they were to be addressed.

The concept of 'positive' health was central in Cilento's writings, especially in his major work on public health, *Blueprint for the Health of the Nation*. It was imperative, he argued, to recognise that health, rather than sickness, was the proper object of medicine. As the state assumed a gradually increasing portion of responsibility for health in the nineteenth century, it came ever closer to 'the ideal that a health service is intended to provide positive health, preventive care and medical aid at need, to every member of the community'.[82] The state had been responsible for basic sanitation and vaccination for many years. The *'intrinsic factors of the hygiene of everyday life'*, however, were 'less and less related to the general practitioner' and most in need of attention.[83] Even if one could avoid disease, malnourishment, unhygienic working conditions and other factors might subtly injure individuals and impair their capacity to work. The embodied subject was seen as being in a dynamic relationship with its environment—an organism with finite reserves of energy and vulnerable to the effects of deprivation and toxic substances. In the context of the economic interests noted above, it was thus important to seek 'the promotion of an optimal state of wellbeing', by intervening in diet, housing, antenatal care, maternal and infant welfare, school and industrial hygiene, physical education and leisure.[84]

The need for physicians to assume greater responsibility for prevention and public health became a theme of social medicine in all its divergent forms.[85] Sand praised the United States for pioneering cooperation between doctors and social workers, but argued that doctors themselves should become social workers.[86] Including prevention and social responsibility in medical education was thus an important reform.[87] In 1937, Cilento reported on the course of the new medical school at the University of Queensland, in which:

---

82 Cilento, *Blueprint for the Health of a Nation*, p. 48.
83 ibid., p. 49. Cilento's emphasis.
84 ibid., p. 74.
85 Zylberman, 'Fewer Parallels than Antitheses,' p. 89.
86 Sand, 'The Rise of Social Medicine,' p. 190.
87 Nigel Oswald, 'Training Doctors for the National Health Service: Social Medicine, Medical Education and the GMC 1936–48,' in Dorothy Porter (ed.), *Social Medicine and Medical Sociology in the Twentieth Century* (Atlanta: Rodopi, 1997), pp. 68–9; Porter, *Health, Civilization and the State*, pp. 291–5.

Preventive medicine is emphasised as strongly as curative medicine, and in which the student will be taught his duty to the State in the matter of community risk and public health responsibilities, as definitely as he will be taught his duty to the individual and his private medical relationships.[88]

Arthur Newsholme, the Chief Medical Officer of the Local Government Board in Britain, had in the 1920s pleaded for family doctors to involve themselves in preventive medicine by providing advice on childrearing, avoiding occupational hazards and adopting healthy habits. The doctor, he argued, must recognise 'himself as an integral part of the entire medical organization for the service of the public'.[89]

This question of the relationship between the doctor, the public and the medical profession was a central theme in American discussions of social medicine, to which figures such as Henry Sigerist, the noted medical historian, and Thomas Parran, the New York State health commissioner and US surgeon general, made significant contributions. The social and environmental effects of industrialisation, the complexity of modern medical knowledge and practice and the increasingly dominant belief that society was responsible for the 'welfare of all its members' were important ideas shaping proposals for reform.[90] For some commentators and activists, the claim that health had roots in social conditions and economic structures had radical implications. If sickness was a consequence of inequality and poverty, the solution appeared to be the radical transformation of social and economic relationships. As Rosenberg and Fee note, however, many radical reformers in America in the 1920s and 1930s reconciled this observation with the belief that the health services of capitalist democracies could also be liberating once access to them was equitable.[91] Thus Sigerist, a prominent advocate of Soviet social medicine, threw himself into debates over the establishment of health centres and the reform of medical education in the United States.

88   Queensland, *Annual Report on the Health and Medical Services of the State of Queensland for the Year 1936–37* (Brisbane, 1938), p. 51.
89   Arthur Newsholme, *Health Problems in Organized Society: Studies in the Social Aspects of Public Health* (London: P. S. King & Son, 1927), pp. 86–9.
90   Sigerist, 'The Physician's Profession through the Ages,' p. 676.
91   Charles Rosenberg, *Explaining Epidemics and Other Studies in the History of Medicine* (Cambridge: Cambridge University Press, 1992), pp. 261–3; Elizabeth Fee, 'Henry E. Sigerist: His Interpretations of the History of Disease and the Future of Medicine,' in Charles Rosenberg and Janet Golden (eds), *Framing Disease: Studies in Cultural History* (New Brunswick, NJ: Rutgers University Press, 1992), p. 299.

Fair access to health care, the distribution of doctors and the role of government were the central topics of a conference the American Academy of Political and Social Science organised in Philadelphia in 1934. James Bossard, a sociologist at the University of Pennsylvania, argued that the American public had become accustomed to government health care in schools, the military and workplaces and now saw protection against disease and the promotion of physical wellbeing as 'rights in a modernized democratic society'.[92] The public health statistician Edgar Sydenstricker spoke about the vast number of people excluded from the services of private practitioners, who, despite congregating in wealthy neighbourhoods, had failed to achieve high incomes. Meanwhile, the nation continued to suffer from preventable diseases and ill health.[93] Thomas Parran similarly noted that the 'medical profession, as at present constituted, increasingly is unable to provide for all the people the minimum essentials of medical care' that were their right.[94] All the contributors argued for greater coordination of medical services that should be available to all citizens and oriented towards disease prevention, the cultivation of health and the reduction of infant mortality. The inevitability of change under the pressure of public demands became a key argument. In an oft-quoted passage, Sigerist argued that 'the physician's position in society is never determined by the physician himself, but by the society he is serving'.[95] By the end of the 1930s, this was becoming a consensus view across the world.[96]

Cilento was scheduled to give a speech entitled 'The State, The Public and the Medical Profession' at the inaugural meeting of the National Health and Medical Research Council (NHMRC) in Hobart on 2 February 1937. In it, he drew directly from the Philadelphia conference to argue that economic and social conditions produced and shaped access to health care and asserted that current international thought demanded that the medical profession become more responsible to the state and for the health of the public. Cilento never gave this speech, however, after representatives of the British Medical Association threatened to walk

---

92   James Bossard, 'A Sociologist Looks at the Doctors,' in *The Medical Profession and the Public: Currents and Counter-currents* (Philadelphia: The American Academy of Political and Social Science, 1934), p. 5.
93   Sydenstricker, 'Medical Practice and Public Needs,' pp. 23–5.
94   Thomas Parran, 'Health Services of Tomorrow,' in *The Medical Profession and the Public: Currents and Counter Currents* (Philadelphia: The American Academy of Political and Social Science, 1934), p. 79.
95   Sigerist, 'The Physician's Profession through the Ages,' p. 676.
96   Gillespie, *The Price of Health*, p. 86.

out of the meeting if he did.[97] Cilento pressed his case later that year in an open letter to the medical profession in the Brisbane *Telegraph*. Echoing Bossard, he argued that young people in Australia had become accustomed to government provision of health care in the army and schools. The private practitioner was finding it increasingly difficult to keep up with developments in knowledge and technology. Plagiarising Sydenstricker, Cilento asserted: 'Medical care is no longer a mysterious and sacred realm, into which only the physician may enter, and at whose doors all others must bow in humility.'[98] In this world of government provision and scientific advancement, the romantic vision of the skilled individual doctor had to give way to recognition of the need for a coordinated and cooperative service to the whole community. His recommendation for hospital reorganisation—including a medical audit, a compulsory year for medical school graduates and increasing government control over staff—reflects this belief. He warned that it was up to doctors to voluntarily take part in determining their place in a new health service or risk having one forced on them.[99]

Yet Cilento always felt—like his American counterparts—that it was possible to encourage greater public service among doctors while preserving the patient's free choice of doctors and the intimacy of the doctor–patient relationship:

> The maintenance of the physician's professional freedom is of cardinal importance, and so also is the maintenance, where possible, of the private relationship between physician and patient, and the patient's free choice of physician. To fit the physician into a scheme, the simplest and most logical way is to appoint physicians on a salary basis.[100]

The proposal for a salaried medical service was to become the central conflict between the profession and state and federal health authorities. Cilento, Cumpston and many other doctors and public health officials envisaged a system of suburban clinics and outpatient centres, where up to 10 practitioners might organise to run group practices on a salaried

---

97 Raphael Cilento, 'The State, the Public and the Medical Profession,' pp. 1–6, Cilento Papers, UQFL44, Box 16, Item 70.
98 Raphael Cilento, 'Open Letter to Medical Men,' 1937, p. 1, Cilento Papers, UQFL44, Box 19, Item 132. In his contribution to the Philadelphia conference, Sydenstricker asserted that one had to reject the notion that medical practice was a 'mysterious and sacrosanct realm into which only the physician may enter'. Sydenstricker, 'Medical Practice and Public Needs,' p. 21.
99 Cilento, 'Open Letter to Medical Men,' p. 1.
100 ibid., p. 2.

basis.[101] During World War II, the Commonwealth Government established the Joint Parliamentary Committee on Social Security, which invited the NHMRC to submit evidence and recommendations on the reorganisation of health services. Cilento and Cumpston were members of a subcommittee that drafted the council's proposals in 1941, which, despite internal differences over whether the Commonwealth or the states would have control, recommended the establishment of a salaried medical service across Australia.[102] Group practice had already gained worldwide support since the opening of the Mayo Clinic in the United States, and advocates argued that it would bring further relief for outpatient clinics at major hospitals, greater teamwork and pooling of knowledge, ease of access for patients and bases from which practitioners could perform duties in preventive medicine for the district. Group practice would also protect the 'so rapidly disappearing' local doctor–patient relationships.[103]

Although Cilento invoked the notion that health was an individual right, national health and efficiency were the avowed priorities of the comprehensive government health service he envisaged. Paul Weindling has challenged the notion that social medicine was a humanistic stance against professional and economic interests. Rather than really analysing health as an outcome of poverty and working conditions, social medicine envisioned technocratic solutions for medicalised socioeconomic problems. In this way, it provided career opportunities and authority for public health officials, while avoiding the question of real social and economic justice. Social medicine, moreover, subjected many aspects of life to intrusion and control.[104] This was certainly true of Cilento's scheme for a complete health program for Australia. Given that some of the most important factors that shaped health were part of everyday life, surveillance of individuals and populations became a major imperative. Many aspects of domestic hygiene, infant care and childrearing became subject to professional and official scrutiny.

---

101 See, for example, L. Jarvis Nye, *Group Practice* (Sydney: Australasian Medical Publishing Company, n.d. [c. 1946–49]).

102 National Health and Medical Research Council, 'An Outline of a Possible Scheme for a Salaried Medical Service,' *The Medical Journal of Australia*, II(25), 20 December 1941, pp. 710–25.

103 Cilento, *Blueprint for the Health of a Nation*, p. 63. For group practice and the details of health politics in Australia, see Gillespie, *The Price of Health*. On the origins of group practice in the United States, see W. Bruce Fye, 'The Origins and Evolution of the Mayo Clinic from 1864 to 1939: A Minnesota Family Practice Becomes an International "Medical Mecca",' *Bulletin of the History of Medicine*, 84(3), 2010, pp. 323–57.

104 Weindling, 'Social Medicine at the League of Nations Health Organisation and the International Labour Office Compared,' pp. 136–7.

Cilento hoped that a medical service that included diet, the environment of childhood, education, working conditions and motherhood would protect individuals and the nation as a whole 'against those insidious departures from health, which lower vitality and efficiency'.[105] Modern preventive medicine, Cilento wrote, 'has embraced every aspect of individual and racial security from food to fertility'.[106] The meaning of health thus shifted away from the simple absence of infectious disease towards the fulfilment of potential fitness and productivity. A truly progressive health service sought 'the deliberate promotion in every individual of the highest mental and physical efficiency of which he is capable'.[107] In *Blueprint for the Health of a Nation*, Cilento defined social medicine as 'an attempt to determine the principles by which circumstances can be scientifically influenced in the interests of the individual and of the race'.[108] The object of Cilento's 'machinery' of health was thus the fitness of the race in Australia. The national community for whose health the state was responsible was thus defined by racial inclusions and exclusions, especially when it came to Indigenous people and non-European migrants.

These ideologies conflated national health and racial fitness and, by the mid-1930s, carried weight in political circles. At the inaugural meeting of the NHMRC in 1937, Billy Hughes, the Commonwealth Minister of Health and former prime minister, told assembled health officials that in improving the nation's health, the council must pursue not 'a negative condition, mere freedom from active disease; but that state of abounding energy and vitality that makes one rejoice and be glad to be alive'. Hughes singled out maternal health as the foundation of 'a strong, numerous and disease-resistant people' and noted the establishment of the Commonwealth Advisory Council on Nutrition.[109] At its fifth session, the NHMRC discussed possibilities for a national physical fitness movement. Then Minister of Health, Harry Foll, told that meeting that 'those countries in Europe which have concentrated on physical development of their young people, have improved the racial standard of the people, both mentally and physically'.[110] In its resolution on fitness, the NHMRC stated:

105 Cilento, 'Open Letter to Medical Men,' p. 1.
106 ibid., p. 1.
107 Cilento, *Blueprint for the Health of a Nation*, p. 91.
108 ibid., p. 91.
109 *Report of the National Health and Medical Research Council*, 1st Session (Canberra: Government Printer, 1937), p. 4.
110 *Report of the National Health and Medical Research Council*, 5th Session, p. 4.

> In the constant struggle for economic survival progress is determined, other resources being equal, by the relative proportions of the fit and the unfit, that is to say, in effect, the percentage of the population ineffective towards national life and survival, by physical infirmity or lack of training.[111]

Calls for 'positive' health and fitness, especially in relation to the status of military recruits, were a fixture of national public health discussions.[112] E. Sydney Morris presented a paper to the fifth session of the NHMRC that stated:

> One of the most potent national urgings towards physical fitness has been the desire to provide a race of strong, virile, stalwart individuals who would provide an invincible bulwark for defence in times of crisis or emergency.[113]

He further noted the importance of physical development and of teaching Australian citizens the importance of 'the will' in shaping the fit body:

> The aim of physical education should be to obtain and maintain the best possible development and functioning of the body as a means to aid the full fruition of mental capacity and of character.[114]

Public health discourse thus emphatically dreamed of a polity in which health and fitness of the race—through proper nutrition, maternal and infant care, education and exercise—reached a perfect maximum.

Given this abiding interest in the deliberate cultivation of the health and fitness of individuals and populations, it is not surprising that some formulations of social medicine had strong eugenic strands.[115] The place of biology and heredity in social and preventive medicine, however, was complicated. Francis Lee Dunham, a consulting psychiatrist and lecturer at Johns Hopkins University, included within the scope of social medicine such practices as 'family restriction among the poor', 'rational and

---

111 ibid., p. 10.
112 Fitness was often noted in proposals for a new national research body in the mid-1930s. C. G. Lambie, D. A. Welsh and Henry Priestly to Earle Page, Minister for Health, 11 March 1935, Papers of Earle Page [hereinafter Page Papers], MS 1633, Folder 564. See also 'Notes on a Deputation Representative of the National Health and Medical Research Council, Waited on Prime Minister, Canberra,' 3 July 1937, p. 2, Page Papers, MS 1633, Folder 563.
113 E. S. Morris, 'Physical Education: An Outline of its Aims, Scope, Methods and Organisation,' n.d., p. 1, Page Papers, MS 1633, Folder 566, Item 9.
114 ibid., p. 5.
115 Weindling, 'Social Medicine at the League of Nations Health Organisation and the International Labour Office Compared,' p. 136.

economic' control of marriage, the encouragement of reproduction among the 'better classes' and maintenance of 'equilibrium' between births and deaths in the interests of food supplies.[116] John Ryle, Professor of Physics at Cambridge University in the 1940s—who, like other proponents of social medicine, emphasised the significance of diet and the domestic and working environments—also spoke enthusiastically about 'Medicine and Eugenics' in his 1938 Galton Lecture. There was a need, he said, for the family doctor to provide advice on reproduction and to become an educator in 'principles of health and healthy breeding and their supreme importance to the family and the race'.[117] Arthur Newsholme, however, was a prominent medical critic of hereditarian views on health:

> Ante-natal infection or toxic poisoning and defects of the environment and of the food of the expectant mother are now recognized as responsible for much disease and for many defects in children which were formerly regarded as the result of heredity.[118]

It is clear, then, that while some in public health circles shared eugenicists' concerns about class, reproduction and genetics, the place of heredity in social and preventive medicine was uncertain and contested. The effects of domestic, school and working environments on health, on the other hand, were always the core element of social medicine.

Hereditarian eugenics and social medicine were not, of course, necessarily opposed. Rather than conceiving two opposed environmental and hereditarian discourses neatly confined to liberal and conservative political persuasions, Stephen Garton has argued that debates over the relative importance of environment and biological inheritance occurred within a shared discourse of degeneration. This discourse contained its own internal sets of contested principles for social action distinct from political ideologies.[119] Thus, feminists pushed for birth control as a means of achieving greater social independence, as did activists seeking environmental progress, which confounds the usual association

---

116 Francis Lee Dunham, *An Approach to Social Medicine* (Baltimore: The Williams & Wilkins Company, 1925), pp. 24–5.

117 John Ryle, 'Medicine and Eugenics,' *The Eugenics Review*, 30(1), 1938, pp. 13–14. See also John Ryle, 'Social Medicine: Its Meaning and Scope,' *British Medical Journal*, II, 1943, pp. 633–6.

118 Newsholme, *Health Problems in Organized Society*, p. 242. See also John M. Eyler, *Sir Arthur Newsholme and State Medicine, 1885–1935* (Cambridge: Cambridge University Press, 1997), pp. 187–98.

119 Stephen Garton, 'Sound Minds in Healthy Bodies: Re-considering Eugenics in Australia, 1914–1940,' *Australian Historical Studies*, 26(103), 1994, p. 166.

of strategies for genetic intervention with conservative political forces.[120] Diana Wyndham has similarly suggested that it was possible to frame intervention in fields such as housing, hygiene, labour conditions, food regulation, drug rehabilitation and other medical provision as eugenic.[121]

In *Nutrition and Numbers*, Cilento noted:

> [E]ach of us differs—each begins life with a different inheritance— an individuality that diverges increasingly as every experience of our physiological being leaves its mark and trace recorded within the body.[122]

Cilento thus affirmed that heredity and environment combined to shape life. Cilento shared Newsholme's misgivings about forms of eugenics that focused on heredity and reproductive regulation, but in a way that reflected distinctly Australian anxieties about racial and national decline. Like many before him, Cilento worried about a falling birth rate that seemed to portend racial and national oblivion.[123] The imperative for 'survival' meant that any state-sponsored restriction of reproduction was misguided. Cilento complained that clinics and other institutions dealing with fertility operated at ideological poles:

> Either they over-advocate birth control, recognising that the decline of the population is nature's method of correcting economic disparities, and that the spacing of births may be a factor of value, but forgetting the major threat to national and cultural survival that the falling birthrate involves; or on the other hand they may be staffed by emotionalists whose sole objective is to multiply marriages and foster fertility for its own sake, and who can see, for example, no calamity but only triumph in two deaf mutes mated.[124]

In 1935, the Secretary of the Queensland Birth Control Association wrote to Cilento extolling the health and social benefits of regulating reproduction. The spacing of births would preserve the health of mother and child and reduce the financial burden of reproduction, while the 'mentally and physically unfit' would have 'no fear of passing on their weaknesses'.[125] Cilento's reply reflected his formulation of social medicine in the Australian context:

---

120 ibid., p. 165.
121 Wyndham, *Eugenics in Australia*, pp. 1–3.
122 Cilento, *Nutrition and Numbers*, p. 19.
123 See, for example, the dire prognostications of racial decline in Bostock and Nye (*Whither Away?*, pp. 10–29), which drew on Cilento's lectures. See also Anderson, *The Cultivation of Whiteness*, p. 160.
124 Cilento, *Blueprint for the Health of a Nation*, p. 98.
125 E. Davidson to Raphael Cilento, 10 March 1935, QSA, Series 12355, Item 8892.

> It is the feeling of the Government that in a country such as this which depends for its survival upon a population of at least five times as great as that which it now holds that endeavours should be directed towards removal of those social factors which at present make children a burden rather than by concentrating upon [a] measure of which the ultimate result is definitely in doubt.[126]

Cilento's main preoccupation as the chief health officer in Queensland was thus with social aspects of health and population that were characteristic of mainstream preventive medicine, including housing and industrial hygiene, but especially maternal and infant welfare and nutrition. Dietary reform, infant feeding, antenatal care, birth and abortion all became significant aspects of public health in Queensland under Cilento, in a way that figured each as the outcome of income, education, ignorance and professional training.

In pursuing maternal and infant welfare as part of a state apparatus, Cilento absorbed other social movements into social medicine. Since the 1880s, a loose coalition of middle-class philanthropists and an emerging cohort of professionals had worked towards solving the problems of falling birth rates and infant mortality.[127] These experts and social elites were broadly concerned with the influence of urbanisation on the health, morality and general welfare of working-class infants and children. Their combination of money, political influence and self-proclaimed expertise helped establish curricula and entire schools dedicated to domestic science, as well as networks of maternal and infant welfare clinics and home visitors.

Such strategies were familiar in Britain, where some voluntary women's associations had established 'lady helpers' in the 1860s who later became part of the state's public health apparatus.[128] In Australia, a city health officer in Sydney, W. G. Armstrong, set up a system of home visitors in 1903.[129] Arthur Newsholme credited home visitors with improving knowledge of infant life, especially regarding problems of nutrition and 'efficient motherhood'.[130] Janet Vaughan, a fellow of the Royal College of Physicians and a prominent British advocate of social medicine in the

---

126 Raphael Cilento to E. Davidson, 14 March 1935, QSA, Series 12355, Item 8892.
127 Reiger, *The Disenchantment of the Home*; Michael Gilding, *The Making and Breaking of the Australian Family* (Sydney: Allen & Unwin, 1991).
128 Porter, *Health, Civilization and the State*, p. 179.
129 Gilding, *The Making and Breaking of the Australian Family*, pp. 88–9.
130 Newsholme, *Health Problems in Organized Society*, p. 88.

1930s, stressed the importance of health visitors in ensuring that babies and mothers received expert supervision as soon after birth as possible.[131] Health visitors came to form an important part of the force of social workers attached to public health and developed their own professional identity through conferences and other meetings.[132] Phyllis Cilento was in many ways emblematic of this new expertise, having studied maternal and child health at the Great Ormond Street Hospital in London in 1919.[133] As President of the Queensland Mothercraft Association, she oversaw the production of booklets on childhood nutrition and became a public advocate for educating girls in 'motherhood' and improving midwife training.[134] Like Raphael Cilento, Vaughan sought to incorporate this field of social work into a public health apparatus:

> We want the health services of which the social workers are an essential part and which in the future must come to be recognised as an essential part to form such a fine net that no individual can fall through it from good health into ill health. I feel the weaving of this net is the function of Social Medicine. There are to be many different strands, but it will be an understanding of Social Medicine which will bring all these strands together to make a whole.[135]

Maternal and infant welfare, which in the twentieth century increasingly became the province of the state, focused on the education of women and girls in motherhood according to scientific principles and the creation of a system through which the state could supervise infant care.

Maternal and infant welfare in Queensland in the 1930s similarly involved concerns about national efficiency. In 1918, the state government established four clinics, while the 1922 Maternity Act led to a significant increase in such infant welfare centres, especially in the coastal railway towns.[136] By mid-1946, there were 170 such centres and branches in

---

131 Janet Vaughan, 'The Medical Services in Slough,' n.d., p. 2, Papers of Dame Janet Vaughan [hereinafter Vaughan Papers], GC/186/4, Wellcome Library, London.
132 See 'Summary of Lectures Given at Summer School at Cambridge, 26th June – 5th July,' Papers of the Health Visitors Association, SA/HVA/D.4/11, Wellcome Library, London.
133 Fisher, *Raphael Cilento*, p. 23.
134 'Lady Cilento Discusses the Falling Birth Rate,' *The Courier-Mail*, [Brisbane], 14 October 1937, p. 22.
135 Janet Vaughan, 'Social Medicine,' n.d., p. 6, Vaughan Papers, GC/186/4.
136 Superintendent to C. E. Chuter, 'Maternal and Child Welfare Service,' n.d., p. 1, QSA, Series 12355, Item 8892. See also Patrick, *A History of Health and Medicine in Queensland*, p. 75. Interest in maternal and infant welfare in Australia preceded World War I, but it grew rapidly into a larger professional service in the 1920s. See Reiger, *The Disenchantment of the Home*, p. 86.

the state.[137] In Queensland, the Labor Government had long claimed maternal and infant welfare as its special domain, so that when Cilento made his first recommendations about collecting all health functions and institutions in one ministry, including infant welfare and baby clinics, his views aligned with existing policy.[138] Official investigations noted the obstacles in the way of attendance at antenatal clinics, including long travel, low incomes and the pressure for some pregnant women to work right up to parturition. A 1937 report thus recommended the appointment of nurses who could visit women in their homes.[139] A. Jefferis Turner, the Director of Infant and Child Welfare, reminded Cilento in 1935:

> The greatest asset of this State is the health of its people. The future of a people depends chiefly on the health of its children … From them will be recruited most of the chronic invalids who fill our hospitals and asylums and inflate the roll of invalid pensioners.[140]

As with hospitals, Queensland pursued maternal and infant welfare as a means of reducing the public burden of sickness and improving national efficiency.

The government's priorities were infant mortality and the birth rate and officials investigated ways of addressing these problems through tightening surveillance and improving popular hygiene knowledge. Cilento instructed Abraham Fryberg, a departmental medical officer, to investigate infant mortality in 1937, with particular attention paid to social contexts and consequences. Originally intending to visit homes, Fryberg had to settle for examining hospital records. He suggested that instances of infant mortality should be divided into those deaths that occurred in the first month and those that occurred after this. Deficiencies in antenatal care were to blame for the first, while the latter were due to poor nutrition and respiratory diseases. Education in infant feeding and domestic hygiene had, Fryberg claimed, reduced mortality of the latter type, but death rates of the former type were still high. Seventy-three of

137 Queensland, *Annual Report on the Health and Medical Services of the State of Queensland for the Year 1945–46* (Brisbane: Government Printer, 1946), p. 85.
138 C. E. Chuter to W. M. Hughes, 29 October 1935, QSA, Series 12355, Item 8892; Raphael Cilento, 'Preliminary Report on the Re-organisation of the Home Department,' p. 23; Virginia Thorley, 'Softly, Softly: How the Mothercraft Association of Queensland Co-existed with Government Policy, 1931–1961,' *Health and History*, 3(2), 2001, pp. 80–4.
139 Abraham Fryberg, 'Infantile Mortality from a Social Aspect,' n.d., p. 3, QSA, Series 12355, Item 8892.
140 A. Jefferis Turner to Raphael Cilento, 22 July 1935; A. Jefferis Turner to Raphael Cilento, 27 May 1935, QSA, Series 12355, Item 8892.

the 195 infant deaths in Brisbane hospitals in 1936–37 were linked to prematurity and hospitals did not always record the exact cause of death. Stillbirths were not recorded at all. Some 103 deaths were firstborns, suggesting the need, Fryberg argued, for a pamphlet concerning antenatal care that could be sent to women within three months of marriage. The state might also, he suggested, withhold baby bonuses if women failed to access available antenatal care.[141] The state's preferred approaches thus included a thorough medical record of the population as well as educational, and sometimes punitive, measures aimed at disciplining that population in hygiene.

Those records that did exist indicated that many infant deaths were due to complications, such as albuminuria and malpresentation, which could be prevented or detected early. Fryberg thus stressed the importance of improving access to antenatal care, by improving the training and skills of nurses and private practitioners attending births, mandating faster notification of premature births, providing visiting nurses and granting allowances for low-income women who might be forced to work until giving birth or who might seek an abortion. This was in addition to increasing the number of maternity hospitals and antenatal clinics, providing obstetrics and paediatrics consultation for general practitioners and extending nursing services in rural areas.[142] A 1940 report similarly noted the importance of making notification of births compulsory within three days instead of the previous limit of 60 days: 'In many cases mistakes had been made and harm done before the nurses were able to visit mothers and their babies.'[143] The upbeat report claimed that state maternal and infant welfare services now reached 90 per cent of mothers and pregnant women in Queensland via personal visits, telephone calls, pamphlets, letters and other publications. With the help of clinics and welfare services, '[m]others have learned the value of natural feeding and have come to regard it as their babies right'.[144] It was imperative to acquire as much data as possible on the life, health and development of mothers and children, and thus of the population. Maternal and infant welfare were thus part of a public health apparatus that combined programs of education with extensive surveillance.[145]

141 Fryberg, 'Infantile Mortality from a Social Aspect,' p. 4.

142 ibid., pp. 1–6.

143 Superintendent to C. E. Chuter, 'Maternal and Child Welfare Service,' 23 July 1940, p. 1, QSA, Series 12355, Item 8892.

144 ibid., p. 2.

145 See Reiger, *The Disenchantment of the Home*, Ch. 4.

Public interest in maternal and infant welfare services remained high, especially among prominent local figures and councils in remote areas of the tropical north and west. Turner frequently received requests for the establishment of either a welfare centre or a travelling nurse in remote towns such as Hughenden, Mossman, Roma and Barcaldine.[146] Some requests emphasised the national imperative of settling the tropics. The Chairman of the Douglas Shire Council informed Turner that local women were enthusiastic about infant welfare services and suggested that a clinic would act as an 'inducement to a further settlement of our undeveloped fertile lands with virile workers and offspring to pave the way'. 'Our ideal of a White Australia must be a living force,' he wrote, 'especially in our tropical areas with its many problems.'[147]

Diet and nutrition were at the core of public health and social medicine in the 1930s, running through maternal and infant welfare and school health in particular. Nutritional research in Britain was beginning to expand and develop knowledge of the relationship between diet and human health in the 1920s. Identifying the specific role of particular vitamins remained a central preoccupation, including the roles of vitamins A and D in disease resistance.[148] There was also a growing interest in the effect of dietary deficiencies on women and pregnancy that reflected concerns about persistently high rates of disability and mortality among pregnant women and infants. A raft of studies emerged suggesting that malnutrition was the chief cause of the various 'toxaemias' of pregnancy.[149] Edward Mellanby, a professor of pharmacology at the University of Sheffield, became a particularly vocal advocate of nutritional reform in Britain. Throughout the 1920s and 1930s, Mellanby spoke often about the impact of deficiencies of vitamins, calcium, iron, phosphorus and other constituents of food on the development of teeth and bones, the

---

146 A. Hodges, Secretary, Hughenden Branch, Queensland Country Women's Association, to A. Jefferis Turner, 10 June 1935; Mrs C. H. Young to A. Jefferis Turner, 18 June 1935; A. Jefferis Turner to Raphael Cilento, 18 June 1935; M. Duncombe to A. Jefferis Turner, n.d., QSA, Series 12355, Item 8892.
147 Secretary, Douglas Shire Council, to A. Jefferis Turner, 1 June 1935, QSA, Series 12355, Item 8892.
148 H. N. Green and Edward Mellanby, 'Vitamin A as an Anti-infective Agent,' *The British Medical Journal*, II(3537), 20 October 1928, pp. 691–6.
149 Lucy Wills, 'Treatment of "Pernicious Anaemia of Pregnancy" and "Tropical Anaemia",' *The British Medical Journal*, I(3676), 20 June 1931, pp. 1059–64; G. W. Theobald, 'The Aetiology and Prevention of the Toxaemias of Pregnancy,' *The British Medical Journal*, II(3790), 26 August 1933, pp. 376–81; Edward Mellanby, 'Nutrition and Child-bearing,' *The Lancet*, 222(5751), 18 November 1933, pp. 1131–7.

health of infants and childhood development.[150] This work, and that of American laboratory investigators such as Elmer McCollum at Johns Hopkins, led to an international consensus on the need for a balanced diet, for mother and child, of fresh fruit and vegetables, eggs, butter and milk—the so-called 'protective foods'.[151]

By the 1930s, nutrition studies had progressed from molecular and physiological research to investigations of the economic and social aspects of diet and health.[152] The League of Nations published a series of reports focused on creating standards in dietary requirements, including daily caloric needs and ideal daily intakes of proteins, carbohydrates, fats, vitamins and minerals. It also sought to outline diets for different sections of society, including women, expectant mothers, children and men engaged in various types of labour.[153] Wallace Aykroyd's study of nutrition and low incomes appeared in the League of Nations Health Organization's *Quarterly Bulletin* in 1933.[154] In 1935, Aykroyd and Etienne Burnet published in the same journal a much larger investigation of nutrition in public health generally. The report asserted that nutrition was as important a subject in public health as infectious disease and water supplies:

> In so far as public health activity is concerned not only to defend populations against disease, but also to create a maximum of physical well-being, nutrition is perhaps the most important subject with which it has to deal.[155]

150 Edward Mellanby, 'Diet and Disease, with Special Reference to the Teeth, Lungs, and Pre-natal Feeding,' *The British Medical Journal*, I(3403), 20 March 1926, pp. 515–19.
151 Mellanby, 'Nutrition and Child-bearing,' p. 1137; Commonwealth of Australia, *Report of the Advisory Council on Nutrition. No. 4* (Canberra: Government Printer, 1937), p. 8; Nutrition Committee of the National Health and Medical Research Council, *Diet and Nutrition for the Australian People* (Sydney: Angus & Robertson, 1943), p. 9. See also Cullather, 'Foreign Policy of the Calorie,' p. 354.
152 Hardy, 'Beriberi, Vitamin B1 and World Food Policy,' pp. 64–6.
153 Weindling, 'Social Medicine at the League of Nations Health Organisation and the International Labour Office Compared,' pp. 144–5.
154 W. R. Aykroyd, 'Diet in Relation to Small Incomes,' *Quarterly Bulletin of the Health Organisation of the League of Nations*, 2, 1933, pp. 130–53.
155 Burnet and Aykroyd, 'Nutrition and Public Health,' p. 328.

Its appeal to the need for 'vigorous' and ideal 'physical development and efficiency' reflected the influence that social medicine and the notion of 'positive' health had attained internationally.[156] A mixed committee of the League of Nations, including Mellanby, published its final report on nutrition in 1937, covering the health, agricultural and economic aspects of diet.[157]

These international investigations of the economic and social aspects of nutrition and the research of Mellanby, McCollum and others were important sources for Cilento and informed discussions of nutrition at national and state levels in Australia.[158] At the first meeting of the NHMRC, Hughes stated:

> I believe that in an ill-balanced dietary [sic] from which vitamins, essential chemical elements and roughage have been eliminated, we have the cause of very much of the ill-health and many of the diseases from which people in this and most civilized countries suffer.[159]

When Cilento presented the Livingston Lectures at Camden College in Sydney in 1936, he asserted: 'Nutrition is, indeed, the chief governing factor in the great parabola of the human life course—the constant chemical activator.'[160] The problem, however, went beyond physiology to include, Cilento argued, 'psychological, agricultural, commercial, and industrial problems that underlie both our culture and world comity'.[161] Cilento shared this perspective on the international dimensions of nutrition with many others. Indeed, it was the Australian representative at the League of Nations, former prime minister Sir Stanley Bruce, who called in 1936 for an international campaign to study diet internationally and alleviate malnutrition and undernourishment by increasing trade in food crops.[162] The Commonwealth Advisory Council on Nutrition, which included Cilento, was formed that year and, in planning local nutritional

---

156 ibid., pp. 327–8.

157 League of Nations, *Final Report of the Mixed Committee of the League of Nations on the Relation of Nutrition to Health, Agriculture and Economic Policy* (Geneva: League of Nations, 1937).

158 Weindling, 'Social Medicine at the League of Nations Health Organisation and the International Labour Office Compared,' p. 144. See papers and notes for Cilento's Camden College lectures in Cilento Papers, UQFL44, Box 17, Item 83. See Earle Page's speech at a meeting of the British Medical Association in Melbourne, 5 September 1935, Page Papers, MS 1633, Folder 564.

159 *Report of the National Health and Medical Research Council*, 1st Session, p. 4.

160 Cilento, *Nutrition and Numbers*, p. 25.

161 ibid., p. 46.

162 Gillespie, *The Price of Health*, pp. 53–4. See also, Bashford, 'World Population and Australian Land,' p. 214.

studies, it adopted methods of the league and the International Labour Organization (ILO). The establishment of the council thus reflected Australian initiatives in the international arena.[163] One of the council's aims was to collect information on the actual nutritional status of Australians. To this end, the council distributed booklets in which housewives were to record family meals, although it admitted that this method tended to record food purchased rather than consumed.[164] The council also initiated a direct medical survey of remote inland communities in Queensland, Victoria and South Australia, in which F. W. Clements, a Commonwealth health officer, made physical examinations of school students and inquired about their diet.[165] The aim was to determine levels of nutritional quality, undernourishment or actual malnutrition through measurements of weight, height, an arm–chest–hip index and x-ray examination of the wrist.

The Nutrition Council urged the states to create their own agencies that would act as local committees. The Queensland Nutrition Council originally fulfilled this role after Cilento, academics, government officials and representatives of the National Council of Women, the Mothercraft Association and other organisations established it in 1935.[166] When the government formed the official State Nutritional Advisory Board, however, the independent council was superseded. The board, on which Cilento served as chairman, was responsible for investigating the standard of nutrition in Queensland, with special reference to schools, public institutions and industry. It could also initiate inquiries into the quality of fruit, vegetables, meat and bread produced in Queensland.

---

163 The council included Cumpston as chairman; Cilento; Douglas Lee, Professor of Physiology, University of Queensland; Sir David Rivett, CEO of the Commonwealth Council for Scientific and Industrial Research (CSIR); Sir George Julius, the Chairman of the CSIR; S. M. Wadham, Professor of Agriculture, University of Melbourne; Professor Harvey Sutton; C. G. Lambie, Professor of Medicine, University of Sydney; W. A. Osbourne, Professor of Physiology, University of Melbourne; Sir C. Stanton Hicks, Professor of Physiology and Pharmacology, University of Adelaide; and Henry Priestly, Professor of Physiology, University of Sydney. See Commonwealth of Australia, *Report of the Advisory Council on Nutrition. No. 2* (Canberra: Government Printer, 1936), p. 5.
164 ibid., pp. 8–11.
165 Commonwealth of Australia, *Report of the Advisory Council on Nutrition. No. 3* (Canberra: Government Printer, 1937), p. 9; Commonwealth of Australia, *Report of the Advisory Council on Nutrition. No. 4*, pp. 9–11.
166 'Preliminary Meeting Queensland Nutrition Council,' 21 July 1936, QSA, Series 14769, Item 86221.

Food had long been a concern of public health authorities, beginning with sanitation concerns over the possible contamination and adulteration of milk in the nineteenth century.[167] Where older sanitarians had been worried about the addition of molasses, water and chalk to milk, or the transmission of infectious diseases, the Queensland board focused on the safety of modern coal-tar dyes used in foods and the value of synthetic proprietary brands of baby food, bread and fruit juice.[168] Douglas Lee, a member of both the Queensland Nutrition Council and the State Nutritional Advisory Board, investigated the vitamin and mineral content of Queensland produce, and his findings suggested it did not suffer from any intrinsic deficiencies that could ever lead to malnutrition or malnourishment.[169] One of the most persistent topics with which the board dealt was the creation of bread standards to govern the production of different kinds of white, wholemeal, brown and wheatgerm bread. Regulations would require that loaves not conforming to these standards had to display labels with their nutritional content. A memorandum on bread standards that Lee submitted to the board noted the higher cost of producing nutritious bread and suggested incentives such as bonuses, concessions in fixed price or weight concessions.[170]

The government's interest in nutrition intersected with domestic science and ideas about public education. Cilento wrote in frustration to one interested citizen:

> One of the difficulties in a democracy is the fact that it is impossible to institute reforms by order, however well recognised the necessity for reform may be. The one thing in which the Australian worker will not tolerate dictation is in the matter of his breakfast table. Education along sound lines appears to be the only solution and it is a very difficult and thankless task.[171]

---

167 Deborah Dwork, 'The Milk Option: An Aspect of the History of the Infant Welfare Movement 1898–1908,' *Medical History*, 31(1), 1987, pp. 31–69; P. J. Atkins, 'Sophistication Detected: Or, the Adulteration of the Milk Supply, 1850–1914,' *Social History*, 16(3), 1991, pp. 320–1.
168 'Minutes of the State Nutritional Advisory Board,' 26 January 1939; 'Minutes of State Nutritional Advisory Board,' 18 May 1938, QSA, Series 14767, Item 86217.
169 Raphael Cilento, 'Report of the State Nutritional Advisory Board,' 1937–38, pp. 2–3, QSA, Series 14767, Item 86217.
170 D. H. K. Lee, 'Bread Standards,' n.d. p. 3, attached to 'Minutes of the State Nutritional Advisory Board,' 20 April 1937, QSA, Series 14767, Item 86217.
171 Raphael Cilento to F. Kemp, 4 September 1936, QSA, Series 14769, Item 86221.

The board dealt with public education about food in a way that reflected established ideas about domestic science and the role of women in cultivating both a hygienic home and a vital nation. Kerreen Reiger and Michael Gilding have both shown how late nineteenth-century industrial capitalism fostered a lasting ideological division of public and domestic spheres, in which the latter came to represent a moral refuge from the strain and debasing competition of the former. Bourgeois discourse strongly gendered these spheres, dictating that the primary duty of mothers was to bear children and provide a domestic environment that ensured the health of her offspring. Reiger and Alison Bashford have also identified a fundamental contradiction in this aspect of modern capitalist culture—namely, that although the domestic female role was supposedly natural and apart from the world of industry, the emerging class of trained experts and professionals disseminating this discourse also insisted on the need for motherhood to be taught according to scientific principles and knowledge. Indeed, the discourse of the female domestic sphere as a space for scientific investigation was an important basis on which many women created a professional career in the public sphere.[172]

Health and nutrition in Queensland clearly reflected these ideologies. The government largely excluded the Queensland Mothercraft Association, formed in 1931, from maternal and infant welfare. The association definitely had a voice, however, in discussions about nutrition. Phyllis Cilento, herself a specialist in maternal and infant welfare and the first president of the Mothercraft Association, was a noted public advocate for including domestic science and hygiene in the state curriculum for schoolgirls.[173] Her prominence in organisations involved in infant welfare enabled her to contribute to the State Nutritional Advisory Board, providing an avenue through which expert women could influence government policy and propaganda on nutrition. W. J. Sachs, a nurse from the Mothercraft Association, provided a paper on 'Domestic Science as a Factor in National Health Service' to a meeting of the board in April 1939 that illustrates the gendered discourse of nutrition and health. Reflecting the penetration of the domestic sphere by scientific principles, Sachs asserted:

---

172 Reiger, *The Disenchantment of the Home*, pp. 62, 216; Alison Bashford, *Purity and Pollution: Gender, Embodiment and Victorian Medicine* (Basingstoke, UK: Macmillan, 1998), pp. 8–16; Alison Bashford, 'Domestic Scientists: Modernity, Gender, and the Negotiation of Science in Australian Nursing, 1880–1910,' *Journal of Women's History*, 12(2), 2000, pp. 132–9.
173 'Ideal Conditions for Motherhood: Lady Cilento Addresses Q.W.E.L.,' *Telegraph*, 18 July 1935, QSA, Series 12355, Item 8892.

Recognition of the chemical nature of food constituents and in particular
the determination of the molecular structures of the vitamins have made
food preparation a science as well as an art. The quantitative estimations
of the laboratory worker now <u>dictate</u> kitchen procedure.[174]

The qualified and up-to-date domestic science teacher, using
demonstrations and lectures, and always a woman, could thus become
the best asset for improving national health as long as received wisdom
bowed to the 'research worker'.[175] The greatest obstacle to good nutritional
health was the 'ignorance' of the housewife and, as the 'girl of to-day is
the mother of the near future', it was crucial to instruct young women in
the principles of a healthy diet. The improved physical condition of future
generations that would result from the instruction of young women in
principles of domestic science, Sachs contended, 'must lead to a "<u>positive</u>
improvement of health, the induction of a more buoyant health and
gains in national health, efficiency and longevity"'.[176] In 1939, Sachs
was a member of a subcommittee of the board, which Phyllis Cilento
chaired, that wrote revisions for the official *Queensland Mothers' Book*,
a government publication that provided instructions for breastfeeding,
weaning and the preparation of artificial feeding mixtures.[177]

Public interest in nutrition in Queensland was significant, but it was
skewed towards the educated middle class. Indeed, one of the chief
problems that health officials identified in the Commonwealth's nutrition
survey was the tendency for those participating to be a select group of
educated women who were already interested in nutrition and domestic
science.[178] While the Commonwealth was responsible for the content and
production of publicity on diet, such as pamphlets and booklets, the state
board was responsible for their distribution to schools and maternal and
infant welfare clinics. Interested citizens and domestic science teachers
frequently wrote to Raphael Cilento requesting copies of pamphlets on
vitamins, milk and fruit and vegetables.[179] Schools would occasionally

---

174 'Domestic Science as a Factor in National Health Service,' n.d., p. 1, QSA, Series 14767,
Item 86217. Sachs's emphasis.

175 ibid., p. 2.

176 ibid., p. 3. Sachs's emphasis.

177 'State Nutritional Advisory Board: Report of Subcommittee to Consider Diets in Queensland
Mothers' Book,' n.d., pp. 1–4, QSA, Series 14767, Item 86217; Thorley, 'Softly, Softly,' pp. 83–4.

178 'State Nutritional Advisory Board: Minutes of Meeting,' 4 March 1938, p. 1, QSA, Series
14767, Item 86217.

179 Jean Casly to Raphael Cilento, 2 December 1940; Mrs J. A. Drynan to Raphael Cilento, 6 June
1941; Sister A. E. McCallum to Raphael Cilento, 12 May 1941; J. A. Adsett to Raphael Cilento,
22 June 1941; Margaret Butterworth to Raphael Cilento, 8 July 1941, QSA, Series 14767, Item 86217.

hold special events to encourage students to think about citizenship through subjects such as hygiene, agriculture and vocational training. The state school at Esk, north-west of Brisbane, organised a Project Club Day in December 1939, during which students were organised into separate groups of boys and girls, each with a chairperson, to prepare short lectures for the rest of the students. The boys were to discuss forestry and the girls domestic hygiene. When the young chairperson of the girls' group addressed the school, she stated: 'It is most desired that we girls should have some knowledge of such very important matters as Health and Nutrition.' Armed with that knowledge of vitamins, the nutritional value of foods and diets, they, the 'future citizens' of Australia, would 'continue to make us a progressive and virile nation'.[180] Cilento was impressed and helped to set up a prize at the Esk school for the best essay on nutrition.[181]

When reformers raised the issue of household income, they often identified 'ignorance' as the most important factor in nutritional problems. In her paper on domestic science for the State Nutritional Advisory Board, Sachs wrote:

> Though noticeable deficiency diseases are not common in Australia, we shall not reach optimal standards of health till the intake of the essential food stuffs is increased. Increased purchasing power, which is so often advocated as a cure for this shortage, will not solve this trouble, while the housewife's ignorance of food values and correct methods of preparation leads her to choose food wrongly and in process of preparation frequently to discard the most valuable part.[182]

In *Nutrition and Numbers*, Cilento acknowledged that low incomes affected diets, yet asserted that 'the poor are often also ignorant, and poor incomes are often associated with crass stupidity in food purchase'.[183] People were creatures of habit, not machines, Cilento insisted, and much had to be done to overcome the 'class consciousness' that made workers aspire to a diet of meat and fewer vitamin-rich foods. There was thus much credence to complaints from trade unions that government investigations into nutrition tended to justify neglect of the question of wages.[184] Indeed, the final report of the Commonwealth Advisory

180 Leona Blank, 'Address,' attached to L. W. Bailey, Head Teacher, to Raphael Cilento, 15 December 1939, QSA, Series 14767, Item 86217.
181 Raphael Cilento to L. W. Bailey, 16 February 1940, QSA, Series 14767, Item 86217.
182 'Domestic Science as a Factor in National Health Service,' p. 3.
183 Cilento, *Nutrition and Numbers*, p. 49.
184 Gillespie, *The Price of Health*, p. 55.

Council on Nutrition pointed to 'faulty selection of diets as the main cause of malnutrition, a selection sometimes necessitated by poverty, but more often the result of ignorance'.[185] The council's conclusions were poorly received. Labour representatives suspected they would justify reductions in wages, while the final report noted that husbands sometimes prevented their wives from recording household meals for the survey.[186] The council's work also faced criticism from economists who noted that the Australian investigations had avoided correlating malnutrition and income—a practice that had been central to international studies.[187] The board and the council essentially sought to address the physiological needs of the community within the framework of a capitalist democracy, reflecting Weindling's claim that social medicine amounted in many countries to the technocratic application of physiology.[188]

Nutrition reflected the larger tendency in public health in Australia and Queensland to combine efforts to develop pervasive mechanisms of surveillance and research with a gendered program of education in health and hygiene. Recognition of the role of various environmental factors—nutrition chief among them—increasingly fostered a conception of health that included notions of 'vitality', energy and physical development. Public health discourse now emphasised that the body was not simply a clean space that invading germs might infect, but also an organism whose development could be impaired. In their life and work, individuals needed quantities of energy that science could calculate. Many factors—such as diet, light, air, exercise, chemicals and germs—operated through life as potential causes of lasting sickness or reduced physical capacity. For health authorities with an interest in economic development and productivity—such as Cilento, Cumpston, Morris and others—achieving maximum individual and collective efficiency led to energetic campaigns to expand a range of measures designed to produce knowledge of individuals and populations and to coordinate mechanisms with which the state could intervene in the health, care and development of infants,

---

185 Commonwealth of Australia, *Final Report of the Advisory Council on Nutrition* (Canberra: Government Printer, 1938), p. 32.
186 ibid., p. 6.
187 James Gillespie, 'The "Marriage of Agriculture and Health" in Australia: The Advisory Council on Nutrition and Nutrition Policy in the 1930s,' in Suzanne Parry (ed.), *From Migration to Mining: Medicine and Health in Australian History* (Darwin: Historical Society of the Northern Territory, 1998), pp. 49–52.
188 Weindling, 'Social Medicine at the League of Nations Health Organisation and the International Labour Office Compared,' p. 137.

schoolchildren and workers. The state, in other words, backed with scientific authority, sought to keep its eye on individuals from life to death, provide protections for them in education and work and transform them into productive citizens.

The city colossus and the tropical jungle: Diet and decline in the 1930s

Cilento was obviously indebted to international discourse, circulating through journals and reports, concerning the state, the medical profession and the community in 'civilised' industrial societies. The particular formulation of social medicine that Cilento developed owed much, however, to his colonial experience and his understandings of modern empire and globalisation. Many of the projects Cilento pursued in Queensland reflected an agenda for medicine he had developed in New Guinea. The nutritional research and reforms he initiated were particularly conspicuous examples of this, as was the assertion that medical knowledge must be at the heart of the governance of populations. Furthermore, Cilento explained sickness and demographic stagnation among white Australians and colonised peoples in the Pacific as a shared experience of economic globalisation. In this sense, he imagined the mind and body of the Australian people in relation to embodied colonial subjects in the Pacific.

Cilento became something of a public intellectual in the 1930s. While still a Commonwealth medical officer, he began giving lectures in which he connected population and health to nutrition and history. In his 1933 Anne MacKenzie Oration, 'The Conquest of Climate', delivered at the Institute of Anatomy in Canberra, Cilento added a historical perspective to his earlier refutations of climatic determinism, arguing that great civilisations had sprung from warm climates in Asia and the Middle East. Progress, he argued, derived not from an inherently superior quality of place, but from 'maintained accord between man and his environment'.[189] Having read Oswald Spengler's *The Decline of the West* and Thomas Malthus's works on population, Cilento became fond of overarching metanarratives involving historical cycles of civilisation, progress and decline. In this, Cilento emphasised the material interaction of food and

---

189 Cilento, 'The Conquest of Climate,' pp. 421–32.

health. In Malthusian population theory, the availability of food placed the most important check on population growth, and Cilento was drawn more and more to a Malthusian historical narrative in which social decline, disease and war were the consequences of population growth that outstripped available food.[190]

Although Malthusian theory had lost popular credibility by the late nineteenth century, Malthusianism did not die off. Rather, as Alison Bashford points out, it migrated from voluntary public activism to twentieth-century academic social science.[191] Twentieth-century demographers pointed to overpopulation, especially in Europe, and stressed the need for balance in the relationship between population, land and available food on a global scale. In fact, many demographers subjected national sovereignty, especially in settler-colonial contexts, to a neo-Malthusian critique that questioned the ethics of claiming land with low population density while denying settlement of that land to foreign subjects.[192] Cilento was thus one of a number of doctors, demographers and other professionals around the world for whom Malthus's ideas about the relationship between food, population and land were a critical intellectual framework for their work in social policy and practice.

Malthusian discourse in Australia was not homogeneous and Cilento's view diverged in important ways from Australian neo-Malthusians, including the government statistician George Handley Knibbs. Neo-Malthusian academics and professionals such as Knibbs and his counterparts overseas causally linked population growth and war, and sought peaceful international solutions to problems of overpopulation, resources and distribution.[193] Nationalism and the 'engines of destruction' built to violently maintain the present distribution of people had to give way, in their view, to peaceful international cooperation in allowing migration from overpopulated areas to those of low population density.[194] This was for Knibbs and other pacifist demographers a moral issue that had clear implications for Australia and the vast sparsely populated areas that it claimed exclusively.

---

190 Such Malthusian perspectives had informed international diplomats since the end of World War I. See Brawley, *The White Peril*, pp. 11–14.
191 Bashford, 'World Population and Australian Land,' pp. 214–15.
192 ibid., pp. 213–14.
193 Brawley, *The White Peril*, p. 12; Bashford, 'World Population and Australian Land,' p. 220.
194 George Handley Knibbs, *The Shadow of the World's Future; Or the Earth's Population Possibilities and the Consequences of the Present Rate of Increase of the Earth's Inhabitants* (London: Ernest Benn Ltd, 1928), p. 72.

Cilento's adherence to Malthusian theory actually hardened his nationalist commitment to white occupation of Australia through increasing and improving the population in the face of potential international racial conflict.[195] A Malthusian process was still in effect in his account, but it outlined a different response. In *Nutrition and Numbers*, the urgency of settling and developing the tropics still derived from the potential for invasion: 'War is still the final arbiter between land-hungry nations on the borders of subsistence, and lethargic peoples in half-developed lands.' It was thus vital to allow science to foster new agricultural and pastoral production that would increase the Australian population beyond a stalemate.[196] In *Blueprint for the Health of a Nation*, Cilento criticised Knibbs's supposed obsession with overpopulation in Europe: 'The only "over-population" that we need fear, or ever have needed to fear is among our enemies.'[197] Although Bashford notes that Knibbs never countenanced anything other than British settlement in Australia, Cilento forcefully emphasised the threat of Asian population growth—an old anxiety expressed in popular, political and academic texts, including serialised stories of invasion, numerous published cartoons and in the works of the American political scientist Lothrop Stoddard and British geographer J. W. Gregory.[198] In a 1936 article on race and population in the Pacific, Cilento argued that Japanese territorial ambitions arose from the pressure of population growth on agricultural land and production. War was a very possible outcome of this interaction.[199] In *Blueprint for the Health of a Nation*, Cilento wrote:

> *The plain fact is that the aging civilisation of Europe with its offshoots in America, Australia, and elsewhere, is pressed on all its borders by the increasing hordes of Mongol and Mongoloid races.*[200]

It was therefore imperative, Cilento argued, to not only assure that Australians attained the status of the 'commando' instead of the 'coolie', but also secure the continent for white settlement through increased fertility.[201] His earlier emphasis on increasing the birth rate and improving the physical quality of Australians thus reflected Cilento's belief in the racial and martial struggle of international politics and history.

195 Gillespie, *The Price of Health*, p. 51.
196 Cilento, *Nutrition and Numbers*, p. 69.
197 Cilento, *Blueprint for the Health of a Nation*, pp. 93–4.
198 Stoddard, *The Rising Tide of Color Against White World-supremacy*; Gregory, *The Menace of Colour*.
199 Cilento, 'Some Problems of Racial Pressure in the Pacific,' p. 42.
200 Cilento, *Blueprint for the Health of a Nation*, p. 93. Cilento's emphasis.
201 ibid., p. 113.

Cilento frequently qualified this insistence on a materialist Malthusian narrative by pointing to psychology and cultural decline. It was not only the availability of food that limited populations, but also the attitude of the upper classes in advanced, urbanised societies. From the early twentieth century, falling birth rates stoked anxieties that remained at a high pitch in Australia. New South Wales established a royal commission into birth rates in 1903 and, in the 1930s, it was still a matter of deep concern for politicians and public health officials. In a speech to the NHMRC, Hughes noted that worldwide declines in birth rates in the civilised world had '[s]pecial and alarming implications for this country':

> Our national motto, 'Advance Australia', is not a boast, but a finger post to national salvation. We can only justify our claim to this great and fertile country by effectively occupying it. Australia must advance and populate, or perish.[202]

Cilento noted falling birth rates in his 'Open Letter' and followed up these warnings about a stagnant population in *Blueprint for the Health of a Nation*.[203] At a conference of officials, hospital staff and representatives of the medical profession convened to discuss abortion in Queensland, Hanlon declared that 'from the point of view of the nation we were approaching race suicide'.[204]

In his lectures, Cilento drew parallels with ancient China, Greece and Rome, where laws designed to increase the birth rate seemed to reflect a fear of 'race suicide'. Cilento deplored women who abandoned their duty as mothers of the race, encouraged by modern urban culture:

> 'The Ibsen woman' of the city Colossus feels, as Bernard Shaw states, that 'unless she repudiates her womanliness, her duty to her husband, to her children, to society, to the law, and to everyone but herself, she cannot emancipate herself.' Instead of children she has 'soul conflicts'; the robust family is something about which to be apologetic; the father of many children is in city life a subject for caricature.[205]

---

202 *Report of the National Health and Medical Research Council*, 1st Session, p. 4.
203 Cilento, 'Open Letter to Medical Men,' p. 1; Cilento, *Blueprint for the Health of a Nation*, pp. 92–3.
204 Notes of a Conference Held on Tuesday, 26 October, n.d., QSA, Series 8400, Item 279715.
205 Cilento, 'Some Problems of Racial Pressure in the Pacific,' p. 46.

Speaking to the Queensland Mothercraft Association, Phyllis Cilento claimed that young married women were 'anxious to evade maternity at whatever cost ... It is we who are failing our nation in our refusal or inability to bear children and replenish and develop our land'.[206] In *Blueprint for the Health of a Nation*, Raphael suggested that urbanisation encouraged an obsession with the acquisition of social status through furniture, clothing and entertainment. The problem of the Australian birth rate was thus in part a psychological effect of city life, which led to neglect of national civic duty.[207] The upshot of industrial and scientific progress, Cilento argued, was the sacrifice of national virility and vigour to effete, and effeminate, urban culture.[208]

Public health discourse of the interwar period harboured ambivalent feelings about modernity that are evident in Cilento's work. Based in the laboratory and associated with science and progress, medicine and public health seemed to epitomise modernity. Yet many worried about the impact of modern society and culture on health and 'vitality'. Nutrition, especially, seemed to Cilento to demonstrate how industrial capitalism and urbanisation affected the health of people in 'civilised' countries. In *Nutrition and Numbers*, he noted how modern production had modified food for 'taste, appearance, portability, storage, or other convenience'.[209] The Queensland State Nutritional Advisory Board paid close attention to synthetic foods and food additives and framed regulations to preserve the nutritional value of urban working-class diets. Commercial production of tinned food, white bread and sweets, and artificial flavouring and colouring, tended to reduce the vitamin content of food available to urban populations. Such developments during the nineteenth century, Cilento wrote, led to 'chronic deficiencies among white workers' that remained in the 1930s.[210]

Cilento expressed such concerns within a wider apprehension about the affects on modernity on national culture. The globalisation of the economy led to the production and importation of canned and dried foods, often

206 *The Courier-Mail*, [Brisbane], 14 October 1937, p. 22.
207 Cilento, *Blueprint for the Health of a Nation*, pp. 96–7. See also Cilento, *Nutrition and Numbers*, pp. 62–70.
208 George Newman, a former Chief Medical Officer of the British Board of Education and Ministry of Health, discussed some of these dynamics between industrialisation, urbanisation and women's attitudes to maternity in a less sensational way in his *The Building of a Nation's Health* (London: Macmillan & Co., 1939), pp. 292–6.
209 Cilento, *Nutrition and Numbers*, p. 34.
210 ibid., p. 34.

containing additives to make them more palatable.[211] Ordinary people, Cilento wrote, were led 'to live upon materials fractionated for the sake of taste, appearance, or convenience, treated by destructive methods, and preserved too long before consumption'.[212] The implications of the modern diet were not limited to health. For Cilento, it reflected the larger sense in which modernity made life artificial—deprived of the 'stimulus' of the struggle against nature that the comforts of city and domestic life had eliminated.[213] A distinction between the natural and the evolving on the one hand and the artificial and the stagnant on the other was important here. Cilento believed people had an innate 'taste' for nutritional value— seen in the way he understood the high value of some foods in New Guinean cultures as a nutritional instinct. In contrast, the metropolitan consumer's enthusiasm for white bread and other foods 'depraved' this instinct.[214] Individuals were being:

> deprived of [their] capacity for selection by the flavours with which food is disguised, and he has been led, moreover, to look for the ready and delusive energy supplied in the form of sugar and starches.[215]

Cilento's ambivalence towards modernity thus focused on the way it appeared to him to disrupt the equilibrium of food and work fostered by being within a 'natural' environment.

In positing a disruption of balanced adaptation to environments, Cilento linked metropolitan modernity and imperialism by comparing the impact of urban modernity on the city dweller with the impact of colonisation on Pacific societies. As discussed in earlier chapters, Cilento attributed much of the sickness and social problems of New Guinea and Fiji in the 1920s to the impact of imperial integration within a global economy. The alienation of land in New Guinea and the growth of a community of Indian peasants in Fiji had severely affected traditional agriculture. Instead of producing and consuming local produce, indigenous people lived on tinned meat and rice. Their vitamin and mineral deficiencies were what primarily determined sickness and declining fertility in these populations. Cilento continued this theme in lectures and articles in the 1930s. 'The overflow

---

211 ibid., p. 42. On the transformations of British food consumption, see Andrew Thompson, *The Empire Strikes Back? The Impact of Imperialism on Britain from the Mid-nineteenth Century* (New York: Pearson Longman, 2005), pp. 45–9.
212 Cilento, *Nutrition and Numbers*, p. 44.
213 ibid., p. 45.
214 ibid., p. 38.
215 ibid., p. 44.

of the West submerged the Pacific in a wave of arrogant commercialism, seeking new markets, raw products, and new homes', balancing these populations 'on a knife-edge of survival'.[216] In *Nutrition and Numbers*, he told his audience that indigenous people were increasingly drawn into the same 'industrial spate' that caused health problems among European workers: 'The growing exploitation of native lands for the production of the primary produce increasingly desired by Europe had very marked effects upon the native populations.'[217] Colonialism, Cilento argued, in drawing indigenous peoples into a global economy, disturbed a diet that, however inferior to an ideal European one, had been part of an equilibrium between population and environment that allowed a people to survive.

Returning to his insistence that cycles of progress and decline turned on material relations of population, subsistence and disease, Cilento likened the disturbance of colonialism to that of urbanisation. The impoverished diet that resulted from both processes led to problems with physical development, endurance and fatigue, as well as lowering resistance to diseases such as malaria and tuberculosis. The difficulty of obtaining adequate and nutritious food:

> may explain the decay of primitive and sophisticated alike, for there is no less evidence that the same conditions occur in people resident in cities, where the difficulties of obtaining a properly balanced diet and live food are marked.[218]

Colonialism in the Pacific and modern urbanisation were equally disorienting for 'primitive' and 'civilised' peoples. For Robert Dixon, texts on tropical medicine were an exemplary instance of the importance of colonial discourse and practice in shaping Australian modernity. Public health officials such as Elkington and Cilento sought to subject European settlers in the Australian tropics to the same apparatuses of surveillance and government developed in India, the Philippines and the Dutch East Indies.[219] At the same time, literature on the tropics, especially the diaries of colonial officials and published travel narratives, reveal anxiety about nervous breakdowns and the dissolution of distinctions between the white and the indigenous subject.[220]

---

216 Cilento, 'Some Problems of Racial Pressure in the Pacific,' p. 46.
217 Cilento, *Nutrition and Numbers*, p. 34.
218 Cilento, 'Some Problems of Racial Pressure in the Pacific,' p. 45.
219 Dixon, *Prosthetic Gods*, pp. 35–7; Anderson, *The Cultivation of Whiteness*, pp. 135–46.
220 Dixon, *Prosthetic Gods*, p. 17. See also Anderson, *Colonial Pathologies*, pp. 130–42.

In Cilento's work, one finds this relationship not just in his work on tropical settlement, but also in his work on Australian public health reform in general and in nutrition especially. Much important research on the constituents of food, especially vitamins, and the effects of dietary deficiencies on human health emerged in colonial settings in India and the Dutch East Indies. These studies would underpin nutrition science and policy around the world in the 1930s.[221] Cilento's own experience in New Guinea had convinced him of the role diet played in health, yet he also drew on new reports and research from Britain, the United States and the League of Nations. That nutrition found an important place in Australian public health in the 1930s thus reflected both Cilento's own experience of colonial governance and the global diffusion of colonial knowledge and practice. Beyond government, however, Cilento also incorporated the 'colonial' into 'Western' subjectivity. In all periods of cultural decline around the world, he wrote:

> The stigmata of frustration follow their typical course, and find an outlet in apathy or exaltation, whether the victim be a native chewing on a betel nut, a Malay *amok*, a city neurasthene, an early Christian of the fifth century welcoming the barbarian sword as a passport to a glorious eternity, or his Egyptian forerunner of 2600 B.C.[222]

In Cilento's account, the physical and psychological 'crisis', to borrow Dixon's terminology, that modernity inflicted on the 'civilised' city dweller was the same crisis that the 'native' faced in the Pacific.[223] Indeed, the decline of Western civilisation tended to reveal in the civilised subject the latent characteristics of the colonial subject. Drawing on one of Spengler's motifs, Cilento represented the decline of civilisations as a pyramid crumbling at the top: 'At the last only the basic primitive blood—the "fellaheen" type—remains, robbed of its virile and progressive elements.'[224] Colonialism, in disrupting traditional diets and entrenching chronic sickness, precipitated the collapse and stagnation of indigenous populations and vitality. In the city, a similar deterioration in the quality of nutrition led also to stagnation and degeneration towards the status of 'the native'.

---

221 McCarrison and Sinclair, *The Work of Sir Robert McCarrison*; Worboys, 'The Discovery of Colonial Malnutrition between the Wars,' pp. 214–15; Hardy, 'Beriberi, Vitamin B1 and World Food Policy,' pp. 61–77.
222 Cilento, 'Some Problems of Racial Pressure in the Pacific,' p. 43.
223 Dixon, *Prosthetic Gods*, pp. 14–15.
224 Cilento, 'Some Problems of Racial Pressure in the Pacific,' p. 43.

Cilento's contribution to public health had a complex genealogy and intellectual framework that reflected the colonial experience and global historical thought that he bore into the 1930s. In Australia, Cilento sought to bring health into the centre of government. He wanted to make it clear that government ought to be first and foremost concerned with the maintenance of individual health and the collective vitality of the nation, since productivity, efficiency, population and defence rested on the health of the population. Health should also be governmental, he argued, in that the state and the medical profession ought to foster health through close management of the exchanges and interactions between environments and individuals, such as their intake of protein, vitamins, air, water, industrial chemicals and exercise. To foster positive health required broad intervention in the daily lives of individuals and families, along with the central coordination of clinics, hospitals, personnel and professional training.

The conception of health that underpinned this insistence on preventive medicine and positive health was fostered in the social and governmental context of colonial New Guinea. Nutrition was the paradigmatic field of investigation in which individuals and populations could be figured as organisms in a dynamic relationship with their environment and amenable to positive intervention and improvement. Several scholars have noted the importance of colonial research in the development of knowledge and understandings of nutrition. Cilento's enthusiasm for dietary reform likewise arose in the colonial setting of New Guinea, which offered an opportunity to bring nutritional knowledge into government regulations. Cilento's efforts at implementing nutritional knowledge through a public health apparatus thus represented not just a derivation of investigations and considerations overseas, but also a policy commitment born of colonial experience.

Cilento's experience of empire fed into a larger vision of world order and history that provided urgency and an intellectual framework for health reform. Commentaries on falling or stagnant birth rates, abortion, sickness or poor physical development in children had long been manifestations of anxiety about national decline among Australian political, social and professional elites. Modernity in this context—conceived in terms of urbanisation, patterns of consumption, mass media and its effects on the health and psychology of Australians—became a topic on which medical professionals felt they could comment. Cilento's articulation of this story placed Australian sickness within a global movement of empire and industrialisation. Australian decline in the metropolis was paired, Cilento argued, with the decline of indigenous societies precipitated by European colonisation in the Pacific Islands. Indeed, empire was an essential part of the globalised industrial economy that had so affected working-class health. All patterns of decline were in fact the same, as injurious environmental factors bled individuals and societies of their initiative and vitality.

6

Social work and world order: The politics and ideology of social welfare at the United Nations

When Cilento went to work for the United Nations Relief and Rehabilitation Administration (UNRRA) in Egypt in May 1945, he left Australia on an aeroplane from Perth, leaving his family behind in Brisbane. In an unpublished memoir of his time at the United Nations, he wrote that, amid fears for the future of 'civilisation', he was 'among the part-realist and part-sentimentalist millions who were eager to silence their doubts and to offer any abilities they might have to advance this long-range bid for altruistic co-operation'.[1] En route to Cairo, he stopped at Colombo, Madras, Hyderabad, Bombay, Ahmadabad, Karachi and Bahrain. Where once Cilento had travelled by train and boat, he now flew above the borders of the globe in a newer manifestation of modernity—one that had posed novel problems for quarantine officials since the early 1930s. On his journey, Cilento confirmed for himself the existence of social and health problems he had observed in Pacific colonies. Flying over Ceylon, he noted that 'areas devoted to the production of the staple crops are tremendous when compared with the straggly areas on which native foodstuffs are cultivated for local consumption'.[2] There was some irony in his comments. Twenty years earlier, Cilento had noted in a report

---

1   Raphael Cilento, 'Escape from UN-reality,' Introduction, p. 3, Cilento Papers, UQFL44, Box 18, Item 107.
2   Raphael Cilento, Diary: 1 May – 16 May 1945, Appointment to UNRRA, 5 May 1945, Cilento Papers, UQFL44, Box 12, Item 26.

on medical services in New Guinea that 'in old established countries, such as Ceylon, it has been recognised that a mere striving towards economic development irrespective of the health of the native population, means disaster'.[3] As in New Guinea and Fiji, he now observed the need for profit from commercial agriculture had sacrificed indigenous agriculture and nutrition.[4]

This critique did not unsettle his belief in the inferiority of non-European peoples. The Indian pilots and crew were 'inclined to sit down helplessly and hopelessly if anything goes wrong', while the planes were 'crowded with every kind of colonial Indian from cafe au lait to cafe noir'.[5] In the wake of news of the German surrender, he noted in his diary:

> The ships in the harbour at Karachi were all dressed in flags and there is a sort of sedate glee about the English area. Karachi's only reaction, however, is 'What about freedom for India? The war is against imperialism no less than against Fascism'.[6]

In describing both the ruin of the world and the voice of anticolonial nationalism, Cilento felt he was moving through a world that was on the brink of epochal change, for better or worse.

Cilento's time in international civil service was convoluted. Between 1945 and 1950, he held several positions with UNRRA and the UN Secretariat. He was initially offered a post in the Balkans as a malariologist for UNRRA in January 1945, but his arrival in Egypt came as a surprise to the Cairo office.[7] When it became clear that responsibility for Greece had since passed from the Cairo office to London, Cilento proceeded to Athens. Yet UNRRA officials in Greece were ambivalent about Cilento's usefulness. When the chief of the UNRRA mission rejected outright his proposals for aerial spraying of dichlorodiphenyltrichloroethane (DDT), it became clear that his expertise would have little outlet.[8] Cilento then went to London to consult with UNRRA's European Regional Office, which appointed him the UNRRA Director for the British Zone of

3   Raphael Cilento, 'Medical Progress and Policy in the Territory of New Guinea,' January 1925, p. 4, NAA: A518, F832/1/3.
4   See Chapters 2 and 3, this volume.
5   Raphael Cilento, Diary: 1 May – 16 May 1945, Appointment to UNRRA, 6 May 1945, Cilento Papers, UQFL44, Box 12, Item 26. Cilento's emphasis.
6   ibid., 9 May 1945.
7   ibid., 10 May 1945. See also Cilento, 'Escape from UN-reality,' p. 9.
8   Cilento, 'Escape from UN-reality,' p. 36.

occupied Germany. He thus became responsible for the displaced persons' camps that held hundreds of thousands of refugees waiting for repatriation or resettlement. In May 1946, Cilento joined the Secretariat of the United Nations at Lake Success in New York, where he oversaw the creation of the International Refugee Organization in his capacity as Director of the Division of Refugees and Displaced Persons. Cilento thus acquired a reputation as an expert in administering refugee relief. During the 1948 Palestinian refugee crisis, he was assigned to direct the Disaster Relief Project and, when he presented a paper at the 1949 UN Social Welfare Seminar in Beirut, it was on the topic of the 'Social Aspects of Any Refugee Problem'.[9]

For most of his career as an international civil servant, Cilento was the Director of the Division of Social Activities within the Department of Social Affairs of the UN Secretariat. The Advisory Social Welfare Programme—one of the first operational functions of the new international organisation—was his responsibility. Under General Assembly Resolution 58, member states could ask the UN Secretariat to provide assistance with social welfare through expert consultants, regional seminars and technical documentation. The program also offered fellowships to help social workers from underdeveloped countries observe the work of welfare departments and social work schools in the United States and Europe. The Department of Social Affairs fostered connections to government welfare agencies and schools of social work and social science, which provided personnel and support for the program. The secretariat thus mobilised the knowledge and expertise of social welfare institutions and agencies in the developed world. It became involved in disseminating or consolidating both practices of social welfare and ideas about the relationship between wellbeing, family, the community and the state. In this respect, it was a kind of development project, but one with a tense and critical relationship to forms of technical assistance and economic development that emerged in the late 1940s.

---

9   Raphael Cilento, 'The Social Aspects of Any Refugee Problem,' Cilento Papers, UQFL44, Box 17, Item 89.

Renewed interest in international history in general has refocused scholars' attention on the United Nations.[10] Historians have been interested in varieties of internationalism and cosmopolitanism, as well as understanding the connections between imperialism, postwar politics and the social sciences. Many officials and those involved in its foundation believed the United Nations' purpose was to maintain an imperial relationship of tutelage between the 'civilised' white world and the 'coloured' rest. Several studies in history, sociology and anthropology have challenged the distinction between prewar colonialism and post-1940 'development'. On one level, postwar inequality in power, social wellbeing and economic prosperity between the global north and south partly derive from the colonial past.[11] On another, studies suggest the linear progress between 'traditional' and 'modern' prescribed in development discourse preserved imperial ideologies concerning the 'sacred trust of civilisation' or the uplift of 'primitive' peoples.[12] Joseph Hodge, for example, has pointed out that large-scale agricultural development projects after World War II were overseen by scientific experts who had previously worked closely with the British Colonial Office on policies designed to counter colonial unrest in the 1920s and 1930s.[13] Many postwar projects that exemplified large-scale, technocratic development, such as the East Africa Groundnut Scheme of the late 1940s, were late British colonial projects.[14]

At the same time, historians have tried to be sensitive to postwar and postcolonial transformations in ideology and practice. Amy Staples has depicted the birth of postwar international development as a departure from imperialism that was fundamentally positive and infused with

10 Sunil Amrith and Glenda Sluga, 'New Histories of the United Nations,' *Journal of World History*, 19(3), 2008, pp. 251–74; Alison Bashford, 'Population, Geopolitics, and International Organizations in the Mid Twentieth Century,' *Journal of World History*, 19(3), 2008, pp. 327–47; Connelly, *Fatal Misconception*; Mazower, *No Enchanted Palace*; Sluga, 'UNESCO and the (One) World of Julian Huxley,' pp. 393–418.

11 Uma Kothari, 'From Colonial Administration to Development Studies: A Post-colonial Critique of the History of Development Studies,' in Uma Kothari (ed.), *A Radical History of Development Studies: Individuals, Institutions and Ideologies* (London: Zed Books, 2005), pp. 48–9.

12 Frederick Cooper and Randall Packard argue that enthusiasm for these transformations did not develop within British colonialism until the 1940s; 'Introduction,' in Frederick Cooper and Randall Packard (eds), *International Development and the Social Sciences* (Berkeley: University of California Press, 1997), pp. 17–18. See also Kothari, 'From Colonial Administration to Development Studies,' p. 49. On the importance of these dichotomies in colonial ideology and development, see Anderson, *Colonial Pathologies*, pp. 183–4.

13 Hodge, *Triumph of the Expert*, pp. 7–10.

14 ibid., pp. 209–14.

international idealism.[15] Frederick Cooper has argued more subtly that postwar decolonisation effectively ended the legitimacy of colonial empires but also cautions against obscuring the complexities of continuity and rupture in this period.[16] Sunil Amrith has argued that an increasing emphasis on technology and administration at the expense of visions of rural social progress reflected the transformation, at least partially, of the world into a system of nation-states preoccupied with economic development.[17]

Cilento was a UN official with both colonial experience and an imperial vision of world order. It is important to pay attention to continuities of imperial power relations and colonial culture in postwar development, but it is also important to keep in mind the tensions between different imperial discourses and practices. That Cilento's colonial experience and ideas would prompt him to critique postwar economic development is indicative of this. In other words, continuities between imperialism and development did not stop Cilento from perceiving a major rupture in the postwar period. Moreover, the United Nations offered projects in social welfare to all developing or wartorn countries, not merely those nation-states in Asia and the Middle East that were emerging from recent decolonisation.[18] A close examination of the ideology and practice of UN social welfare services, both at headquarters in New York and in particular national missions, illustrates the way in which colonial representations of backwardness and modernity persisted within an administrative framework that reflected a postcolonial world order of sovereign and equal nation-states.

In late 1948, within a few years of Resolution 58, the United Nations began taking on economic development, just as the United States was beginning to expand its web of bilateral aid under president Harry S. Truman's Point IV program.[19] With the ascent of economic development,

<hr />

15   Amy Staples, *The Birth of Development: How the World Bank, Food and Agriculture Organization and the World Health Organization Changed the World, 1945–65* (Kent, OH: Kent State University Press, 2006), pp. 1–2.
16   Frederick Cooper, *Colonialism in Question: Theory, Knowledge, History* (Berkeley: University of California Press, 2005), pp. 19–20.
17   Amrith, *Decolonizing International Health*, pp. 47–8.
18   Kothari notes also that, despite their colonial genealogy, development projects were not a simple extension of colonial rule, since development projects were not inevitable after decolonisation. Kothari, 'From Colonial Administration to Development Studies,' pp. 49–50.
19   US Department of State, *Point Four: Cooperative Program for Aid in the Development of Economically Underdeveloped Areas* (Washington, DC: Office of Public Affairs, 1950). See also Cooper and Packard, 'Introduction,' pp. 8–9.

social welfare experts sought to negotiate a place for their knowledge. They suggested ways in which they could facilitate the economic and social transformation of underdeveloped communities while simultaneously offering a critique of rapid social change among purportedly backward peoples. Cilento felt that the social welfare work of the United Nations ought to continue the paternal tutelage that he had promoted in the still-colonial Pacific Islands, where improved health and social change should occur away from the effects of rapid and substantial economic transformation. When Cilento resigned from the United Nations, he cited as his biggest grievance not only the in-principle equality of nations and races that was emerging in the general assembly, but also the way in which social progress and the 'uplift' of colonial discourse had been trampled under the desire of nation-states to rapidly modernise and develop. Cilento's career at the United Nations thus underscores how this historical moment, between the war and the early 1950s, saw not simple continuity or rupture, but rather the restructuring of a select set of colonial discourses and practices within a politically transformed world.

The world in transition

Cilento came to international social welfare by accident, having initially been appointed to UNRRA as a malaria expert. Dr Wilbur Sawyer, a former director of the International Health Board (IHB) of the Rockefeller Foundation and of the Australian Hookworm Campaign from 1919 to 1922, became involved in planning postwar health work for UNRRA.[20] Cilento later recalled that Sawyer phoned to offer him a role in the Balkans to prevent the spread of malaria from Egypt to Greece.[21] After initial British planning for an anticipated postwar humanitarian crisis, a new impetus from the United States led to the formation of UNRRA in November 1943, which took over organising disease control and material relief for displaced persons. The bulk of the resources and experts involved

---

20   Raphael Cilento, 'Hookworm Work and Control in Australia,' *Report of the Federal Health Council of Australia*, 4, 1930, p. 65.
21   'Interview with Sir Raphael Cilento, Tropical Medicine Specialist,' Interview by Mel Pratt, 7 March 1971, Transcript, National Library of Australia [hereinafter NLA], Canberra, pp. 31–2. On the complex history of the 1942–44 malaria epidemic in Egypt, see Timothy Mitchell, *The Rule of Experts: Egypt, Techno-politics, Modernity* (Berkeley: University of California Press, 2002), Ch. 1.

in its operations also came from the United States.[22] With the cessation of hostilities, UNRRA began providing emergency clothing, blankets, food and shelter to millions of displaced persons in Europe, South-East Asia and China, while also working to prevent epidemics of typhus, malaria and other diseases. After this massive initial distribution of aid, UNRRA took on a broader role in reconstruction. Missions were established in several countries, where UNRRA worked to rehabilitate local economies and institutions by providing child welfare services, occupational training and employment services.[23]

Cilento's first encounter with UNRRA did not impress him. When he arrived at the Cairo office, it had lost all record of his appointment. Cilento eventually made it to Greece in May 1945, just months after British troops and the armed forces of the left-wing National Liberation Front (EAM) had fought in Athens. The size and popularity of the leftist resistance had grown enormously during the war, as it provided infrastructure and social services to many communities.[24] After the withdrawal of German and Italian forces, the British sought a return to the monarchy as the best chance of securing a friendly, anticommunist state, and tried to exclude the EAM from any role in shaping or forming a government. When the British demanded that the Greek People's Liberation Army (ELAS) demobilise while insisting that other minor resistance groups remain armed, the EAM called for a strike and ELAS forces descended on Athens. British prime minister Winston Churchill authorised British troops to actively engage the ELAS, claiming they were seeking to seize power. As Philip Minehan suggests, however, it seems unlikely that this was the case and the British were simply seeking to suppress a left-wing organisation that had enjoyed significant popularity during the war.[25]

In this context of ongoing political tension, Cilento found much in UNRRA's activities to criticise. An agreement in March left UNRRA in a nonpartisan advisory role, giving responsibility for the distribution of

---

22   Amrith, *Decolonizing International Health*, pp. 55–6; Daniel G. Cohen, 'Between Relief and Politics: Refugee Humanitarianism in Occupied Germany 1945–1946,' *Journal of Contemporary History*, 43(3), 2008, pp. 437–9; Katerina Gardikas, 'Relief Work and Malaria in Greece, 1943–1947,' *Journal of Contemporary History*, 43(3), 2008, pp. 493–8; Flora Tsilaga, '"The Mountain Laboured and Brought Forth a Mouse": UNRRA's Operations in the Cyclades Islands, c.1945–46,' *Journal of Contemporary History*, 43(3), 2008, p. 527.
23   Cohen, 'Between Relief and Politics,' pp. 439–42.
24   Philip B. Minehan, *Civil War and World War in Europe: Spain, Yugoslavia, and Greece, 1936–1949* (New York: Palgrave Macmillan, 2006), pp. 148–53.
25   ibid., pp. 210–11.

material aid to the Greek state. UNRRA had insisted on such a position to avoid a popular backlash against an association with British forces, yet its remove from actual operations made its work difficult and its role ambiguous.[26] The Greek Government that had returned from exile in Egypt had little authority in many parts of the country and little capacity to deal with economic reconstruction.[27] Cilento recalled that, in relinquishing a role in providing practical aid with tools, livestock and other materials vital to restarting local production, UNRRA had appeared useless to military authorities, local officials and the public.[28] In the Cyclades Islands, Cilento noted, extreme malnutrition crippled the population, yet in an environment of corruption and inefficiency UNRRA was largely powerless to ease the situation and black markets flourished.[29]

Cilento quickly became redundant. The American chief of the UNRRA mission in Greece rejected outright his proposal for aerial spraying in Crete using DDT. The powerful new insecticide had been used extensively in Sicily, Egypt and Ceylon during the war, but UNRRA balked at prohibitive costs, political ramifications and shortages of personnel.[30] Daniel E. Wright, the Chief Sanitary Engineer for the UNRRA mission in Greece, who had worked in the country for the Rockefeller Foundation in the 1930s, shared Cilento's enthusiasm for DDT and had planned a nationwide house-to-house spraying campaign. Yet Wright was also jealous of the Rockefeller legacy and had argued against taking foreign malaria specialists to Greece in the belief that American philanthropic involvement in the 1930s had left behind a corps of well-trained local personnel.[31]

A frustrated Cilento left Greece to discuss these problems at UNRRA's European Regional Office in London. He encountered resistance there as well, but the London office also needed someone to help coordinate anti-typhus work in Germany. After meeting with the Australian Director-General of the European Regional Office, Commander Robert Jackson, and a long administrative quagmire, Cilento eventually arrived in the

---

26 Gardikas, 'Relief Work and Malaria in Greece,' p. 502.
27 Tsilaga, '"The Mountain Laboured and Brought Forth a Mouse",' p. 527.
28 Cilento, 'Escape from UN-reality,' pp. 19–22.
29 ibid., pp. 29–30.
30 ibid., p. 36. On the wartime use of DDT, see Amrith, *Decolonizing International Health*, pp. 48–50.
31 Cilento, 'Escape from UN-reality,' pp. 34–5. See also Gardikas, 'Relief Work and Malaria in Greece,' p. 503.

British Zone of occupied Germany, serving initially as the Chief Health Officer and then as zone director.[32] Cilento was in charge of attempts to manage the flow of displaced persons and typhus, using an array of camps and medical techniques, including dusting people and clothes with DDT as they crossed the *cordon sanitaire*. The favoured policy of the occupying powers for dealing with displaced persons was repatriation, yet not all were convinced that they would be safe or find opportunities for employment in Eastern Europe.[33] While some accepted repatriation, others opted for resettlement in Germany or abroad in the United States and other lands, including Palestine.[34]

Cilento's work in Germany was thus an attempt to manage a problem population and it spoke to modern ambitions of administrative order over life. UNRRA's work in Germany, as Daniel G. Cohen has noted, was part of a shift from voluntary participation in international welfare to organised and professional planning of relief and development.[35] Refugees, soldiers and other displaced persons were, as in the aftermath of World War I, potential bearers of the lice that carried typhus and therefore threatened the spread of epidemics.[36] 'An unorganized mass movement of these people, attempting to return to their homes', stated one UNRRA publication, 'would reduce war-enfeebled transportation facilities to chaos, would clog roads, and would lead to misery, starvation, and the spread of epidemics'.[37] Jewish inmates of labour and concentration camps were also seen as reservoirs of disease. During Cilento's term as zone director, UNRRA developed plans for mobile x-ray teams to survey the extent of tuberculosis among displaced persons.[38] Cilento in fact administered an apparatus of DDT dusting teams, food depots along

---

32   Fisher, *Raphael Cilento*, p. 181.

33   Raphael Cilento, 'Memorandum: Zone Directive,' n.d.; 'Memorandum: Repatriation of Polish D.P.s,' Col. E. T. Penfold, UNRRA District Director, 30 Corps District, 9 February 1946, S-0422-0011-0003, United Nations Archives [hereinafter UNA]. See also Cilento, 'The Social Aspects of Any Refugee Problem,' p. 24.

34   Some in fact asserted that they were from Palestine, regardless of their real nationality. See Director, UNRRA Team 806, to UNRRA Field Supervisory Officer, 43rd (W) Division, BAOR, 21 May 1946, S-0422-0002-07, UNA.

35   Cohen, 'Between Relief and Politics,' pp. 437–9.

36   On the post–World War I epidemics, see Weindling, 'Introduction,' p. 8; Paul Weindling, *Epidemics and Genocide in Eastern Europe 1890–1945* (Oxford: Oxford University Press, 2000), pp. 145–6; Patrick Zylberman, 'Civilizing the State,' pp. 31–2.

37   United Nations Relief and Rehabilitation Administration [hereinafter UNRRA], *UNRRA: Organization, Aims, Progress* (Washington, DC: UNRRA, 1944), p. 2.

38   Dr J. Balfour Kirk, Assistant Director of Relief Services, to Raphael Cilento, 4 October 1945, S-0422-0002-05, UNA.

main routes, assembly centres, camps, selective billeting and repatriation trains—all designed to calculate the health risk of population movements and provide systems of surveillance and medical screening.

The aim of camps in this context was to regulate the movement of people and reintroduce them to orderly, settled life. In a lecture on administering refugee relief, Cilento recommended that refugees in camps be afforded self-government as soon as possible so as to recognise 'the dignity and social consciousness of the individual'.[39] Cilento cited the example of a camp director who prided himself on its discipline and order, only to witness his charges break every window in revolt.[40] UNRRA officials similarly stressed that the displaced persons camps were self-governing. Yet some among the regional and local UNRRA teams saw the displaced persons camps, with their regular sick parades, as sites of surveillance and discipline as well.[41] On one occasion, an UNRRA officer called in local military units to a camp where Polish inmates protested the distribution of Red Cross parcels. While the army enforced martial law for 36 hours to 'restore order', camp officials conducted interrogations, separated families, single men and women and placed 'doubtful characters' in separate sections.[42] A 1955 report of the United Nations Educational, Scientific and Cultural Organization (UNESCO) similarly stressed the need to subject refugees to these kinds of controls in the interests of managing groups with such potential for disorder.[43] The camps, along with the repatriation trains and DDT teams, were thus part of a larger apparatus designed to regulate the flow of people, thus minimising disruptions and disorder.[44]

Political questions were not completely subordinate to administration. Citizenship status and the demands of communist states in Eastern Europe exerted considerable influence on whether people were granted displaced person status and on patterns of repatriation. Screening processes at displaced persons collection depots and camps sought out former enemy

39   Cilento, 'The Social Aspects of Any Refugee Problem,' p. 11. Cilento's emphasis.
40   ibid., p. 11–12.
41   Mark Wyman, DPs: Europe's Displaced Persons, 1945–1951 (Ithaca, NY: Cornell University Press, 1989), p. 41; Cohen, 'Between Relief and Politics,' p. 443.
42   C. B. Grier, Director UNRRA Team 800, Augustdorf, to District Director, 460 UNRRA HQ, Iserlohn, 29 June 1946, S-0423-0002-01, UNA. On the disciplinary nature of internal institutional divisions, see Bashford and Strange, 'Isolation and Exclusion in a Modern World,' pp. 9–10.
43   Cohen, 'Between Relief and Politics,' p. 443.
44   UNRRA's work with refugees thus resembles a Foucauldian apparatus of security. Michel Foucault, Security, Territory, Population: Lectures at the College de France, 1977–1978, trans. Michael Senellart (New York: Picador, 2004), pp. 18–20.

collaborators, who were ineligible for humanitarian aid.[45] Cilento's early experience with postwar political chaos and emergency relief reinforced his right-wing political views. The problems in Greece, for example, were complex. Besides the sheer destruction of the economy, the procedures UNRRA used to measure levels of indigence were inaccurate, leaving many exposed to privation. The opportunistic refusal of local millers in the Cyclades to use all of the relief grain they received also contributed further to malnutrition.[46] Yet Cilento was quick to blame communist agitation and the absence of middle-class leadership. On Greece, he later wrote:

> The Communists, cleverly sowing dissension by defaming every local leader who aimed at stability on a national basis, and by glorifying ambitious and impressionable juniors who found a ready welcome in their 'People's National Army', urged the masses ever closer to hysteria and panic.[47]

As discussed in the previous chapter, Cilento's belief that progress depended on expert leadership in medicine, education and social welfare, as well as the cooperation of ordinary citizens, fostered strong anticommunism and indeed a suspicion of democracy itself. The communists in Europe, he wrote, were now conducting a 'ruthless elimination of men of status, and of those who showed any capacity for leadership among the bourgeoisie'.[48] Cilento's emphasis on a strong state and the harmonious arrangement of society under expert, middle-class leadership thus reinforced his political alignment as he waded deeper into international service.

Cilento's resignation from UNRRA took effect in May 1946; he complained that policy directives and conflicts had undermined his authority. He almost immediately received an offer to become the Director of the Division of Refugees and Displaced Persons in the UN Secretariat, where he would be responsible for establishing the Preparatory Commission of the International Refugee Organization (PCIRO).[49] Cilento's hopes of becoming the first director of this organisation were dashed when the American representative Arthur Altmeyer was elected

---

45 Cohen, 'Between Relief and Politics,' pp. 443–6.
46 Tsilaga, '"The Mountain Laboured and Brought Forth a Mouse",' pp. 527–44.
47 Cilento, 'Escape from UN-reality,' p. 15. Cilento's emphasis.
48 ibid., p. 44.
49 Fisher, *Raphael Cilento*, pp. 215–16; Raphael Cilento to Andrew Cordier, Executive Assistant to the Secretary-General, 20 December 1946; Raphael Cilento to A. D. K. Owen, Acting Secretary-General, 22 January 1947, RAG-2/73/1/01, Box 1, UNA.

executive secretary of the PCIRO at its first meeting.[50] An opportunity for a more permanent and responsible position in international affairs had slipped away. The Secretary-General of the United Nations, Trygvie Lie, however, offered Cilento the position of Director of the Division of Social Activities. Charged with administering the United Nations' emerging responsibilities for international social welfare, Cilento occupied this post until he resigned from the United Nations in 1951.

Social welfare advisory services: Social work, nationalism and international society

The UN Advisory Social Welfare Services, established under General Assembly Resolution 58(1) in December 1946, were initially adopted to maintain the work of UNRRA, which was scheduled to cease operations by 31 December 1946. Yet the welfare work of the United Nations quickly became a larger program. The Social Commission, created to advise the Economic and Social Council, recommended at its first meeting in early 1947 that the UN Secretariat adopt some of the functions of the League of Nations, with an emphasis on establishing a permanent system of fellowships and instructors. It also asserted, however, that the United Nations should take a more 'positive role' than had the league.[51] Adopting a long-range view, the Social Commission aimed to propagate modern, professional and state-run welfare services modelled on those of the developed world and especially the United States. A draft report of the Social Commission declared that it was 'urgent to take immediate steps with a view to promoting international action in welfare work'.[52] It went further, stating that the social welfare program was:

> The first experiment by the United Nations in rendering practical field service to the people of the different nations.
>
> … The development of these advisory services in the field of social welfare therefore provides a most important opportunity of demonstrating in a practical manner the interest and concern of the United Nations Organization itself in meeting human needs through an effective service

50   The United States had been expected to dominate the committee, which comprised only eight small countries, some of them American dependencies. See W. Moderow, Director Representing the Secretary-General, Geneva, to Henri Laugier, 18 February 1947, RAG-2/73/1/01, Box 1, UNA; Fisher, *Raphael Cilento*, p. 226.

51   United Nations [hereinafter UN], *The Yearbook of the United Nations, 1946–7* (Lake Success, NY: UN Department of Public Information, 1947), p. 516.

52   'Social Commission: Draft General Report,' 1 February 1947, p. 7, S-0441-0073-01, UNA.

provided by its Secretariat. The Commission recognized that these advisory services will be the cornerstone of a permanent social welfare service emanating from the United Nations.[53]

In adopting the functions of both the League of Nations and UNRRA, the UN social welfare program revived longstanding international concerns, such as narcotics and trafficking in women and children, and intersected with the more recent ascension of American ambition, money and expertise.[54]

The Department of Social Affairs was part of an institutional structure that implied both the unity and the distinctiveness of economic and social issues. The Economic and Social Council (ECOSOC) was the third major body of the United Nations, alongside the General Assembly and the Security Council, and was responsible for shaping operational activities. Separate social and economic commissions, which respective social and economic departments in the secretariat supported, assumed most of this responsibility.[55] Cilento's division worked alongside others dedicated to human rights, narcotics and population, and itself consisted of sections for social welfare, migration, health, refugees, living standards, family protection and social defence. It thus covered a wide field, including housing, child welfare, juvenile delinquency, social security and public assistance, social work training, community organisation, rehabilitation, policy, planning, research and statistics, among other areas. Many of these were inherited from the League of Nations and, in some cases, such as population and demography, the United Nations simply absorbed league personnel and research material.[56] The scope of the social affairs department was thus extremely broad, incorporating many of the interests of other international organisations, including the International Labour Organization (ILO) and specialised agencies of the United Nations such as the World Health Organization (WHO) and UNESCO. Although much emphasis was placed on cooperation, such overlaps could lead to tensions in the field, such as when ILO personnel in Iran claimed the United Nations had been 'trespassing'.[57]

---

53 ibid., p. 18.
54 Cohen, 'Between Relief and Politics,' pp. 437–9.
55 The Department of Social Affairs also directly served ECOSOC, various other commissions on population, human rights, the status of women and narcotic drugs and the Third Committee of the General Assembly respecting education, demography, human rights, refugees, human rights and other matters. UN, *Yearbook of the United Nations 1946–7*, p. 619.
56 Bashford, 'Population, Geopolitics, and International Organizations in the Mid Twentieth Century,' p. 331.
57 'Minutes of Inter-departmental Meeting on Technical Assistance,' 5 December 1949, RAG-2/336/02(1), Part B, UNA.

Plate 6.1 Cilento in 1947
Source: National Archives of Australia: A1200, L9026.

Advisory services under Resolution 58 fell into four categories, each of which could be provided only on the receipt of specific requests from national governments. First, the United Nations could provide experts in social welfare to act as consultants. Consultants spent anywhere from a month to a few years attached to a government department, providing advice on social security legislation, government policy, the establishment of schools of social work or welfare centres, the initiation of pilot projects in social research or welfare services or the modernisation of administration. Second, it could grant fellowships to nominated social workers, enabling them to travel to study welfare practices and social work curricula in welfare agencies and schools in the United States and Western Europe. Third, it could give advice and demonstrations in the manufacture of prosthetic limbs and provide technical documentation. The secretariat was also responsible for organising regional seminars on social welfare, at which a range of foreign experts and local social workers could meet to learn about and discuss various aspects of welfare in regions thought to have common problems. By 1950, the United Nations had organised multiple seminars in Latin America, Asia, Eastern Europe and the Middle East.[58]

For its part, the social work profession hoped its ideas and methods would find a prominent place in the United Nations on a long-term basis.[59] *The Social Service Review*, a journal for American social workers, kept a close eye on proceedings at the UN Social Commission. Ellen Potter, a doctor and President of the National Conference of Social Work, argued that social workers had:

> developed a philosophy and a technical competence [and were] united … in a quest for that place in the new world order in which social workers individually and collectively shall be able to render their maximum contribution to the welfare of mankind.[60]

58   United Nations Department of Social Affairs, *Training for Social Work: An International Survey* (New York: United Nations, 1950), pp. 69–72.

59   Smith Simpson, 'International Organization in the Area of Social and Humanitarian Problems,' *The Social Service Review*, 19(1), 1945, pp. 9–12.

60   Ellen C. Potter, 'The Year of Decision for Social Work,' *The Social Service Review*, 19(3), 1945, pp. 297–8.

George F. Davidson, the Deputy Minister of Welfare in Canada, narrated a history of social welfare ascending through levels of government responsibility until it became a national concern. It was only left for it to assume a role in 'predisposing the peoples of the world to peaceful and co-operative ways of life'.[61] Social workers thus felt that their role in providing social 'security' for a national citizenry was relevant to international peace and stability. In July 1946, representatives from several American welfare agencies and the US Department of State met with Henri Laugier, the Assistant Secretary-General in Charge of Social Affairs, and Charles Alspach, an UNRRA official who would later become chief of the social services section under Cilento. The delegation emphasised the desirability of a permanent social commission and a subcommittee of welfare agencies that would meet with Laugier to discuss the ways in which they could assist with providing staff and consultants.[62]

Cilento had long believed that social workers should be involved in a broad and coordinated program of health and welfare. In the interwar years, he had embraced holistic and social notions of health. Diet, housing, working conditions, income and leisure contributed to the energy and strength—the 'positive health'—of individuals and therefore populations and the nation. A medical service that relied primarily on private services and aimed at cure instead of prevention was unsatisfactory. Like many other public health officials across the world, Cilento argued that the state must assume responsibility for developing and coordinating a broad health service that could positively shape the lives of individuals and families beyond the hospital and the general practitioner. The state, in other words, would make a 'deliberate attempt to develop to the full the mental and physical capacities of every individual'.[63] Social workers had a vital role to play in such a public health apparatus. As Cilento argued in *Blueprint for the Health of a Nation*, those professionals who would carry out the work of visiting homes to check on convalescents or to provide advice on the feeding and care of children were vital for such a coordinated attempt at cultivating health.[64]

---

61 George F. Davidson, 'International Horizons for Health and Welfare,' *The Social Service Review*, 22(3), 1948, p. 280.
62 'Notes on Meeting of National Committee on International Organisation for Social Welfare,' 16 July 1946, pp. 1–3, S-0544-0009-0002, UNA.
63 Cilento, *Blueprint for the Health of a Nation*, p. 109.
64 ibid., p. 109.

Cilento brought these values with him to the United Nations. In a 1949 paper for the anniversary of the New York School of Social Work, he argued that in the midst of postwar social, political and economic disruptions it was important that methods of reducing poverty and improving standards of living 'embrace all those activities that lie between the recognized fields of health, education, and labour that we call "social welfare"'.[65] Despite attempts by American representatives in San Francisco to limit the scope of action for a new international health organisation, interwar advocates of social medicine, including US surgeon general Thomas Parran and Croatian health official Andrija Stampar, managed to put diet, housing and working conditions on the agenda of the WHO.[66]

Cicely D. Williams, a WHO official, sent an article to Cilento in 1949, emphasising that medicine must 'make and keep people healthy' by looking beyond the patient to 'his work, his house, his family, his education, and all the variegated factors which have influenced his life and his well being'.[67] Every aspect of the whole life of the individual—usually a man or a boy—was in this view the object of intervention by experts and the state. The social medicine that Cilento had championed throughout the 1930s and 1940s was thus enshrined at the United Nations as the orthodox view of health, the individual and society.

Public health reformers had been urging a closer relationship between social workers, public health services and the state since the 1920s. Richard Cabot, a doctor and former president of the American National Conference of Social Work, suggested in 1919 that social workers should be 'distinctly recognized as *part of the machinery*' of hospitals and attached firmly to public health agencies and institutions.[68] Social workers, in contrast, sought to protect their distinctive professional and scientific status and gradually developed their own academic and institutional existence in the interwar years.[69] Despite this, most insisted on the interrelatedness

---

65   Raphael Cilento, 'The World Moves towards Professional Standards in Social Work,' in *Social Work as Human Relations: Anniversary Papers of the New York School of Social Work and the Community Service Society of New York* (New York: Columbia University Press, 1949), p. 228.

66   Amrith, *Decolonizing International Health*, pp. 73–5.

67   'Child Health and Child Welfare,' Cicely D. Williams, Maternal and Child Health Section, World Health Organization, to Raphael Cilento, 5 July 1949, S-0441-0103-05, UNA.

68   Richard C. Cabot, *Social Work: Essays on the Meeting-ground of Doctor and Social Worker* (Boston: Houghton Mifflin Company, 1919), pp. 3–4. Cabot's emphasis.

69   Elizabeth MacAdam, *The Equipment of the Social Worker* (London: George Allen & Unwin, 1925), pp. 16–22; Mary Antoinette Cannon and Philip Klein (eds), *Social Casework: An Outline for Teaching* (New York: Columbia University Press, 1933), pp. 20–4.

of health, education, employment, housing and other social factors and increasingly recognised the need for the coordination of public health and social work under the aegis of the state.[70] Among the medical and social professionals in the UN Secretariat and specialised agencies, this became the orthodoxy that underpinned their work in the international arena.

Many scholars have argued that, despite the persistence of colonial rule in Africa and the Pacific, the dominant political ideology of the postwar period enshrined the nation-state as the central unit of world order, with all the tensions and contradictions over ethnic diasporas and alternative subjectivities this entailed. The United Nations itself on some level embodied this, yet cultivating a strong central state was also a political priority within postcolonial governments in Asia.[71] Partha Chatterjee has argued that developing Western 'governmental technologies' of discipline and surveillance, such as censuses and surveys, became central aspirations of postcolonial governments.[72] Extending this account beyond the nation, Sunil Amrith has argued that the dominant form of internationalism in postcolonial Asia—which finally triumphed at the 1955 Bandung Conference—emphasised cooperative and altruistic circulation of these governmental practices between sovereign states. An alternative vision of Asian cosmopolitanism fell out of favour.[73] Such a relationship to international society and its institutions reflected the emergence of national sovereignty and statehood as the chief priorities of postcolonial states across Asia, especially after the political and human crises of Indian Partition and various armed conflicts in late 1947.[74]

The need to equip developing states with the tools of modern government underpinned the UN social welfare program. 'International aid should be so planned as to enable the recipient country eventually to face by herself her urgent need for well-organized and well-equipped social services', read one early report.[75] The United Nations framed the Advisory Social Welfare

70　MacAdam, *The Equipment of the Social Worker*, pp. 156–8; Cannon and Klein, *Social Casework*, pp. 35–7, 44–6. See also Kathleen Woodroofe, *From Charity to Social Work in England and the United States* (London: Routledge & Keegan Paul, 1962), pp. 158–60.
71　Kelly and Kaplan, *Represented Communities*, pp. 4–6.
72　Partha Chatterjee, *The Politics of the Governed: Reflections on Popular Politics in Most of the World* (New York: Columbia University Press, 2004), pp. 34–7.
73　Sunil Amrith, 'Asian Internationalism: Bandung's Echo in a Colonial Metropolis,' *Inter-Asia Cultural Studies*, 6(4), 2005, pp. 558–60.
74　Amrith, *Decolonizing International Health*, pp. 79–82.
75　'Assumption by the United Nations of Certain Advisory Social Welfare Functions of UNRRA: Report and Recommendations of the Secretary-General,' 7 November 1946, p. 5, S-0441-0073-01, UNA.

Programme as one of long-term national development, in which a society of neighbourly nations would provide support to each other. Material that Cilento's division submitted for the secretary-general's report to the Social Commission stated:

> Social questions constitute an immense series of subjects of constantly increasing importance in the international sphere. This results from an increasing willingness on the part of nations to assist their nationals, as individuals or groups, to attain more satisfactory relationships and higher standards of living in accordance with their desires and capacities, and in harmony with the community in which they live.[76]

In short, the aim was to 'help recipient countries help themselves'.[77] By requiring that national governments request assistance from the United Nations and identify the specific fields—such as child welfare, juvenile delinquency, social legislation, training or administration—in which it was needed, the UN social welfare program reinforced the primacy and autonomy of the nation-state in the postwar world.

To provide expert consultants and fellowships, the Department of Social Affairs developed ties with a variety of schools of professional social work and social science, such as the New York School of Social Work, and with government social welfare agencies around the world, such as the US Federal Security Agency and the South African Council for Child Welfare.[78] The UN Secretariat used these contacts to attach fellows to various agencies and to secure expert personnel. Harry M. Cassidy, the Director of the School of Social Work at the University of Toronto, Henning Friis, an official from the Danish Ministry of Social Work, and Elizabeth Clarke, an employee of the US Children's Bureau, for example, all worked as consultants for the United Nations abroad.[79] In drawing personnel directly from institutions and agencies primarily concerned

---

76   Raphael Cilento to Henri Laugier, 5 June 1947, S-0544-0011-11, UNA.
77   United Nations Department of Social Affairs, *International Advisory Social Welfare Services* (Lake Success, NY: United Nations, 1949), p. 1.
78   Martin Hill, Special Adviser to Secretary-general, to Katherine Lenroot, Children's Bureau, Federal Security Agency, Social Security Administration, 23 September 1948; Lenroot to Martin Hill, 3 September 1948; Charles Alspach to Dr William Haber, University of Michigan, 23 September 1948; Miss L. M. MacKenzie, South African Council for Child Welfare, to Raphael Cilento, 25 May 1948, S-0441-0090-08, UNA; Katherine Lenroot to Raphael Cilento, 13 June 1947, S-0472-0075-0003, UNA. See also Raphael Cilento to General Omar Bradley, Director, Veterans' Administration, Washington, 16 June 1947, S-0472-0075-0003, UNA.
79   See Egypt reports, S-0441-0092-01, UNA; Charles Alspach to Russell Cook, Bureau of Personnel, Federal Security Agency, 23 August 1948, S-0441-0090-0008, UNA.

with local or national welfare in developed countries, the UN program thus aimed to transfer concepts and practices of social work and welfare around the world.

UN social welfare consultants were typically embedded within a government agency, where their primary task was to advise governments on legislation, personnel training and other aspects of social welfare. Egypt assigned Cassidy and Friis to the Ministry of Social Affairs. Cassidy was to carry out a complete review of social work training in the country, while Friis—although he was interested in population, child welfare and rehabilitation of the disabled—spent much of his time developing a social security scheme at the request of the government.[80] In Ecuador, Anna MacAuliffe, George Narensky and Clarke were attached to the Ministry for Welfare and Labor. MacAuliffe conducted a complete review of existing welfare conditions and services. With the aim of drawing a 'good view of real status of living standards of the people: salaries, housing, food, family relations, family problems; economic basis of behaviour problems', she interviewed local officials and academics, examined legislation, toured institutions and even considered model villages.[81]

The Philippines mission included an especially diverse group of consultants working on a broad range of fields in a country that had suffered during the war and had recently emerged from US colonial rule. The consultants there were associated with the social welfare commissioner Asuncion Perez, who held a degree in sociology from the University of Wisconsin. Perez, and agencies such as the Philippine Relief and Trading Rehabilitation Administration and the National Development Company, was particularly involved in shaping the work of UN personnel. In this early phase of UN social welfare assistance, consultants often blurred the line between what were considered economic and what were considered social matters. Irene Murphy, the American chief consultant, had previously worked for the Detroit Department of Public Welfare and the Detroit Council of Social Agencies. In the Philippines, she helped draft social security legislation and plans for home industries designed to supplement rural incomes.[82] Most of the work, however, focused on

---

80   'Report of the United Nations Adviser on Social Welfare to the Government of Egypt,' 1 April – 15 May 1950, S-0441-0092-01, UNA.

81   Anna MacAuliffe, 'Report,' 28 September – 28 October 1948, pp. 5–6, S-0441-0091-07, UNA.

82   Irene Murphy, 'Field Report of the United Nations Social Affairs Office in the Philippines,' 16 August – 15 September 1947; Irene Murphy, 'Rehabilitation of Home Industries,' 27 September 1947, S-0441-0095-01, UNA.

recognised matters of social welfare. Maria Albano, a Brazilian graduate of the New York School of Social Work, taught short courses in social casework for existing Philippines welfare personnel. Andree Roche, from France, worked on developing vocational and physical rehabilitation through hospitals and welfare institutions, while Theresa Wardell, from Australia, specialised in juvenile delinquency.[83] The consultants—part of a global network mobilising social welfare experts—all reported to Cilento, who was responsible for providing them with support in the form of documentation and materials.[84] He would also on occasion request that expert personnel collect information on the general state of social work training and welfare provision.[85] UN consultants thus provided a service to sovereign states while also helping the United Nations to construct a picture of the state of social welfare on a global scale.

Continuities between colonial rule and post-independence development were manifest in UN social welfare work in the Philippines in several ways. The consultants themselves had backgrounds in colonial service or society. Roche, for example, had previously served as a government inspector in Algeria.[86] Murphy had worked with the American Philippines War Relief, a private philanthropic organisation, yet she was also the sister-in-law of Frank Murphy, the Governor-General of the Philippines in the mid-1930s, and her personal representations of society and culture in late colonial Asia drew familiar images. Her description of the governor's mansion at Baguio, for example, was a familiar colonial tableaux: 'Five houseboys in their white uniforms with red crest on the coat, served the grand dinner.'[87] Elsewhere, she described arriving in Shanghai en route to the Philippines:

> As soon as the ship anchored in the dirty, yellow river the little junks came clamoring around. Whole families with babies and grandmothers live all their lives on these dirty barges.

---

83   Asuncion Perez, 'Circular,' attached to Asuncion Perez to Irene Murphy, 2 October 1947, S-0441-0095-01, UNA.

84   Andree Roche to Raphael Cilento, 21 April 1948, S-0441-0095-02, UNA.

85   Irene Murphy, 'Field Report of United Nations Senior Consultant on Social Affairs,' 16 November – 15 December 1947, pp. 5–6, S-0441-0095-01, UNA; M. Josephina R. Albano, 'Field Report of UN Consultant on Social Affairs,' 16 December 1947 – 15 January 1948, p. 2, S-0441-0095-02, UNA.

86   Henri Laugier to Alberto Tarchiani, Italian Ambassador to the United States, 27 June 1947, S-0544-0009-13, UNA.

87   Irene Murphy to Aunt Irene, 26 December 1933, Papers of Irene Ellis Murphy [hereinafter Murphy Papers], 851917 Aa 2, Box 1, Bentley Historical Library, University of Michigan.

Like other observers, Murphy highlighted how non-Europeans not only ignored hygiene boundaries between the clean and the contaminated, but also seemed content with low standards of living:

> It's a matter of the survival of the fittest and if a baby lives more than a few weeks I guess it lives to be a hundred. They drink the river water, throw their waste into it and swim in it![88]

Murphy thus, like Cilento, brought to postwar social welfare direct experience of colonial social relations and distinctions between hygienic backwardness and modernity.

The Philippines mission marginalised the broader community and nonstate agencies, including the Catholic Church and charities, in favour of the state and professional experts. The political context in which they worked was largely absent in the consultants' reports, especially the armed Hukbalahap guerillas active in rural areas, whom the right-wing government of president Manuel Roxas sought to repress.[89] In the Philippines, as in Egypt, agrarian unrest stemmed from dissatisfaction with the concentration of landownership among a few elite families, yet land reform was largely off the table in postcolonial politics.[90] UN welfare consultants were sometimes uncomfortable, however, about the large-scale agricultural and industrial development projects that became the defining features of international development and which left a litany of social disruption and failure.[91] Irene Murphy, in fact, warned against the mechanisation of agriculture in the Philippines, which, given its impact on rural labour, would be 'socially revolutionary' in areas where patterns of land tenure already produced 'daily bloodshed and civil war'.[92] As Timothy Mitchell has suggested, modern development's claims about leading societies through periods of violence to one of ordered rule often obscures ongoing violence.[93]

---

88   Irene Murphy to Helen Ellis, 27 November 1933, Murphy Papers, 851917 Aa 2, Box 1.
89   Benedict J. Kerkvliet, *The Huk Rebellion: A Study of Peasant Revolt in the Philippines* (Berkeley: University of California Press, 1977), pp. 143–50; Dennis Merrill, 'Shaping Third World Development: US Foreign Aid and Supervision in the Philippines, 1948–53,' *The Journal of American–East Asian Relations*, 2(2), 1993, p. 137.
90   Merrill, 'Shaping Third World Development,' p. 142. On Egypt, see Mitchell, *The Rule of Experts*, pp. 38–9.
91   James Ferguson, *The Anti-politics Machine: 'Development,' Depoliticization, and Bureaucratic Power in Lesotho* (Minneapolis: University of Minnesota Press, 1994), pp. 8–9; Mitchell, *The Rule of Experts*, pp. 41–2; Sluga, 'UNESCO and the (One) World of Julian Huxley,' pp. 410–11.
92   Irene Murphy, 'Field Report of United Nations Senior Consultant on Social Affairs Philippines,' 15 October – 15 November 1947, pp. 3–4, S-0441-0095-01, UNA.
93   Mitchell, *The Rule of Experts*, p. 79.

That social welfare was ideally a state service, with professionally trained personnel, was a core understanding of the permanent staff of the secretariat and consultants in the field. Cilento told an audience of social workers in New York in 1949 that the separation of social work from voluntary, charitable and religious institutions was most advanced in the United States. In contrast, wealthy elites and religious leaders in Latin America, the Middle East and elsewhere resisted the development of state-based, professional social welfare services. Cilento noted, however, that there were others in developing countries who felt the need to adopt 'organized social welfare services based on New World concepts of social work',[94] in which the chief aim was

> the constant and enlightened endeavour to insure that the influence of the individual upon the community, and of the community upon the individual, shall be toward a constantly improving standard of living.[95]

He finally placed social work in an international frame:

> The eyes of the world are upon social work, and the heavy responsibility that rests upon its advocates and practitioners is to show first that it is truly 'social' and, secondly, that it 'works'; and, moreover, that it has within itself the flexibility and the potentialities to cope successfully with all the problems of human life and endeavour, as one by one they emerge, more and more definitely, from the social confusion of our present period of transition.[96]

Cilento had initiated a global survey of concepts of social work in that year. The resulting report, *Training for Social Work: An International Survey*, described the United Nations' efforts to increase knowledge about social services around the world as an extension of the work of the League of Nations and other interwar international organisations.[97] It noted that there were no established standards for the training of social workers anywhere, even in the United States. The ultimate development of social welfare, however, was a professional service for 'broad social planning for the prevention of economic insecurity and for the promotion of social well-being', available to each individual '*to assist him in achieving his full potentialities for productive and satisfying living*'.[98] Other countries and

94 Cilento, 'The World Moves towards Professional Standards in Social Work,' p. 231.
95 ibid., p. 237.
96 ibid., p. 239.
97 United Nations Department of Social Affairs, *Training for Social Work*, pp. 2–3.
98 ibid., p. 10. Original emphasis.

professions were coming around to the importance of investigating and intervening in emotional and physical development, education, work and family life:

> [T]here is demonstrably an inherent logic in the movement from unorganised personal 'charity' available to disadvantaged members of the community, towards professional 'service' potentially available to all members of the community.[99]

Social work was integrative, seeking to tie together the school, clinic, hospital, employment office, court and community centre, and seeking to see each individual's health and emotional life in relation to their whole 'pattern of social relationships'.[100]

UN welfare consultants shared this understanding of their work as cultivating values, personnel and institutions of state social work in the field. In Ecuador, Anna MacAuliffe reported to Cilento in 1948: 'The profession of Social Worker is rather new in the country and therefore not yet well understood.'[101] Her meetings with the Department of Labor had become opportunities for in-service training in 'professional social service'.[102] In Egypt, Cassidy gave lectures at Alexandria on the professionalisation of social work while conducting a survey on social work training in the country. The program of the first Conference of Social Workers in the Philippines reiterated the UN definition of social policy, which 'must be intimately concerned with the life of the whole community and not only with particular sections of it'. The standard of living across the whole community was central:

> The standard to be attained is the well-being of all members of the community so as to enable each one to develop his personality, in accordance with the needs of the community, and at the same time to enjoy, from youth to old age, as full a life as may be possible.[103]

In an explanatory note to a draft bill for provision of assistance to dependent children, Irene Murphy wrote that Western nations had for the past 50 years:

99 ibid., pp. 13–14.
100 ibid., p. 14.
101 Anna MacAuliffe, 'Report,' 28 September – 28 October 1948, p. 14, S-0441-0091-07, UNA.
102 Anna MacAuliffe, 'Monthly Report,' October 1949, p. 1, S-0441-0091-07, UNA.
103 'Program,' 1st Conference of Social Workers, 16–31 October 1947, S-0441-0095-01, UNA.

Assumed the responsibility for adequate and regular assistance to their economically dependent citizens, particularly the children, through public assistance, social security, or social insurance. The modern tendency has found expression in the replacement of the casual charity of the earlier centuries with a stable and democratic social security program organized and maintained along scientific lines.

Appealing to the government, she declared:

The Republic of the Philippines cannot remain indifferent to these progressive movements abroad. The enactment of this bill would give the Philippines the distinct honor of being the first country in Asia to have adopted a social security program for children.[104]

There was thus a clear insistence on modernising the role and apparatuses of the state in the way they provided for a polity that was explicitly national.

Developing the state's capacity to govern appealed to Filipino politicians and bureaucrats for whom a modern and independent Philippines had been a long-term goal. US colonial policy in the Philippines had emphasised the importance of education, including medicine and nursing, from the beginning, while the incorporation of trained indigenous elites in government accelerated in the 1920s. American officials always reserved the right, however, to judge whether Filipinos had attained the capacity for self-government. Some, in fact, claimed that Filipino deficiencies in knowledge of hygiene and administration were profoundly racial, making national independence a distant prospect.[105] Yet trained Filipino officials worked hard to challenge dismissive American discourse by divorcing ideas about modernity from race. In this way, they could frame perceived backwardness in the Philippines as a matter of class difference and education.[106] In nursing and community work through welfare centres, for example, women found a role in nation-building that was for the most part a Filipino initiative. If such work partly augmented the surveillance capacities of the American colonial state in the Philippines, indigenous nurses and welfare officials also framed it as both liberating and service to the developing nation.[107]

---

104 'An Act to Grant Aid to Dependent Children, Explanatory Note,' n.d., S-0441-0095-02, UNA.
105 Paul Kramer, *The Blood of Government: Race, Empire, the United States and the Philippines* (Chapel Hill, NC: University of North Carolina Press, 2006), pp. 308–12.
106 Anderson, *Colonial Pathologies*, pp. 187–203.
107 See Catherine Ceniza Choy, *Empire of Care: Nursing and Migration in Filipino American History* (Durham, NC: Duke University Press, 2003), pp. 31–2; Bonnie McElhinny, 'Producing the A-1 Baby: Puericulture Centers and the Birth of the Clinic in the U.S.-occupied Philippines, 1906–1946,' *Philippine Studies*, 57(2), 2009, pp. 219–60.

When UN experts arrived there had thus been a long history of Filipino officials seeking progressive national development. Asuncion Perez sent a circular letter to private welfare agencies after the arrival of the UN consultants:

> For many of us who would have liked to have had foreign study in order to modernize our programs in accordance with prevailing world standards these consultants bring to our door a cross-section of international experience.[108]

UN consultants also reported a thirst for knowledge among local social workers. Delegates at the first Conference of Social Workers, although 'untrained', were, wrote Irene Murphy, 'hard-working people who had grappled with the complexities of a war-destroyed society. They felt a prestige in the title of "social worker" which had been conferred on them'. Conference discussions were 'filled with riotous, eager animation'. 'A controversy about a rejected child, marital problems, insufficient income, etc., became a subject in which all wanted to speak pro and con.' At the end of the conference, the students 'responded to us with the warmth and gratitude of those who cherish their teachers'.[109]

In developing state welfare institutions and capacities, UN consultants were continuing a longer process. In 1921, Filipino officials organised the first National Conference on Infant Mortality and Public Welfare and established the Office of Public Welfare. By 1930, there were over 350 puericulture centres providing services to local communities. Modelled on French institutions, these centres performed functions familiar in Britain, the United States and Australia. The staff measured and weighed babies and children to monitor physical development, gave lectures on hygiene and made house-to-house visits to survey family size and health, diet, income, expenditure, housing and other aspects of domestic life.[110] In many ways, UN consultants were simply reconstructing these trends in personnel and institutions interrupted by the war. Maria Albano established the Institute of Social Case Work, which offered popular short courses in social work methodologies, including homes visits, interviews,

---

108 'Circular,' attached to Asuncion Perez to Irene Murphy, 2 October 1947, S-0441-0095-01, UNA.
109 Irene Murphy, 'Field Report of United Nations Senior Consultant on Social Affairs—Philippines,' 15 October – 15 November 1947, pp. 2–3, S-0441-0095-01, UNA.
110 McElhinny, 'Producing the A-1 Baby,' pp. 231–48.

record keeping and family histories.[111] Andree Roche hoped to set up more organised and extensive record keeping at hospitals, including the trial employment of a social worker at a major hospital.[112]

A census undertaken of the towns of Lipa and Vigan in late 1947 and early 1948 is an especially interesting case of the continuities between US colonial administration and the UN program in the Philippines. Murphy suggested the census might demonstrate the importance of social data in a country lacking postwar information on population, urbanisation, dependency, infirmity and income. She also suggested that students from the local high school conduct the census, in which they would collect information on family size, income, schooling, daily rice consumption, mortality, physical defects and other data.[113] The project would, Albano reported, 'provide a practical exercise in citizenship for high school students in the fields of social studies and social research'.[114] In these respects, this demonstration census bore a strong resemblance to the American colonial census undertaken between 1903 and 1905. As in the case of Vigan and Lipa, the US Government employed Filipinos to perform the census in local areas. Foreshadowing Albano's language, General William Howard Taft had declared that the census would 'therefore form a test of the capacity of the Filipinos to discharge a most important function of government'. As Vicente Rafael observes, the 1903–05 census was both an exercise in colonial tutelage in the technical work of self-government and:

> A stage upon which Filipinos were to be represented as well as represent themselves as subjects of a colonial order: disciplined agents actively assuming their role in their own subjugation and maturation.[115]

111 Maria Albano, 'Field Report of UN Consultant on Social Affairs—Philippines,' 2 October – 15 November 1947, S-0441-0095-01, UNA.
112 Andree Roche, 'National Emergency Hospital: Proposal for a Programme on Social Work and Occupational Therapy,' n.d., S-0441-0095-01, UNA.
113 Irene Murphy, 'Field Report of United Nations Senior Consultant on Social Affairs—Philippines,' 15 October – 15 November 1947, p. 5; Social Census Form, n.d., S-0441-0095-01, UNA.
114 Maria Albano, 'Prospectus of Social Census of Vigan–Lipa,' n.d., in 'Field Report of United Nations Consultant on Social Affairs—Philippines,' 16 November – 15 December 1947, S-0441-0095-01, UNA.
115 Vicente L. Rafael, *White Love and Other Events in Filipino History* (Durham, NC: Duke University Press, 2000), p. 26.

There is also a strong echo here of the values underpinning the Project Club Day at Esk High School in Queensland, described in the previous chapter, in which students were asked to speak about the contributions they could make to national development. Cilento was at the same time seeking to increase the legibility of the population for the state in Queensland. The entwining of citizenship with disciplined participation in cultivating social welfare thus underscores the entanglement of colonial and national frameworks in these postcolonial UN programs.

Ambitions for national statehood were perfectly compatible with the internationalism of the peaceful exchange of developmental knowledge between sovereign nation-states. Indeed, this view of sovereign nation-states sharing technologies of governance flourished among many postcolonial governments in Asia in the late 1940s and 1950s.[116] As McElhinny argues in the context of the Philippines, independent engagement by colonised peoples with an international community of scientific and technical knowledge suggests that historians should avoid a simple conflation of colonial and national biopolitics.[117] UN personnel in the Philippines hoped that the census, as an instance of such exchange, might encourage internationalism and goodwill towards the United Nations. The consultants in the Philippines had hoped to present the students involved in the Vigan and Lipa censuses with UN certificates, yet reports suggest that headquarters at Lake Success baulked at this. While Murphy agreed with headquarters on some of the technical issues, she also reported that 'students and officials are still anxious to have a United Nations Certificate in order to feel a personal participation in an otherwise abstract world organization'.[118] Yet it is clear that, for many Filipinos, the aspiration to nationhood demanded engagement with international institutions and norms. At a public ceremony celebrating completion of the Lipa census, J. Alex Katigbak, a teacher at the Mabini Academy, remarked that the teachers and students were 'duty bound' to assist the consultants as citizens of a member nation of the United Nations:

> It is an honor and a distinction to have worked for the United Nations and feel that you have done a bit [to] help the United Nations realize one of its big humanitarian aims.

---

116 Amrith, 'Asian Internationalism,' pp. 558–9.
117 McElhinny, 'Producing the A-1 Baby,' p. 252.
118 Irene Murphy, 'Field Report of United Nations Senior Consultant on Social Affairs— Philippines,' 16 November – 15 December 1947, p. 7, S-0441-0095-01, UNA.

He further noted:

> For the first time, the great bulk of our people heard of the United Nations or see it work actually, with their own eyes. The United Nations has gone home to them to prove to us all that the United Nations Organization is alive, dynamic, and vital.[119]

The United Nations and recipient nations thus framed the social welfare program in terms of a world order of sovereign nation-states sharing strategies for positively shaping the lives of individuals and families, improving standards of living and cultivating the happiness and political stability of populations. At a conference of social workers, Roche told her audience that 'your presence here today, coming from all parts of the Philippines, is a picture of unity of your nation, for studying [the] best solutions of your social problems'.[120] The titles of consultants' radio addresses also stressed international cooperation and the role of social welfare in preserving peace.[121] Albano told her audience that the United Nations acted because it was 'aware that peace cannot be built in a world inhabited by hungry and unhappy individuals'.[122] In an earlier broadcast, Albano echoed the rhetoric of neighbourly international society:

> We, the people of the world, realized that war brings 'untold sorrow to mankind' and got together in an effort to create a better world. We all belong to this organization—the United Nations—and we have a great contribution to give to the advancement of all people.[123]

The UN social welfare program was thus aimed at developing an international harmony of social and economic progress. In doing so, the program internationalised the ethos of social medicine that Cilento and many others had elaborated in the 1930s.

119 J. Alex Katigbak, Speech, in Maria Albano, 'Field Report of UN Consultant on Social Affairs—Philippines,' 16 February – 31 March 1948, S-0441-0095-02, UNA.
120 Andree Roche, Address to Conference of Social Workers, attached to 'Summary of Activities,' 15 October – 15 November 1947, S-0441-0095-01, UNA.
121 Andree Roche, 'A Picture of Social Security Plans among United Nations Members,' Radio address, 22 September 1947; Teresa Wardell, 'Your Neighbours Australia and New Zealand,' Radio address, 29 September 1947; Maria Albano, 'Brazil—Your Neighbour is 15 Thousand Miles Away,' Radio address, 13 October 1947, S-0441-0095-01, UNA.
122 Maria Albano, Radio address, in 'Field Report of UN Consultant on Social Welfare,' 16 January – 15 February 1948, S-0441-0095-02, UNA.
123 Maria Albano, 'Brazil—Your Neighbour is 15 Thousand Miles Away,' Radio address, 13 October 1947, p. 1, S-0441-0095-01, UNA.

Empire, population and world order

Cilento at times expressed the purpose of the social welfare program in the same idealist terms of postwar liberal internationalism. Yet his ideological framework also reflected imperial conceptions of world order. Cilento had previously worked with international organisations to coordinate colonial government in the Pacific Islands, where states framed cooperation in health as meeting an obligation to improve and uplift indigenous people. Perhaps more importantly, coordination of preventive health measures also aimed to ensure healthy indigenous labour and prevent immigration of 'coloured' races that might threaten 'white' civilisation. Cilento had imagined indigenous people in the Pacific as nations, yet the idea that they were ready for independent statehood was, to him, absurd. Racial hierarchies and tutelage of 'backward' peoples by the 'civilised' were thus at the centre of Cilento's internationalism.

The core development concept that national communities must progress from a premodern and 'traditional' form of social organisation and government to a civilised modern one had roots in colonial discourse. Frederick Lugard, for example, as Governor of Hong Kong before World War I, insisted that advanced states were obliged to accelerate development in return for the colonial resources that underpinned European and American progress.[124] By the 1930s, trained indigenous personnel had administered public health in the Philippines for decades and, although they eschewed racial explanations for disease and poverty, they maintained an emphasis on the need to educate and transform the 'masses' through forms of surveillance, education and discipline.[125]

For Filipino social workers trained in the colonial period, such as Asuncion Perez, modernisation along international guidelines was the guiding principle for postcolonial development. The voices of Filipino social workers in the late 1940s reveal how the traditional–modern distinction informed their practices. In a final paper written for Maria Albano's short course on social casework, one student described visiting the family of a boy who was found sleeping with 24 others under a church.

---

124 See Far Eastern Association of Tropical Medicine, *Transactions of the Second Biennial Congress, held at Hong Kong, 1912* (Hong Kong: Noronha & Co., 1914), pp. 3–4.
125 Anderson, *Colonial Pathologies*, pp. 191–3.

In a manner familiar from texts on sanitation in nineteenth-century Britain and twentieth-century tropical medicine, Filipino social workers linked morality, disease and the spaces the working classes inhabited:

> Their house is a make-shift affair, nestling amidst unshapely houses that squeeze in one upon the other, giving little space for the entrance of fresh air and direct sunlight … [whilst most] of the residents in the neighborhood seem to belong to the lowest strata of social life.

This was especially disturbing given their proximity to better residences on Avenida Rizal:

> It is, indeed, strange to find only a few steps from that center of culture and pretension, a glaring contrast where no drop of civilization seems to have been extended.[126]

The nationalist preoccupation with development thus reproduced many of the discursive constructions, relationships of power and forms of government that had taken shape under colonial rule.

Recent histories have shown that many internationalists saw intergovernmental organisations as the best way to preserve the imperial relationship between white civilisation and the rest of the world.[127] Mark Mazower has highlighted how many architects of the League of Nations and the United Nations, such as the South African politician and military leader Jan Smuts and the liberal scholar Alfred Zimmern, sought to preserve an imperial world order. Despite some differences, Smuts, Zimmern and others agreed on the need for moral world leadership and a measure of international cooperation in benevolent governance of 'primitive' territories. International organisations, in their understanding, ought to protect and disseminate 'civilisation', which they understood to be the democratic freedoms and obligations in which non-European people needed tutelage.[128] Glenda Sluga has similarly shown how the early cosmopolitanism of UNESCO, under the leadership of Julian Huxley, continued to insist that the 'white race' had special responsibilities that came with its 'civilised' status to uplift backward races. Indeed, cosmopolitan models of internationalism that emerged during World War II sought to expand citizenship and rights through existing empires.[129]

126 Fortunata del Rosario, 'Final Paper,' February 1948, pp. 1–4, S-0441-0095-02, UNA.
127 Morefield, *Covenants without Swords*, pp. 105–7.
128 Mazower, *No Enchanted Palace*, pp. 22, 40–1.
129 Sluga, 'UNESCO and the (One) World of Julian Huxley,' pp. 405–7.

These visions of the beneficent endowment of backward peoples with modern knowledge, education and government had long been at the heart of imperial discourse, in a way that also assumed that the whole world should benefit from empire.[130] Such ideas were very much alive in the United Nations. Henri Laugier, the Assistant Secretary-General in Charge of Social Affairs and Cilento's immediate superior, wrote that, around the world, there were likely to be reserves of unexploited resources that were of 'paramount' concern for underdeveloped countries and for 'the whole of mankind'.[131] For Laugier, the role of the United Nations, beyond diplomacy, was to generate knowledge of the world's resources and maximise their exploitation. The imperial relationship between 'civilisation' and backward peoples would thus continue:

> When there are regions and nations whose physical, intellectual, and moral development lags behind the general pace of civilization, immediate concrete measures can doubtless be taken to help them along the path of human progress.[132]

Important members of the permanent staff of the United Nations thus framed the operational activities of the secretariat in terms that were common in imperial discourses of indigenous transformation, uplift and improvement.

Cilento's imperial internationalism rested on ingrained belief in racial hierarchy and concerns about postwar threats to the 'civilised' world order and the paternalist traditions of empire. For him, the UN social welfare programs should reflect colonial tutelage and pursue gradual development. He shared with Zimmern and Smuts a commitment to an internationalism that insisted on the need for 'civilised' nations to aid the development of 'backward' peoples. Cilento's reference to the gulf in civilisation between colonising and colonised peoples in the 1920s and his assertion of the latter's incapacity for self-government echoed strongly the imperialism of British liberalism, as did the writings of Hubert Murray and Edmund Piesse.[133] Yet Cilento's vision of world order was far less sanguine about international relations than the liberal internationalism of

---

130 Lugard, *The Dual Mandate in British Tropical Africa*, p. 617.
131 Henri Laugier, 'The First Step in the International Approach to the Problems of Underdeveloped Areas,' *Milbank Memorial Fund Quarterly*, 26(3), 1948, p. 257.
132 ibid., p. 256.
133 See Chapter 2, this volume. See also Mehta, *Liberalism and Empire*, pp. 81–5; Morefield, *Covenants without Swords*, pp. 105–7.

thinkers such as Zimmern.[134] Cilento explicitly rejected hope for 'universal reconciliation between nations' in favour of a more martial understanding of international relations rooted in his preoccupation with population and its relationship to conflict.[135]

The writings of Thomas Malthus had shaped Cilento's thinking since the 1930s and, in public lectures and articles, he imposed a cyclical metanarrative on history that hinged on a Malthusian account of population and subsistence. Population, Cilento reminded his audiences, always outstripped subsistence. This in turn put pressure on available land and encouraged various deliberate restrictions on population growth or attempts to relieve population pressure through migration or expansion. In a 1936 lecture on 'Some Problems of Racial Pressure in the Pacific', Cilento argued that Japanese expansion and the threat of war in the region rested on such population pressures on agricultural land and productivity. Drawing on Japanese scholarship, Cilento noted that a ban on contraception and an increase in food production after the Meiji Restoration had caused a surge in population growth. Faced with a choice between decreased living standards, population control and expansion, 'Japan has chosen the only alternative consistent with her exalted nationalism—she has extended to the Equator in the South'.[136] Cilento thus explained the Pacific conflict that many thought was inevitable within a framework of natural laws and social science.

Cilento's understanding of the postwar world and the responsibilities of the United Nations in it remained grounded in these concerns about population growth. In a 1948 paper for a Milbank Memorial Fund roundtable discussion, Cilento framed the UN social welfare program as an effort to ameliorate the effects of growing populations on standards of living in Asia and their geopolitical consequences. 'The problem of civilization is definitely the problem of population', he wrote, and: 'The problem of population is the accessibility or availability of subsistence.'[137] In New Guinea, he claimed, the encroachment of European commerce, law and culture disrupted systems of child sacrifice that had maintained demographic equilibrium for generations. At the same time, malnutrition and disease had caused drastic demographic decline in many areas. Pacific

---

134 Mazower, *No Enchanted Palace*, pp. 71–7.
135 Cilento, *Nutrition and Numbers*, p. 69.
136 Cilento, 'Some Problems of Racial Pressure in the Pacific,' p. 46.
137 Cilento, 'Underdeveloped Areas in Social Evolutionary Perspective,' p. 292.

populations were recovering but in a transformed society. America had opened Japan to the global economy in the 1850s and 1860s, particularly to new modes of agricultural production that, along with cessation of official contraceptive policies, caused the population to jump from 28 million to 68 million by 1938. 'The population graph, however, drawn from 1810 to 1940,' Cilento wrote, 'shows in the most graphic form not only the rise and fall of populations, but the history of every nation indicated, and the pre-factors of every major war'.[138] History was thus 'the story of a succession of balanced economies upset from time to time by a new factor making for a massive increase in productive power'—a cyclical narrative of stable equilibrium and chaotic transition.[139]

The Middle East and South-East Asia were areas of particular concern regarding postwar population growth. Cilento listed Pakistan, Indonesia, Malaya, Indochina, the Philippines and China, among others, as areas where World War II had not restricted this growth:

> [W]hatever procedures are introduced at this stage to limit population or to rationalize the population/subsistence ratio, cannot prevent the growth of population within the next fifty years to a critical and explosive degree.

Many of these countries had only gained independence from colonial powers in the late 1940s, their people 'infused with a new stimulus, a new inspiration towards individualism, and an aim at all costs to protect these new-found freedoms'.[140] Cilento claimed to have talked to rickshaw pullers and plantation workers in Asia who freely expressed their own confidence and the West's lost prestige. These demographic tendencies would, if not seriously addressed, 'necessarily become a threat to every specialized frontier of culture and civilization'.[141] When this happened, the 'solemn stupidities of treaty obligations' would mean little.[142] The social scientific lens that Cilento brought to bear on the early postwar years thus linked anticolonial and postcolonial political movements to dangerous tendencies in population biology.

Cilento was here reiterating old anxieties about the threat 'the East' posed to peace and white civilisation. Politicians, scholars, scientists, labour leaders and the press had, since the mid-nineteenth century, represented

---

138 ibid., pp. 298–9.
139 ibid., p. 295.
140 ibid., p. 296.
141 ibid., p. 299.
142 ibid., p. 296.

Asian societies as swarming, unclean 'hordes' that threatened to descend on Europe, America and Australia, bringing disease, immorality and degradation.[143] Christian Geulen has examined how visions of global order developed at the apex of modern imperialism and racial thought. Race, Geulen argues, provided a complete way of understanding the world, not just Self and Other, as European empires expanded and interacted with one another.[144] Such racial discourse—particularly anxiety about the 'yellow peril'—was thus increasingly transnational in character, seeming to bind together the Anglo-Saxon worlds.[145] Of course, there was more to debates and population science than this vision of racial conflict. As Alison Bashford notes, interwar organisations such as the International Institute of Intellectual Cooperation were concerned with the more general global relationship between population growth, land and geopolitics, especially in the context of German, Italian and Japanese claims to territorial expansion and the Nazi notion of *lebensraum*, or living space.[146] When demographers after World War II argued for the removal of immigration restrictions, which had been fundamental to some visions of imperial world order, the relationship between population, land and war remained an important conceptual underpinning.[147] Few after the late 1940s took expectations of a race war seriously, especially since the postcolonial hardening of national boundaries and political divisions in Asia made the notion of a 'swarming' East look outmoded and pan-Asian internationalism beaten.[148]

Confidence in the ability of the social sciences to manipulate the natural laws of global geopolitics had not, however, faded. Postwar demographers still feared population growth and its potential to cause new wars, while abandoning the explicit racism of Nazi conceptions of living space and the interwar discourse of the yellow peril.[149] Cilento appealed to the authority of international organisations, arguing that the United Nations must address the looming threat of population growth in underdeveloped countries to peace and 'civilisation'. If the range of social welfare services available in the UN social welfare program was intended to enlarge the

---

143 Evans, '"Pigmentia",' pp. 103–24; Connelly, *Fatal Misconception*, pp. 33–5.
144 Geulen, 'The Common Grounds of Conflict,' pp. 69–72.
145 Lake and Reynolds, *Drawing the Global Colour Line*, pp. 289–90.
146 Bashford, 'Population, Geopolitics, and International Organizations in the Mid Twentieth Century,' pp. 337–8.
147 ibid., p. 344.
148 Amrith, 'Asian Internationalism,' pp. 559–61; Mazower, *No Enchanted Palace*, pp. 186–7.
149 Connelly, *Fatal Misconception*, pp. 116–18.

capacity of nation-states to provide for their populations, they were also part of a broader effort to shape the outlook of peoples who were achieving political independence:

> It is the obligation to direct the activities, the intentions and the ideas of the peoples of these huge undeveloped areas in such a way that when they become a dominant factor in the scheme of things, as they will, their actions will be along lines that experience has proved to be the most progressive socially.[150]

Like UN welfare consultants, Cilento saw the provision of social welfare as an effort to build the capacity of states to govern their populations and improve standards of living. At the heart of this work was the confidence that expertise and knowledge would allow the United Nations and member states to reduce or ameliorate poverty. As seen in the examples of Ecuador, Egypt and the Philippines, this was largely a technical enterprise focused on social security legislation, surveys, record keeping, education and employment services. But Cilento was also suggesting that, while international assistance in social welfare operated on a national basis, its most important aim was to address the same regional population growth that had agitated so many scientists and political figures in the preceding decades.

The UN Advisory Social Welfare Services shared many of the characteristics of later development projects. They were not monolithic, but instead were made up of a shifting network of personnel, institutions and agencies, giving them the kind of multivalent and dispersed character that Frederick Cooper and Randall Packard have described.[151] The ideas and objectives of consultants were not necessarily the same as Cilento's and local elites were often the ones who set the agenda for the welfare program. Yet there were conceptual elements shared across both the welfare program and postwar economic development, especially between the 1940s and the 1970s. UN officials and recipient governments preferred to deploy expert knowledge to help strengthen centralised states that would be responsible for the wealth and wellbeing of their people. Government would be technical and administrative, focused not on politics but on official interventions in health, education, employment and wellbeing.

---

150 Cilento, 'Underdeveloped Areas in Social Evolutionary Perspective,' p. 298.
151 Cooper and Packard, 'Introduction,' pp. 1–41.

In affecting this transformative growth, the United Nations and international society were beneficently guiding underdeveloped nations along a path to modernity.[152]

Competing projects: Social welfare and economic development

It may have been only a matter of time, but, by 1949, the spotlight that social welfare had enjoyed for a few years had shifted to economic development. In December 1948, the UN General Assembly passed Resolution 200(III): 'Technical Assistance for Economic Development'. Like Resolution 58, this one established a program of expert missions, fellowships, local technical training and seminars. Yet it signalled, as Amrith has suggested, a shift away from social objectives to a preoccupation with increasing economic productivity above all else.[153] The United Nations' entry into economic development prompted discussions on how the departments of economic and social affairs could collaborate more closely. In February 1949, Cilento prepared a memorandum on social welfare services that rejected rigid distinctions between the economic and the social: 'All forms of economic development have social improvement as their ultimate goal; all forms of social improvement finally contribute to economic development.'[154] US president Truman had just called for an internationally coordinated effort to reduce poverty and promote economic development in underdeveloped regions. After hearing a proposal from the United States, ECOSOC resolved in March to instruct secretary-general Lie to report on a 'comprehensive plan for an expanded co-operative programme of technical assistance for economic development … paying due attention to questions of a social nature which directly condition economic development'.[155] It was anticipated that a larger, comprehensive program of development would emerge from the United Nations.

---

152 These characteristics of the work of UN social welfare services are echoed in many later development projects. See Ferguson, *The Anti-politics Machine*, pp. 9–10; Cooper and Packard, 'Introduction,' pp. 17–18; Mitchell, *The Rule of Experts*, pp. 39–42; James Scott, *Seeing Like a State: How Certain Schemes to Improve the Human Condition Have Failed* (New Haven, CT: Yale University Press, 1998), pp. 4–6.
153 Amrith, *Decolonizing International Health*, pp. 84–6.
154 Henri Laugier to David Owen, Assistant Secretary-General in Charge of Economic Affairs, 25 February 1949, RAG-2/335/01 Part A, UNA.
155 United Nations Economic and Social Council, 'Technical Assistance for Economic Development,' Resolution of 4 March 1949, 8th Session, RAG-2/335/01, Part A, UNA.

Voices in the Social Commission, General Assembly and the Department of Social Affairs were all at pains to emphasise consideration of social matters alongside economic growth. Alva Myrdal, the new Director of the Department of Social Affairs, reminded staff that 'the social programme must be conceived as an integral and inseparable part of the total programme, in each region and in each project'.[156] In an informal statement made to the Social Commission in May 1949, she portrayed economic development as a social project: 'The objectives of all economic development are largely and predominantly social. Economic development is only a means of achieving improvement in the social welfare of all people.' Economic development, implicitly conceived of here as industrialisation, must be made 'in harmony with social objectives'.[157] Concern about the disruptive social consequences of industrialisation and urbanisation became a common refrain of social affairs officials. A secretariat memorandum for the Social Commission in March 1950 stated that urbanisation tended to 'breed disease, delinquency and other social evils'.[158] In proposing a conference on social problems encountered in the course of economic development projects, Donald McGranahan, from the cultural activities section of social affairs, similarly noted that such projects threatened the disintegration of community and family life, the breakdown of old mores and an increase in juvenile delinquency.[159] Laugier reminded Lie that the resolution of the ECOSCO had stated how important it was to 'take account of the probable consequences of proposed projects for economic development in terms of the welfare of the population as a whole'.[160]

If social welfare officers at the United Nations harboured concerns about the social consequences of economic development, the 'social questions' with which they were concerned often referred to welfare services that would actually facilitate industrialisation and urbanisation. Development projects often aimed at the social and cultural transformation of peasants and 'traditional' communities, which represented a blockage in the way

---

156 Alva Myrdal to All Directors, 15 March 1949, p. 3, RAG-2/335/01, UNA.

157 Alva Myrdal, 'Technical Assistance: Informal Statement of Views Made by Mrs Alva Myrdal,' Social Commission, 4th Session, 17 May 1949, p. 2, RAG-2/335/01 Part A, UNA.

158 'Social Projects to be Provided by the United Nations under the Expanded Programme of Technical Assistance for the Economic Development of Under-developed Countries,' Memorandum by Secretariat for Social Commission, 6th session, 14 March 1950, p. 8, RAG-2/184/4/02, UNA.

159 'Proposed Conference on Social Problems Encountered and Methods Found Effective in Raising Standards of Living in Under-developed Areas,' n.d. p. 7, attached to Donald McGranahan to Alva Myrdal, 16 November 1949, RAG-2/184/4/02, Box 1, UNA.

160 Henri Laugier to Tygvie Lie, 28 October 1949, RAG-2/335/01 Part A, UNA.

of modern political, social and economic organisation.[161] When the Department of Social Affairs suggested contributions it could make to the expanded program of technical assistance, Gustavo Duran advised that his section could prepare social scientific studies of 'rigid tribal and kinship organization, ignorance, superstition, ancient habits' and other 'major social conditions that impede modern economic development'.[162] McGranahan's proposed conference was intended to investigate social conditions that impeded development, such as 'uneconomic customs and taboos', ignorance and 'backwardness'.[163] General Assembly Resolution 222(IX) stated that the Expanded Programme of Technical Assistance required projects that 'mitigate the social problems … that may arise as a concomitant of economic change'. The secretariat thus felt that some social institutions and customs were 'holding back development' and that 'effective economic development may depend upon the introduction of certain social reforms'.[164] Despite their misgivings about economic development, social welfare personnel at the United Nations clearly wanted to give their expertise to a larger project of transformation, in which the social sciences would become instruments for spreading modern, 'civilised' modes of production, property and culture.

Texts on imperial medicine and governance in the early twentieth century had stressed the civilising impact of European rule. Empire, it was claimed, had stopped constant tribal war and oppression in primitive society.[165] Warwick Anderson, for example, has shown how medical discourse in the Philippines constructed a dichotomy of 'primitive' and 'modern', between which there was a single trajectory. For American colonial officials, it was the duty of civilised nations such as the United States to slowly guide backward peoples between these two poles.[166] As shown in previous chapters, Cilento's colonialism had similarly imagined a gulf between the Pacific Islands and the attainments of European civilisation. The reformist

---

161 Cooper and Packard, 'Introduction,' pp. 17–18. See also Chatterjee, *The Politics of the Governed*, pp. 31–3; Kothari, 'From Colonial Administration to Development Studies,' p. 49.
162 Gustavo Duran to Henri Laugier, 28 February 1949, RAG-2/335/01 Part A, UNA.
163 'Proposed Conference on Social Problems Encountered and Methods Found Effective in Raising Standards of Living in Under-developed Areas,' n.d., pp. 5–6, RAG-2/184/4/02, Part A, UNA.
164 'Social Projects to be Provided by the United Nations under the Expanded Programme of Technical Assistance for the Economic Development of Under-developed Countries,' Memorandum by Secretariat for Social Commission, 6th session, 14 March 1950, pp. 10–12, RAG-2/184/4/02, UNA.
165 See Lugard, *The Dual Mandate*, p. 617; Pearson and Mouchet, *The Practical Hygiene of Native Compounds in Tropical Africa*, p. viii.
166 Anderson, *Colonial Pathologies*, pp. 182–4.

discourse of empire that informed the creation of the League of Nations mandates stressed the importance of suppressing the kinds of customs that were deemed 'repugnant to the general principles of humanity'.[167]

Despite these affinities between colonial and development discourse, Cilento instead saw the emergence of technical assistance as a break from an earlier imperial internationalism and he left the United Nations in disgust in 1950. At the heart of Cilento's discontent was rising anticolonialism and antiracism in the General Assembly.[168] In particular, Cilento felt that economic development as practised through the technical assistance program trampled on the best traditions of British imperialism, while simply replacing colonial governance with the kind of economic hegemony he traced to the mid-nineteenth-century Pacific.[169] In a letter to Australian prime minister Robert Menzies, Cilento related how, in the anticolonial atmosphere of the General Assembly: 'It was impossible for most people with experience of British territories to hear without impatience and anger the emotional rubbish produced by speakers in many of these meetings.' He attacked theories of colonial underdevelopment as 'jejune', writing:

> Any reference to the great steps taken towards the development of native races in such areas, or any sane recognition of the need to progress by slow stages when introducing backward populations to industrialization and its manifold perils, were viewed with suspicion and denounced by the USSR, the USA, and all the minor states of Middle and Latin America, and of the Middle and Far East.[170]

In his letter, Cilento echoed the likes of Jan Smuts, Alfred Zimmern and others who had modelled a civilised world order on the British Empire. He especially railed against American and Soviet attempts to break down the 'solidarity and status of the British Commonwealth of Nations'.[171] Indeed, Cilento argued, American money and ambition influenced the United Nations to the extent that the new world order simply promised entrenched American domination:

---

167 Commonwealth of Australia, *Report to the League of Nations on the Administration of the Territory of New Guinea, 1921–2* (Melbourne: Commonwealth of Australia, 1923), p. 47.
168 Mazower, *No Enchanted Palace*, p. 185.
169 See Chapter 2, this volume.
170 Raphael Cilento to Robert Menzies, 11 September 1950, p. 1, Cilento Papers, UQFL44, Box 4, Item 11.
171 ibid., p. 2.

The policy for Technical Assistance, though giving lip-service to social development and safeguards, seems likely in practice to tend only towards the establishment of an economic hegemony for the international financier on the ruins of the British and other empires.[172]

In defending British imperialism, of course, Cilento ignored the British colonial development projects of the late 1940s and early 1950s that epitomised the imperial capitalism he had critiqued in the 1920s.[173] Yet Cilento was not merely objecting to attacks on the British Empire. The drift towards American hegemony, he argued, undermined the cultivation of an internationalised social scientific improvement in standards of living. In his account, American capital flowing through bilateral arrangements, rather than a truly international program, had fostered suspicion that the United Nations' work was cover for American intrusions designed to protect private investment and maximise returns.[174] If a UN project, he wrote, 'disguises the economic ambitions of another country, it is not only unnecessary but it may be politically corrupt in the international sense'.[175] Cilento's critique of the technical assistance program, and the increasing dominance of American capital, thus reflected his earlier criticism of imperial capitalism. In New Guinea, Fiji and while flying over Ceylon, he had condemned over-alienation and exploitation of land for commercial agriculture for sacrificing the health and wellbeing of indigenous peoples. At the United Nations, therefore, his critique of technical assistance as one form of imperialism rested on his commitment to another.

Cilento remained a critic of the United Nations on his return to Australia. In 'Escape from UN-Reality', he wrote that he 'had salvaged at least some shreds of my intellectual sincerity, sapped by six years of attrition'.[176] During a 1952 debate on ABC Radio on the subject of 'Is the United Nations Worth While?', Cilento spoke in the negative. He was quick to assert that he did not wish to attack the ideal of international cooperation in the maintenance of peace. Rather, he focused his attack on the United Nations' structure and prevailing ideals. The equality of sovereign nation-states was an especially bad defect to Cilento, who had long insisted that racial hierarchies were obviously real. 'Could you agree', he asked

172 ibid., p. 2.
173 Hodge, *Triumph of the Expert*, pp. 209–22; Sluga, 'UNESCO and the (One) World of Julian Huxley,' pp. 410–12.
174 Hodge, *Triumph of the Expert*, p. 3.
175 ibid., p. 5.
176 Cilento, 'Escape from UN-reality,' p. 1.

rhetorically, 'that Liberia or Costa Rica should have a casting vote as to whether there should be peace or war in the world? Of course not—neither could anyone else'.[177]

The Soviet Union had stymied progress with its veto in the Security Council and voting in the General Assembly had degenerated into political bloc voting.[178] As shown in previous chapters, Cilento had long believed that individuals who were trained, afforded an elevated status as professionals and dedicated to a life of service were the true source of progress. Improvements in welfare came not from democracy or human rights, but from expertise, initiative and centralised authority. For Cilento, the United Nations represented, in its capitulation to notions of rights and racial equality, a rupture with an ideal world order in which international cooperation would maintain and extend a progressive imperial governance.

Reflecting on his postwar international service, Cilento commented that one of the 'tragedies' of the early years of the United Nations was that its most capable staff were 'elbowed aside by opportunists' or 'reluctantly decided that their work still lay in the national fields they had tilled for so long and so lovingly'.[179] This was obviously self-referential and perhaps a way of dealing with his frustration at being prevented from reaching a higher position at one of the specialised agencies, especially the WHO.[180] Despite his criticism of 'job-seekers', he had always been ambitious himself. Yet here was also the genuine dismay of a former colonial official who was deeply invested in the social mission of empire and committed to a segregated world order predicated on racial and cultural hierarchy. Cilento had previously entertained a kind of cultural relativism. Writing in 1933 against climatic theories of race, he noted how past civilisations had lost themselves in the conceit that their climate was ideal: 'this national belief in national superiority has been a universal delusion', as were a string of related beliefs:

> The white man degenerates as he approaches the equator; that heat and cold rule character and govern the destiny of races; that skin colour is a sure guide to intellect; and, most emphatically, that the land of his

177 'Is the United Nations Worth While?,' The Nation's Forum of the Air, Australian Broadcasting Company, 3 December 1952, p. 3, Cilento Papers, UQFL44, Box 18, Item 99.
178 ibid., p. 4.
179 Cilento, 'Escape from UN-reality,' Preface.
180 Fisher, Raphael Cilento, p. 203.

forefathers was, is, and always will be the ideal and unique source for the production of ideal men and the original repository of civilization and culture.[181]

'Civilisation' is here not intrinsic but 'ephemeral'—'a matter of maintained accord between man and his environment'.[182] Yet it was also self-evident to Cilento that the 'white' man—understood as something more than Anglo-Saxon—had attained cultural and scientific heights that outstripped the 'coloured' peoples of the world. This insistence on the gulf between modern white society and backward peoples underpinned his belief that an empire of protection and tutelage was the only moral and practical way of ordering the world.

The social welfare program at the United Nations was for Cilento an opportunity for international cooperation in this kind of empire. He had consistently criticised the dominance of commercial interests in imperial governance in the 1920s and 1930s. The rapid integration of 'primitive' peoples into a world economy was, in his view, perilous for all concerned. The duty of civilised societies was to shield those peoples from the socially disintegrating effects of global capitalism while also gradually transforming them culturally, socially and politically. Cilento's critique of the UN technical assistance program—an element in the lopsided development of agriculture and industry that, since the 1950s, has largely failed to reduce poverty—was thus based on his commitment to a paternalistic stream of imperialism.

There were obvious continuities between colonial administration and social development programs. The notion that there was one linear trajectory towards modernity had been a feature of colonial discourse generally and found frequent expression in the UN social welfare program. Moreover, many post-independence governments sought to consolidate powerful centralised states capable of providing for and governing populations through the known mechanisms of surveillance and discipline that national and colonial states had developed over the previous 50 years. The structure of the program, however, assumed the sovereignty and independence of many peoples who imperialists such as Cilento and Smuts had previously claimed lacked the capacity for self-government.

181 Cilento, 'The Conquest of Climate,' p. 424.
182 ibid., p. 424.

Colonial ideology and practice, in other words, were maintained within a new political world order that represented a rupture with older imperial internationalisms.

By the 1950s, the world seemed to be leaving people like Cilento behind. Walter Crocker, another Australian in the UN Secretariat, noted that he, Cilento and a number of other idealistic types left the United Nations around the same time, conscious that they had largely been 'defeated'.[183] Marilyn Lake, Henry Reynolds and Mark Mazower have noted that people such as Smuts and Cilento, who valued an international order predicated on racial hierarchy and the moral leadership of the British Empire, were increasingly pushed aside within the United Nations as it became a forum for anticolonialism and development. The United Nations became, in other words, an arena for a political, economic and ideological struggle that increasingly pushed Smuts and Cilento to the margins.[184]

---

183 Walter Crocker, *The Role of Sir Raphael Cilento at the United Nations* (Brisbane: University of Queensland Press, 1985), p. 3.
184 Lake and Reynolds, *Drawing the Global Colour Line*, pp. 343–53; Mazower, *No Enchanted Palace*, pp. 183–5.

Epilogue

Towards the end of his unpublished autobiography, 'The World, My Oyster', Cilento claimed that his views on the recent history of the world were akin to those of Albert Schweitzer, the Alsatian doctor and theologian who worked in Africa during the 1920s and 1930s:

> Schweitzer says that if there were any sort of possibility that primitive people could live by and for themselves, we could leave them to themselves, but as things are world trade which has reached them is a fact against which both we and they are powerless and he goes on to point out that it is true, but tragic that the interests of colonization and civilization are often in direct opposition. He concludes that the best thing for primitive peoples would have been that, in such seclusion from world trade as is possible and under intelligent administration, they should rise by slow development from being nomads and semi-nomads to be agriculturalists and artisans, permanently settled on their own soil. He affirms that this has been rendered impossible because these people will not now let themselves be withheld from the chance of earning money by selling goods or materials to the agents of world trade.[1]

Cilento here conceded that paternalistic imperialism had developed untenable contradictions between a desire to quarantine 'primitive' indigenous peoples from the effects of international capital while inevitably absorbing colonial labour and resources into a global economy. In other words, the common ideal of rooting nations in their own soil was becoming impossible in the face of mobilising people, goods and capital on regional and global scales.

Yet Cilento could not shake the feeling that really distinct peoples existed within a hierarchy of races that ought to live separately. In the context of the Australian Labor Party's abandonment of 'white Australia' and increasing

---

1   Raphael Cilento, 'The World, My Oyster,' Ch. 10, p. 4, Cilento Papers, UQFL44, Box 1, Item 4.

Asian immigration in the 1960s, Cilento again became involved in right-wing politics. In a lecture delivered in his absence to the Australian League of Rights in the early 1970s, he warned of the threat to health and social order posed by the 'dilution of our RACIAL blood'. Gesturing to the racial politics and violence of postwar Britain and the United States, he reasserted that peaceful multiracial societies were impossible.[2] Violence and conflict, Cilento argued in apocalyptic tones, were the inevitable results of racial mixing that must be prevented. That Cilento remained committed to such views underscores the extent to which he failed to adapt to changing political and social realities.[3]

Cilento was a product of imperial networks of education, public service and research. He moved through colonial spaces alongside scientific literature, epidemiological data and ideas about public health practices, while pathogens continued to make their own way through the islands scattered between Malaya and New Zealand. Much of his thinking about the nature of health took shape in New Guinea and Malaya before reverberating throughout the reforms he promoted in Australia. His career thus highlights the dynamic exchange of public health ideas and practices between colonies in South-East Asia, the Pacific Islands and Australia.

At the same time, Australia has been the centre of gravity in this story. A range of material and cultural connections drew the Pacific Islands together, but Cilento's imperialism sought to orient them towards Australia. This particular expression of the Pacific region, in other words, imagined power relations as resting on the dissemination of expert knowledge from institutions, such as the Australian Institute of Tropical Medicine (AITM). On another level, Cilento always folded his experience and understanding of the Pacific into his work in Australia. Cilento proposed applying techniques of categorisation and institutional segregation used in New Guinea to Aboriginal people and disease in Queensland. In fact, he compared his ideal situation in the Australian tropics with systems for managing indentured labour in the Pacific. In discussing the significance of public health reform in Australia, Cilento invoked not only the prospect of war in the Pacific, but also discursively incorporated sickness and decline among Pacific Islanders into his representations of white Australian health and illness. As Pacific history, therefore, this book has

---

2   Cilento, *Australia's Racial Heritage*, p. 8.
3   Finnane, 'Cilento, Sir Raphael West (Ray) (1893–1985).'

been concerned both with health and government in the Pacific Islands and with how Cilento's colonial imagination incorporated the Pacific into the national settler-colonial politics and discourse of health in Australia.

When he was appointed to the United Nations, Cilento brought an imperial vision of world order to postwar international civil service. He hoped that the United Nations' Advisory Social Welfare Services would be part of a wider effort to maintain 'backwards' peoples and territories in a relationship of tutelage to the 'civilised' world. Rather than diplomatic negotiation of borders, Cilento argued, these interventions in standards of living and social 'evolution' were what would ensure peace in the midst of rapid population growth, economic development and cultural transformation. The structure of the program reflected the postwar system of sovereign and increasingly decolonised nation-states. It was, however, the enthusiasm for industrialisation among postcolonial states, the United Nations and other development agencies in the late 1940s that prompted Cilento's disillusionment with postwar internationalism. Newly independent states in Asia and the Middle East, Cilento asserted, were not ready for the transformations of industrialisation and statehood. Indeed, Cilento would later declare that the postwar world rested on edifices of human rights and racial equality that were fundamentally mistaken.

As successive Australian governments dismantled the White Australia Policy in the late 1960s and 1970s, Cilento began repeating old claims about the inevitability of conflict in a mixed society. These sentiments were the latest expression of his awareness that different political and moral norms were changing the world around him. The atmosphere of postwar Karachi, the development of Cold War antagonisms and the flowering of human rights and anticolonial discourse in the UN General Assembly were to him all signs that his ideals and certainties would no longer govern the world. This did not mean, of course, that racism ceased shaping social policy and discourse or international relations. Development regimes and institutions established after World War II at least partially preserved imperial relationships of power, while decolonisation was a protracted process across Africa and the Pacific. Many of the Pacific Islands remain formal or informal colonies of France or the United States. Despite Cilento's fears, the dominance of national development and welfare meant that collective ways of framing rights largely overshadowed human rights until the 1970s.[4] The institutionalisation of Indigenous people also persisted in Australia long after the war and its effects still linger in the present. National borders remain important as racism and imperial legacies continue to shape regimes for the management and exclusion of foreign bodies. The ongoing legacies of colonialism and a reactionary surge in racial nationalism in many parts of the world today, in other words, belie Cilento's own pessimistic belief that the world was moving beyond his ideals.

---

4   Samuel Moyn, *The Last Utopia: Human Rights History* (Cambridge, MA: Belknap Press, 2010), pp. 2–4.

Bibliography

Primary sources

Unpublished material: Archives and manuscripts

Fryer Library, University of Queensland
Papers of Sir Raphael Cilento, UQFL44.

National Archives of Australia
A1: Correspondence Files, Department of Home and Territories.

A1928: Correspondence Files, Department of Health.

A452: Correspondence Files, Department of Territories.

A457: Correspondence Files, Department of the Prime Minister.

A518: Correspondence Files, Territories Branch, Department of the Prime Minister.

A6119: Personal Files, Australian Security Intelligence Organisation.

C1942: Minutes of the Advisory Council of the School of Public Health and Tropical Medicine, Office of the Director of the School of Public Health and Tropical Medicine.

SP1061/1: General Correspondence, Australian Institute of Tropical Medicine/ School of Public Health and Tropical Medicine.

Queensland State Archives
Series 505: Correspondence Files, Office of the Chief Protector of Aboriginals.

Series 4356: Batch Files, Department of Health and Home Affairs.

Series 5263: General Correspondence, Office of the Home Secretary.

Series 8241: Miscellaneous Records, Department of Health and Home Affairs.

Series 8400: Special Batches, Department of Health and Home Affairs.

Series 8767: Circulars Received from the Chief Protector of Aboriginals, Chief Protector, Herberton.

Series 12355: Director-General's Correspondence and Papers, Health and Medical Services Branch, Department of Health and Home Affairs.

Series 14767: Correspondence and Papers, State Nutritional Advisory Board.

Series 14769: Queensland Nutrition Council Correspondence and Papers, Health and Medical Services Branch, Department of Health and Home Affairs.

National Library of Australia
Papers of Earle Page, MS 1633.

Papers of Edmund Leolin Piesse, MS 882.

Papers of Ernest William Pearson Chinnery, MS 766.

Papers of John Howard Lidgett Cumpston, MS 613.

United Nations Archives and Records Centre, New York
Records series system

S-0422: Subject Files of Assembly Centres and Camps of Central Registry of the British Zone, Occupied Germany.

S-0423: Subject Files, Rhine and Westphalia.

S-0441: Registry Files, Social Welfare Functions.

S-0472: Registry Files, Department of Social Affairs.

S-0544: Department of Social Affairs.

Records group system

RAG-2/73: Preparatory Committee of the International Refugee Organization.

RAG-2/184: UN/UNESCO Conference on Social Aspects of Economic Development.

RAG-2/335: Technical Assistance for Social Welfare.

RAG-2/336: Technical Assistance for Economic Development.

National Archives of the United Kingdom
Colonial Office Records

CO 717/1: Federated Malay States, Original Correspondence, January–March 1920.

CO 717/4: Federated Malay States, Original Correspondence, September–October 1920.

Wellcome Library, London
Papers of Dame Janet Vaughan, GC/186.

Papers of the Health Visitors Association, SAHVA.

Papers of Sir Leonard Rogers, PP/ROG.

Bentley Historical Library, University of Michigan, Ann Arbor, MI, USA
Papers of Irene Ellis Murphy, Bentley Historical 851917 Aa 2.

Records of the London School of Hygiene and Tropical Medicine
Register No. 7.

American Philosophical Society Library, Philadelphia, PA, USA
Papers of Victor George Heiser, Mss.B.H357.

Government reports, papers and debates
Annual Report on the Health and Medical Services of the State of Queensland, 1946.

New Guinea Gazette.

Report of the Advisory Council on Nutrition, Nos 2–4, 1936–37.

Report of the Federal Health Council of Australia, 1927–34.

Report of the National Health and Medical Research Council, 1937–38.

Report to the League of Nations on the Administration of the Mandated Territory of New Guinea, 1923–29.

The Official Yearbook of the Commonwealth, 1922.

Western Australia Parliamentary Debates, 1936.

Newspapers and periodicals

The Advertiser [Adelaide, SA].

The Argus [Melbourne, Vic.].

British Medical Journal.

The Courier-Mail [Brisbane, QLD].

The Medical Journal of Australia.

Morning Bulletin [Rockhampton, QLD].

Science.

Sydney Morning Herald.

Transactions of the Australasian Medical Congress.

Published articles, books, journals and reports

Andrews, C. F., *Indian Indentured Labour in Fiji* (Perth: The Colortype Press, 1918).

Anigstein, Ludwik, 'Malaria and *Anopheles* in Siam: Report on a Study Tour,' *Quarterly Bulletin of the Health Organisation of the League of Nations*, 1(2), 1932, pp. 233–308.

Australian Institute of Tropical Medicine, *Collected Papers* (Townsville, QLD: Australian Institute of Tropical Medicine, 1914–30).

Aykroyd, W. R., 'Diet in Relation to Small Incomes,' *Quarterly Bulletin of the Health Organisation of the League of Nations*, 2, 1933, pp. 130–53.

Balfour, Andrew, *War Against Tropical Disease: Being Seven Sanitary Sermons Addressed to All Interested in Tropical Hygiene and Administration* (London: Bailliere, Tindall & Cox, 1920).

Barrett, James W., *The Twin Ideals: An Educated Commonwealth. Volume II* (London: H. K. Lewis & Co. Ltd, 1918).

Barrett, James W., 'Can Tropical Australia be Peopled by a White Race?,' *The Margin*, 1, 1925, pp. 28–32.

Bleakley, J. W., 'The Aboriginals and Half-castes of Central Australia and North Australia,' *Commonwealth Parliamentary Papers*, 2, 1929, pp. 1159–225.

Bleakley, J. W., 'Report of the Aboriginal Department for 1934,' *Queensland Parliamentary Papers*, 1, 1935, pp. 975–98.

Bleakley, J. W., *The Aborigines of Australia: Their History, Their Habits, Their Assimilation* (Brisbane: The Jacaranda Press, 1961).

Bossard, James, 'A Sociologist Looks at the Doctors,' in *The Medical Profession and the Public: Currents and Counter-currents* (Philadelphia: The American Academy of Political and Social Science, 1934), pp. 1–10.

Bostock, John and L. Jarvis Nye, *Whither Away? A Study of Race Psychology and the Factors Leading to Australia's National Decline*, 2nd edn (Sydney: Angus & Robertson, 1936).

Breinl, Anton, *Tropical Diseases: Report by Dr Breinl, Director of the Australian Institute of Tropical Medicine, Townsville, on the Results of His Journey to the Northern Ports of Queensland* (Melbourne: Commonwealth of Australia, 1910).

British Solomon Islands Protectorate, *Annual Medical and Sanitary Report* (Suva: Government Printer, 1927).

British Solomon Islands Protectorate, *Annual Medical and Sanitary Report* (Suva: Government Printer, 1928).

British Solomon Islands Protectorate, *Annual Medical and Sanitary Report* (Suva: Government Printer, 1935).

Burnell, G. H. and John McKee, *Survey Report No. 12: A Hookworm Survey of the South-eastern Part of the Rockhampton District* (Brisbane: Hookworm Campaign, 1921).

Burnet, E. and W. R. Aykroyd, 'Nutrition and Public Health,' *Quarterly Bulletin of the Health Organisation of the League of Nations*, 4(2), 1935, pp. 323–474.

Burton, John Wear, *The Fiji of To-day* (London: Charles H. Kelly, 1910).

Burton, John Wear, *Our Task in Papua* (London: The Epworth Press, 1926).

Cabot, Richard C., *Social Work: Essays on the Meeting-ground of Doctor and Social Worker* (Boston: Houghton Mifflin Company, 1919).

Cannon, Mary Antoinette and Philip Klein (eds), *Social Casework: An Outline for Teaching* (New York: Columbia University Press, 1933).

Charlton, Noel B., *Completed Area Report No. 18: The Control of Hookworm Disease in Cairns and Vicinity and in the Yarrabah and Mona Mona Aboriginal Missions, North Queensland* (Brisbane: Hookworm Campaign, 1923).

Charlton, Noel B., *Completed Area Report No. 19: The Control of Hookworm Disease in the Cooktown Area of North Queensland, Including a Special Report on the Cape Bedford Mission Station* (Brisbane: Hookworm Campaign, 1923).

Cilento, Phyllis, *My Life* (Sydney: Methuen Haynes, 1987).

Cilento, Raphael, 'Preventive Medicine and Hygiene in the Tropical Territories under Australian Control,' *Report of the Sixteenth Meeting of the Australasian Association for the Advancement of Science*, 1924, pp. 672–84.

Cilento, Raphael, 'Observations on the Working White Population of Tropical Queensland,' *Health*, 4(1, 3), 1926, pp. 5–14.

Cilento, Raphael, *The White Man in the Tropics: With Especial Reference to Australia and its Dependencies* (Melbourne: Government Printer, 1926).

Cilento, Raphael, *The Causes of the Depopulation of the Western Islands of the Territory of New Guinea* (Canberra: Government Printer, 1928).

Cilento, Raphael, 'The White Settlement of Tropical Australia,' in P. D. Phillips and G. L. Wood (eds), *The Peopling of Australia* (Melbourne: Macmillan & Co., 1928), pp. 222–45.

Cilento, Raphael, 'Hookworm Work and Control in Australia,' *Report of the Federal Health Council of Australia*, 4, 1930, pp. 65–9.

Cilento, Raphael, 'The Future of Tropical Settlement,' *Church of England College Annual (Brisbane Diocese)*, 1931, pp. 41–4.

Cilento, Raphael, 'Review of the Position of Tropical Medicine and Hygiene in Australia,' *Report of the Federal Health Council of Australia*, 5, 1931, pp. 20–33.

Cilento, Raphael, 'The Value of Medical Services in Relation to Problems of Depopulation,' *The Medical Journal of Australia*, II(16), 15 October 1932, pp. 480–3.

Cilento, Raphael, 'Australia's Orientation,' *Health Bulletin*, 35–6, 1933, pp. 1039–65.

Cilento, Raphael, 'The Conquest of Climate,' *The Medical Journal of Australia*, (I)14, 8 April 1933, pp. 421–32.

Cilento, Raphael, 'Brief Review of Leprosy in Australia and its Dependencies,' in *Report of the Federal Health Council*, 7th Session, 1934, pp. 19–23.

Cilento, Raphael, *Nutrition and Numbers: The Livingstone Lectures* (Sydney: Camden College, 1936).

Cilento, Raphael, 'Some Problems of Racial Pressure in the Pacific,' *British Medical Journal (Supplement)*, I(3917), 1 February 1936, pp. 42–6.

Cilento, Raphael, *Blueprint for the Health of a Nation* (Sydney: Scotow Press, 1944).

Cilento, Raphael, 'Underdeveloped Areas in Social Evolutionary Perspective,' *The Milbank Memorial Fund Quarterly*, 26(3), 1948, pp. 292–9. doi.org/10.2307/3348238.

Cilento, Raphael, 'The World Moves towards Professional Standards in Social Work,' in *Social Work as Human Relations: Anniversary Papers of the New York School of Social Work and the Community Service Society of New York* (New York: Columbia University Press, 1949), pp. 222–39.

Cilento, Raphael and Clem Lack, *Triumph in the Tropics: An Historical Sketch of Queensland* (Brisbane: Smith & Paterson, 1959).

Cilento, Raphael, *Australia's Racial Heritage* (Adelaide: The Australian Heritage Society [Australian League of Rights], 1972).

Colony of Fiji, *Report of the Commission Appointed to Inquire into the Decrease of the Native Population* (Suva: Colony of Fiji, 1897).

Commonwealth of Australia, 'Report of the International Pacific Health Conference,' *Commonwealth Parliamentary Papers*, 5, 1926, pp. 803–920.

Commonwealth of Australia, *Aboriginal Welfare: Initial Conference of Commonwealth and State Aboriginal Authorities Held at Canberra, 21st to 23rd April 1937* (Canberra: Government Printer, 1937).

Cook, Cecil, *The Epidemiology of Leprosy in Australia* (Melbourne: Government Printer, 1927).

Crocker, Walter, *The Role of Sir Raphael Cilento at the United Nations* (Brisbane: University of Queensland Press, 1985).

Cronin, Archibald J., *The Citadel* (London: Victor Gollancz, 1939).

Cumpston, J. H. L., 'The Australian Institute of Tropical Medicine,' *The Medical Journal of Australia*, I(15), 1923, pp. 398–400.

Cumpston, J. H. L., 'Depopulation of the Pacific,' *Proceedings of the Pan-Pacific Science Congress*, 2(4), 1923, pp. 1389–94.

Davidson, George F., 'International Horizons for Health and Welfare,' *The Social Service Review*, 22(3), 1948, pp. 279–85. doi.org/10.1086/636888.

Dunham, Francis Lee, *An Approach to Social Medicine* (Baltimore: The Williams & Wilkins Company, 1925).

Elkin, A. P., 'A Policy for the Aborigines,' *The Morpeth Review*, 3(25), October 1933, pp. 29–35.

Elkin, A. P., *Citizenship for the Aborigines: A National Aboriginal Policy* (Sydney: Australasian Publishing Company, 1944).

Elkington, J. S. C., *Tropical Australia: Is It Suitable for a Working White Race?* (Melbourne: Commonwealth of Australia, 1905).

Far Eastern Association of Tropical Medicine, *Transactions of the Second Biennial Congress, Held at Hong Kong, 1912* (Hong Kong: Noronha & Co., 1914).

Federated Malay States, *Medical Report for the Year 1919* (Kuala Lumpur: Federated Malay States, 1920).

Federated Malay States, *Medical Report for the Year 1921* (Kuala Lumpur: Federated Malay States, 1922).

Gilks, J. L. and J. B. Orr, 'The Nutritional Condition of the East African Native,' *The Lancet*, 209(5402), 12 March 1927, pp. 560–2. doi.org/10.1016/S0140-6736(00)75124-5.

Government of Queensland, *Annual Report on the Health and Medical Services of the State of Queensland for the Year 1936–37* (Brisbane: Government of Queensland, 1938).

Grant, Madison, *The Passing of the Great Race, or the Racial Basis of European History* (London: G. Bell & Sons, 1917).

Green, H. N. and Edward Mellanby, 'Vitamin A as an Anti-infective Agent,' *British Medical Journal*, II(3537), 20 October 1928, pp. 691–6. doi.org/10.1136/bmj.2.3537.691.

Gregory, J. W., *The Menace of Colour* (London: Seeley Service & Co. Ltd, 1925).

Heydon, G. A. M., 'Malaria at Rabaul,' *The Medical Journal of Australia*, II(24), 15 December 1923, pp. 625–33.

Hogbin, H. Ian and Camilla Wedgwood, *Development and Welfare in the Western Pacific* (Sydney: Australian Institute of International Affairs, 1943).

Huntington, Ellsworth, *West of the Pacific* (New York: Charles Scribner's Sons, 1925).

Johnson, James, *The Influence of Tropical Climates on European Constitutions*, 2nd edn (London: T. & G. Underwood, 1818).

Kennedy, Marnie, *Born a Half-caste* (Canberra: Australian Institute of Aboriginal Studies, 1985).

Knibbs, George Handley, *The Shadow of the World's Future; Or the Earth's Population Possibilities and the Consequences of the Present Rate of Increase of the Earth's Inhabitants* (London: Ernest Benn Ltd, 1928).

Lambert, Sylvester, *Completed Area Report No. 1: The Control of Hookworm Disease in the Bowen District, Queensland* (Brisbane: Hookworm Campaign, 1920).

Lambert, Sylvester, *A Doctor in Paradise* (Melbourne: Georgian House, 1941).

Laugier, Henri, 'The First Step in the International Approach to the Problems of Underdeveloped Areas,' *Milbank Memorial Fund Quarterly*, 26(3), 1948, pp. 256–9. doi.org/10.2307/3348233.

League of Nations, *Final Report of the Mixed Committee of the League of Nations on the Relation of Nutrition to Health, Agriculture and Economic Policy* (Geneva: League of Nations, 1937).

League of Nations Health Organization, *Report by the Medical Director on the Work of the Health Organization Since October 1927* (Geneva: League of Nations, 1928), pp. 1–16.

League of Nations Permanent Mandates Commission, *Minutes of the 11th Session* (Geneva: League of Nations, 1927).

Lind, James, *An Essay on Diseases Incidental to Europeans in Hot Climates: With the Method of Preventing their Fatal Consequence*, 5th edn (London: J. Murray, 1792).

London School of Tropical Medicine, *Prospectus* (London: E. G. Berryman & Sons, 1921).

Lugard, Frederick, *The Dual Mandate in British Tropical Africa* (Edinburgh: William Blackwood & Sons, 1926).

MacAdam, Elizabeth, *The Equipment of the Social Worker* (London: George Allen & Unwin, 1925).

McCarrison, Robert and Hugh M. Sinclair, *The Work of Sir Robert McCarrison* (London: Faber & Faber, 1953).

Mellanby, Edward, 'Diet and Disease, with Special Reference to the Teeth, Lungs, and Pre-natal Feeding,' *British Medical Journal*, I(3403), 20 March 1926, pp. 515–19.

Mellanby, Edward, 'Nutrition and Child-bearing,' *The Lancet*, 222(5751), 18 November 1933, pp. 1131–7.

Meston, Archibald, *Queensland Aboriginals: Proposed System for their Improvement and Preservation* (Brisbane: Government of Queensland, 1895).

Meston, Archibald, *Report on the Aboriginals of Queensland* (Brisbane: Government Printer, 1896).

Murray, Hubert, *Papua of To-day, or an Australian Colony in the Making* (London: P. S. King & Son, 1925).

National Health and Medical Research Council, 'An Outline of a Possible Scheme for a Salaried Medical Service,' *The Medical Journal of Australia*, II(25), 20 December 1941, pp. 710–25.

Newman, George, *The Building of a Nation's Health* (London: Macmillan & Co., 1939).

Newsholme, Arthur, *Health Problems in Organized Society: Studies in the Social Aspects of Public Health* (London: P. S. King & Son, 1927).

Nutrition Committee of the National Health and Medical Research Council, *Diet and Nutrition for the Australian People* (Sydney: Angus & Robertson, 1943).

Nye, L. Jarvis, *Group Practice* (Sydney: Australasian Medical Publishing Company, n.d. [c. 1946–49]).

Parran, Thomas, 'Health Services of Tomorrow,' in *The Medical Profession and the Public* (Philadelphia: The American Academy of Political and Social Science, 1934), pp. 75–87.

Pearson, A. and R. Mouchet, *The Practical Hygiene of Native Compounds in Tropical Africa: Being Notes from the Experience of the First Eighteen Years of European Work in the Katanga* (London: Bailliere, Tindall & Cox, 1923).

Pearson, Charles, *National Life and Character: A Forecast* (London: Macmillan & Co., 1894).

Pearson, H., *Activities of Hookworm Campaign Unit No. 1 in the Northern Rivers District of New South Wales, 1926* (Brisbane: Hookworm Campaign, 1926).

Pearson, H., *An Investigation into the Epidemiology of Hookworm Disease in the Atherton Area, N.Q.* (Brisbane: Hookworm Campaign, 1926).

Pitt-Rivers, George Henry Lane-Fox, *The Clash of Cultures: An Anthropological and Psychological Study of the Laws of Racial Adaptability* (London: George Routledge & Sons, 1927).

Pockley, F. Antill, 'Presidential Address,' *Transactions of the Australasian Medical Congress*, 9, 1911, pp. 82–99.

Potter, Ellen C., 'The Year of Decision for Social Work,' *The Social Service Review*, 19(3), 1945, pp. 297–309.

Proud, J. C. Rookwood, *World Peace, the League and Australia* (Melbourne: Robertson & Mullens, 1936).

Report of the Select Committee on Aborigines (British Settlements) (Cape Town: C. Struik, 1966).

Rivers, W. H. R., 'The Psychological Factor,' in W. H. R. Rivers (ed.), *Essays on the Depopulation of Melanesia* (Cambridge: Cambridge University Press, 1922), pp. 84–114.

Roberts, Stephen, *Population Problems of the Pacific* (London: George Routledge & Sons, 1927).

Roberts, Stephen, 'Racial and Labour Problems,' in F. W. Eggleston (ed.), *The Australian Mandate for New Guinea: Record of Round Table Discussion* (Melbourne: Macmillan & Co., 1928), pp. 74–84.

Ryle, John, 'Medicine and Eugenics,' *The Eugenics Review*, 30(1), 1938, pp. 9–19.

Ryle, John, 'Social Medicine: Its Meaning and Scope,' *British Medical Journal*, II, 1943, pp. 633–6.

Sand, Rene, 'The Rise of Social Medicine,' *Modern Medicine*, 1, 1919, pp. 189–91.

Sigerist, Henry, 'The Physician's Profession through the Ages,' *Bulletin of the New York Academy of Medicine*, 9(12), 1933, pp. 661–76.

Simpson, Smith, 'International Organization in the Area of Social and Humanitarian Problems,' *The Social Service Review*, 19(1), 1945, pp. 1–23.

Stampar, Andrija, *Serving the Cause of Public Health: Selected Papers of Andrija Stampar*, ed. M. D. Grmek (Zagreb: University of Zagreb, 1966).

Stoddard, Lothrop, *The Rising Tide of Color Against White World-supremacy* (New York: Charles Scribner's Sons, 1921).

Straits Settlements, *Annual Report on the Medical Department for the Year 1927* (Singapore: Government Printer, 1928).

Sydenstricker, Edgar, 'Medical Practice and Public Needs,' in *The Medical Profession and the Public: Currents and Counter-currents* (Philadelphia: The American Academy of Political and Social Science, 1934), pp. 21–30.

Theobald, G. W., 'The Aetiology and Prevention of the Toxaemias of Pregnancy,' *British Medical Journal*, II(3790), 26 August 1933, pp. 376–81.

United Nations, *The Yearbook of the United Nations 1946–7* (New York: Department of Public Information, 1947).

United Nations Department of Social Affairs, *International Advisory Social Welfare Services* (Lake Success, NY: United Nations, 1949).

United Nations Department of Social Affairs, *Training for Social Work: An International Survey* (New York: United Nations, 1950).

United Nations Relief and Rehabilitation Administration, *UNRRA: Organization, Aims, Progress* (Washington, DC: UNRRA, 1944).

United States Department of State, *Point Four: Cooperative Program for Aid in the Development of Economically Underdeveloped Areas* (Washington, DC: Office of Public Affairs, 1950).

Weihen, A. Wallace, 'The Medical Inspection of Immigrants to Australia,' *Transactions of the Australasian Medical Congress*, 9, 1911, pp. 635–45.

Wills, Lucy, 'Treatment of "Pernicious Anaemia of Pregnancy" and "Tropical Anaemia",' *British Medical Journal*, I(3676), 20 June 1931, pp. 1059–64.

Theses

Cilento, Raphael W., 'A Correlation of Some Features of Tropical Preventive Medicine, and their Application to the Tropical Areas under Australian Control' (Doctor of Medicine thesis, University of Adelaide, 1922).

Secondary sources

Articles

Adas, Michael, 'Contested Hegemony: The Great War and the Afro–Asian Assault on the Civilizing Mission,' *Journal of World History*, 15(1), 2004, pp. 31–63. doi.org/10.1353/jwh.2004.0002.

Akami, Tomoko, 'A Quest to be Global: The League of Nations Health Organization and Inter-colonial Regional Governing Agendas of the Far Eastern Association of Tropical Medicine 1910–25,' *The International History Review*, 38(1), 2015, pp. 1–23. doi.org/10.1080/07075332.2015.1018302.

Amrith, Sunil, 'Asian Internationalism: Bandung's Echo in a Colonial Metropolis,' *Inter-Asia Cultural Studies*, 6(4), 2005, pp. 557–69. doi.org/10.1080/1464 9370500316869.

Amrith, Sunil and Glenda Sluga, 'New Histories of the United Nations,' *Journal of World History*, 19(3), 2008, pp. 251–74. doi.org/10.1353/jwh.0.0021.

Anderson, Warwick, 'Geography, Race and Nation: Remapping "Tropical" Australia, 1890–1930,' *Historical Records of Australian Science*, 11(4), 1997, pp. 457–63. doi.org/10.1071/HR9971140457.

Anderson, Warwick, 'The Colonial Medicine of Settler States: Comparing Histories of Indigenous Health,' *Health and History*, 9(2), 2007, pp. 144–54. doi.org/10.2307/40111579.

Anderson, Warwick, 'Ambiguities of Race: Science on the Reproductive Frontier of Australia and the Pacific between the Wars,' *Australian Historical Studies*, 40(2), 2009, pp. 143–60. doi.org/10.1080/10314610902849302.

Anderson, Warwick, 'Making Global Health History: The Postcolonial Worldliness of Biomedicine,' *Social History of Medicine*, 27(2), 2014, pp. 372–84. doi.org/10.1093/shm/hkt126.

Anderson, Warwick and Hans Pols, 'Scientific Patriotism: Medical Science and National Self-fashioning in Southeast Asia,' *Comparative Studies in Society and History*, 54(1), 2012, pp. 93–113.

Arnold, David, 'Tropical Governance: Managing Health in Monsoon Asia, 1908–1938,' Working Paper No. 116 (Singapore: Asia Research Institute Seminar Series, 2009).

Atkins, P. J., 'Sophistication Detected; Or, the Adulteration of the Milk Supply, 1850–1914,' *Social History*, 16(3), 1991, pp. 317–39. doi.org/10.1080/0307 1029108567811.

Bain, 'Atu, 'A Protective Labour Policy? An Alternative Interpretation of Early Colonial Labour Policy in Fiji,' *The Journal of Pacific History*, 23(2), 1988, pp. 119–36. doi.org/10.1080/00223348808572584.

Barona, Joseph L., 'Nutrition and Health: The International Context during the Inter-war Crisis,' *Social History of Medicine*, 21(1), 2008, pp. 87–105. doi.org/10.1093/shm/hkm114.

Bashford, Alison, 'Domestic Scientists: Modernity, Gender, and the Negotiation of Science in Australian Nursing, 1880–1910,' *Journal of Women's History*, 12(2), 2000, pp. 127–46. doi.org/10.1353/jowh.2000.0033.

Bashford, Alison, '"Is White Australia Possible?" Race, Colonialism and Tropical Medicine,' *Ethnic and Racial Studies*, 23(2), 2000, pp. 248–71. doi.org/10.1080/014198700329042.

Bashford, Alison, 'Global Biopolitics and the History of World Health,' *History of the Human Sciences*, 19(1), 2006, pp. 67–88. doi.org/10.1177/0952695106062148.

Bashford, Alison, 'Nation, Empire, Globe: The Spaces of Population Debate in the Interwar Years,' *Comparative Studies in Society and History*, 49(1), 2007, pp. 170–201. doi.org/10.1017/S0010417507000448.

Bashford, Alison, 'Population, Geopolitics, and International Organizations in the Mid Twentieth Century,' *Journal of World History*, 19(2), 2007, pp. 327–47.

Bashford, Alison, 'World Population and Australian Land: Demography and Sovereignty in the Twentieth Century,' *Australian Historical Studies*, 38(130), 2007, pp. 211–27. doi.org/10.1080/10314610708601243.

Bayly, C. A., Sven Beckert, Matthew Connelly, Isabel Hofmeyr, Wendy Kozol and Patricia Seed, 'AHR Conversation: On Transnational History,' *American Historical Review*, 111(5), 2006, pp. 1440–65.

Blackburn, Kevin, 'White Agitation for an Aboriginal State in Australia (1925–1929),' *Australian Journal of Politics and History*, 45(2), 1999, pp. 157–80. doi.org/10.1111/1467-8497.00060.

Blake, Thom, 'Deported … At the Sweet Will of the Government: The Removal of Aborigines to Reserves in Queensland 1897–1939,' *Aboriginal History*, 22, 1998, pp. 51–61.

Cahill, Peter, 'Chinese in Rabaul: 1921 to 1942—Normal Practices, or Containing the Yellow Peril?,' *The Journal of Pacific History*, 31(1), 1996, pp. 72–91. doi.org/10.1080/00223349608572807.

Cameron-Smith, Alexander, 'Australian Imperialism and International Health in the Pacific Islands,' *Australian Historical Studies*, 41(1), 2010, pp. 57–74. doi.org/10.1080/10314610903317614.

Carillo, Ana Maria and Anne-Emmanuelle Birn, 'Neighbours on Notice: National and Imperial Interests in the American Public Health Association, 1872–1921,' *Canadian Bulletin of Medical History*, 25(1), 2008, pp. 225–54. doi.org/10.3138/cbmh.25.1.225.

Chappell, David, 'Active Agents versus Passive Victims: Decolonized Historiography or Problematic Paradigm,' *The Contemporary Pacific*, 7(2), 1995, pp. 303–26.

Cohen, Daniel G., 'Between Relief and Politics: Refugee Humanitarianism in Occupied Germany 1945–1946,' *Journal of Contemporary History*, 43(3), 2008, pp. 437–49. doi.org/10.1177/0022009408091834.

Cox, Leonie, 'Fear, Trust and Aborigines: The Historical Experience of State Institutions and Current Encounters in the Health System,' *Health and History*, 9(2), 2007, pp. 70–92. doi.org/10.2307/40111576.

Cullather, Nick, 'Foreign Policy of the Calorie,' *American Historical Review*, 112(2), 2007, pp. 337–64. doi.org/10.1086/ahr.112.2.337.

Curtin, Philip D., '"The White Man's Grave": Image and Reality, 1780–1850,' *The Journal of British Studies*, 1(1), 1961, pp. 94–110. doi.org/10.1086/385437.

Deacon, Harriet, 'Racial Segregation and Medical Discourse in Nineteenth-century Cape Town,' *Journal of Southern African Studies*, 22(2), 1996, pp. 287–308. doi.org/10.1080/03057079608708492.

Deacon, Harriet, 'Racism and Medical Science in South Africa's Cape Colony in the Mid-to-late Nineteenth Century,' *Osiris*, 15, 2000, pp. 190–206. doi.org/10.1086/649326.

Dwork, Deborah, 'The Milk Option: An Aspect of the History of the Infant Welfare Movement 1898–1908,' *Medical History*, 31(1), 1987, pp. 31–69. doi.org/10.1017/S0025727300046317.

Ernst, Waltraub, 'Beyond East and West: From the History of Colonial Medicine to a Social History of Medicine(s) in South Asia,' *Social History of Medicine*, 20(3), 2007, pp. 505–24. doi.org/10.1093/shm/hkm077.

Evans, Raymond, '"Fallen among Thieves": Aboriginal Labour and State Control in Inter-war Queensland,' *Labour History*, 69, 1995, pp. 115–30. doi.org/10.2307/27516394.

Evans, Richard, '"A Menace to this Realm": The New Guard and the New South Wales Police, 1931–32,' *History Australia*, 5(3), 2008, pp. 76.1–76.20.

Finnane, Mark, 'Cilento, Sir Raphael West (Ray) (1893–1985),' *Australian Dictionary of Biography. Online Edition* (Canberra: The Australian National University, 2006). Available from: www.adb.online.anu.edu.au/biogs/A170212b.htm.

Fye, W. Bruce, 'The Origins and Evolution of the Mayo Clinic from 1864 to 1939: A Minnesota Family Practice Becomes an International "Medical Mecca",' *Bulletin of the History of Medicine*, 84(3), 2010, pp. 323–57. doi.org/10.1353/bhm.2010.0019.

Gardikas, Katerina, 'Relief Work and Malaria in Greece, 1943–1947,' *Journal of Contemporary History*, 43(3), 2008, pp. 493–508. doi.org/10.1177/0022009408091837.

Garton, Stephen, 'Sound Minds in Healthy Bodies: Re-considering Eugenics in Australia, 1914–1940,' *Australian Historical Studies*, 26(103), 1994, pp. 163–82. doi.org/10.1080/10314619408595958.

Giannuli, Dimitra, '"Repeated Disappointment": The Rockefeller Foundation and the Reform of the Greek Public Health System,' *Bulletin of the History of Medicine*, 72(1), 1998, pp. 47–72. doi.org/10.1353/bhm.1998.0054.

Hardy, Anne, 'Beriberi, Vitamin B1 and World Food Policy, 1925–1970,' *Medical History*, 39, 1995, pp. 61–77. doi.org/10.1017/S0025727300059482.

Harrison, Mark, 'Disease, Diplomacy and International Commerce: The Origins of International Sanitary Regulation in the Nineteenth Century,' *Journal of Global History*, 1, 2006, pp. 197–217. doi.org/10.1017/S1740022806000131.

Harrison, Mark, 'A Global Perspective: Reframing the History of Health, Medicine and Disease,' *Bulletin of the History of Medicine*, 89, 2015, pp. 639–89. doi.org/10.1353/bhm.2015.0116.

Henningham, Nikki, '"Hats Off, Gentlemen, to Our Australian Mothers!" Representations of White Femininity in North Queensland in the Early Twentieth Century,' *Australian Historical Studies*, 32(117), 2001, pp. 311–21. doi.org/10.1080/10314610108596167.

Hermann, Elfriede and Wolfgang Kempf, 'Introduction to Relations in Multicultural Fiji: The Dynamics of Articulations, Transformations and Positionings,' *Oceania*, 75(4), 2005, pp. 309–25. doi.org/10.1002/j.1834-4461.2005.tb02893.x.

Hodges, Sarah, 'The Global Menace,' *Social History of Medicine*, 25(3), 2011, pp. 719–28. doi.org/10.1093/shm/hkr166.

Huggins, Jackie, 'White Aprons, Black Hands: Aboriginal Domestic Servants in Queensland,' *Labour History*, 69, 1995, pp. 188–95. doi.org/10.2307/27516398.

Hyslop, Anthea, 'A Question of Identity: J. H. L. Cumpston and Spanish Influenza, 1918–1919,' *ACH: The Journal of the History of Culture in Australia*, 16, 1997, pp. 60–76.

Johnson, Ryan, 'European Cloth and "Tropical" Skin: Clothing Material and British Ideas of Health and Hygiene in Tropical Climates,' *Bulletin of the History of Medicine*, 83(3), 2009, pp. 530–60. doi.org/10.1353/bhm.0.0252.

Johnson, Ryan, 'The West African Medical Staff and the Administration of Imperial Tropical Medicine, 1902–14,' *The Journal of Imperial and Commonwealth History*, 38(3), 2010, pp. 419–39. doi.org/10.1080/03086 534.2010.503396.

Jolly, Margaret, 'Epilogue: Multicultural Relations in Fiji—Between Despair and Hope,' *Oceania*, 75(4), 2005, p. 418–30. doi.org/10.1002/j.1834-4461.2005. tb02900.x.

Kerin, Rani, '"Natives Allowed to Remain Naked": An Unorthodox Approach to Medical Work at Ernabella Mission,' *Health and History*, 8(1), 2006, pp. 80–99. doi.org/10.2307/40111530.

Kessler-Harris, Alice, 'Why Biography?,' *American Historical Review*, 114(3), 2009, pp. 625–30. doi.org/10.1086/ahr.114.3.625.

King, David and Malcolm Vick, 'Keeping 'Em Down: Education on Palm Island under Queensland's Aboriginal Acts,' *History of Education Review*, 23(1), 1994, pp. 1–18.

Kramer, Paul and John Plotz, 'Pairing Empires: Britain and the United States, 1857–1947,' *Journal of Colonialism and Colonial History*, 2(1), 2001, pp. 1–8. doi.org/10.1353/cch.2001.0008.

Lake, Marilyn, 'White Man's Country: The Transnational History of a National Project,' *Australian Historical Studies*, 34(122), 2003, pp. 346–63. doi.org/ 10.1080/10314610308596259.

Lake, Marilyn, '"The Brightness of Eyes and Quiet Assurance Which Seems to Say American": Alfred Deakin's Identification with Republican Manhood,' *Australian Historical Studies*, 38(129), 2007, pp. 32–51. doi.org/ 10.1080/10314610708601230.

Lake, Marilyn and Vanessa Pratt, '"Blood Brothers". Racial Identification and the Right to Rule—The Australian Response to the Spanish–American War,' *Australian Journal of Politics and History*, 54(1), 2008, pp. 16–27. doi.org/ 10.1111/j.1467-8497.2008.00481.x.

McElhinny, Bonnie, 'Producing the A-1 Baby: Puericulture Centers and the Birth of the Clinic in the U.S.-occupied Philippines, 1906–1946,' *Philippine Studies*, 57(2), 2009, pp. 219–60.

McGregor, Russell, 'Drawing the Local Colour Line: White Australia and the Tropical North,' *The Journal of Pacific History*, 47(3), 2012, pp. 329–46. doi.org/10.1080/00223344.2012.692549.

Manela, Erez, 'A Pox on Your Narrative: Writing Disease Control into Cold War History,' *Diplomatic History*, 34(2), 2010, pp. 299–323. doi.org/10.1111/j.1467-7709.2009.00850.x.

Marks, Shula, 'What is Colonial about Colonial Medicine? And What Has Happened to Imperialism and Health?,' *Social History of Medicine*, 10(2), 1997, pp. 205–19. doi.org/10.1093/shm/10.2.205.

Merrill, Dennis, 'Shaping Third World Development: US Foreign Aid and Supervision in the Philippines, 1948–53,' *The Journal of American–East Asian Relations*, 2(2), 1993, pp. 137–59. doi.org/10.1163/187656193X00022.

Moore, Andrew, 'The New Guard and the Labour Movement, 1931–35,' *Labour History*, 89, 2005, pp. 55–72. doi.org/10.2307/27516075.

Nasaw, David, 'AHR Roundtable: Historians and Biography—Introduction,' *American Historical Review*, 114(3), 2009, pp. 573–8. doi.org/10.1086/ahr.114.3.573.

O'Brien, Patricia, 'Remaking Australia's Colonial Culture? White Australia and its Papuan Frontier 1901–1940,' *Australian Historical Studies*, 40(1), 2009, pp. 96–112. doi.org/10.1080/10314610802663043.

Packard, Randall, 'The "Healthy Reserve" and the "Dressed Native": Discourses on Black Health and the Language of Legitimation in South Africa,' *American Ethnologist*, 16(4), 1989, pp. 686–703. doi.org/10.1525/ae.1989.16.4.02a00050.

Parker, Andrew, 'A "Complete Protective Machinery": Classification and Intervention through the Australian Institute of Tropical Medicine, 1911–1928,' *Health and History*, 1, 1999, pp. 182–201. doi.org/10.2307/40111343.

Parsons, Meg, 'Fantome Island Lock Hospital and Aboriginal Venereal Disease Sufferers 1928–45,' *Health and History*, 10(1), 2008, pp. 41–62. doi.org/10.2307/40111593.

Pedersen, Susan, 'Back to the League of Nations,' *American Historical Review*, 112(4), 2007, pp. 1091–117. doi.org/10.1086/ahr.112.4.1091.

Pedersen, Susan, 'Getting Out of Iraq in 1932: The League of Nations and the Road to Normative Statehood,' *American Historical Review*, 115(4), 2010, pp. 975–1000. doi.org/10.1086/ahr.115.4.975.

Roe, Michael, 'The Establishment of the Australian Department of Health: Its Background and Significance,' *Historical Studies*, 17(67), 1976, pp. 176–92. doi.org/10.1080/10314617608595546.

Salvatore, Nick, 'Biography and Social History: An Intimate Relationship,' *Labour History*, 87, 2004, pp. 187–92. doi.org/10.2307/27516005.

Saunders, Suzanne, 'Isolation: The Development of Leprosy Prophylaxis in Australia,' *Aboriginal History*, 14(2), 1990, pp. 168–81.

Sealy, Anne, 'Globalizing the 1926 International Sanitary Convention,' *Journal of Global History*, 6, 2011, pp. 431–55. doi.org/10.1017/S1740022811000404.

Sluga, Glenda, 'UNESCO and the (One) World of Julian Huxley,' *Journal of World History*, 21(3), 2010, pp. 393–418. doi.org/10.1353/jwh.2010.0016.

Stoler, Ann Laura, 'Tense and Tender Ties: The Politics of Comparison in North American History and (Post) Colonial Studies,' *The Journal of American History*, 88(3), 2001, pp. 829–65. doi.org/10.2307/2700385.

Strange, Carolyn, 'Transgressive Transnationalism: Griffith Taylor and Global Thinking,' *Australian Historical Studies*, 41(1), 2010, pp. 25–40. doi.org/10.1080/10314610903317606.

Stuart, Annie, 'Contradictions and Complexities in an Indigenous Medical Service: The Case of Mesulame Taveta,' *The Journal of Pacific History*, 41(2), 2006, pp. 125–43. doi.org/10.1080/00223340600826029.

Stuart, Annie, 'We Are All Hybrid Here: The Rockefeller Foundation, Sylvester Lambert, and Health Work in the Colonial South Pacific,' *Health and History*, 8(1), 2006, pp. 56–79. doi.org/10.2307/40111529.

Thompson, Roger, 'Making a Mandate: The Formation of Australia's New Guinea Policies 1919–1925,' *The Journal of Pacific History*, 25(1), 1990, pp. 68–84. doi.org/10.1080/00223349008572626.

Thorley, Virginia, 'Softly, Softly: How the Mothercraft Association of Queensland Co-existed with Government Policy, 1931–1961,' *Health and History*, 3(2), 2001, pp. 80–93. doi.org/10.2307/40111406.

Tsilaga, Flora, '"The Mountain Laboured and Brought Forth a Mouse": UNRRA's Operations in the Cyclades Islands, c. 1945–46,' *Journal of Contemporary History*, 43(3), 2008, pp. 527–45. doi.org/10.1177/0022009408091839.

Tyrrell, Ian, 'American Exceptionalism in an Age of International History,' *American Historical Review*, 96(4), 1991, pp. 1031–55. doi.org/10.2307/2164993.

Walker, David, 'Climate, Civilization and Character in Australia, 1880–1940,' *Australian Cultural History*, 16, 1997, pp. 77–95.

Wolfe, Patrick, 'Settler Colonialism and the Elimination of the Native,' *Journal of Genocide Research*, 8(4), 2006, pp. 387–409. doi.org/10.1080/14623520601056240.

Worboys, Michael, 'The Colonial World as Mission and Mandate: Leprosy and Empire, 1900–1940,' *Osiris*, 15, 2000, pp. 207–18. doi.org/10.1086/649327.

Zylberman, Patrick, 'Fewer Parallels than Antitheses: Rene Sand and Andrija Stampar on Social Medicine, 1919–1955,' *Social History of Medicine*, 17(1), 2004, pp. 77–92. doi.org/10.1093/shm/17.1.77.

Books and chapters in edited collections

Amos, Keith, *The New Guard Movement 1931–1935* (Melbourne: Melbourne University Press, 1976).

Amrith, Sunil, *Decolonizing International Health: India and Southeast Asia 1930–65* (Basingstoke, UK: Palgrave Macmillan, 2006). doi.org/10.1057/9780230627369.

Anderson, Warwick, *The Cultivation of Whiteness: Science, Health and Racial Destiny in Australia* (Melbourne: Melbourne University Press, 2002).

Anderson, Warwick, 'Postcolonial Histories of Medicine,' in Frank Huisman and John Harley Warner (eds), *Locating Medical History: The Stories and their Meanings* (Baltimore: Johns Hopkins University Press, 2004), pp. 285–306.

Anderson, Warwick, *Colonial Pathologies: American Tropical Medicine, Race, and Hygiene in the Philippines* (Durham, NC: Duke University Press, 2006).

Arnold, David (ed.), *Imperial Medicine and Indigenous Societies* (Manchester: Manchester University Press, 1988).

Arnold, David, *Colonizing the Body: State Medicine and Epidemic Disease in Nineteenth-century India* (Berkeley: University of California Press, 1993).

Attwood, Bain, *Rights for Aborigines* (Sydney: Allen & Unwin, 2003).

Austin, Tony, *Never Trust a Government Man: Northern Territory Aboriginal Policy 1911–1939* (Darwin: Northern Territory University Press, 1997).

Ballantyne, Tony and Antoinette Burton, 'Empires and the Reach of the Global,' in Emily Rosenberg (ed.), *A World Connecting: 1870–1945* (Cambridge, MA: Belknap Press, 2012), pp. 285–431.

Banivanua-Mar, Tracey and Penelope Edmonds, 'Introduction: Making Space in Settler Colonies,' in Tracey Banivanua Mar and Penelope Edmonds (eds), *Making Settler Colonial Space: Perspectives on Race, Place and Identity* (Basingstoke, UK: Palgrave Macmillan, 2010), pp. 1–24.

Bashford, Alison, *Purity and Pollution: Gender, Embodiment and Victorian Medicine* (Basingstoke, UK: Macmillan, 1998). doi.org/10.1057/9780230501249.

Bashford, Alison, *Imperial Hygiene: A Critical History of Colonialism, Nationalism and Public Health* (Basingstoke, UK: Palgrave Macmillan, 2004).

Bashford, Alison, *Global Population: History, Geopolitics, and Life on Earth* (New York: Columbia University Press, 2014).

Bashford, Alison and Maria Nugent, 'Leprosy and the Management of Race, Sexuality and Nation in Tropical Australia,' in Alison Bashford and Claire Hooker (eds), *Contagion: Epidemics, History and Culture from Smallpox to Anthrax* (Sydney: Pluto Press, 2002), pp. 106–28.

Bashford, Alison and Carolyn Strange, 'Isolation and Exclusion in a Modern World: An Introductory Essay,' in Alison Bashford and Carolyn Strange (eds), *Isolation: Places and Practices of Exclusion* (London: Routledge, 2003), pp. 1–19.

Battersby, Paul, 'Mapping Australasia: Reflections on the Permeability of Australia's Northern Maritime Borders,' in Anna Shnukal, Guy Ramsey and Yuriko Nagata (eds), *Navigating Boundaries: The Asian Diaspora in Torres Strait* (Canberra: Pandanus Books, 2004), pp. 13–32.

Bell, Heather, *Frontiers of Medicine in the Anglo-Egyptian Sudan 1899–1940* (Oxford: Clarendon Press, 1998).

Bennett, Judith, 'Holland, Britain and Germany in Melanesia,' in K. R. Howe, Robert C. Kiste and Brij V. Lal (eds), *Tides of History: The Pacific Islands in the Twentieth Century* (Sydney: George Allen & Unwin, 1994), pp. 40–70.

Bizzo, Maria Letitia Galluzzi, 'Postponing Equality: From Colonial to International Nutritional Standards, 1932–1950,' in Veronika Lipphardt and Alexandra Widmer (eds), *Health and Difference: Rendering Human Variation in Colonial Engagements* (New York: Berghahn Books, 2016), pp. 129–48.

Blake, Thom, *A Dumping Ground: A History of the Cherbourg Settlement* (Brisbane: University of Queensland Press, 2001).

Boehmer, Elleke, *Empire, the National and the Postcolonial, 1890–1920* (Oxford: Oxford University Press, 2002).

Brawley, Sean, *The White Peril: Foreign Relations and Asian Immigration to Australasia and North America, 1919–1978* (Sydney: UNSW Press, 1995).

Briscoe, Gordon, *Counting, Health and Identity: A History of Aboriginal Health and Demography in Western Australia and Queensland, 1900–1940* (Canberra: Aboriginal Studies Press, 2003).

Brown, Lawrence, 'Inter-colonial Migration and Refashioning of Indentured Labour: Arthur Gordon in Trinidad, Mauritius and Fiji (1866–1880),' in Alan Lester and David Lambert (eds), *Colonial Lives Across the British Empire: Imperial Careering in the Long Nineteenth Century* (Cambridge: Cambridge University Press, 2006), pp. 204–27.

Buckley, K. and K. Klugman, *'The Australian Presence in the Pacific': Burns Philp 1914–1946* (Sydney: George Allen & Unwin, 1983).

Burton, Antoinette, 'Introduction: On the Inadequacy and Indispensability of the Nation,' in Antoinette Burton (ed.), *After the Imperial Turn: Thinking with and through the Nation* (Durham, NC: Duke University Press, 2003), pp. 1–23.

Caine, Barbara, *Biography and History* (Basingstoke, UK: Palgrave Macmillan, 2010). doi.org/10.1007/978-1-137-10740-4.

Chatterjee, Partha, *The Politics of the Governed: Reflections on Popular Politics in Most of the World* (New York: Columbia University Press, 2004).

Choy, Catherine Ceniza, *Empire of Care: Nursing and Migration in Filipino American History* (Durham, NC: Duke University Press, 2003). doi.org/10.1215/9780822384410.

Clifford, James, '"Hanging Up Looking Glasses at Odd Corners": Ethnobiographical Prospects,' in Daniel Aaron (ed.), *Studies in Biography* (Cambridge, MA: Harvard University Press, 1978), pp. 41–56.

Connelly, Matthew, *Fatal Misconception: The Struggle to Control World Population* (Cambridge, MA: Harvard University Press, 2008).

Conrad, Sebastian and Dominic Sachsenmaier (eds), *Competing Visions of World Order: Global Moments and Movements, 1880s–1930s* (Basingstoke, UK: Palgrave Macmillan, 2007). doi.org/10.1057/9780230604285.

Cooper, Frederick, *Colonialism in Question: Theory, Knowledge, History* (Berkeley: University of California Press, 2005).

Cooper, Frederick and Randall Packard, 'Introduction,' in Frederick Cooper and Randall Packard (eds), *International Development and the Social Sciences* (Berkeley: University of California Press, 1997), pp. 1–41.

Cresciani, Gianfranco, *Fascism, Anti-fascism and Italians in Australia, 1922–1945* (Canberra: Australian National University Press, 1980).

Curthoys, Ann, 'Genocide in Tasmania: The History of an Idea,' in A. Dirk Moses (ed.), *Empire, Colony, Genocide: Conquest, Occupation, and Subaltern Resistance in World History* (Oxford: Berghahn Books, 2008), pp. 229–52.

Curthoys, Ann and Marilyn Lake, 'Introduction,' in Anne Curthoys and Marilyn Lake (eds), *Connected Worlds: History in Transnational Perspective* (Canberra: ANU E Press, 2006), pp. 5–20.

Deacon, Desley, Penny Russell and Angela Woollacott, 'Introduction,' in Desley Deacon, Penny Russell and Angela Woollacott (eds), *Transnational Ties: Australian Lives in the World* (Canberra: ANU E Press, 2008), pp. xiii–xxi.

De Bevoise, Ken, *Agents of Apocalypse: Epidemic Disease in the Colonial Philippines* (Princeton, NJ: Princeton University Press, 1995). doi.org/10.1353/book. 29603.

Denoon, Donald, *Public Health in Papua New Guinea: Medical Possibility and Social Constraint, 1884–1984* (Cambridge: Cambridge University Press, 1989). doi.org/10.1017/CBO9780511563447.

Denoon, Donald, 'The Idea of Tropical Medicine and its Influence in Papua New Guinea,' in Roy MacLeod and Donald Denoon (eds), *Health and Healing in Tropical Australia and Papua New Guinea 1911–1930* (Townsville, QLD: James Cook University, 1991), pp. 12–22.

Denoon, Donald, with Stewart Firth, Jocelyn Linnekin, Malama Meleisea and Karen Nero (eds), *The Cambridge History of the Pacific Islanders* (Cambridge: Cambridge University Press, 2004).

Dixon, Robert, *Prosthetic Gods: Travel, Representation and Colonial Governance* (Brisbane: University of Queensland Press, 2001).

Dobry, Michel, 'Desperately Seeking "Generic Fascism": Some Discordant Thoughts on the Academic Recycling of Indigenous Categories,' in Antonio Costas Pinto (ed.), *Rethinking Fascism: Comparative Perspectives* (Basingstoke, UK: Palgrave Macmillan, 2011), pp. 53–84.

Docker, John, 'Are Settler Colonies Inherently Genocidal? Re-reading Lemkin,' in A. Dirk Moses (ed.), *Empire, Colony, Genocide: Conquest, Occupation, and Subaltern Resistance in World History* (Oxford: Berghahn Books, 2008), pp. 81–101.

Dubin, Martin David, 'The League of Nations Health Organisation,' in Paul Weindling (ed.), *International Health Organisations and Movements, 1918–1939* (Cambridge: Cambridge University Press, 1995), pp. 56–80.

Dureau, Christine M., 'Mutual Goals? Family Planning on Simbo, Western Solomon Islands,' in Margaret Jolly and Kalpana Ram (eds), *Borders of Being: Citizenship, Fertility, and Sexuality in Asia and the Pacific* (Ann Arbor: University of Michigan Press, 2001), pp. 232–61.

Dwork, Deborah, *War is Good for Babies and Other Young Children: A History of the Infant and Child Welfare Movement in England, 1898–1918* (London: Tavistock Publications, 1987).

Eatwell, Roger, *Fascism: A History* (London: Chatto & Windus, 1995).

Eatwell, Roger, 'Ideology, Propaganda, Violence and the Rise of Fascism,' in Antonio Costa Pinto (ed.), *Rethinking the Nature of Fascism: Comparative Perspectives* (Basingstoke, UK: Palgrave Macmillan, 2011), pp. 165–85.

Edmond, Rod, *Leprosy and Empire: A Medical and Cultural History* (Cambridge: Cambridge University Press, 2006). doi.org/10.1017/CBO9780511497285.

Edmonds, Penelope, 'Dual Mandate, Double Work: Land, Labour and the Transformation of Native Subjectivity, 1908–1940,' in Patricia Grimshaw and Russell McGregor (eds), *Collisions of Culture and Identities: Settlers and Indigenous People* (Melbourne: Melbourne University Press, 2006), pp. 127–37.

Edmonds, Penelope, *Urbanizing Frontiers: Indigenous Peoples and Settlers in 19th-century Pacific Rim Cities* (Vancouver: UBC Press, 2010).

Ellinghaus, Katherine, *Taking Assimilation to Heart: Marriages of White Women and Indigenous Men in the United States and Australia* (Lincoln: University of Nebraska Press, 2006). doi.org/10.2307/j.ctt1djmhvp.

Evans, Raymond, '"Pigmentia": Racial Fears and White Australia,' in A. Dirk Moses (ed.), *Genocide and Settler Society: Frontier Violence and Stolen Indigenous Children in Australian History* (New York: Berghahn Books, 2007), pp. 103–24.

Evans, Raymond, Kay Saunders and Kathryn Cronin, *Race Relations in Colonial Queensland: A History of Exclusion, Exploitation and Extermination* (Brisbane: University of Queensland Press, 1988).Eyler, John M., *Sir Arthur Newsholme and State Medicine, 1885–1935* (Cambridge: Cambridge University Press, 1997).

Farley, John, *Bilharzia: A History of Imperial Tropical Medicine* (Cambridge: Cambridge University Press, 1991).

Farley, John, *To Cast Out Disease: A History of the International Health Division of the Rockefeller Foundation (1913–1951)* (Oxford: Oxford University Press, 2004).

Fee, Elizabeth, 'Henry E. Sigerist: His Interpretations of the History of Disease and the Future of Medicine,' in Charles Rosenberg and Janet Golden (eds), *Framing Disease: Studies in Cultural History* (New Brunswick, NJ: Rutgers University Press, 1992), pp. 297–317.

Ferguson, James, *The Anti-politics Machine: 'Development,' Depoliticization, and Bureaucratic Power in Lesotho* (Minneapolis: University of Minnesota Press, 1994).

Firth, Stewart, 'Colonial Administration and the Invention of the Native,' in Donald Denoon with Stewart Firth, Jocelyn Linnekin, Malama Meleisea and Karen Nero (eds), *The Cambridge History of the Pacific Islanders* (Cambridge: Cambridge University Press, 2004), pp. 253–88.

Fisher, Fedora Gould, *Raphael Cilento: A Biography* (Brisbane: University of Queensland Press, 1994).

Fitzgerald, Ross, *From 1915 to the Early 1980s: A History of Queensland* (Brisbane: University of Queensland Press, 1984).

Foucault, Michel, *Security, Territory, Population: Lectures at the College de France, 1977–1978*, trans. Michael Senellart (New York: Picador, 2004).

Franklin, Margaret-Ann and Isobel White, 'The History and Politics of Aboriginal Health,' in Janice Reid (ed.), *The Health of Aboriginal Australia* (Sydney: Harcourt Brace Jovanovich, 1991), pp. 1–36.

Ganter, Regina, 'Coloured People: A Challenge to Racial Stereotypes,' in Anna Shnukal, Guy Ramsey and Yuriko Nagata (eds), *Navigating Boundaries: The Asian Diaspora in Torres Strait* (Canberra: Pandanus Books, 2004), pp. 219–45.

Ganter, Regina, *Mixed Relations: Asian–Aboriginal Contact in North Australia* (Perth: University of Western Australia Press, 2006).

Geulen, Christian, 'The Common Grounds of Conflict: Racial Visions of World Order 1880–1940,' in Sebastian Conrad and Dominic Sachsenmaier (eds), *Competing Visions of World Order: Global Moments and Movements, 1880s–1930s* (New York: Palgrave Macmillan, 2007), pp. 69–96.

Gilding, Michael, *The Making and Breaking of the Australian Family* (Sydney: Allen & Unwin, 1991).

Gillespie, James, *The Price of Health: Australian Governments and Medical Politics 1910–1960* (Cambridge: Cambridge University Press, 1991). doi.org/10.1017/CBO9780511470189.

Gillespie, James, 'The Rockefeller Foundation, the Hookworm Campaign and a National Health Policy in Australia, 1911–1930,' in Roy MacLeod and Donald Denoon (eds), *Health and Healing in Tropical Australia and Papua New Guinea 1911–1930* (Townsville, QLD: James Cook University, 1991), pp. 64–87.

Gillespie, James, 'The "Marriage of Agriculture and Health" in Australia: The Advisory Council on Nutrition and Nutrition Policy in the 1930s,' in Suzanne Parry (ed.), *From Migration to Mining: Medicine and Health in Australian History* (Darwin: Historical Society of the Northern Territory, 1998), pp. 44–54.Gillion, K. L., *The Fiji Indians: Challenge to European Dominance 1920–1946* (Canberra: Australian National University Press, 1977).

Grant, Kevin, 'Human Rights and Sovereign Abolitions of Slavery, c. 1885–1956,' in Kevin Grant, Philippa Levine and Frank Trentmann (eds), *Beyond Sovereignty: Britain, Empire and Transnationalism, c. 1880–1950* (Basingstoke, UK: Palgrave Macmillan, 2007), pp. 80–102.

Grant, Kevin, Philippa Levine and Frank Trentmann (eds), *Beyond Sovereignty: Britain, Empire and Transnationalism, c. 1880–1950* (Basingstoke, UK: Palgrave Macmillan, 2007). doi.org/10.1057/9780230626522.

Gray, Geoffrey, *A Cautious Silence: The Politics of Australian Anthropology* (Canberra: Aboriginal Studies Press, 2007).

Griffin, Roger, *The Nature of Fascism* (London: Routledge, 1993).

Gussow, Zachary, *Leprosy, Racism, and Public Health: Social Policy in Chronic Disease Control* (Boulder, CO: Westview Press, 1989).

Haebich, Anna, *Broken Circles: Fragmenting Indigenous Families 1800–2000* (Fremantle, WA: Fremantle Arts Centre Press, 2000).

Haebich, Anna, '"Clearing the Wheat Belt": Erasing the Indigenous Presence in the Southwest of Western Australia,' in A. Dirk Moses (ed.), *Genocide and Settler Society: Frontier Violence and Stolen Indigenous Children in Australian History* (New York: Berghahn Books, 2007), pp. 267–89.

Hall, Catherine, *Civilising Subjects: Metropole and Colony in the English Imagination 1830–1867* (Cambridge: Polity Press, 2002).

Hall, Stuart, 'When Was the "Post-colonial"? Thinking at the Limit,' in Iain Chambers and Lidia Curti (eds), *The Post-colonial Question: Common Skies, Divided Horizons* (London: Routledge, 1996), pp. 242–60.

Hamlin, Christopher, 'State Medicine in Great Britain,' in Dorothy Porter (ed.), *The History of Public Health and the Modern State* (Amsterdam: Rodopi, 1994), pp. 132–64.

Harloe, Lorraine, 'Anton Breinl and the Australian Institute of Tropical Medicine,' in Roy MacLeod and Donald Denoon (eds), *Health and Healing in Tropical Australia and Papua New Guinea* (Townsville, QLD: James Cook University, 1991), pp. 35–46.

Harrison, Mark, *Public Health in British India: Anglo-Indian Preventive Medicine, 1859–1914* (Cambridge: Cambridge University Press, 1994).

Harrison, Mark, *Climates and Constitutions: Health, Race, Environment and British Imperialism in India, 1600–1850* (Delhi: Oxford University Press, 1999).

Haynes, Douglas M., *Imperial Medicine: Patrick Manson and the Conquest of Tropical Disease* (Philadelphia: University of Pennsylvania Press, 2001).

Headrick, Daniel G., *Tools of Empire: Technology and European Imperialism in the Nineteenth Century* (New York: Oxford University Press, 1981).

Hempenstall, Peter, 'Releasing the Voices: Historicizing Colonial Encounters in the Pacific,' in Robert Borofsky (ed.), *Remembrance of Pacific Pasts: An Invitation to Remake History* (Honolulu: University of Hawai'i Press, 2000), pp. 43–61.

Hiery, Hermann, *The Neglected War: The German South Pacific and the Influence of World War I* (Honolulu: University of Hawai'i Press, 1995).

Hodge, Joseph Morgan, *Triumph of the Expert: Agrarian Doctrines of Development and the Legacies of British Colonialism* (Athens, OH: Ohio University Press, 2007).

Hopkins, A. G. (ed.), *Globalization in World History* (New York: W. W. Norton & Co., 2002).

Inglis, Amirah, *The White Women's Protection Ordinance: Sexual Anxiety and Politics in Papua* (London: Sussex University Press, 1974).

Iriye, Akira, *Global Community: The Role of International Organizations in the Making of the Contemporary World* (Berkeley: University of California Press, 2002).

Irving, Helen, *To Constitute a Nation: A Cultural History of Australia's Constitution* (Cambridge: Cambridge University Press, 1997).

Jolly, Margaret, 'Other Mothers: Maternal "Insouciance" and the Depopulation Debate in Fiji and Vanuatu 1890–1930,' in Kalpana Ram and Margaret Jolly (eds), *Maternities and Modernities: Colonial and Postcolonial Experiences in Asia and the Pacific* (Chicago: University of Chicago Press, 1998), pp. 177–212.

Jolly, Margaret, 'Infertile States: Person and Collectivity, Region and Nation in the Rhetoric of Pacific Population,' in Margaret Jolly and Kalpana Ram (eds), *Borders of Being: Citizenship, Fertility, and Sexuality in Asia and the Pacific* (Ann Arbor: University of Michigan Press, 2001), pp. 262–306.

Jones, Margaret, *Health Policy in Britain's Model Colony: Ceylon (1900–1948)* (New Delhi: Orient Longman, 2004).

Kaplan, Martha, *Neither Cargo nor Cult: Ritual Politics and the Colonial Imagination* (Durham, NC: Duke University Press, 1995). doi.org/10.1215/9780822381914.

Kelly, John D. and Martha Kaplan, *Represented Communities: Fiji and World Decolonization* (Chicago: University of Chicago Press, 2001).

Kelm, Mary-Ellen, *Colonizing Bodies: Aboriginal Health and Healing in British Columbia 1900–50* (Vancouver: University of British Columbia Press, 1998).

Kerkvliet, Benedict J., *The Huk Rebellion: A Study of Peasant Revolt in the Philippines* (Berkeley: University of California Press, 1977).

Kidd, Rosalind, *The Way We Civilise* (Brisbane: University of Queensland Press, 2005).

Kothari, Uma, 'From Colonial Administration to Development Studies: A Post-colonial Critique of the History of Development Studies,' in Uma Khotari (ed.), *A Radical History of Development Studies: Individuals, Institutions and Ideologies* (London: Zed Books, 2005), pp. 47–66.

Kramer, Paul, *The Blood of Government: Race, Empire, the United States and the Philippines* (Chapel Hill, NC: University of North Carolina Press, 2006).

Lake, Marilyn and Henry Reynolds, *Drawing the Global Colour Line: White Men's Countries and the Question of Racial Equality* (Melbourne: Melbourne University Press, 2008). doi.org/10.1017/CBO9780511805363.

Lal, Brij V., *Broken Waves: A History of the Fiji Islands in the Twentieth Century* (Honolulu: University of Hawai'i Press, 1992).

Lal, Brij V., 'The Passage Out,' in K. R. Howe, Robert C. Kiste and Brij V. Lal (eds), *Tides of History: The Pacific Islands in the Twentieth Century* (Sydney: Allen & Unwin, 1994), pp. 435–61.

Lal, Brij V., '*Girmit*, History, Memory,' in Brij V. Lal (ed.), *Bittersweet: The Indo-Fijian Experience* (Canberra: Pandanus Books, 2004), pp. 1–29.

Lambert, David and Alan Lester, 'Imperial Spaces, Imperial Subjects,' in David Lambert and Alan Lester (eds), *Colonial Lives Across the British Empire: Imperial Careering in the Long Nineteenth Century* (Cambridge: Cambridge University Press, 2006), pp. 1–31.

Levine, Philippa, *Prostitution, Race, and Politics: Policing Venereal Disease in the British Empire* (New York: Routledge, 2003).

Lipphardt, Veronika and Alexandra Widmer, 'Introduction: Health and Difference—Rendering Human Variation in Colonial Engagements,' in Veronika Lipphardt and Alexandra Widmer (eds), *Health and Difference: Rendering Human Variation in Colonial Engagements* (New York: Berghahn Books, 2016), pp. 1–19.

Loos, Noel, *Invasion and Resistance: Aboriginal–European Relations on the North Queensland Frontier 1861–1897* (Canberra: Australian National University Press, 1982).

Lyons, Maryinez, *The Colonial Disease: A Social History of Sleeping Sickness in Northern Zaire, 1900–1940* (Cambridge: Cambridge University Press, 1992). doi.org/10.1017/CBO9780511583704.

Lyttelton, Adrian, *The Seizure of Power: Fascism in Italy 1919–1929*, 3rd edn (London: Routledge, 2004).

McGrath, Ann, *Born in the Cattle: Aborigines in Cattle Country* (Sydney: Allen & Unwin, 1987).

McGrath, Ann, 'The Golden Thread of Kinship: Mixed Marriages between Asians and Aboriginal Women during Australia's Federation Era,' in Penny Edwards and Shen Yuanfang (eds), *Lost in the Whitewash: Aboriginal–Asian Encounters in Australia, 1901–2001* (Canberra: ANU Humanities Research Centre, 2003), pp. 37–58.

McGregor, Russell, *Imagined Destinies: Aboriginal Australians and the Doomed Race Theory, 1880–1939* (Melbourne: Melbourne University Press, 1997).

McGregor, Russell, 'Governance, Not Genocide: Aboriginal Assimilation in the Postwar Era,' in A. Dirk Moses (ed.), *Genocide and Settler Society: Frontier Violence and Stolen Indigenous Children in Australian History* (New York: Berghahn Books, 2007), pp. 290–311.

MacIntyre, Stuart, *The Oxford History of Australia: The Succeeding Age, 1901–1942. Volume 4* (Melbourne: Oxford University Press, 1986).

MacIntyre, Stuart, *A Concise History of Australia* (Cambridge: Cambridge University Press, 1999).

McKeown, Adam, *Melancholy Order: Asian Migration and the Globalization of Borders* (New York: Columbia University Press, 2008).

MacLeod, Roy and Milton J. Lewis (eds), *Disease, Medicine and Empire: Perspectives on Western Medicine and the Experience of European Expansion* (London: Routledge, 1988).

Manderson, Lenore, 'Wireless Wars in the Eastern Arena: Epidemiological Surveillance, Disease Prevention and the Work of the Eastern Bureau of the League of Nations Health Organisation, 1925–1942,' in Paul Weindling (ed.), *International Health Organisations and Movements, 1918–1939* (Cambridge: Cambridge University Press, 1995), pp. 109–33.

Manderson, Lenore, *Sickness and the State: Health and Illness in Colonial Malaya, 1870–1940* (Cambridge: Cambridge University Press, 1996).

Manela, Erez, *The Wilsonian Moment: Self-determination and the International Origins of Anticolonial Nationalism* (New York: Oxford University Press, 2007).

Manning, Patrick, *Migration in World History* (New York: Routledge, 2005).

Martinez, Julia and Adrian Vickers, *The Pearl Frontier: Indonesian Labor and Indigenous Encounters in Australia's Northern Trading Network* (Honolulu: University of Hawai'i Press, 2015).

Matsuda, Matt, 'The Pacific,' *American Historical Review*, 111(3), 2006, pp. 758–80. doi.org/10.1086/ahr.111.3.758.

Mazower, Mark, *No Enchanted Palace: The End of Empire and the Ideological Origins of the United Nations* (Princeton, NJ: Princeton University Press, 2009).

Mazower, Mark, *Governing the World: The History of an Idea* (New York: The Penguin Press, 2012).

Mehta, Uday Singh, *Liberalism and Empire: A Study in Nineteenth Century British Liberal Thought* (Chicago: University of Chicago Press, 1999).

Minehan, Philip B., *Civil War and World War in Europe: Spain, Yugoslavia, and Greece, 1936–1949* (New York: Palgrave Macmillan, 2006).

Mitchell, Timothy, *The Rule of Experts: Egypt, Techno-politics, Modernity* (Berkeley: University of California Press, 2002).

Moore, Andrew, *The Secret Army and the Premier: Conservative Paramilitary Organisations in New South Wales 1930–32* (Sydney: UNSW Press, 1989).

Moore, Clive, *New Guinea: Crossing Boundaries and History* (Honolulu: University of Hawai'i Press, 2003).

Morefield, Jeanne, *Covenants without Swords: Idealist Liberalism and the Spirit of Empire* (Princeton, NJ: Princeton University Press, 2005).

Moyn, Samuel, *The Last Utopia: Human Rights History* (Cambridge, MA: Belknap Press, 2010).

Oswald, Nigel, 'Training Doctors for the National Health Service: Social Medicine, Medical Education and the GMC 1936–48,' in Dorothy Porter (ed.), *Social Medicine and Medical Sociology in the Twentieth Century* (Atlanta: Rodopi, 1997), pp. 59–80.

Packard, Randall, 'Visions of Postwar Health and their Impact on Public Health Interventions in the Developing World,' in Frederick Cooper and Randall Packard (eds), *International Development and the Social Sciences: Essays on the History and Politics of Knowledge* (Berkeley: University of California Press, 1997), pp. 93–118.

Packard, Randall, *The Making of a Tropical Disease: A Short History of Malaria* (Baltimore: The Johns Hopkins University Press, 2007).

Paisley, Fiona, *Loving Protection? Australian Feminism and Aboriginal Women's Rights, 1919–1939* (Melbourne: Melbourne University Press, 2000).

Parry, Suzanne, 'Tropical Medicine and Colonial Identity in Northern Australia,' in Mary P. Sutphen and Bridie Andrews (eds), *Medicine and Colonial Identity* (London: Routledge, 2003), pp. 103–24.

Patrick, Ross, *A History of Health and Medicine in Queensland 1824–1960* (Brisbane: University of Queensland Press, 1987).

Payne, Stanley G., *A History of Fascism, 1914–1945* (Madison: University of Wisconsin Press, 1995).

Pedersen, Susan, 'Settler Colonialism at the Bar of the League of Nations,' in Caroline Elkins and Susan Pedersen (eds), *Settler Colonialism in the Twentieth Century: Projects, Practices, Legacies* (New York: Routledge, 2005), pp. 113–34.

Pedersen, Susan, *The Guardians: The League of Nations and the Crisis of Empire* (Oxford: Oxford University Press, 2015). doi.org/10.1093/acprof:oso/9780199570485.001.0001.

Porter, Dorothy, 'Introduction,' in Dorothy Porter (ed.), *Social Medicine and Medical Sociology in the Twentieth Century* (Atlanta: Rodopi, 1997), pp. 1–31.

Porter, Dorothy (ed.), *Social Medicine and Medical Sociology in the Twentieth Century* (Atlanta: Rodopi, 1997).

Porter, Dorothy, *Health, Civilization and the State: A History of Public Health from Ancient to Modern Times* (London: Routledge, 1999).

Prasad, Rajendra, *Tears in Paradise: A Personal and Historical Journey, 1879–2004* (Auckland: Glade Publishers, 2004).

Pratt, Mary Louise, *Imperial Eyes: Travel Writing and Transculturation* (London: Routledge, 1992).

Price, Charles A., *The Great White Walls Are Built: Restrictive Immigration to North America and Australasia 1836–1888* (Canberra: Australian Institute of International Affairs/Australian National University Press, 1974).

Probyn-Rapsey, Fiona, '"Uplifting" White Men: Marriage, Maintenance and Whiteness in Queensland, 1900–1910,' *Postcolonial Studies*, 12(1), 2009, pp. 89–106. doi.org/10.1080/13688790802616365.

Rafael, Vicente L., *White Love and Other Events in Filipino History* (Durham, NC: Duke University Press, 2000).

Reiger, Kerreen, *The Disenchantment of the Home: Modernizing the Australian Family 1880–1940* (Melbourne: Oxford University Press, 1985).

Reynolds, Henry, *North of Capricorn: The Untold Story of Australia's North* (Sydney: Allen & Unwin, 2003).

Reynolds, Henry, *Nowhere People* (Melbourne: Viking, 2005).

Reynolds, Henry and Dawn May, 'Queensland,' in Ann McGrath (ed.), *Contested Ground: Australian Aborigines under the British Crown* (Sydney: Allen & Unwin, 1995), pp. 168–207.

Roe, Michael, *Nine Australian Progressives: Vitalism in Bourgeois Social Thought, 1890–1960* (Brisbane: University of Queensland Press, 1984).

Rosenberg, Charles, *Explaining Epidemics and Other Studies in the History of Medicine* (Cambridge: Cambridge University Press, 1992).

Rowse, Tim, *White Flour, White Power: From Rations to Citizenship in Central Australia* (Cambridge: Cambridge University Press, 1998). doi.org/10.1017/CBO9780511518287.

Scott, James, *Seeing Like a State: How Certain Schemes to Improve the Human Condition Have Failed* (New Haven, CT: Yale University Press, 1998).

Simmonds, Alecia, Anne Rees and Anna Clark, 'Testing the Boundaries: Reflections on Transnationalism in Australian History,' in Alecia Simmonds, Anne Rees and Anna Clark (eds), *Transnationalism, Nationalism, and Australian History* (Singapore: Palgrave Macmillan, 2017), pp. 1–14.

Sluga, Glenda, *Internationalism in the Age of Nationalism* (Philadelphia: University of Pennsylvania Press, 2013).

Smith, Neil, *American Empire: Roosevelt's Geographer and the Prelude to Globalization* (Berkeley: University of California Press, 2003).

Shnukal, Anna, Guy Ramsey and Yuriko Nagata, 'Introduction,' in Anna Shnukal, Guy Ramsey and Yuriko Nagata (eds), *Navigating Boundaries: The Asian Diaspora in Torres Strait* (Canberra: Pandanus Books, 2004), pp.1–13.

Staples, Amy, *The Birth of Development: How the World Bank, Food and Agriculture Organization and the World Health Organization Changed the World, 1945–65* (Kent, OH: Kent State University Press, 2006).

Stern, Alexandra Minna, 'Yellow Fever Crusade: US Colonialism, Tropical Medicine, and the International Politics of Mosquito Control, 1900–1920,' in Alison Bashford (ed.), *Medicine at the Border: Disease, Globalization and Security, 1850 to the Present* (Basingstoke, UK: Palgrave Macmillan, 2006), pp. 41–59.

Stoler, Ann Laura, *Carnal Knowledge and Imperial Power: Race and the Intimate in Colonial Rule* (Berkeley: University of California Press, 2002).

Stoler, Ann Laura and Frederick Cooper, 'Between Metropole and Colony: Rethinking a Research Agenda,' in Ann Laura Stoler and Frederick Cooper (eds), *Tensions of Empire: Colonial Cultures in a Bourgeois World* (Berkeley: University of California Press, 1997), pp. 1–56. Thomas, Nicholas, *Colonialism's Culture: Anthropology, Travel and Government* (Cambridge: Polity Press, 1994).

Thompson, Andrew, *The Empire Strikes Back? The Impact of Imperialism on Britain from the Mid-nineteenth Century* (New York: Pearson Longman, 2005).

Thompson, Roger, *Australian Imperialism in the Pacific: The Expansionist Era 1820–1920* (Melbourne: Melbourne University Press, 1980).

Thompson, Roger, *Australia and the Pacific Islands in the 20th Century* (Melbourne: Australian Scholarly Publishing, 1998).

Tomes, Nancy, *The Gospel of Germs: Men, Women and the Microbe in American Life* (Cambridge, MA: Harvard University Press, 1998).

Toth, Stephen, *Beyond* Papillon*: The French Overseas Penal Colonies, 1854–1952* (Lincoln: University of Nebraska Press, 2006).

Vaughan, Megan, *Curing their Ills: Colonial Power and African Illness* (Stanford, CA: Stanford University Press, 1991).

Walker, David, *Anxious Nation: Australia and the Rise of Asia, 1850–1939* (Brisbane: University of Queensland Press, 1999).

Waterhouse, Richard, *The Vision Splendid: A Social and Cultural History of Rural Australia* (Fremantle, WA: Curtin University Press, 2005).

Weindling, Paul, *Health, Race and German Politics between National Unification and Nazism, 1870–1945* (Cambridge: Cambridge University Press, 1989).

Weindling, Paul, 'Introduction: Constructing International Health between the Wars,' in Paul Weindling (ed.), *International Health Organisations and Movements, 1918–1939* (Cambridge: Cambridge University Press, 1995), pp. 1–16.

Weindling, Paul, 'Social Medicine at the League of Nations Health Organisation and the International Labour Office Compared,' in Paul Weindling (ed.), *International Health Organisations and Movements, 1918–1939* (Cambridge: Cambridge University Press, 1995), pp. 134–53.

Weindling, Paul (ed.), *International Health Organisations and Movements, 1918–1939* (Cambridge: Cambridge University Press, 1995). doi.org/10.1017/CBO9780511599606.

Weindling, Paul, *Epidemics and Genocide in Eastern Europe 1890–1945* (Oxford: Oxford University Press, 2000). doi.org/10.1093/acprof:oso/9780198206910.001.0001.

Weir, Christine, 'An Accidental Biographer? On Encountering, Yet Again, the Ideas and Actions of J. W. Burton,' in Brij V. Lal and Vicki Luker (eds), *Telling Pacific Lives: Prisms of Process* (Canberra: ANU E Press, 2008), pp. 215–25.

White, Richard, *Inventing Australia: Images and Identity, 1688–1980* (Sydney: Allen & Unwin, 1981).

Wilkinson, Lise and Anne Hardy, *Prevention and Cure: The London School of Hygiene and Tropical Medicine, A 20th Century Quest for Global Public Health* (London: Kegan Paul, 2001).

Wolfe, Patrick, 'Islam, Europe and Indian Nationalism: Towards a Postcolonial Transnationalism,' in Ann Curthoys and Marilyn Lake (eds), *Connected Worlds: History in Transnational Perspective* (Canberra: ANU E Press, 2006), pp. 233–65.

Wolfers, Edward P., *Race Relations and Colonial Rule in Papua New Guinea* (Sydney: Australia and New Zealand Book Company, 1975).

Woodroofe, Kathleen, *From Charity to Social Work in England and the United States* (London: Routledge & Keegan Paul, 1962).

Woollacott, Angela, 'Postcolonial Histories and Catherine Hall's *Civilising Subjects*,' in Anne Curthoys and Marilyn Lake (eds), *Connected Worlds: History in Transnational Perspective* (Canberra: ANU E Press, 2006), pp. 63–74.

Worboys, Michael, 'The Emergence of Tropical Medicine: A Study in the Establishment of a Scientific Speciality,' in Gerard Lemaine, Roy MacLeod, Michael Mulkay and Peter Weingart (eds), *Perspectives on the Emergence of Scientific Disciplines* (The Hague: Mouton & Co., 1976), pp. 75–98.

Worboys, Michael, 'The Discovery of Colonial Malnutrition between the Wars,' in David Arnold (ed.), *Imperial Medicine and Indigenous Societies* (Manchester: Manchester University Press, 1988), pp. 208–25.

Worboys, Michael, 'Manson, Ross, and Colonial Medical Policy: Tropical Medicine in London and Liverpool, 1899–1914,' in Roy MacLeod and Milton J. Lewis (eds), *Disease, Medicine, and Empire: Perspectives on Western Medicine and the Experience of European Expansion* (London: Routledge, 1988), pp. 21–37.

Wray, Matt, *Not Quite White: White Trash and the Boundaries of Whiteness* (Durham, NC: Duke University Press, 2006). doi.org/10.1215/97808 22388593.

Wyman, Mark, *DPs: Europe's Displaced Persons, 1945–1951* (Ithaca, NY: Cornell University Press, 1989).

Wyndham, Diana, *Eugenics in Australia: Striving for National Fitness* (London: The Galton Institute, 2003).

Yarwood, A. T., 'Sir Raphael Cilento and *The White Man in the Tropics*,' in Roy MacLeod and Donald Denoon (eds), *Health and Healing in Tropical Medicine in Australia and Papua New Guinea* (Townsville, QLD: James Cook University, 1991), pp. 47–63.

Zylberman, Patrick, 'Civilizing the State: Borders, Weak States and International Health in Modern Europe,' in Alison Bashford (ed.), *Medicine at the Border: Disease, Globalization and Security, 1850 to the Present* (Basingstoke, UK: Palgrave Macmillan, 2006), pp. 21–40.

Theses

Brown, David, '"Before Everything, Remain Italian": Fascism and the Italian Population of Queensland 1910–1945' (PhD Thesis, University of Queensland, 2008).

Kidd, Rosalind, 'Regulating Bodies: Administrations and Aborigines in Queensland 1840–1988' (PhD Thesis, Griffith University, 1994).

Parsons, Meg, 'Spaces of Disease: The Creation and Management of Aboriginal Health and Disease in Queensland 1900–1970' (PhD Thesis, University of Sydney, 2008).

Watson, Joanne, 'Becoming Bwgcolman: Exile and Survival on Palm Island Reserve, 1918 to the Present' (PhD Thesis, University of Queensland, 1993).

www.ingramcontent.com/pod-product-compliance
Lightning Source LLC
Chambersburg PA
CBHW040819280326
41926CB00093B/4592